AF879032

ASCENT
CENTER FOR TECHNICAL KNOWLEDGE

Autodesk® Inventor® CAM 2024 Milling Fundamentals

Learning Guide

Mixed Units - 1st Edition

ASCENT - Center for Technical Knowledge®
AutoCAD® Inventor® CAM 2024
Milling Fundamentals
Mixed Units - 1st Edition

Prepared and produced by:

ASCENT Center for Technical Knowledge
630 Peter Jefferson Parkway, Suite 175
Charlottesville, VA 22911

866-527-2368
www.ASCENTed.com

Lead Contributor: Jennifer MacMillan

ASCENT - Center for Technical Knowledge (a division of Rand Worldwide Inc.) is a leading developer of professional learning materials and knowledge products for engineering software applications. ASCENT specializes in designing targeted content that facilitates application-based learning with hands-on software experience. For over 25 years, ASCENT has helped users become more productive through tailored custom learning solutions.

We welcome any comments you may have regarding this guide, or any of our products. To contact us please email: feedback@ASCENTed.com.

AS-INV2401-MFND1MU-SG // IS-INV2401-MFND1MU-SG

Contents

Preface

The *Autodesk® Inventor® CAM 2024: Milling Fundamentals* guide focuses on instructing new users on how to use the Inventor CAM add-on to create milling toolpaths. The guide begins with an introduction to the overall Inventor interface and explains how to manipulate your 3D model to change its orientation and view display. Through additional hands-on, practice-intensive curriculum, you will learn the key skills and knowledge required to take the 3D model, set it up in the CAM environment, and assign the 2D and 3D milling toolpaths needed to generate the CNC code required by milling machines.

Topics Covered

- Navigate the Inventor software interface to locate and execute commands.
- Use the model orientation commands to pan, zoom, rotate, and look at a model.
- Assign visual styles to your models.
- Locate, modify, and create tools in the Tool Library.
- Set up machining operations using Inventor CAM.
- Create 2D Milling, 3D Milling and Drilling toolpaths using the Inventor CAM interface.
- Use the Simulation option to visualize toolpaths.
- Import a tool library.
- Create a toolpath template.
- Post process an Inventor CAM setup to output the CNC code required to machine a model.

Prerequisites

- Access to the 2024.0 version of the software, to ensure compatibility with this guide. Future software updates that are released by Autodesk may include changes that are not reflected in this guide. The practices and files included with this guide are not compatible with prior versions (e.g., 2023).
- As an introductory guide, *Autodesk® Inventor® CAM 2024: Milling Fundamentals* does not assume prior knowledge of Autodesk Inventor CAM. However, this guide will not provide instructional content on how to create 3D models using the Inventor modeling tools. Its focus is solely on generating 2D and 3D milling and drilling toolpaths once models are created. The *Autodesk® Inventor® 2024: Introduction to Solid Modeling* guide should be used to learn to create 3D models.

- It is recommended that users have prior experience with the Windows operating system, knowledge of 3D model creation/modification, and an understanding of the CNC milling process.

Note on Software Setup

This guide assumes a standard installation of the software using the default preferences during installation. Lectures and practices use the standard software templates and default options for the Content Libraries.

Lead Contributor: Jennifer MacMillan

With a dedication for engineering and education, Jennifer has spent over 25 years at ASCENT managing courseware development for various CAD products. Trained in Instructional Design, Jennifer uses her skills to develop instructor-led and web-based training products as well as knowledge profiling tools.

Jennifer has achieved the Autodesk Certified Professional certification for Inventor and is also recognized as an Autodesk Certified Instructor (ACI). She enjoys teaching the training courses that she authors and is also very skilled in providing technical support to end-users.

Jennifer holds a Bachelor of Engineering Degree as well as a Bachelor of Science in Mathematics from Dalhousie University, Nova Scotia, Canada.

Jennifer MacMillan has been a Lead Contributor for Autodesk Inventor CAM: Milling Fundamentals (previously released as *Autodesk Inventor: Introduction to 2D Milling*) since 2019.

In This Guide

The following highlights the key features of this guide.

Feature	Description
Practice Files	The Practice Files page includes a link to the practice files and instructions on how to download and install them. The practice files are required to complete the practices in this guide.
Chapters	A chapter consists of the following: Learning Objectives, Instructional Content, Practices, Chapter Review Questions, and Command Summary. • **Learning Objectives** define the skills you can acquire by learning the content provided in the chapter. • **Instructional Content**, which begins right after Learning Objectives, refers to the descriptive and procedural information related to various topics. Each main topic introduces a product feature, discusses various aspects of that feature, and provides step-by-step procedures on how to use that feature. Where relevant, examples, figures, helpful hints, and notes are provided. • **Practice** for a topic follows the instructional content. Practices enable you to use the software to perform a hands-on review of a topic. It is required that you download the practice files (using the link found on the Practice Files page) prior to starting the first practice. • **Chapter Review Questions**, located close to the end of a chapter, enable you to test your knowledge of the key concepts discussed in the chapter. • **Command Summary** concludes a chapter. It contains a list of the software commands that are used throughout the chapter and provides information on where the command can be found in the software.
Appendices	Appendices provide additional information to the main course content. It could be in the form of instructional content, practices, tables, projects, or skills assessment.

Practice Files

To download the practice files for this guide, use the following steps:

1. Type the URL *exactly as shown below* into the address bar of your Internet browser to access the Course File Download page.

   Note: If you are using the ebook, you do not have to type the URL. Instead, you can access the page by clicking the URL below.

   https://www.ascented.com/getfile/id/camaldulensisPF

2. On the Course File Download page, click the **DOWNLOAD NOW** button, as shown below, to download the .ZIP file that contains the practice files.

3. Once the download is complete, unzip the file and extract its contents.

   The recommended practice files folder location is:
   C:\Autodesk Inventor CAM 2024 Milling Fundamentals Practice Files

   Note: It is recommended that you do not change the location of the practice files folder. Doing so may cause errors when completing the practices.

Chapter 1

Introduction to Autodesk Inventor CAM

The Inventor CAM add-on to the Autodesk® Inventor® software is an integrated computer-aided manufacturing (CAM) solution that is used to generate the toolpaths that are needed to create the Numerical Control (NC) data and subsequently manufacture your models. In this chapter, you will review the standard Inventor interface and model manipulation techniques and then learn the new interface items that are unique to the Inventor CAM environment. To complete the chapter, you will learn to use the Simulation option to visually confirm how the model will be machined prior to post processing the NC code.

Learning Objectives

- Load a project file and open Autodesk Inventor files.
- Navigate the software interface to locate and execute commands.
- Use the model orientation commands to pan, zoom, rotate, and look at a model.
- Assign visual styles to your models.
- Understand various manufacturing terms and the general workflow that will be used in this guide.
- Use the Simulation option to visualize the toolpaths that are created in Inventor CAM.

1.1 Getting Started with Inventor

Home Page

When you launch the Autodesk Inventor software, the *Home* page displays, as shown in Figure 1–1. This page enables you to activate a project file, create a new file, open files from the recently used list, or browse for a specific file and open it. Figure 1–1 displays the *Home* page with the Default project active. Note that it doesn't show any previously opened files; as files are opened, they will appear in this list.

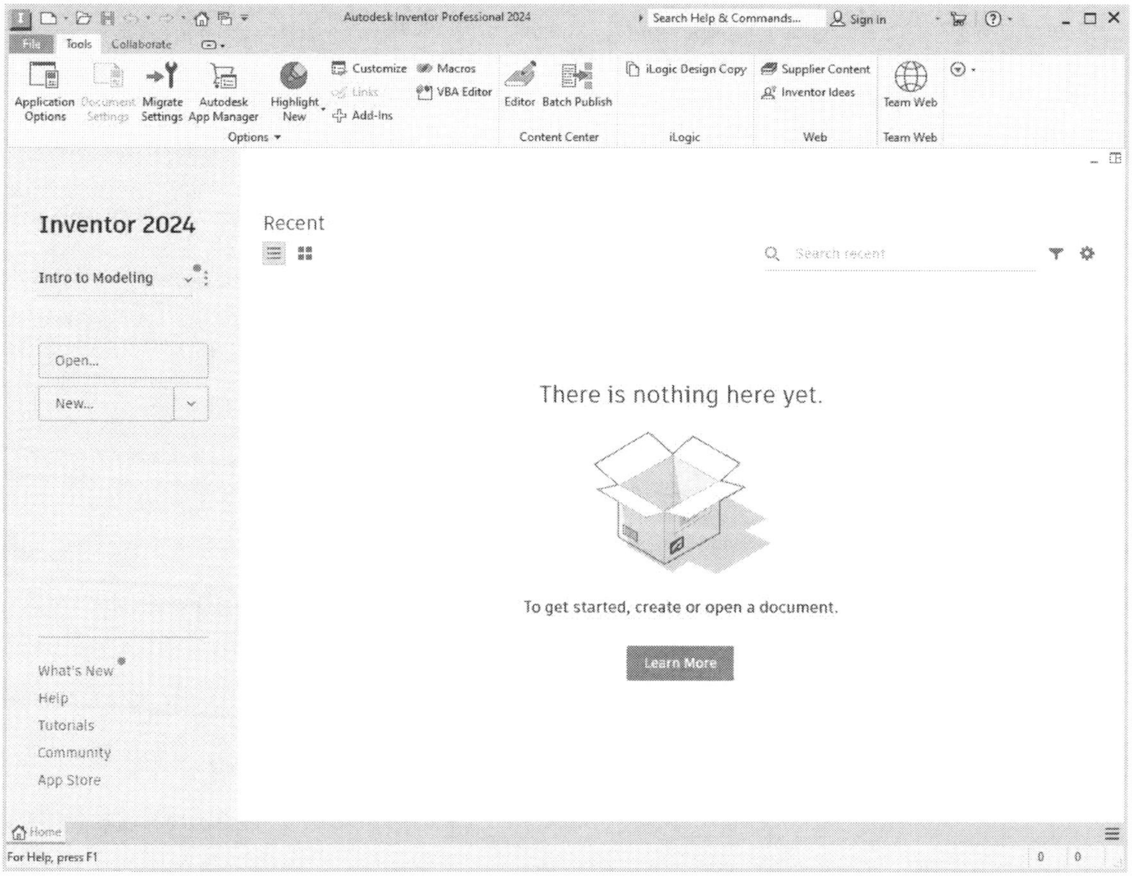

Figure 1–1

Opening Files

Files can be opened using a number of different methods in the Autodesk Inventor software. Use one of the following methods to open an existing file:

- On the *Home* page, select **Open**.
- Click (Open) in the Quick Access Toolbar at the top of the interface.
- In the **File** menu, select **Open>Open**, or select a file from the **File** menu's Recent list.

For all but the recent document methods, the Open dialog box opens. Navigate to the required file, select it, and click **Open**. The (Find Files) button in the Open dialog box can also be used to find a file to be opened.

Hint: Home Tab

The *Home* tab is available even when files are open. To return to the *Home* page, select the *Home* tab at the bottom of the Inventor graphics window, as shown in Figure 1–2.

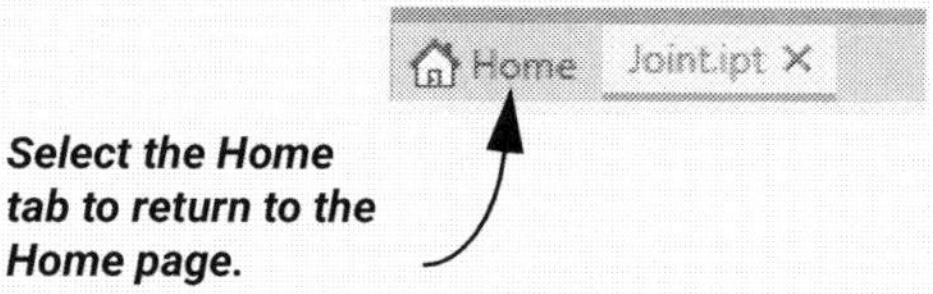

Figure 1–2

Recent List

The *Recent* area on the *Home* page lists previously opened files for the active project and enables you to open files directly from this list. List View ( ) displays the file names in a list format and Grid View ( ) displays the files as thumbnail images. Use any one of the following methods to open files in either view:

- Double-click on the files name or the thumbnail image.
- In List View, right-click on the file name and select **Open**. Alternatively, click adjacent to the Pinned column and select **Open**.
- In Grid View, hover over the thumbnail image, select , and select **Open**.

*Note: The **Open with options** option enables you to open specific Model State or Design View representations in the file. This will be discussed in a later topic.*

Additional tools in the Recent list include:

- Sorting files by selecting column headers in the List View or selecting the **Sort by** option in the Grid View. These enable you to sort by Name, Location, or Date Modified.
- Clicking (pin icon) in the Pinned column in the List View or on the thumbnail image to add a recent document to the pinned list so that it is listed at the top of the list.
- If you are using the Autodesk Vault software, a file status column displays in the *Recent* area.

Hint: Controlling the number of Listed Recent Documents

By default, a maximum of 50 recent documents are listed in the *Recent* area of the Home page. To remove a file in List View, right-click on its file name and select **Remove from Recent**. Alternatively, in Grid View, hover over the thumbnail image, select ⋮, and select **Remove from Recent**. To change the default number of files, click **Tools** > (Application Options), and on the *General* tab, change the value for the **Maximum number of recent documents**.

Project Files

If you work as part of a design team, managing access to the shared Autodesk Inventor data is crucial. Incorporating project files enables you to organize and access the files that are used. A project file is a text file that has an .IPJ format. At a fundamental level, a project file specifies the locations of the files in the project and maintains all of the required links to the files. When you open a model, the paths specified in the active project are searched to find all of the referenced files. At a more advanced level, project files can specify library locations and set many options. Project Files are discussed in more depth later in this guide.

How To: Load a Project File

1. Use one of the following methods to open the Projects dialog box to load a project:
   - On the Home page, select ⋮ (Projects and Settings) > **Settings**.
   - Click (Projects) in the Quick Access Toolbar at the top of the interface.
   - In the **File** menu, select **Manage>Projects**.
   - In the New or Open dialog boxes, click **Projects**.
2. Click **Browse** and navigate to the location of the project file. Select it and click **Open**. The Projects dialog box updates and a checkmark displays next to the new project name, indicating that it is the active project.
3. Click **Done** to close the Projects dialog box.

Once a project has been loaded it remains listed as an available project. A previously loaded project can be activated by:

- Double-clicking on its name in the Projects dialog box, or
- Expanding the Projects drop-down list (⌄) on the *Home* page (as show in Figure 1–3) and selecting the project name.

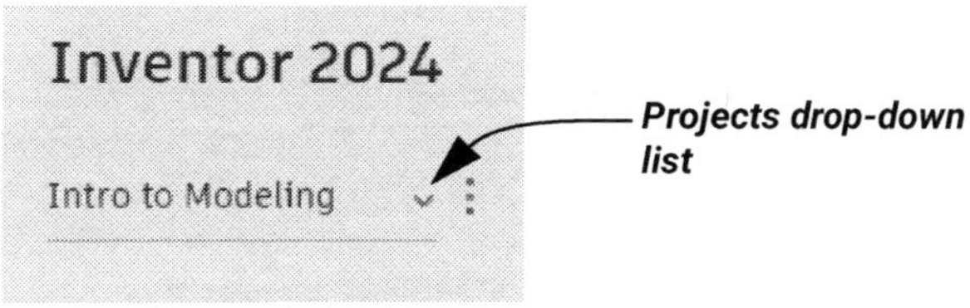

Figure 1–3

Additional options are available in the lower left corner of that Home page that enable you to review the What's New documentation for the latest software release, online Help and Tutorial documents, as well as links to the Inventor Community forum and App Store.

Autodesk Inventor Interface

Once a file has been opened, the interface updates to include additional elements. These are consistent among the various environments. The Part environment and many of the interface elements are shown in Figure 1–4.

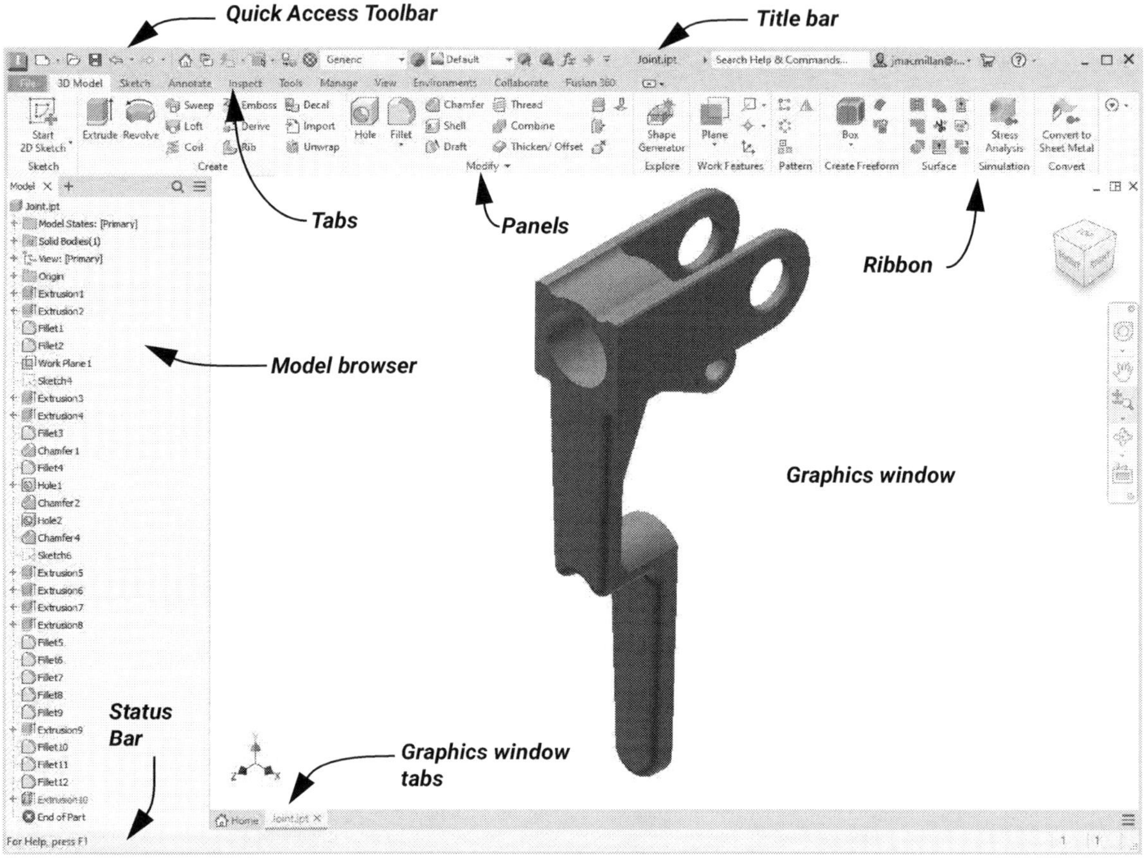

Figure 1–4

The following interface elements exist in the Part environment and the other Autodesk Inventor environments.

Title Bar

The title bar at the top of the interface displays the name of the current active file.

Ribbon/Tabs/Panels

The ribbon provides access to commands and settings. The ribbon is divided into tabs and they are further subdivided into panels. The tabs that are available vary depending on the mode that is currently active. All commands are listed in panels. Many commands can also be accessed by right-clicking on a feature in the model or in the Model browser. In Figure 1–5, the *3D Model* tab is active. Sketch, Create, and Modify are some of the panels in this tab.

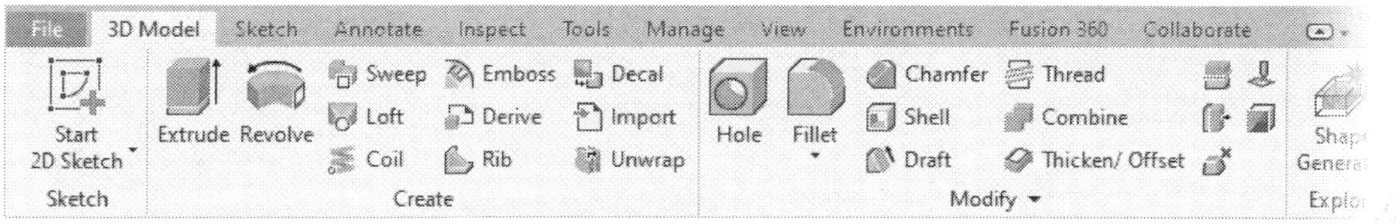

Figure 1–5

- Commands can be hidden in either compressed panels or commands. To expand hidden commands, click on the panel or command name, as shown for the Modify panel and **Start 2D Sketch** command in Figure 1–6.

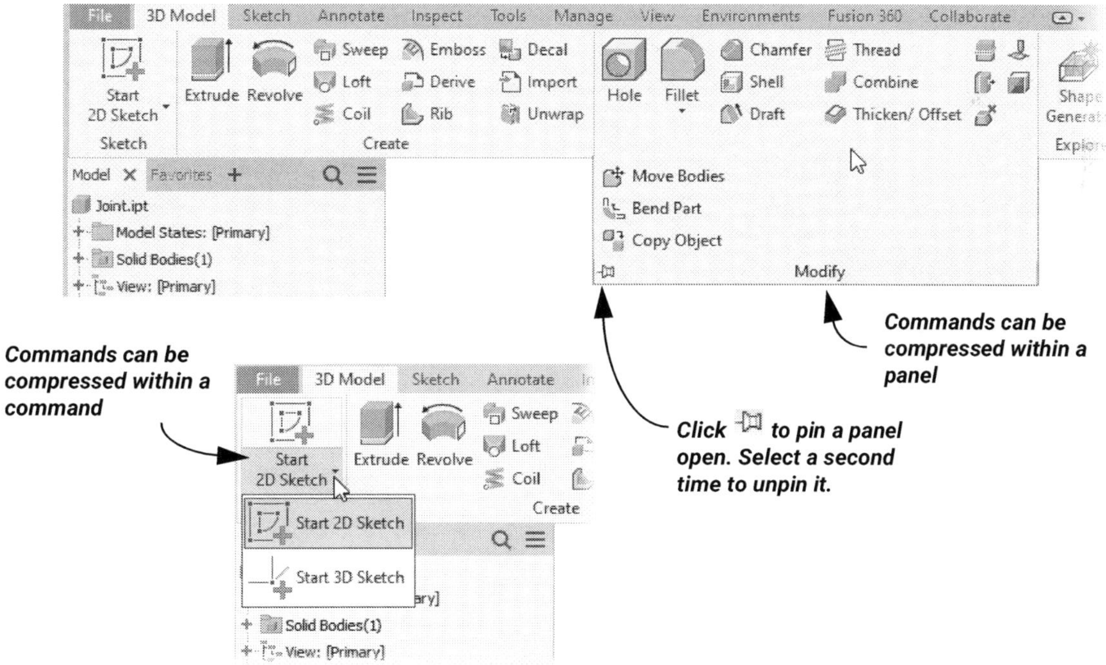

Figure 1–6

- Only commonly accessed panels display by default. To customize which panels display, expand (Show panels) at the end of each tab and select from the available list, as shown in Figure 1–7. Alternatively, you can right-click on the ribbon, expand **Show Panels**, and then select a panel.

Figure 1–7

Graphics Window

Open files are displayed and can be directly manipulated in the graphics window. As individual files are opened, they display listed as tabs along the bottom of the graphics window. Select a tab name to display it. In the example shown in Figure 1–8, a model, drawing, and *Home* tab are shown. The active model is **Joint.ipt**. Hover over the tab to access a thumbnail preview.

Figure 1–8

- Generally, maximizing each window provides the most modeling space. As required, you can minimize and resize windows, or click (Documents Menu) in the bottom right of the graphics window and use (Arrange), (Horizontal Tile), and (Vertical Tile) to customize your graphics window layout.

Quick Access Toolbar

Commonly accessed commands are available at the top of the software window in the Quick Access Toolbar, as shown in Figure 1–9.

Figure 1–9

- Click on the right of the Quick Access Toolbar to customize the toolbar. Alternatively, you can right-click on any command on the ribbon and select **Add to Quick Access Toolbar**.
- The selection filter in the Quick Access Toolbar enables you to filter entities, features, or components so that you can only select that type of object.
- The (Undo) and (Redo) drop-down lists provide you with a list of previously-completed actions that were performed on the model. To jump forward or back to a point in the model's history, select it in from the drop-down list.

Model Browser

The Model browser lists all of the features or components in your models, in order of creation. The Model browser is a powerful tool that can be used to complete any of the following actions:

- Select features.
- Access commonly used options (e.g., **Delete**, or **Edit**).
- Search for features.
- Edit features.
- Display information on features.
- Change the order of features (click and drag).
- Open components in an assembly.
- Open drawings of components.
- Create drawings of parts and assemblies.
- Investigate relationships between features and components.

In the Model browser (shown in Figure 1–10), each feature is identified by its name and a symbol that identifies the feature type. Expandable nodes reveal additional information on the features.

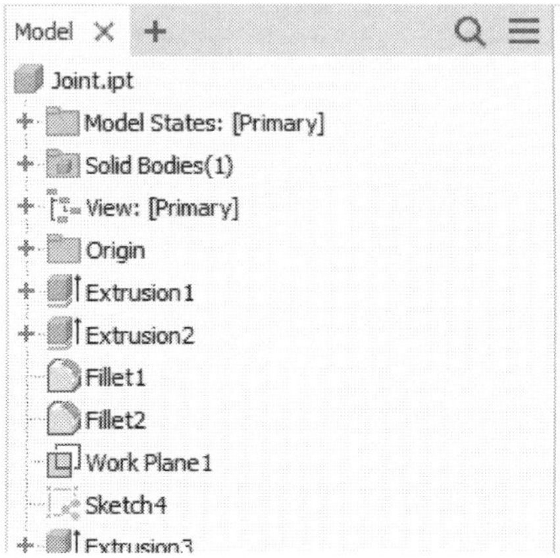

Figure 1–10

- The header of the Model browser indicates the active panel. Model is the panel that displays by default. Click + to expand the list of available panels.
  - For part models, you can activate the iLogic or Favorites panels.
  - For assemblies, you can activate the iLogic, Favorites, or Representation panels to help view model information.
  - For assemblies you can also toggle between an Assembly or Modeling view.
- Click in the Model browser header to access the quick search panel. A search is conducted as you type in keywords. In an assembly model, the quick search also provides access to the and icons, which enable you to filter unresolved and out of date data respectively.
- Click in the Model browser header to access options to expand and collapse the browser nodes, conduct an advanced search, disable the ability to edit values in the Model browser (assemblies only), set display preferences, or access help.

  ***Note:** The Model browser can be displayed or removed from the interface. To control its display, enable or disable the tool in the User Interface drop-down list (View tab>Windows panel).*

Status Bar

The Status Bar displays messages that are related to the active command. For example, in a sketch, the Status Bar can display information related to sketching, dimensioning, and constraining an entity.

Modeling Tools

The marking menu and feature creation controls are commonly used in the design process.

Marking Menu

The marking menu provides alternative access to commands. When you right-click in the graphics window, a radial marking menu and a vertical menu display. Both menus provide quick access to commonly used, context-sensitive commands.

- The marking menu consists of eight wedges that contain different commands. To activate a marking menu command, move the cursor in the direction of the command so that it is highlighted (as shown on the right in Figure 1–11) and select it.

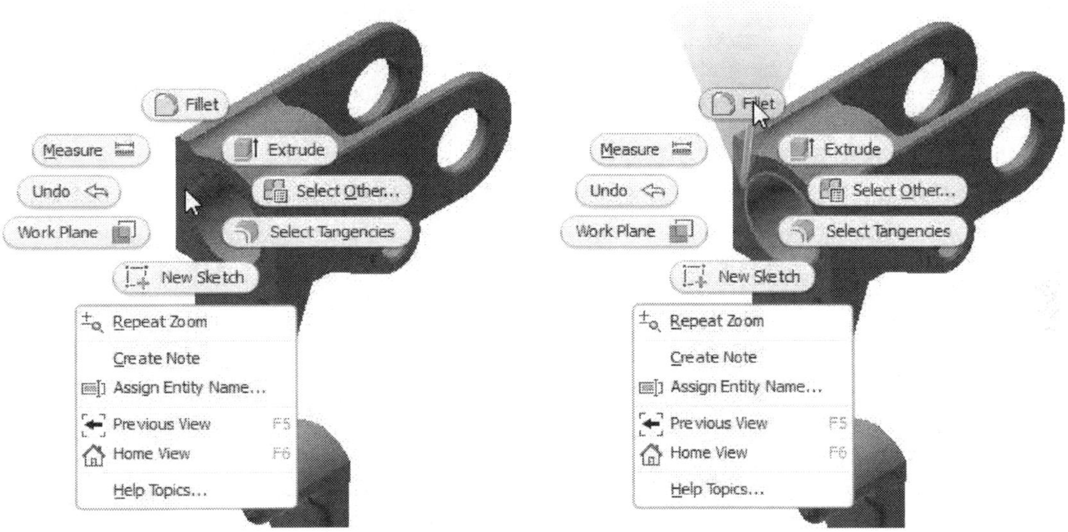

Figure 1–11

- As you become familiar with the marking menu commands, you can use gesturing behavior to initiate commands. To gesture, click and hold the right mouse button, immediately drag the cursor in the direction of the required marking menu wedge to create a trail, and release the mouse button. If these operations are completed in 250 milliseconds, the selected wedge is briefly displayed to confirm that the operation has been performed.
- To close the marking menu, you can start another command, select away from the marking menu, or press <Esc>.

  ***Note:** The marking menu can be customized using the **Customize** option in the Tools tab. This is covered later in this learning guide.*

Feature Creation Controls

When you create a feature, you must define a variety of properties. Depending on the feature type being created, you can define these using the Properties panel, a Feature dialog box, or the mini-toolbar.

- In the example shown in Figure 1–12, a Hole feature is being created and it uses the Properties panel to define all the hole properties. Dimensional values and references can also be defined directly on the model geometry.

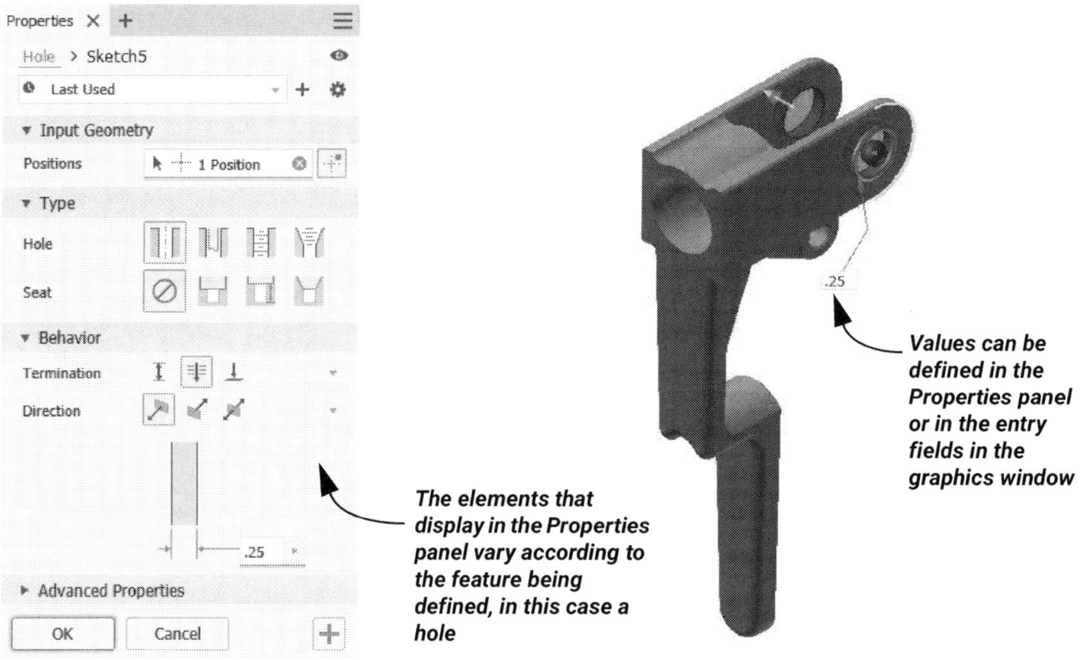

Figure 1–12

Note: *Autodesk is slowly transitioning all feature creation controls to the Properties panel interface. As of the 2024 Inventor release, this has not yet been completed.*

- In the example shown in Figure 1–13, a Chamfer feature is being created and the Chamfer dialog box and its mini-toolbar are displayed. Options can be selected in either location.

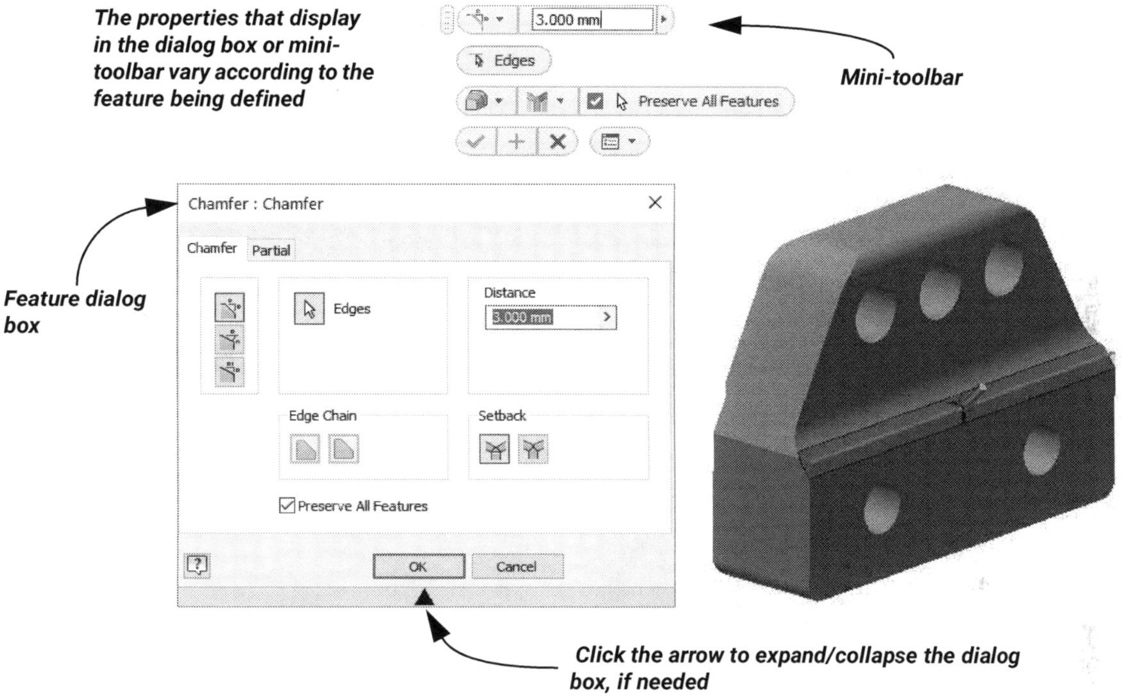

Figure 1–13

Hint: Mini-Toolbar Display

By default, the display of the mini-toolbar is toggled off. To toggle on its display, on the *View* tab, expand **User Interface** and enable the **Mini-Toolbar** option in the list of interface items. The use of the mini-toolbar is optional. In this learning guide, you will toggle it on and learn how to use it. The mini-toolbar is only available for features that use the Feature dialog box. They are not available when creating features that use the Properties panel.

Accessing Help

A number of different tools are available to get help with the software:

- To access context-sensitive help (when available), click [?] in any active Feature dialog box or click ≡ (Advanced Settings Menu)>**Help** in a Properties panel.
- Hover the cursor over a command name to display a tooltip, as shown in Figure 1–14. Some tooltips provide a video demonstration in place of a static image.

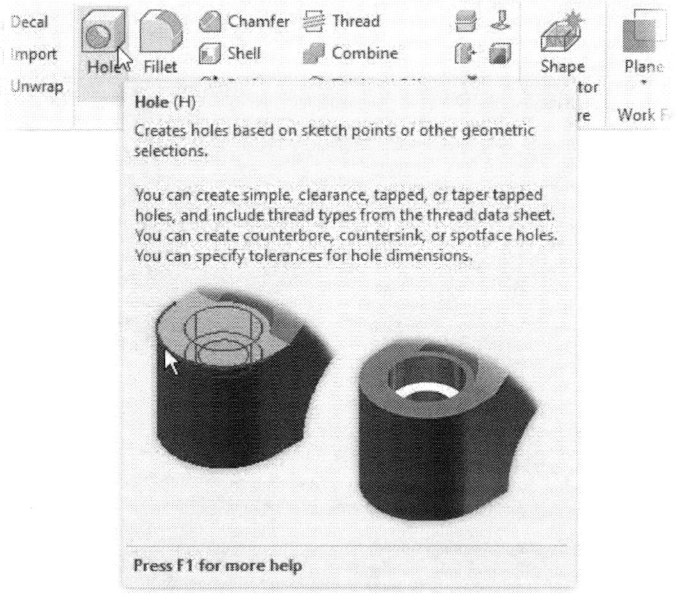

Figure 1–14

- If you are connected to the Internet, you can use Online Help. To access the Help documentation, click ⓘ (Help) in the top-right corner of the interface, click **Help** on the Home page, or press <F1>. Use the *Search* tab to enter a topic to search for or browse the available topics in the Help window.
- The Help documents can be installed locally. This installation is done in the software load point to ensure that it located when required. Once installed, in the Application Options dialog box>*General* tab, enable **Installed Local help**.
- Enter text in the *<Search Help & Commands>* field in the title bar to search for a keyword or phrase. The resulting list updates as you are typing and is divided based on the type of the result (e.g., commands, help articles, support articles, discussion groups, etc). If you press <Enter> after entering a keyword or phrase, the Help files are loaded.

1.2 Model Manipulation in Inventor

Model Orientation

When working with Autodesk Inventor models, being able to manipulate their orientation and display style helps you to better visualize them. The interface elements that control this are shown in Figure 1–15.

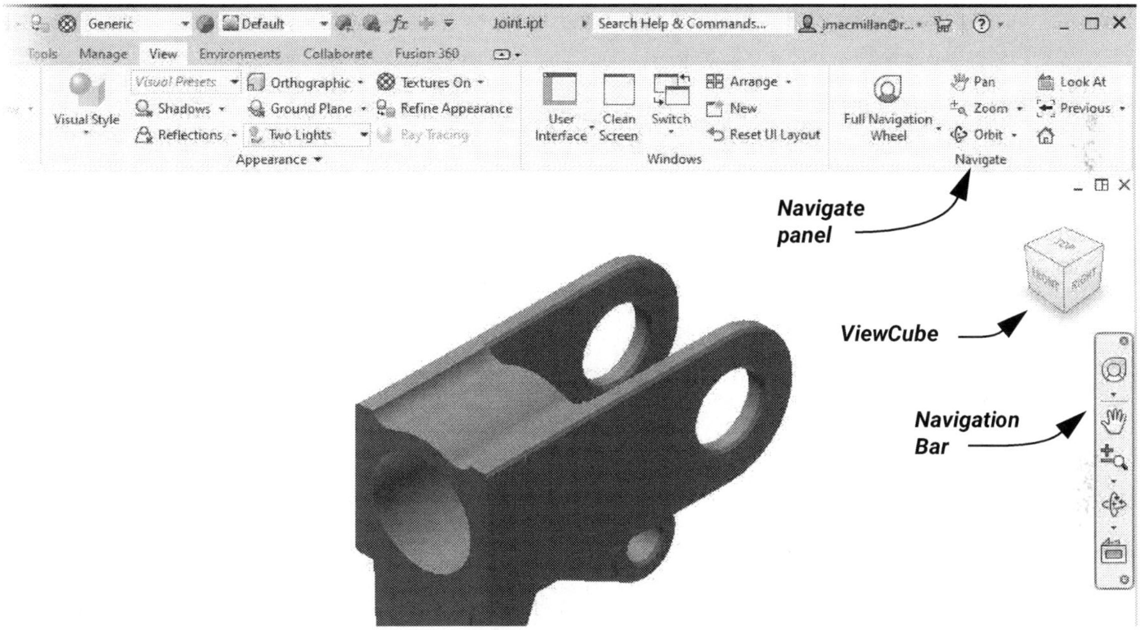

Figure 1–15

A model can be oriented using the software's pan, zoom, rotate and ViewCube controls.

Pan a Model

The **Pan** command moves a model in the graphics window in any direction planar to the screen.

How To: Pan a Model

1. Click (Pan) in the *View* tab>Navigate panel or in the Navigation Bar.
2. Press and hold the left mouse button.
3. Move the mouse to drag the model.

   Note: *You can also pan a model by pressing and holding the middle mouse button while dragging the mouse, or by holding <F2> and panning with the left mouse button.*

Rotate a Model

The **Orbit** command rotates a model around the center of the window, free in all directions, or around the X- or Y-axis.

How To: Rotate a Model

1. Click (Orbit) in the *View* tab>Navigate panel or in the Navigation Bar. The Rotate symbol (a circle) displays on the screen. The appearance of the cursor changes based on the location of the cursor relative to this circle.
2. Drag the cursor to the required orientation.
   - To rotate freely, move the cursor inside the circle. The cursor appearance changes to . Click and hold the left mouse button and then rotate the model in any direction.
   - To rotate about the horizontal axis, move the cursor to the top or bottom handle of the circle symbol. The cursor appearance changes to . Press and hold the left mouse button and rotate the model about the Y-axis.
   - To rotate about the vertical axis, move the cursor to the left or right handle of the circle symbol. The cursor appearance changes to . Press and hold the left mouse button and drag horizontally.
   - To rotate about an axis through the center of the circle symbol (normal to the screen), move the cursor to the rim of the circle symbol. The cursor appearance changes to . Drag the mouse to rotate. To change the center of the rotation, click inside or outside the circle to set the new center.
   - To stop rotating, click again to clear it. Alternatively, while still in the orbit circle, move the cursor away from the model until displays, and click in the graphics window.

   Note: *You can also press and hold <F4> to rotate using the rotate symbol.*

As an alternative to using the (Orbit) tool, you can press and hold <Shift> and use the middle mouse button to rotate the model. Using this method, the model is rotated about a pivot point that appears in the graphics window. Where the pivot point will appear on the model depends on the following:

- If the full model displays in the graphics window, the pivot point is the model geometry center.
- If the model is only partially displayed in the graphics window, the pivot point snaps to the nearest edge/face/vertex.
- If the model is fully panned outside the graphics window, the pivot point is at the cursor location.

Zoom a Model

The **Zoom** command zooms in and out on the model, on a specific entity, or on an area. The available zoom types are shown in Figure 1–16.

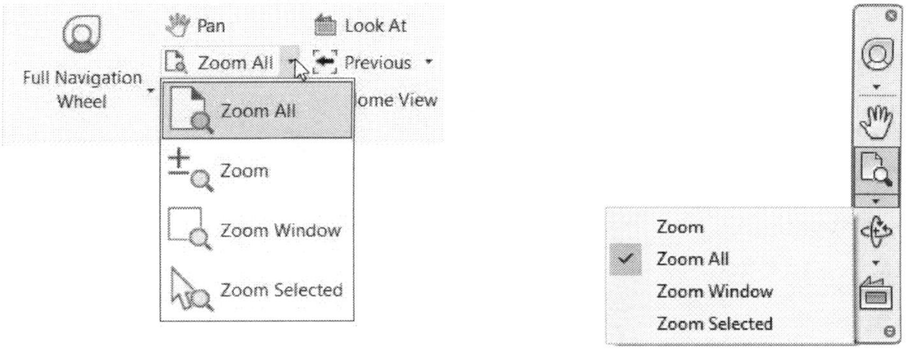

Figure 1–16

How To: Zoom in a Model

1. In the *View* tab>Navigate panel or the Navigation Bar, expand the zoom controls and click **Zoom**.
2. Press and hold the left mouse button.
3. Move the cursor down to zoom in, and up to zoom out.

   Note: *You can also press and hold <F3> to zoom.*

How To: Zoom to a Specific Entity

1. In the *View* tab>Navigate panel or the Navigation Bar, expand the zoom controls and click **Zoom Selected**.
2. Select the entity.

When zooming to an edge or vertex (not a surface), the order in which you select the entity and toolbar icon is important. Clicking the icon, and then clicking on a point on the entity positions the entity in the center of the screen, and maintains the current zoom level. Selecting the reverse (the entity and then clicking the icon), causes the software to zoom to the selected entity. When zooming on a surface, the order of selection does not have an impact.

How To: Zoom to an Area

1. In the *View* tab>Navigate panel or the Navigation Bar, expand the zoom controls and click **Zoom Window**.
2. Select a location on the model using the left mouse button to define the corner of the bounding box zoom area.
3. Drag the mouse to draw a box over the area to zoom.
4. Press or release the left mouse button when the box has been drawn.

Refit the Model

In the *View* tab>Navigate panel or the Navigation Bar, expand the zoom controls and click **Zoom All**. The view returns to its default zoom level and the model is centered in the graphics window.

Look At

To orient a face parallel to the screen, click (Look At) in the *View* tab>Navigate panel or in the Navigation Bar, and select the face. The model reorients and displays the selected face parallel to the screen. In the example shown in Figure 1–17, a face was selected and was reoriented using this command.

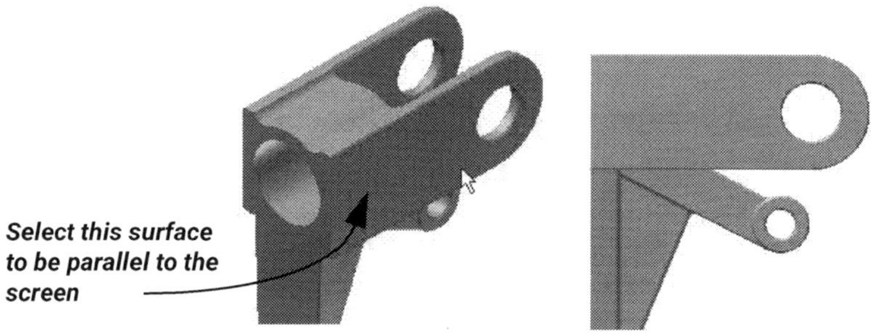

Figure 1–17

ViewCube

As an alternative to the **Look At** command, you can use ViewCube functionality to orient a model face parallel to the screen. By default, the ViewCube displays in the top-right corner of the graphics window, as shown on the left in Figure 1–18. When you hover your mouse over the ViewCube in its 2D or 3D orientation, you can return to the Home view or access additional orientation options.

Figure 1–18

The ViewCube enables the following:

- Select any of the sides of the cube to display the parallel view that is associated with it (**Front**, **Right**, **Bottom**, etc.). Edges can also be selected on the ViewCube to reorient the model.
- Set the type of view to **Orthographic**, **Perspective**, or **Perspective with Ortho Faces** by right-clicking on the ViewCube and selecting the required option.
- Return to a Home view by clicking , which displays at the top-left of the ViewCube when you hover the cursor over it. Initially the Home view is the default isometric orientation.
- Set a new Home view for your model by right-clicking on the ViewCube and selecting **Select Current View as Home**.
- Select and drag a surface on the ViewCube to rotate. If in a 2D orientation, select the rotation arrows that appear.

  Note: *To display the ViewCube settings, right-click on it and select* ***Options****. The ViewCube Options dialog box enables you to control the location, size, default ViewCube orientation, etc. The orientation enables you to select two parallel origin planes to define the orientation.*

Full Navigation Wheel

The Full Navigation Wheel (shown in Figure 1–19) provides an alternative to the *View* tab and Navigation Bar commands for zooming, panning, and rotating. The **Rewind** command on the wheel enables you to navigate through previous views.

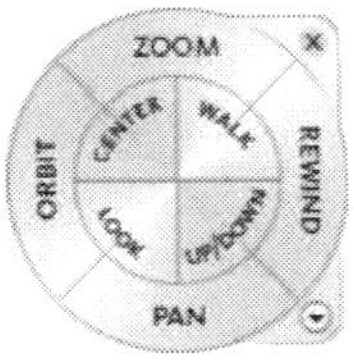

Figure 1–19

The Full Navigation Wheel moves with the cursor to provide access to the navigation tools.

How To: Use the Navigation Tool

1. Enable the tool by clicking  (Full Navigation Wheel) in the *View* tab>Navigate panel or in the Navigation Bar. The Full Navigation Wheel displays attached to the mouse.
2. Press and hold the mouse on a command (e.g., **Zoom**).
3. Move the cursor to change the view as required.
4. Release the mouse button to end the navigation command.
5. Click  or the **x** in the top-right corner of the tool to close the Full Navigation Wheel.

   Note: *In addition to the* ***Zoom****,* ***Orbit****,* ***Pan****, and* ***Rewind*** *commands, other more advanced tools are available on the inner ring of the Full Navigation Wheel that are not covered in this guide.*

Model Display

By default, new models created using the default templates display as **Shaded with Edges**. However, other visual styles can be assigned. All visual styles are available in the *View* tab> Appearance panel as shown in Figure 1–20.

Note: *The ability to use many of the styles depends on your computer's graphics hardware.*

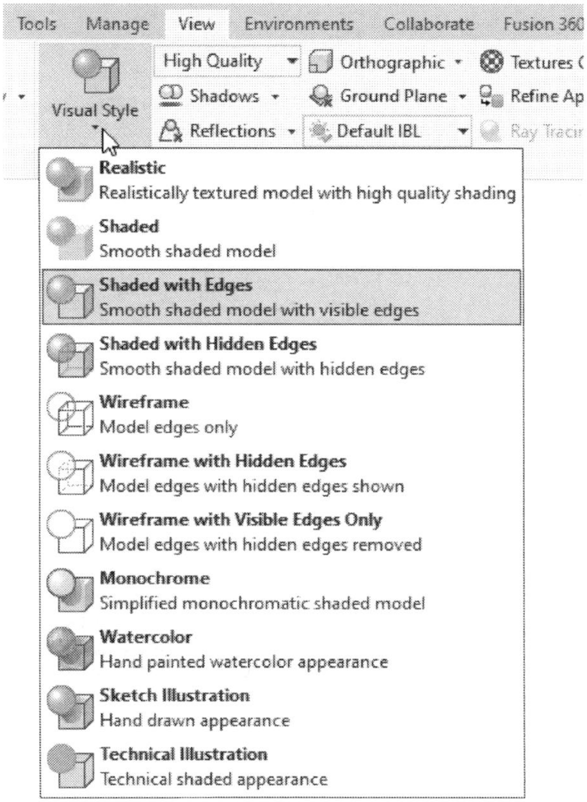

Figure 1–20

Note: *The* ***Realistic*** *setting is dependent on the color and lighting settings that are applied in the model. When using this style you can also incorporate Ray Tracing to further enhance model display. Additionally, the watercolor and illustration settings provide artistic, hand-painted, and drawn representations of the model.*

Figure 1–21 shows some examples of the available visual styles.

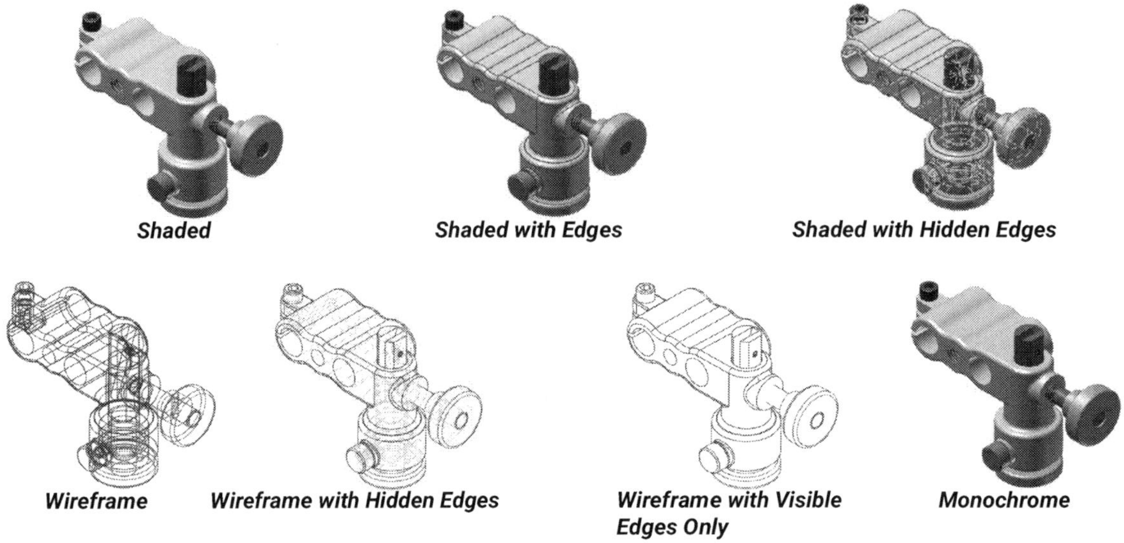

Figure 1–21

Sketched Entity Selection

There are several ways to select sketched entities for editing. Consider using any of the following:

- To select an individual object in a sketch, select it using the left mouse button.
- To add additional objects to the selection set, hold <Ctrl> or <Shift> and left-click additional objects.
- Select and drag a boundary box from left to right around objects (as shown in Figure 1–22) to select them. Only objects that are entirely enclosed in the window are selected. This is called the Window Selection technique.

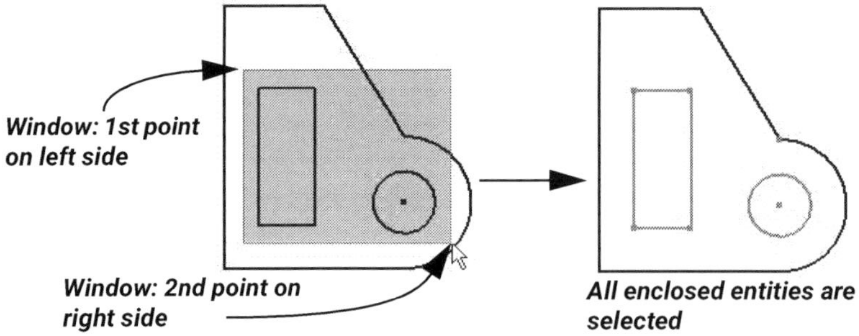

Figure 1–22

- Select and drag a boundary box from right to left around objects (as shown in Figure 1–23) to select them. Objects are selected if they are entirely enclosed in the window, or if any part of the object crosses the sketched border. This is called the Crossing Selection technique.

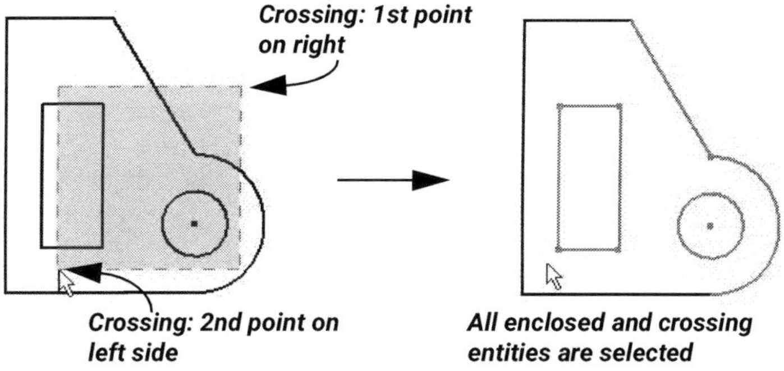

Figure 1–23

Note: *If you drag a boundary box in the wrong direction (i.e., start a window instead of a crossing), select a second point so that the sketched area is empty, and start again.*

- To clear objects, you can hold <Ctrl> or <Shift> and individually select entities, or use the window or crossing techniques to select entities. To clear all of the objects, click in a blank space in the graphics window.

Tangent Entity Selection

To quickly select tangent entities (edges or faces) in a model, right-click on an entity and select **Select Tangencies**, as shown Figure 1–24. As an alternative to using the context menu to access the command, you can also double-click on the entity to quickly select all tangent entities.

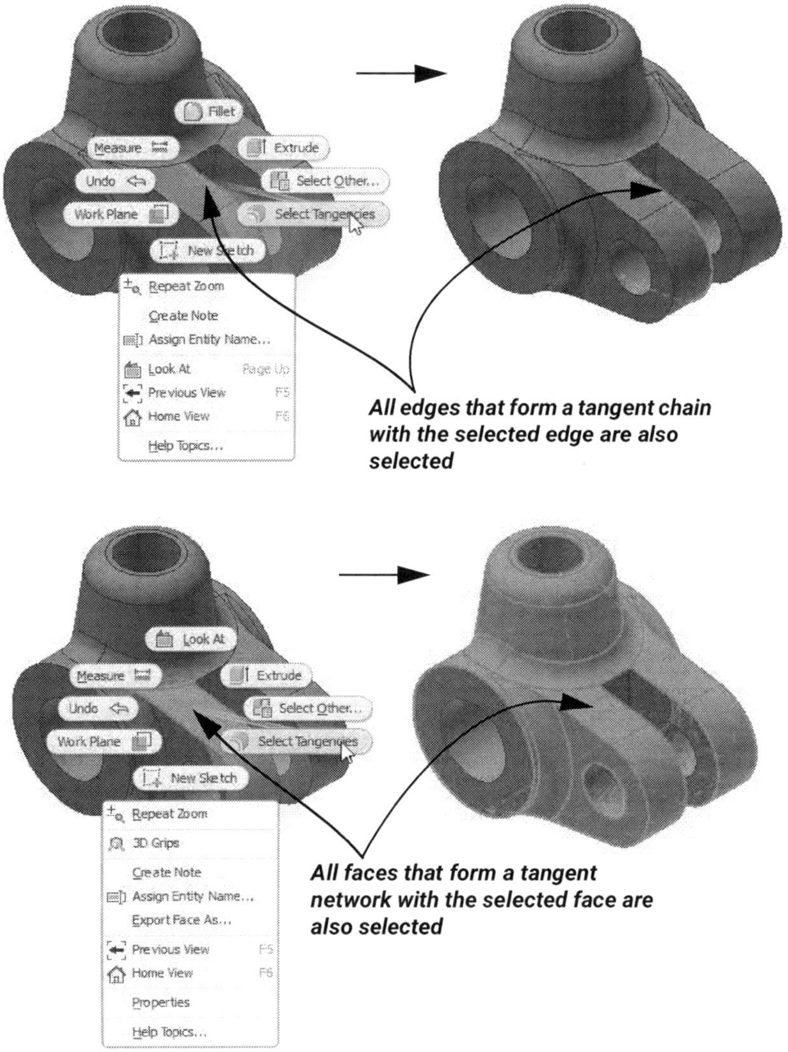

Figure 1–24

Selecting Hidden Entities or Features

To select hidden entities or features, hover the cursor over an object until a drop-down list displays, or right-click and select **Select Other** to open the drop-down list. The list displays all of the shown and hidden features and entities based on the current cursor location, as shown in Figure 1–25. Scroll through the drop-down list and select the required entity when it is highlighted. Alternatively, you can also use the middle mouse button to scroll through the shown and hidden features.

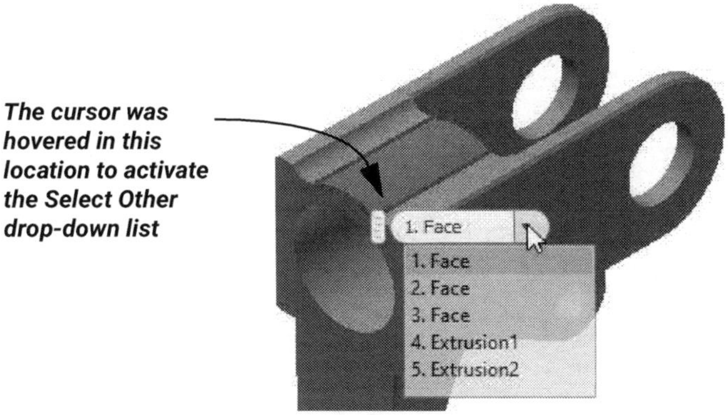

Figure 1–25

Selection Filter

The selection filter in the Quick Access Toolbar enables you to filter entities, features, or components so that you can only select that type of object. For example, if you select **Select Face and Edges**, you can only select the faces or edges on the model. The options that display in the drop-down list vary depending on the current mode. Part mode options display as shown in Figure 1–26. To quickly access the filter options without having to use the Quick Access Toolbar, press and hold <Shift> as you right-click in the main window.

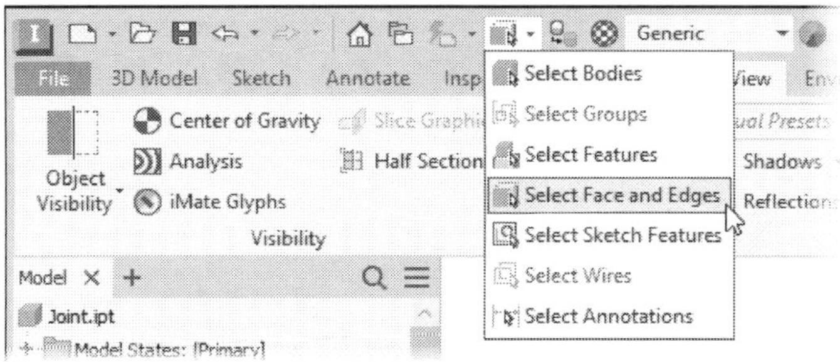

Figure 1–26

Suppressing Features

As you work on a complex part, you might find it difficult to identify or select features in the graphics window. You can simplify the appearance of a model by suppressing a feature to make it temporarily invisible. To suppress a feature, right-click on it in the Model browser and select **Suppress Features**, as shown on the left in Figure 1–27. If you suppress a feature, all of its dependent features are also suppressed. Suppressed features and any of their dependent features are displayed in gray and are crossed out in the Model browser, as shown on the right in Figure 1–27.

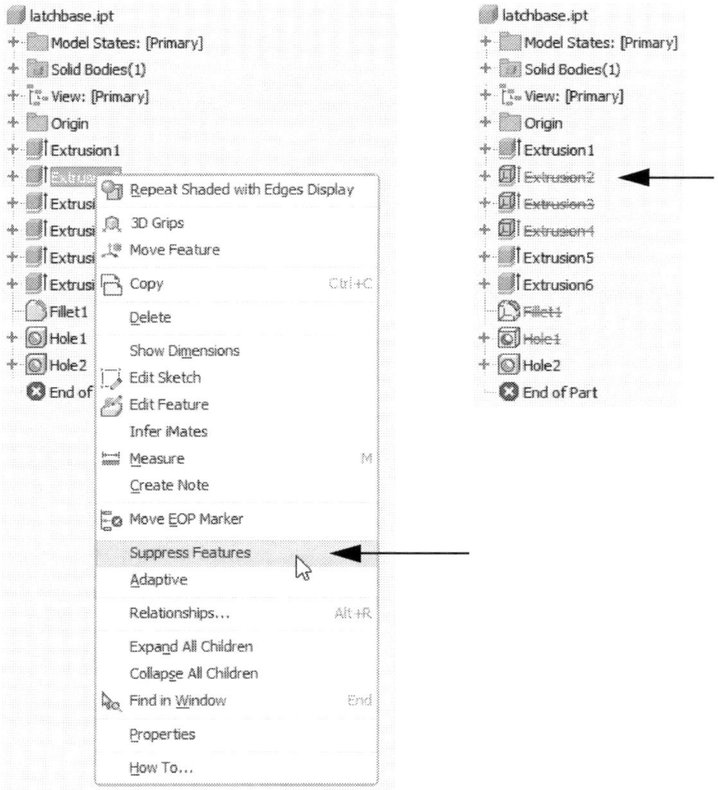

Figure 1–27

> ***Note:*** *You can select features for suppression directly in the graphics window if the* ***Select Features*** *feature priority setting is set.*

To unsuppress a feature, right-click on the feature in the Model browser and select **Unsuppress Features**. The dependent features that were suppressed are also unsuppressed.

1.3 Introduction to Autodesk Inventor CAM

Autodesk Inventor CAM is an add-on tool that is available for the Autodesk Inventor software product. Inventor CAM is an integrated computer-aided manufacturing (CAM) solution that allows users to generate toolpaths for their models quickly and easily within the same application that was used to design the 3D CAD model. It supports 2D, 3D, 3+2 Milling, 5x simultaneous Milling, and Turning functions. With both the design and manufacturing solution integrated into the one software package, changes that are made to the design model can be easily reflected in the generated toolpath and NC data.

Manufacturing Terms

The following table defines some of the important Inventor CAM manufacturing terms that are used regularly in this course. All terms are discussed further throughout the guide.

Design Model	The 3D finished model that is being manufactured
Stock	The starting material that is used to create the finished geometry. The stock is also known as the workpiece.
Fixture	The part or assembly that is used to hold and orient the workpiece during the manufacturing process
Work Coordinate System (WCS)	The coordinate system that locates both the program start position (0,0,0) for the CL data and the workpiece orientation with respect to the machine. The positive Z-axis must always point away from the machine fixture.
Tool	The piece of hardware on the machine that creates cuts in the workpiece (e.g., Flat Endmill, Drill, Bore)
Tool Holder	The piece of hardware on the machine that holds the tool while machining the model
Operation	The information for a set of NC sequences using one particular machine
NC Sequence	The information specific to one particular toolpath, such as cut parameters, cut motion, or tool motion. It also holds retract surface and coordinate system information.
CL Data (Cutter Location Data)	The output from an NC sequence or operation that shows the location of the cutter control point(s)
Setup Sheet	The HTML-generated file that provides an overview of the NC program for the CNC operator
Post Process	The conversion of the ASCII CL data file produced by the software into NC-code
NC-code/G-code/ N-code	The code that can be read by the machine's control system to cut the model. The terms are used interchangeably. In the case of G-code, the lines of code contain the letter G, and for N-code, they contain the letter N. The post-processing step determines the code that is output and is dependent on what the machine being used requires.

General Inventor CAM Workflow

The following steps describe an overview of the process involved in using the Inventor CAM add-in to create CNC code to manufacture your design model. This overview acts as a reference to use throughout this guide. All stages are discussed further in related topics.

1. Create or import the design model that is to be manufactured.
2. Create the first setup for the operation in the Inventor CAM environment. This includes:
    - selecting the NC machine that will be used,
    - defining the operation type (e.g., Milling, Turning, Mill/Turn, Cutting),
    - selecting the work coordinate system (WCS) on the model,
    - selecting the model (if the default selection is not as required),
    - selecting any fixture geometry that is to be avoided, and
    - defining the stock that is to be used to machine the model.
3. Define toolpath(s) based on the setup's operation type (e.g., Face, 2D Pocket, 2D Contour, Groove).
4. Preview the toolpath to verify it was created accurately.
5. Post process the CL data file to generate an NC program that the NC machine can interpret.

    Note: *Multiple setups can be created, as needed, in the same design model.*

Once the NC program file is generated, you can send the data to the NC machine to manufacture the model.

1.4 The Autodesk Inventor CAM Interface

The Inventor CAM interface is the same as that used when creating the 3D model. The only difference is that, once installed, the *CAM* tab is available in the ribbon and the CAM browser can be accessed, as shown in Figure 1–28.

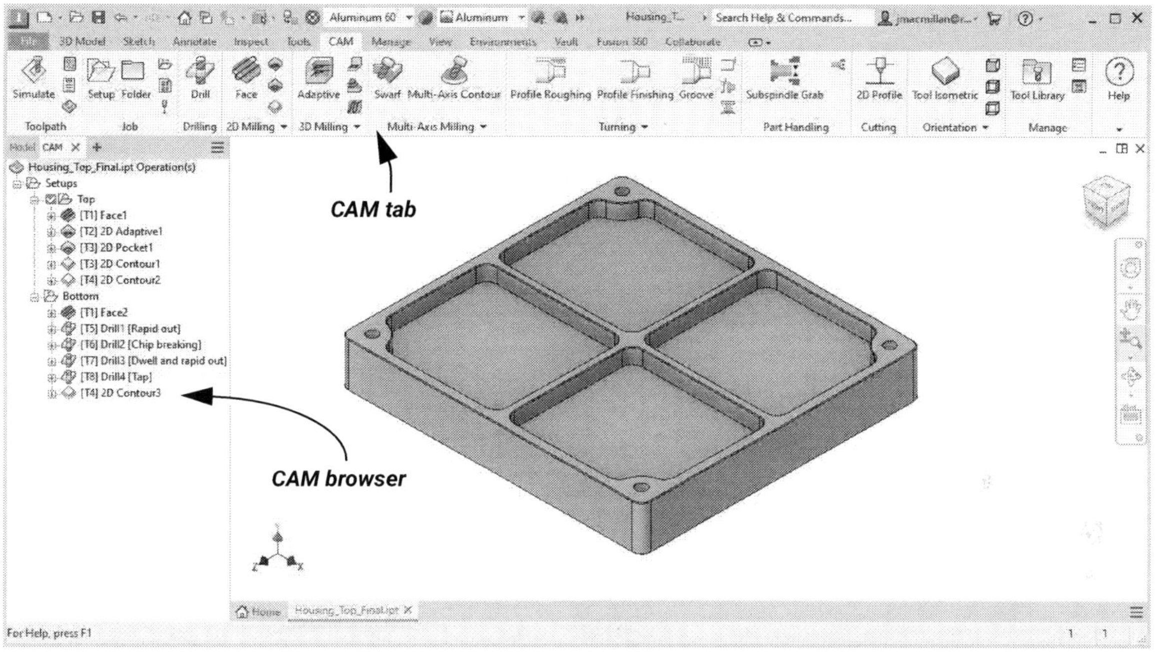

Figure 1–28

CAM Tab

The *CAM* tab is only available if the Autodesk Inventor CAM add-in is installed. This tab provides access to all of the tools that you will need to set up your manufacturing model, define and simulate your toolpaths, and post process the data to generate the required NC code for your CNC machines. Figure 1–29 shows the options that are available when the *CAM* tab is selected. The options displayed are for the Inventor CAM Ultimate add-on. The panels that are displayed on this ribbon vary depending on the CAM add-on package that is installed.

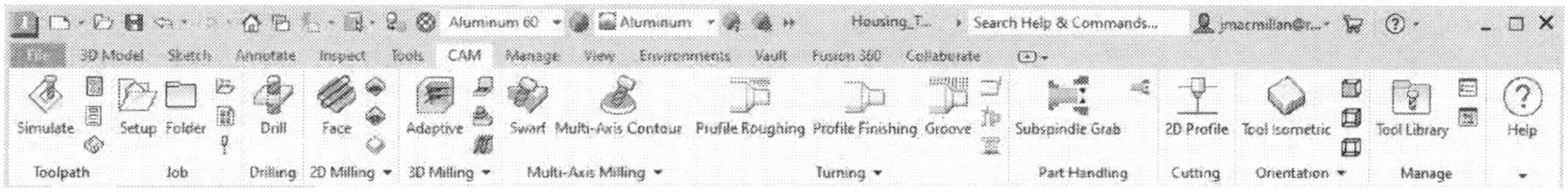

Figure 1–29

CAM Browser

The CAM browser is where all of the CAM operations are listed and organized according to each defined setup. This browser is only available once a setup has been created in the model.

If the CAM browser is not displayed once a setup has been assigned, click + to expand the list of available tabs and select **CAM**.

The CAM browser can contain multiple setups to accurately define the machining processes that are required. Figure 1–30 shows a CAM browser that has two setups. There are five toolpaths in Setup1and five toolpaths in Setup2.

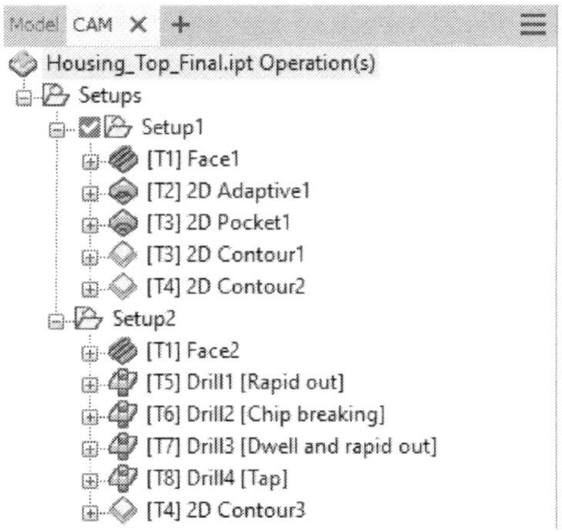

Figure 1–30

- The active setup is identified with the ☑ icon adjacent to the setup name. All new sequence operations that are assigned get added automatically to the setup that is identified as the default folder. To assign the default folder, right-click on the setup name and select **Default Folder**. When a new setup is created, it is automatically set as the default folder.
- Expand a toolpath node to display information on its tool, WCS, and size, as shown in Figure 1–31.

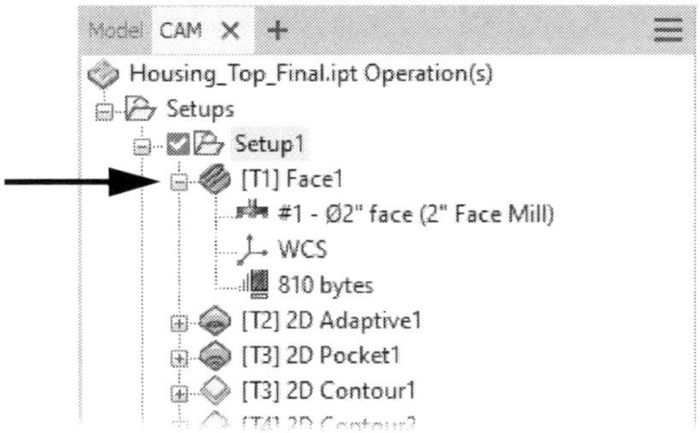

Figure 1–31

- Contextual right-click menus are available in the CAM browser by selecting on the file's Operation(s) node (top of the list), the setup nodes, or the toolpaths. Examples of these menus are shown in Figure 1–32. In general, the contextual options provide quick access to the options in the ribbon; however, they do provide some additional options that allow you to show log messages (**Show Logs**) and assign notes uniquely to a setup or toolpath (**Edit Notes**).

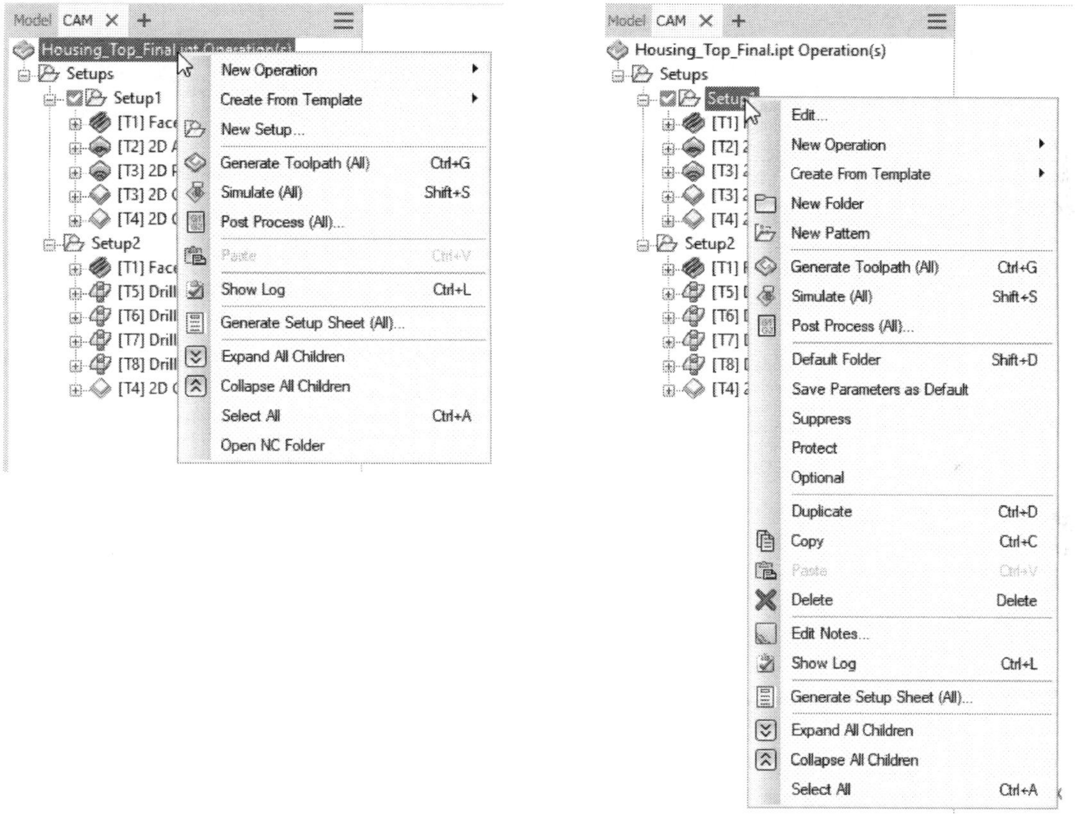

Figure 1–32

- Double-clicking any node name will open the palette used to create it. You can edit the options within the palette to modify the item.
- All of the node names (setup or toolpath) can be renamed. Single-click to select it and then slowly select it again to rename it. Consider using names that will help identify or describe the item.

Palettes

Inventor CAM uses a palette interface for machining setups, creating toolpaths, and running simulations.These palettes are shown in Figure 1–33. Each of these palettes display different tabs that are used to define the options available.

Depending on the width of your pallet and the number of tabs, the tab name may or may not be displayed.

In the Toolpath palette, there are five tabs so only the icons are displayed at this width.

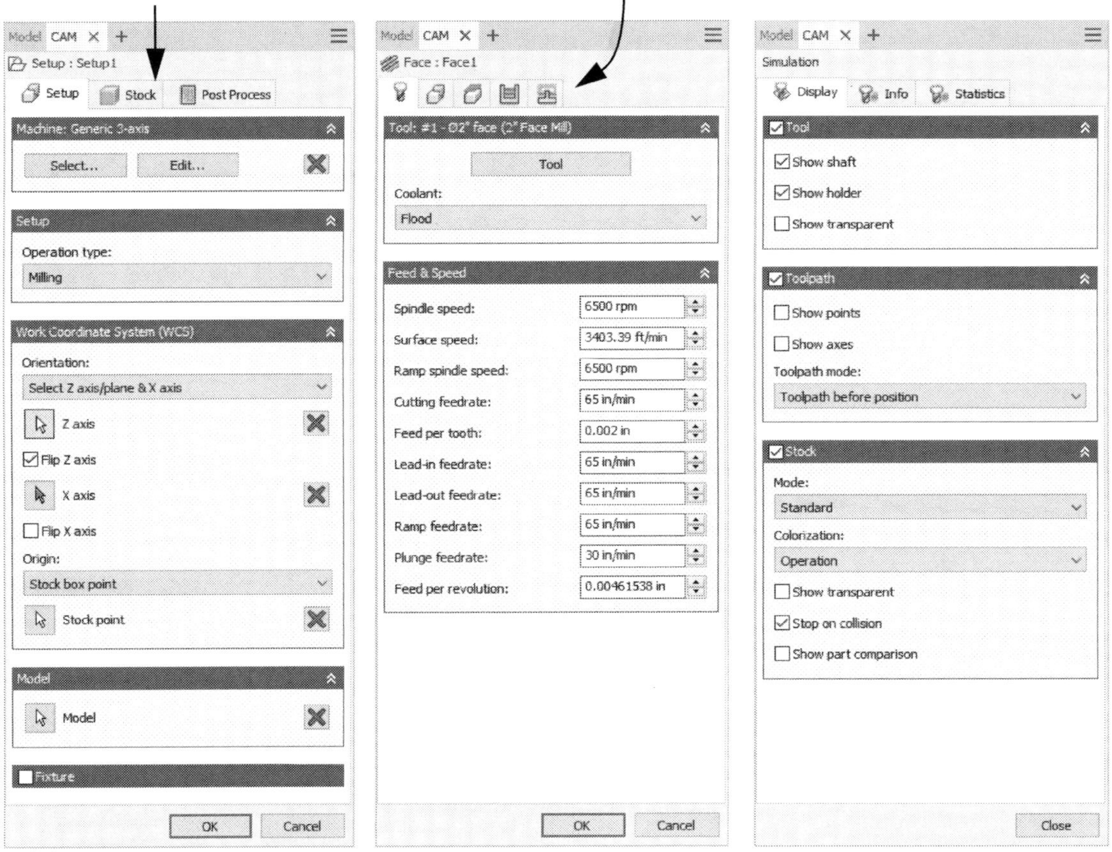

Setup Palette ***Toolpath Palette*** ***Simulation Palette***

Figure 1–33

The different tabs and options are discussed in more detail throughout this guide.

Graphics Window

The graphics window is the main working area of the model. In addition to displaying the 3D model, in the CAM environment, it displays the stock, work coordinate system (WCS), and toolpath movements that have been created in the model. The display of these items is based on the items selected in the CAM browser once a setup(s) and toolpath(s) have been created.

- To display the stock and WCS for a setup, select the setup name in the CAM browser, as shown in Figure 1–34. This allows you to quickly preview the setup and verify that the stock and WCS have been assigned properly.

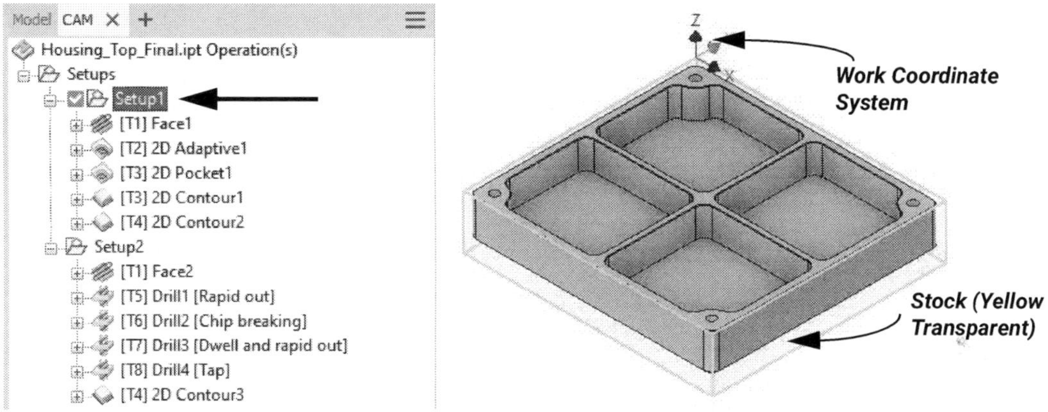

Figure 1–34

- To display a toolpath in the graphics window, select the toolpath name in the CAM browser. The toolpath movements are color coded (as shown in Figure 1–35):
  - Cutting paths are displayed in blue.
  - Lead-in moves are displayed in green.
  - Rapid moves are displayed in yellow.
  - Spiral plunge paths are displayed in red.
  - The start and end of the toolpath are indicated by a red and green triangle, respectively.

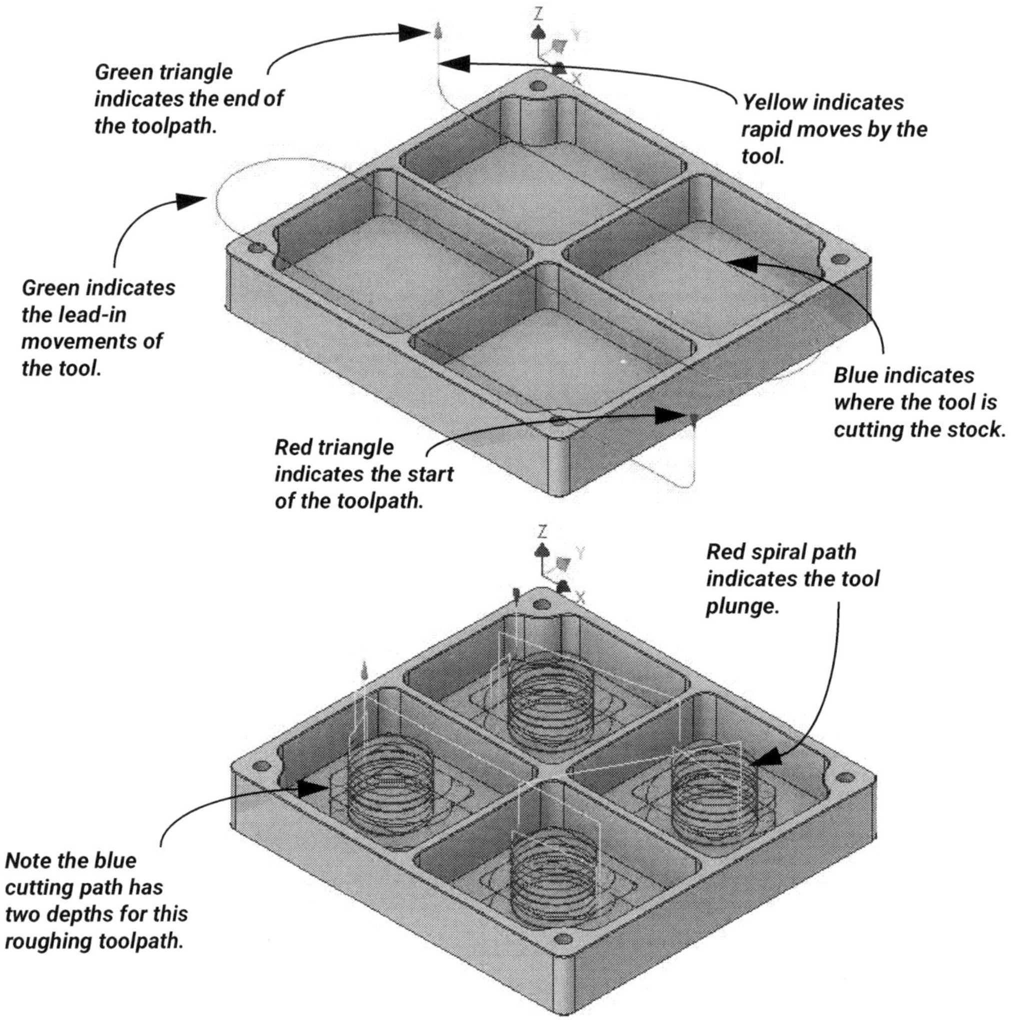

Figure 1–35

Note: *Multiple toolpaths can be displayed at one time by pressing and holding <Ctrl> while selecting the toolpath names in the CAM browser.*

The CAM Simulation environment is also displayed in the graphics window. This is discussed in detail in a later topic.

Preferences

There are a number of preference options that you can set to configure the CAM environment.

To access these options, in the Manage panel, click (Options). The CAM Options dialog box opens as shown in Figure 1–36. Enable or disable the options, as required, on the *User Interface* and *Browser* tabs.

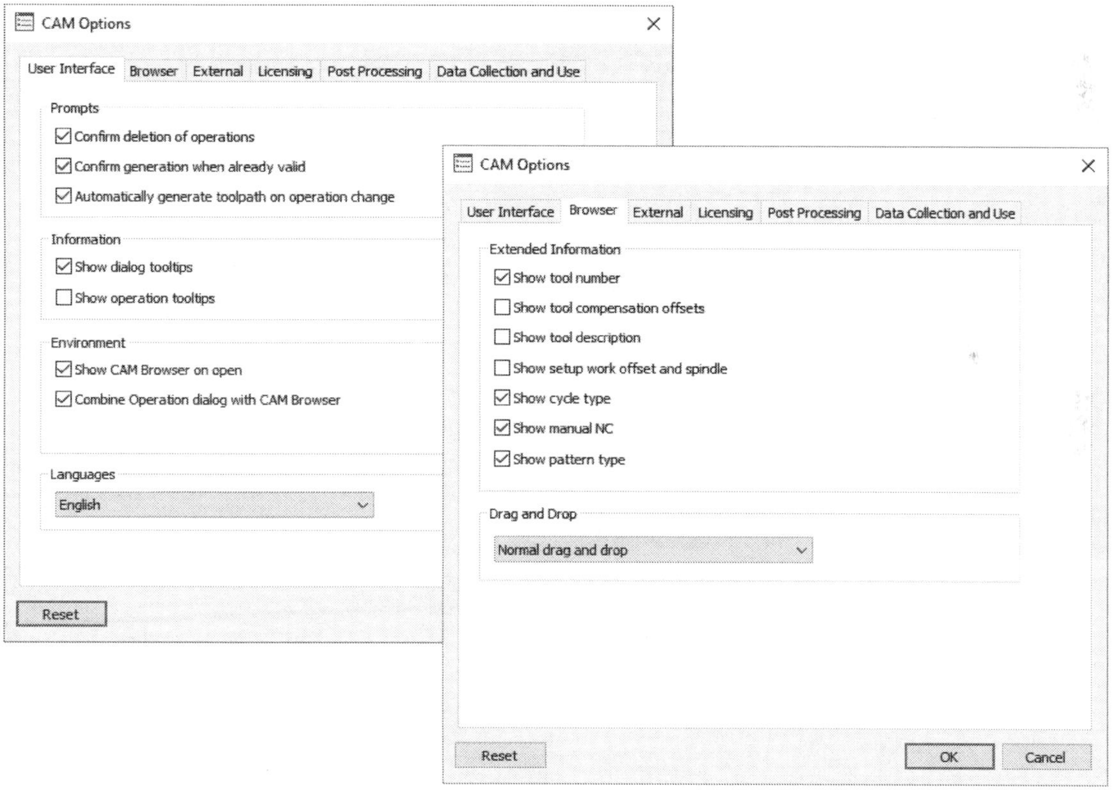

Figure 1–36

1.5 Simulating CAM Operations

The **Simulate** option enables you to visually preview toolpaths in the graphics window to help confirm that they have been set up properly. This section discusses the options in this environment that control the display as well as the playback and speed of the simulation. A simulation can be run on any of the following:

- **Operation** - Select the file's Operation(s) node at the top of the CAM browser to simulate the entire operation.
- **Setup** - Select a setup node in the CAM browser to simulate all of the toolpaths in the selected setup.
- **Toolpath** - Select a toolpath node in the CAM browser to simulate the single selected toolpath. Multiple toolpaths can be simulated at the same time by pressing and holding <Ctrl> prior to activating the simulation option.

To enable this environment, select an item in the CAM browser and then in the *CAM* tab>Toolpath panel, click (Simulate). Once active, the Simulation palette and Simulation Player Timeline appear. Depending on the width of your palette, the tab name beside the icon may or may not be displayed. The icon will always be displayed.

Simulation Palette

The Simulation palette opens as shown in Figure 1–37. The (Display) tab is active by default. This tab controls the display of the Tool, Toolpath, and Stock in the graphics window during the simulation.

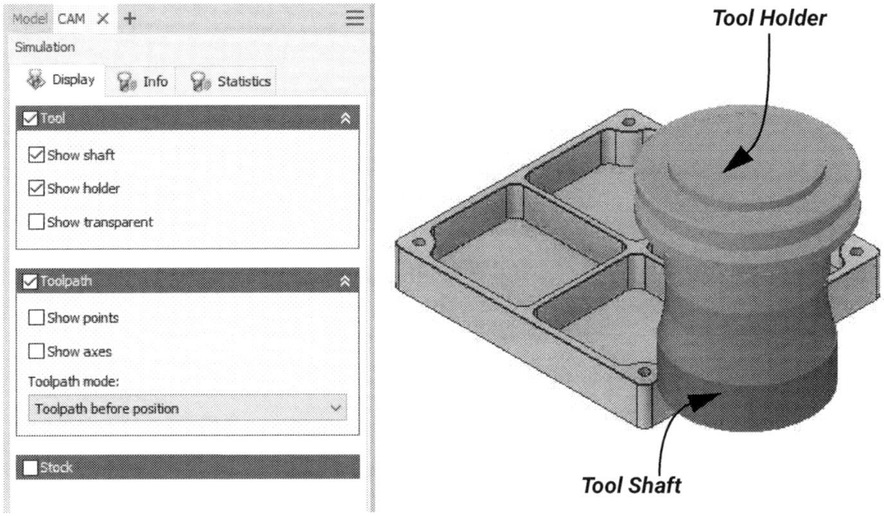

Figure 1–37

Review the following regarding the *Display* tab:

- By default, the **Tool** is set to display in a simulation. The shaft and holder for the tool are displayed as solid; however, the **Show Transparent** option can also be enabled to help with visualization. The tool's shaft and holder can be toggled on and off as required.
- By default, the **Toolpath** is set to display as the simulation is displayed. The Toolpath mode drop-down list can be used to control the path's display before, during, and after the tool traces the path.

  Note: *The toolpaths that are displayed help visualize the path of the tool. They display using the same color scheme as if you selected an operation in the CAM browser that was previously discussed.*

- By default, the **Stock** is not set to be displayed. This can be enabled to display the stock (green) during the simulation. If enabled, additional stock options are available, as shown in Figure 1–38.

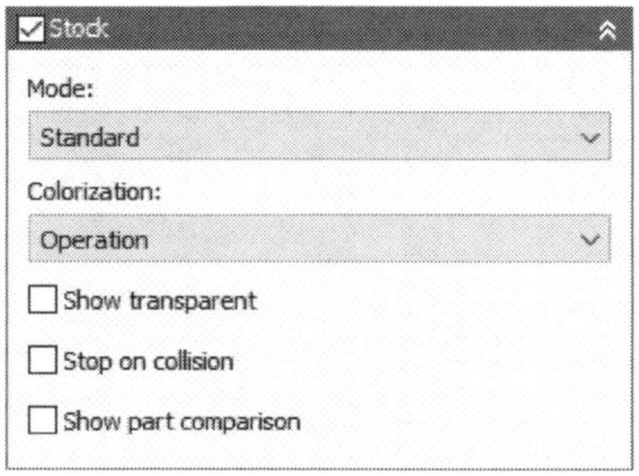

Figure 1–38

  - The Colorization drop-down list controls the color by tool, by operation, or simply display as the material color.
  - Select **Show transparent** to set the Stock to display transparently. Clear the option to return to solid display.
  - Select **Stop on collision**. This option is valuable to test that the manufacturing operations do not produce any collision between the shaft, holder, and fixture. This option does not detect gouges that would be made into the model by too much stock removal.
  - Select **Show part comparison** to compare the stock and part with one another after the toolpath is complete. Red indicates a gouge of the part and blue indicates an excess of stock.
- The tool that is displayed changes depending on the location of the marker in the simulation player timeline. If only a single toolpath is selected to be simulated, only a single tool is displayed.

The (Info) tab in the Simulation palette provides you with additional information at specific points on the simulation player timeline. These include general information about the position, operation type, and verification data. The specific values that are displayed depend on where the playback marker is located. The values in this tab constantly change throughout the simulation. Figure 1–39 shows an example of the values that are displayed.

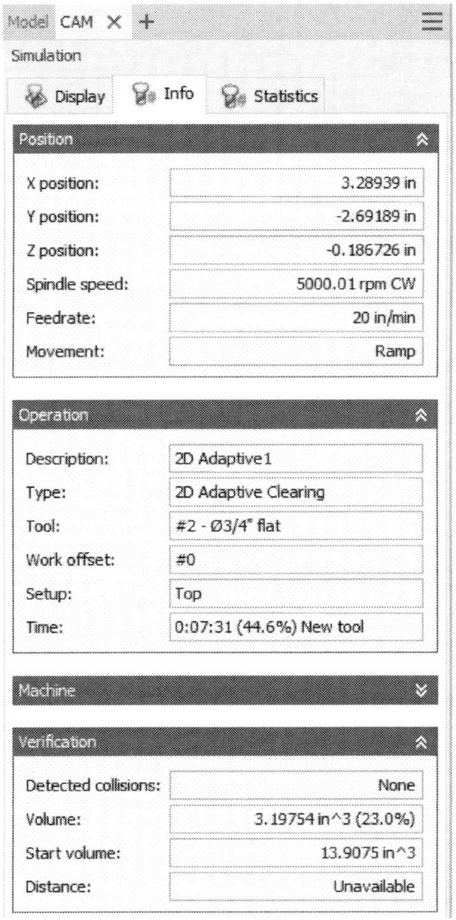

Figure 1–39

The (Statistics) tab in the Simulation palette provides you statistics for the selected operations/toolpaths. For example, to display the overall statistics for multiple setups with multiple toolpaths, you must have preselected the top-level operation to be simulated. The statistics show the overall machining time, distance, number of selected operations being simulated, and number of tool changes required, similar to that shown in Figure 1–40.

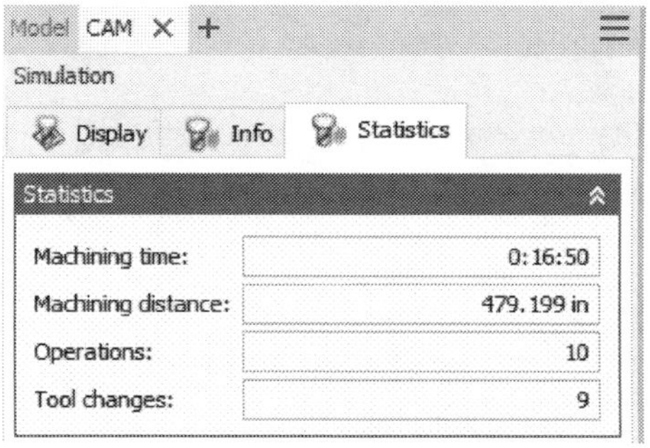

Figure 1–40

Simulation Player and Timeline

The simulation player and simulation player timeline (as shown in Figure 1–41) appear at the bottom of the graphics window when you activate the Simulation environment.

Figure 1–41

The simulation player timeline displays the operations that will be played in the simulation. In this situation, because the file's Operation(s) node was selected, it will play all operations in both setups. The current operation is displayed in green, while the remaining are displayed in alternating shades of gray to distinguish each change in operation.

- Information on an operation (as shown in Figure 1–42) can be displayed by hovering the cursor over an operation. If an operation encounters a collision, a red line appears through the operation in which it occurs.

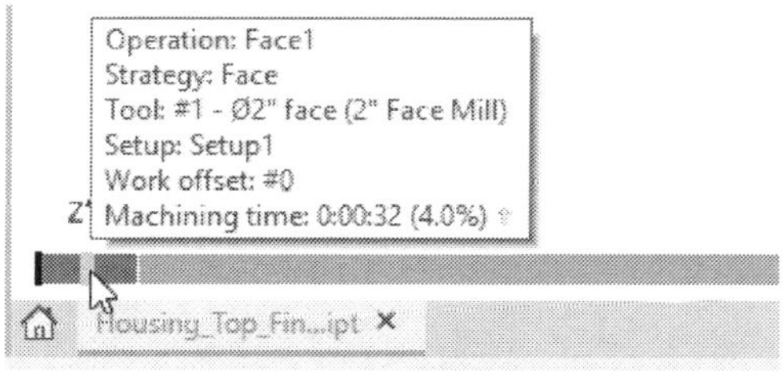

Figure 1–42

- Click  (Play) in the simulation player to play all selected operations/setups/toolpaths. Note how, as they are played, material is removed from the stock/solid model to simulate the machining of the model. The additional playback controls are described in Figure 1–43.

  The Play button switches to a  (Pause) button once playing.

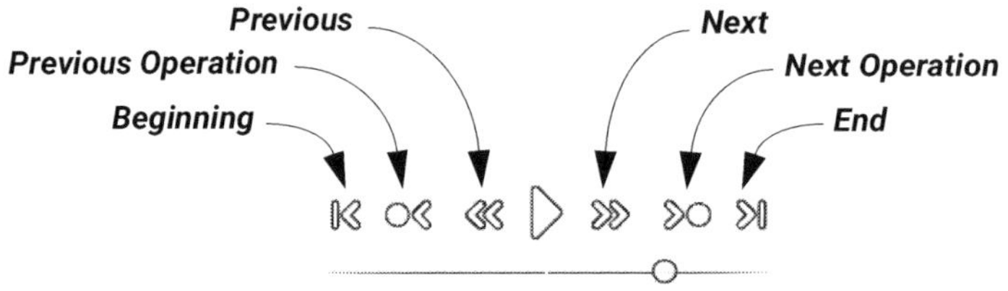

Figure 1–43

- Speed control can be manipulated while the simulation is in progress. To control the speed of the playback, select the circular control under the simulation player (as shown in Figure 1–44) and drag it to the right to increase the speed or to the left to reduce the speed. The playback reverses once you drag past the midpoint on the line.

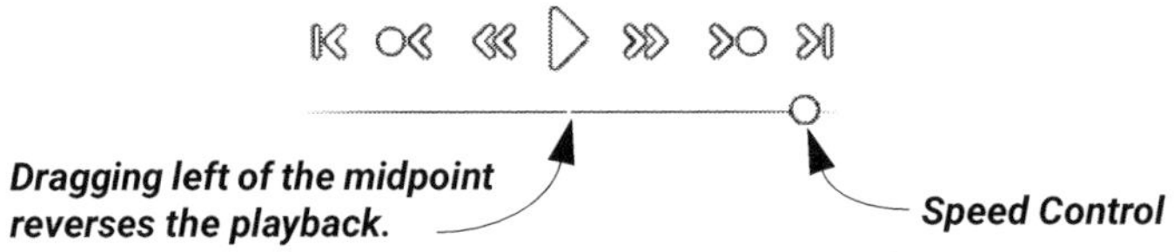

Figure 1–44

Once the simulation has completed, you will notice that all selected operations/setups/toolpaths are visible in the graphics window. For example, in Figure 1–45 the file's Operation(s) node was selected for simulation, so all toolpaths in both Setup1 and Setup2 are shown.

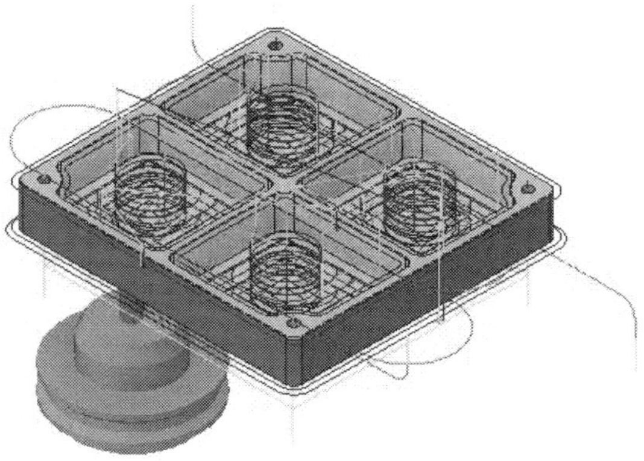

Figure 1–45

Click **Close** in the Simulation palette to close it once the simulation has been reviewed.

Practice 1a
Getting Started

Practice Objectives

- Navigate the Inventor interface to access the Inventor CAM environment.
- Review the Inventor CAM ribbon and CAM browser.
- Review setup parameters and toolpath operations that have been created in an Inventor model.
- Use the Simulation tools in Inventor CAM to display individual operations, multiple operations, an entire setup, and multiple setups.

In this practice, you will use the tools in Inventor CAM to review the manufacturing operations that have been added to an Inventor model to machine it.

Task 1: Open a model.

1. If the Autodesk Inventor software is not already open, select **Start>Autodesk>Autodesk Inventor 2024>Autodesk Inventor 2024** or double-click on the **Autodesk Inventor 2024** icon on the desktop.
2. On the Home page, select ⋮ (Projects and Settings) > **Settings**.
3. Click **Browse**, navigate to *C:\Autodesk Inventor CAM 2024 Milling Fundamentals Practice Files* (or the directory to which you extracted the files) and select **InventorCAM.ipj**. Click **Open** to assign it as the active project file, setting the folder that contains the required models as the Workspace. Close the dialog box.

4. Open **Housing_Top.ipt**. The model and associated Model browser displays as shown in Figure 1–46.

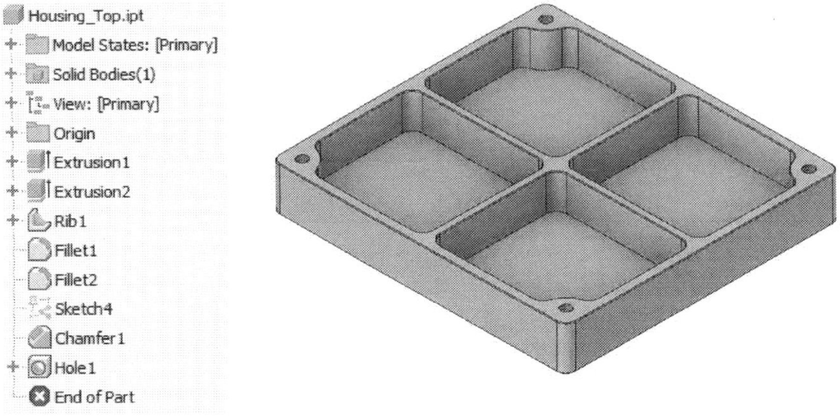

Figure 1–46

5. If the model does not display in the Shaded with Edges display style, in the *View* tab>Appearance panel, expand Visual Style and click **Shaded with Edges**. This display style can be helpful when selecting references and reviewing operations in the CAM environment.

Task 2: Zoom in and out on the model using the Zoom command.

1. Select the *View* tab, if not already active. Locate the Navigate panel. It contains all of the commands that you can use to manipulate the location and orientation of the model.

2. In the Navigate panel, click (Zoom), as shown in Figure 1–47. In some situations, similar commands are compressed in a panel and you must expand commands to access them.

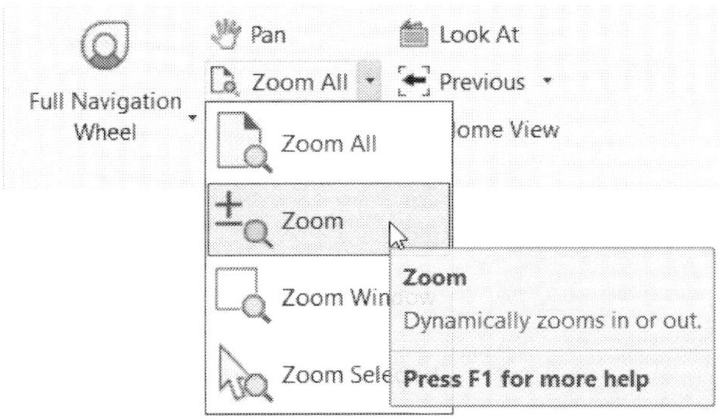

Figure 1–47

3. Move the cursor to the graphics window, click and hold the left mouse button, and move the mouse downward to zoom in and upward to zoom out.

4. Click (Zoom) again in the Navigate panel to toggle it off. You can also use the mouse scroll wheel to zoom in or out. To zoom to a specific area on the model, hover your cursor over the area prior to using the scroll wheel.

5. As an alternative to the *View* tab>Navigate panel, you can manipulate the model display using the options in the Navigation Bar on the right side of the graphics window. As with the Navigate panel, you need to expand the zoom options. Expand the Zoom command grouping in the Navigation Bar and click **Zoom All**, as shown in Figure 1–48.

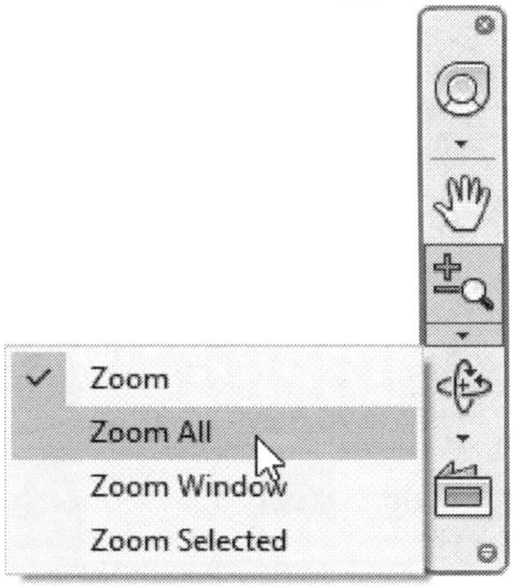

Figure 1–48

6. The model should refit to the center of the screen. If not, click (Zoom All) in the Navigation Bar.

Task 3: Zoom in on an area of the model and zoom out on the model.

1. Expand the zoom commands in the Navigation Bar and select **Zoom Window**.
2. Select a location on the model using the left mouse button to define a corner of the bounding box zoom area.
3. Drag the mouse to draw a box over the area to zoom.
4. Click or release the left mouse button again when the box is the required size. The model zooms in on the area defined by the sketched bounding box.
5. Expand the zoom commands in the Navigation Bar and **Zoom All** to refit the model in the center of the screen.

6. You can also zoom to a selected feature, face, or edge. Ensure that **Select Face and Edges** is selected in the Filter drop-down list in the Quick Access Toolbar, as shown in Figure 1–49.

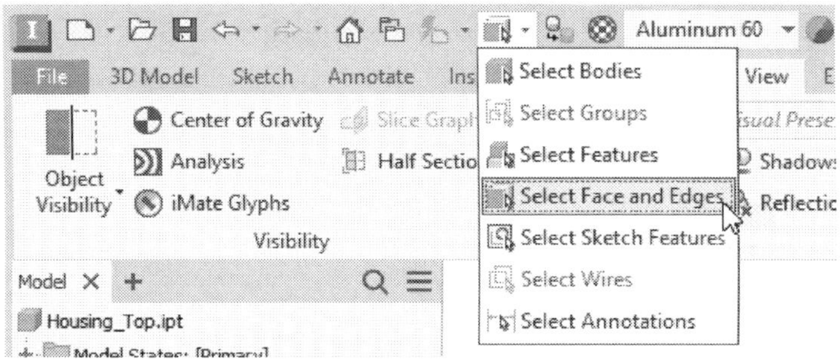

Figure 1–49

7. Expand the zoom commands in the Navigation Bar and select **Zoom Selected**. Hover your cursor over the face of one of the holes and, once prompted, select **Face** to zoom into the selected hole.

Note: *To zoom in on a face, you can also select the face first, then click (Zoom Selected).*

8. As an alternative to using the **Zoom All** command in the Navigation Bar, you can also double-click on the scroll wheel to zoom all.
9. Select an edge anywhere on the model and then select **Zoom Selected**. The result zooms and centers the edge in the graphics window. Alternatively, you can select a face to zoom in the same way.

Note: *When zooming in on an edge, the order in which you select the entity and the command is important and may change the displayed result.*

10. Use either of the **Zoom All** options to refit the model in the center of the screen.

Task 4: Pan the model using the Pan command.

1. In the Navigate panel or Navigation Bar, click (Pan).
2. Click and hold the left mouse button.
3. Move the mouse to drag the model.
4. Refit the model in the center of the screen.

Task 5: Rotate the model using the Orbit command.

1. In the Navigate panel or Navigation Bar, click (Orbit). A circle displays on the screen. The appearance of the cursor changes depending on its location relative to the circle.
2. Move the cursor inside the circle. The cursor appearance changes to .
3. Click and hold the left mouse button and rotate the model freely in any direction.
4. Release the mouse button and move the cursor outside the circle. The cursor appearance changes to .
5. Click and hold the left mouse button to rotate about an axis through the center of the circle symbol (normal to the screen).

   Note: *To change the center of the rotation, double-click inside or outside the circle to set the new center location.*

6. Move the cursor to the line at the top of the circle. The cursor appearance changes to .
7. Click and hold the left mouse button and rotate the model about the horizontal axis.
8. Move the cursor to the line at the right or left side of the circle. The cursor appearance changes to .
9. Click and hold the left mouse button and rotate the model about the vertical axis.

   Note: *While you are still in the orbit circle, you can also disable the **Orbit** command by moving the cursor away from the model until displays and then clicking in the graphics window.*

10. Move the cursor over the ViewCube and click in the top-left corner of the ViewCube (as shown in Figure 1–50) to orient the model into its Isometric Home view (3D). Alternatively, you can right-click and select **Home View** to orient the model in the same way. Note that (Zoom All) only refits the model in the center of the screen while maintaining the same orientation.

Figure 1–50

Task 6: Rotate the model using the ViewCube or keyboard.

As an alternative to using (Orbit), you can use the ViewCube or keyboard to rotate a model.

1. Ensure that (Orbit) is toggled off. Click and hold the left mouse button anywhere on the ViewCube and drag the mouse. Move the mouse away from the ViewCube to stop rotating.
2. Press and hold <F4>. By keeping <F4> depressed, the cursor behaves as it did when (Orbit) was active. Release <F4> to stop rotating.
3. Hold <Shift> and the middle mouse button and drag to rotate the model. Release <Shift> to stop rotating.
4. In the Navigate panel, click (Full Navigation Wheel) to enable the Full Navigation Wheel. Click and hold the left mouse button on the **Orbit** navigation command. Drag the mouse to rotate the view as required.
5. Click (Full Navigation Wheel) again to close the Full Navigation Wheel. The selection of the method to use to rotate the model is based on user preference.
6. Click in the ViewCube to orient the model into its Isometric Home view, or right-click and select **Home View**.
7. Click the **X** icon in the top-right corner of the Navigation Bar to toggle off its display.
8. In the *View* tab>Windows panel, expand **User Interface**. Select the box next to **Navigation Bar** to return it to the display. The remaining options enable you to control the display of the Model browser (Model), ViewCube, Status Bar, Document Tabs, and other interface tools.

Task 7: Orient the model.

1. In the Navigate panel or Navigation Bar, click (Look At) to orient a model face parallel to the screen. Select a face on the model to orient it into a 2D orientation.
2. Note that the ViewCube has reoriented. Click to orient the model to its Isometric Home view. The (Look At) command can help to orient faces that are not parallel with the origin planes. However, the ViewCube is a more efficient option for orienting into views that are parallel with the origin work planes.

3. Select the **RIGHT** face in the ViewCube, as shown in Figure 1–51. The model orients into a 2D orientation without having to select a face on the model.

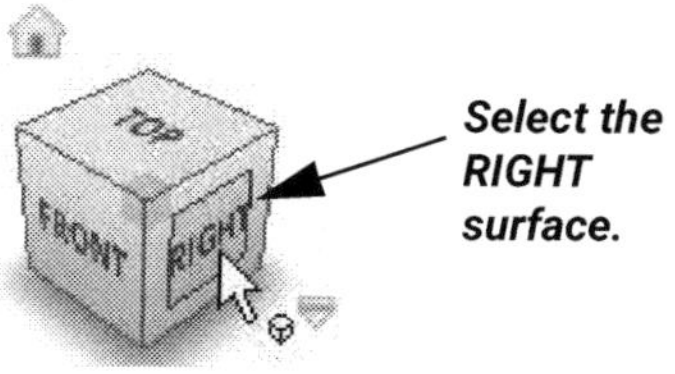

Figure 1–51

4. With the model still in a 2D orientation, move the mouse back over the ViewCube. It displays as shown in Figure 1–52. Select either of the rotating arrows to rotate the model while remaining in the RIGHT view.

Figure 1–52

5. Click any of the four triangular icons on the ViewCube to change to a different orientation.
6. Practice orienting the model into different orientations. You can also select edges of the ViewCube for orienting.
7. Click [home icon] to orient the model into its Isometric Home view.

Task 8: Review the CAM interface.

The **Housing_Top.ipt** model is to be machined from aluminum stock. In this task, you will review the model's features and properties and become familiar with the tools that will be used to create the machining operations.

1. In the Quick Access Toolbar at the top of the software interface, note that **Aluminum 6061** is the assigned material for the model, as shown in Figure 1–53.

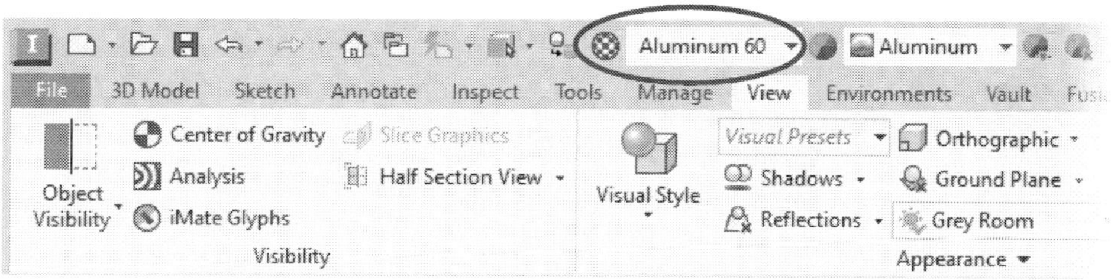

Figure 1–53

2. Review the Model browser and note all the features that were used to create the geometry for the housing.
3. In the graphics window, rotate the model to review the top and bottom (as shown in Figure 1–54). Note that there will need to be operations performed on both the top and bottom to manufacture the design.

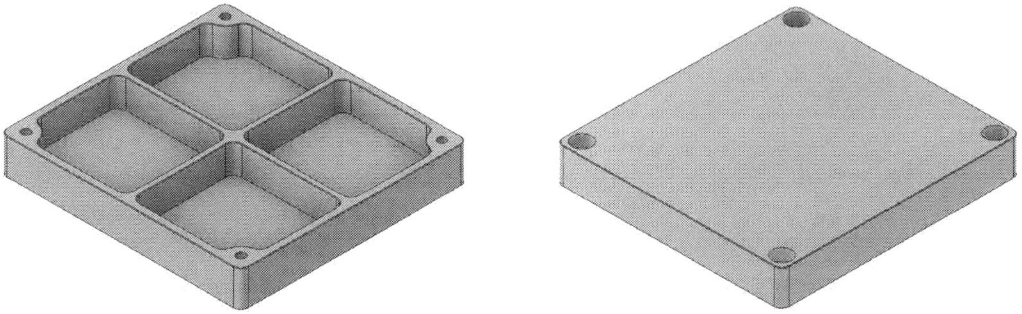

Figure 1–54

4. In the ribbon, select the *CAM* tab. It appears as shown in Figure 1–55. This tab provides the functionality that you will need to set up the model for manufacturing, add operations, simulate the operations, post process, etc. The ribbon is divided into panels that contain all the commands. For example, the Toolpath panel groups all the commands for displaying, generating, and post processing the operations, and many of the other tabs group the manufacturing operations by type (2D Milling, 3D Milling, Turning, etc.).

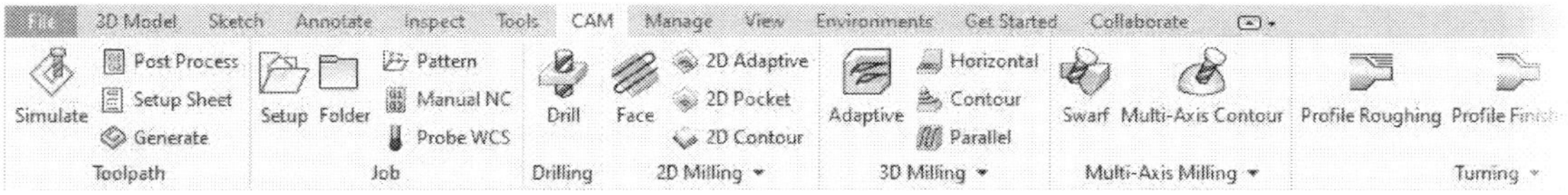

Figure 1–55

5. Close the model. This model will be used in upcoming exercises as you learn to set up and add manufacturing operations.

Task 9: Review the manufacturing setup in a completed model.

In this task, you will open a completed version of the model and review the manufacturing setup and operations that have been assigned. The intent of this is to get you familiar with the operations that you will be creating in upcoming exercises.

1. Open **Housing_Top_Final.ipt**.

2. Note that because the model has had manufacturing operations added to it, it immediately opens the *CAM* tab and the CAM browser (as shown in Figure 1–56).

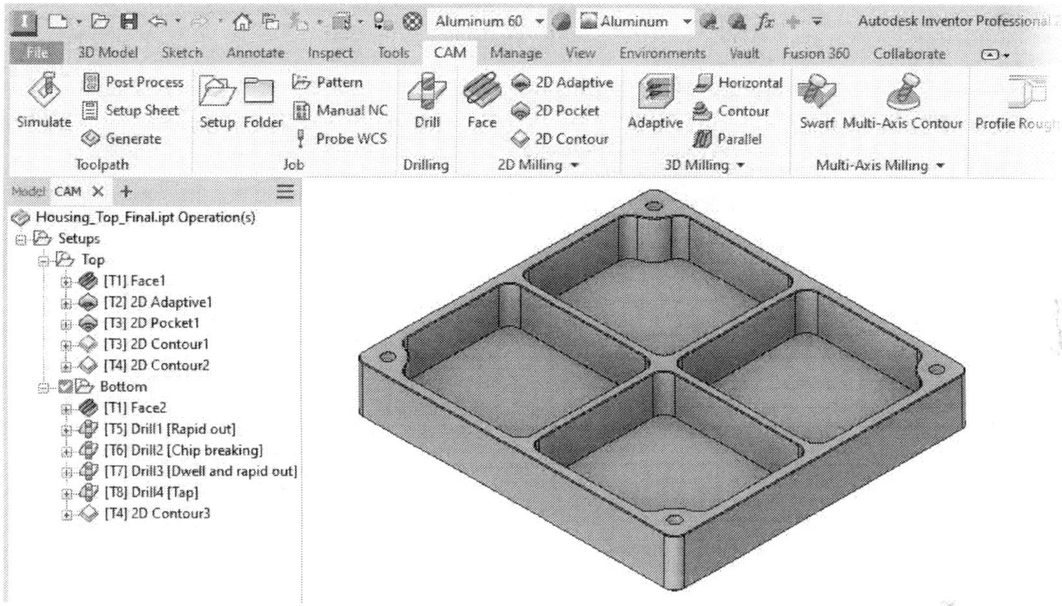

Figure 1–56

3. Select the *3D Model* tab. Although there are machining operations in the model, it does not prevent you from making changes or adding additional features.

4. In the Model browser, click **X** to close the CAM browser. This can be closed to simplify the display, if needed.

5. To reopen the CAM browser, click + in the browser's header and select **CAM**, as shown in Figure 1–57.

Figure 1–57

6. In the CAM browser, note that there are two setups. **Top** represents the operations that will be completed on the top of the model and **Bottom** are the operations for the bottom.
7. Select **Top** in the CAM browser. The stock that was assigned to the setup is displayed, as is the Work Coordinate System (WCS).

8. Right-click on **Top** in the CAM browser and select **Edit**. The Setup palette appears. It is broken into three tabs: (Setup), (Stock), and (Post Process). The *Setup* and *Stock* tabs are shown in Figure 1–58. Review the following:

   - On the *Setup* tab, the *Operation type* is set to **Milling**, the WCS *Orientation* was defined by selecting a Z and X direction (**Select Z axis/plane & X axis**), and the WCS was defined.
   - On the *Stock* tab, the *Mode* is set so that the stock is set relative to the size of the model geometry (**Relative size box**). Side and top offset values are **0.04 in** and the bottom offset is set as **0.25 in**. The larger bottom offset was done to account for the stock needed to hold the workpiece in the fixture.

Note: *The Post Process tab will be discussed later in this guide.*

Depending on the width of your palette, the tab name beside the icon may or may not be displayed. The icon will always be displayed.

Figure 1–58

9. Click **Cancel** at the bottom of the Setup palette to close it.
10. In the **Top** setup, select **[T1] Face1**. The facing operation that was created to machine off the top of the stock is displayed in the graphics window, as shown in Figure 1–59. By default, the toolpath movements are colored:
    - Cutting paths are displayed in blue.
    - Lead-in moves are displayed in green.
    - Rapid moves are displayed in yellow.
    - The start and end of the toolpath are indicated by a red triangle and a green triangle, respectively.

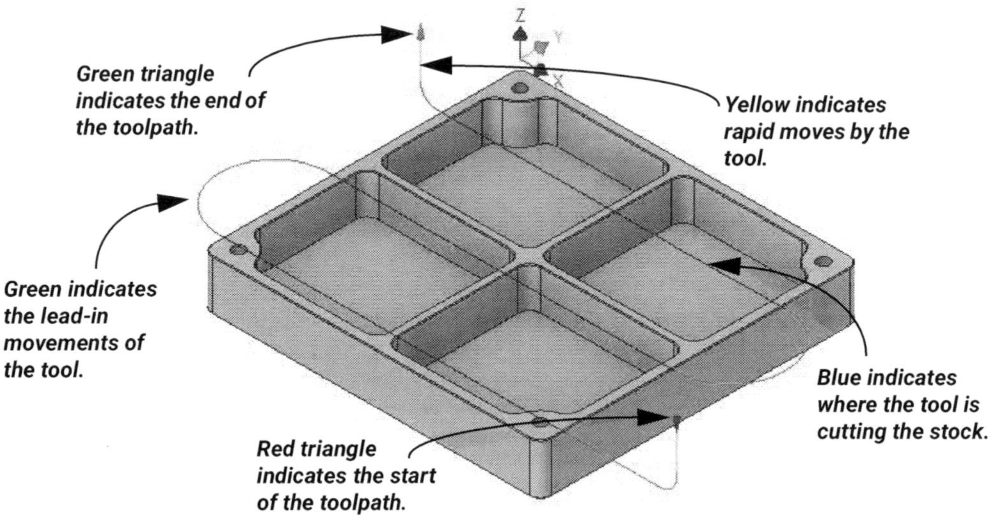

Figure 1–59

Note: *Some machines may have limited memory. In these cases, reviewing the size of the toolpath can be helpful to ensure it can be run without having to send the CNC code to the machine separately.*

11. Select ⊞ adjacent to **[T1] Face1** in the CAM browser to expand it (as shown in Figure 1–60). The items listed for this operation indicate it will be performed using a 2" Face Mill, references the WCS that was established in the setup, and lists its size in bytes.

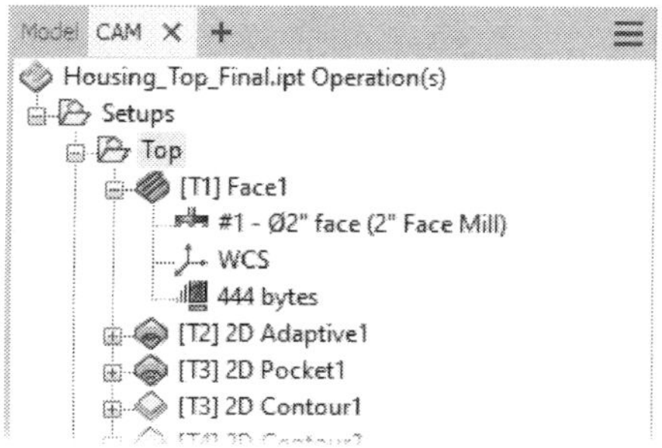

Figure 1–60

12. In the **Top** setup, select **[T2] 2D Adaptive1**. This operation is a roughing operation that is being used to remove all but 0.02 in of stock in the four internal pockets. The toolpath is displayed using the same color scheme; however, a red spiral path is displayed indicating the tool plunge, as shown in Figure 1–61. Note the blue cutting path has two depths for this roughing operation.

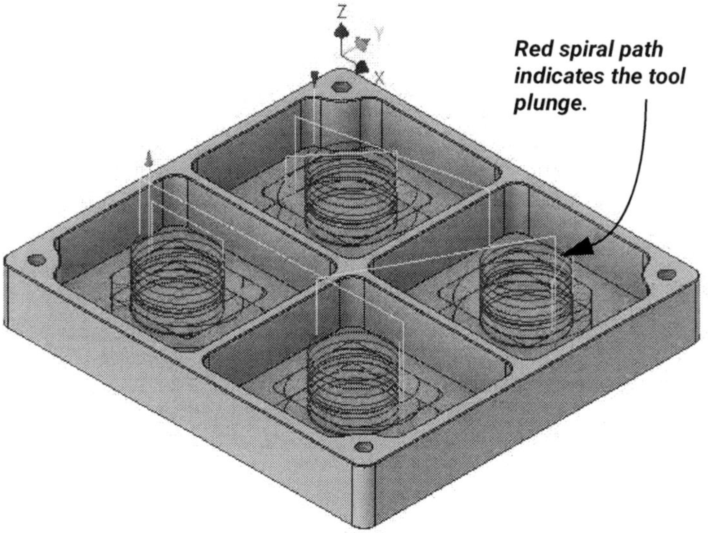

Figure 1–61

13. Continue to select the remaining three operations in the **Top** setup. The five operations combine to fully define the operations that are required to machine the top of the aluminum stock.
    - The **2D Pocket1** operation is a finishing operation for each of the four pockets.
    - The **2D Contour1** operation is a finishing operation that removes the 0.04 in. stock around the outside of the model.
    - The **2D Contour2** operation is a finishing operation that creates a chamfer on all the sharp edges on the top of the model.
14. Select the **Bottom** setup and rotate the model to a view similar to that shown in Figure 1–62. This will allow you to review and display the remaining operations that are to be executed on the bottom of the model.

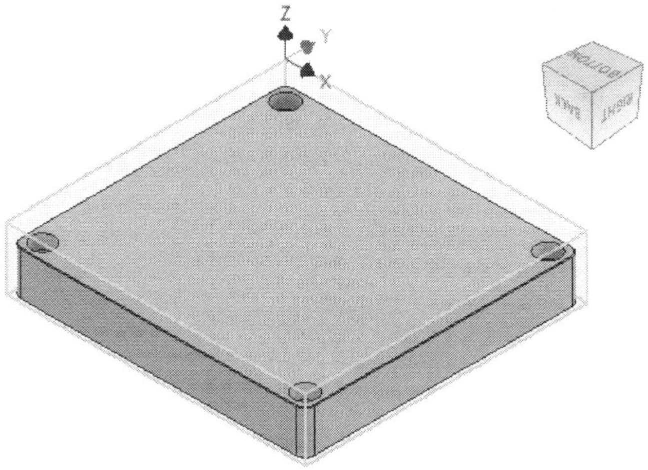

Figure 1–62

Note: *The Bottom setup was created with the understanding that the CNC machine operations in the* ***Top*** *setup were complete, the machine was stopped, and the workpiece was manually flipped. Because of this, a new setup was required to properly define the WCS and stock. This will be discussed in more detail in the next chapter.*

15. In the **Bottom** setup, select and review the five operations.
    - The **Face2** operation is a facing operation to remove the 0.25 in. stock from the bottom of the model.
    - The **Drill1**, **Drill2**, **Drill3**, and **Drill 4** operations all work consecutively to create and tap the four counterbore holes.
    - The **2D Contour3** operation is a finishing operation that creates a chamfer on the sharp edge around the bottom of the model.
16. Press and hold <Ctrl> and select multiple operations in the **Bottom** setup. Note how all the toolpaths are displayed together. Operations can be selected in either setup at once, if necessary.

Task 10: View a simulation of the operations.

In this task, you will use the **Simulate** option to visually preview the toolpaths in the models. You will learn to customize the simulation so that the display of stock, tool, and toolpath are controlled, as well as learn how to use the playback and speed controls.

1. In the CAM browser, right-click on the **Top** setup and select **Default Folder** to set the Top setup as the active setup.
2. Return the model to its default Home view.
3. At the top of the CAM browser, select the **Housing_Top_Final.ipt Operation(s)** node. This ensures that any operations that were previously selected are cleared and that all operations will be played in the simulation.

4. In the CAM ribbon>Toolpath panel, click (Simulate). The Simulation palette opens as shown in Figure 1–63. The *Display* tab is active by default. Review the following:

   Note: *The toolpaths that are displayed help visualize the path of the tool. They display using the same color scheme as if you selected an operation in the CAM browser that was previously discussed.*

   - By default, the **Tool** is set to display in a simulation. The shaft and holder for the tool are displayed as solid; however, the **Show transparent** option can also be enabled to help with visualization.
   - By default, the **Toolpath** is set to display as the simulation is displayed.
   - By default, the **Stock** is not set to be displayed.
   - The tool that is displayed changes depending on the location of the marker in the simulation player timeline. In Figure 1–63, the tool for the first facing toolpath (Face1) is being displayed.

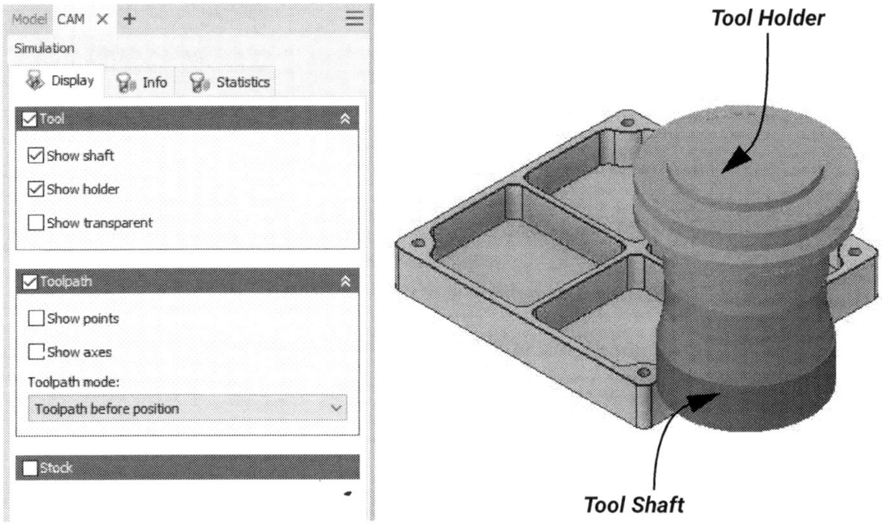

Figure 1–63

5. Enable the **Stock** option at the bottom of the Simulation palette. The stock appears as solid geometry around the model, as shown in Figure 1–64.

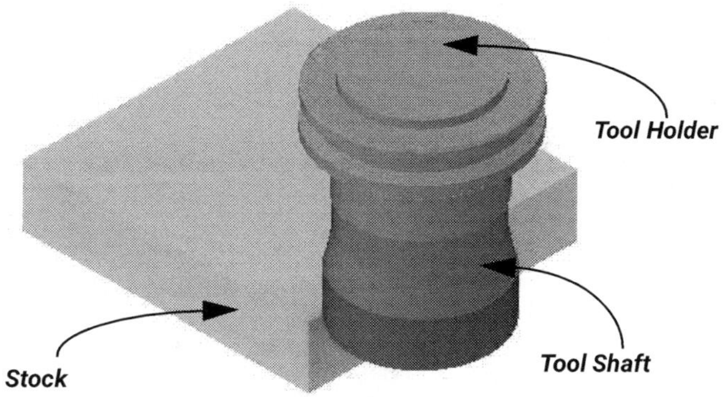

Figure 1–64

Note: *Autodesk Inventor maintains the selected display options the next time a simulation is run. Depending on your computer, your default settings may vary.*

6. In the *Stock* area, select **Show transparent** to set the stock to display transparently. Clear the option to return to solid display.
7. Select **Stop on collision**. This option is valuable to test that the manufacturing operations do not produce any collision between the shaft, holder, and fixture. This option does not detect gouges that would be made in the model by too much stock removal.
8. Locate the simulation player timeline and simulation player at the bottom of the graphics window, as shown in Figure 1–65.

Figure 1–65

Note: *If an operation encounters a collision, a red line appears through the operation in which it occurs.*

9. The simulation player timeline displays the operations that will be played in the simulation. In this situation, because the **Housing_Top_Final.ipt Operation(s)** node was selected, it will play all operations in both setups. The current operation is displayed in green, while the remaining operations are displayed in alternating shades of gray to distinguish each change in operation. Hover your cursor over the first operation, currently displayed in green. A window appears, as shown Figure 1–66, providing information on the operation.

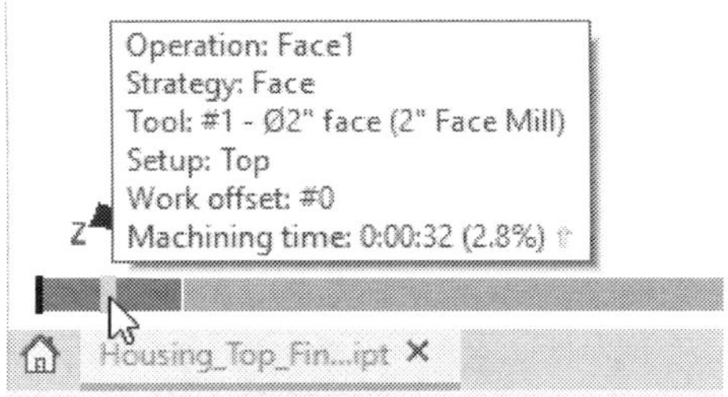

Figure 1–66

10. Hover your cursor over the second operation and review its information window. Note that the length of each operation in the operation timeline is relative to its machining time.

11. Click ▷ in the simulation player to play all operations. Note how as the operations are played, material is removed from the stock to simulate the machining of the model.

12. To control the speed of the playback, select the circular control under the simulation player, as shown in Figure 1–67. Drag it to the right to increase the speed or to the left to reduce the speed. Once you drag it past the midpoint on the line, the playback reverses.

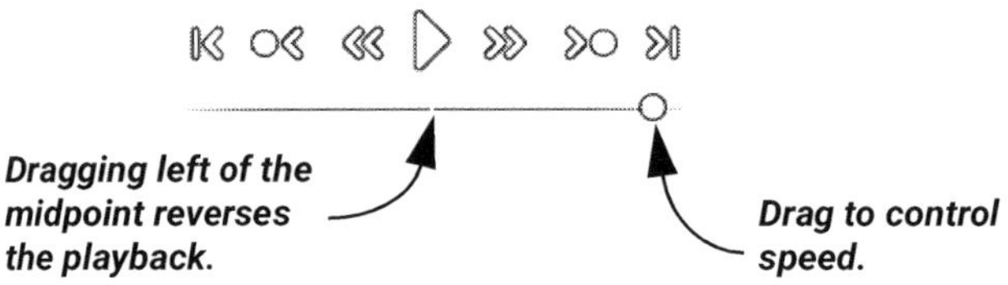

Figure 1–67

Note: *Speed control can be manipulated while the simulation is in progress. Select a location on the timeline to skip to that point in the simulation.*

13. Once the simulation has completed, you will notice that all toolpaths for both the Top and Bottom setups are visible in the graphics window, as shown in Figure 1–68.

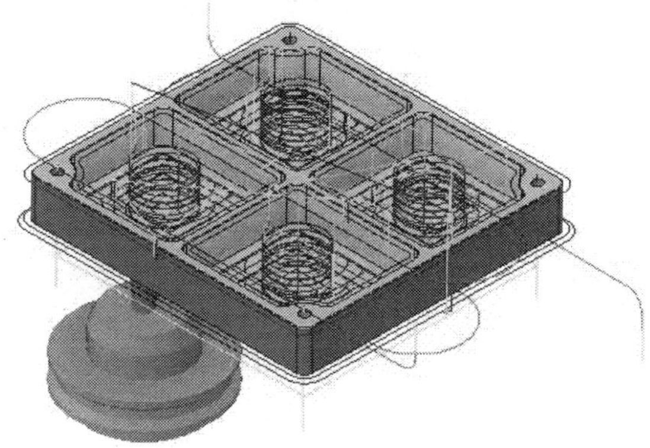

Figure 1–68

14. In the simulation player, select the different control buttons to test their behaviors. Each option is described in Figure 1–69.

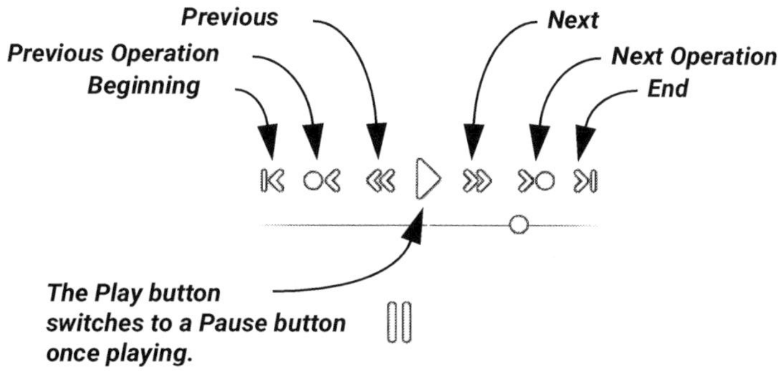

Figure 1–69

15. Once the simulation has been reviewed, click **Close** at the bottom of the Simulation palette.

Task 11: Make a change to the model.

In this task, you will make a change to the model that will affect a machining operation that has been created. Once the change is made, you will return to the CAM environment and learn how this change affects the current operations.

1. Select the *Model* tab in the browser. This enables you to access the features that were used to create the geometry.
2. Right-click on **Extrusion2** and select **Edit Feature**. The Properties panel that was used to create the geometry appears.
3. Change the *Depth* value to **0.2 in**. Click **OK**. The geometry updates as shown in Figure 1–70.

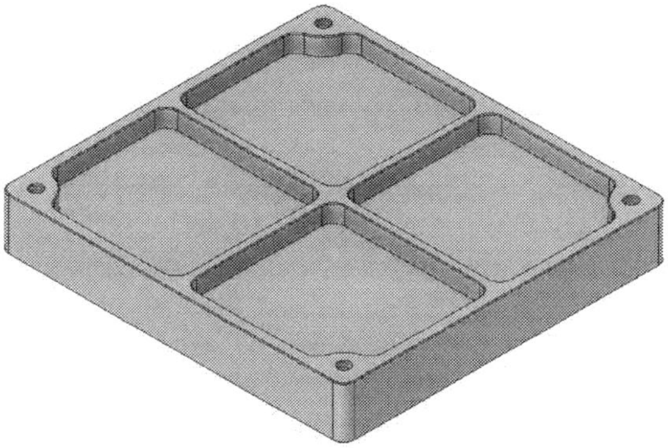

Figure 1–70

4. Select the *CAM* tab in the browser. Note that all the operations are appearing with a red x through them, as shown in Figure 1–71. This indicates that they are out of date.

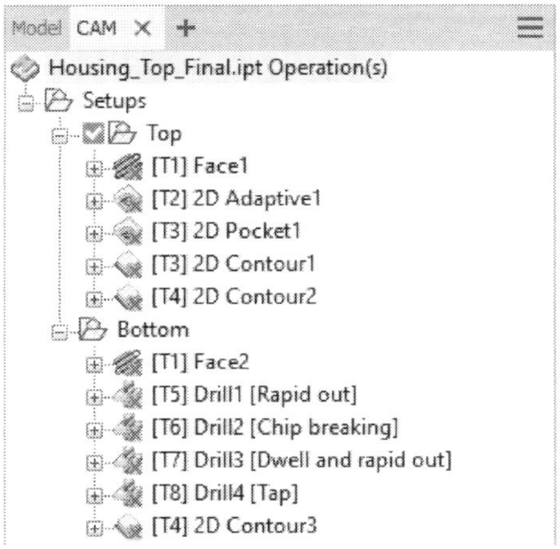

Figure 1–71

5. Ensure that the **Housing_Top_Final.ipt Operation(s)** node is selected at the top of the CAM browser.

6. In the Toolpath panel, click (Generate). All of the toolpaths update to reflect the modeling change.

7. Select the **2D Adaptive1** operation. The toolpath displays in the graphics window, as shown in Figure 1–72. Note how now the plunge has updated and only one depth is used to rough out the aluminum in the four pockets.

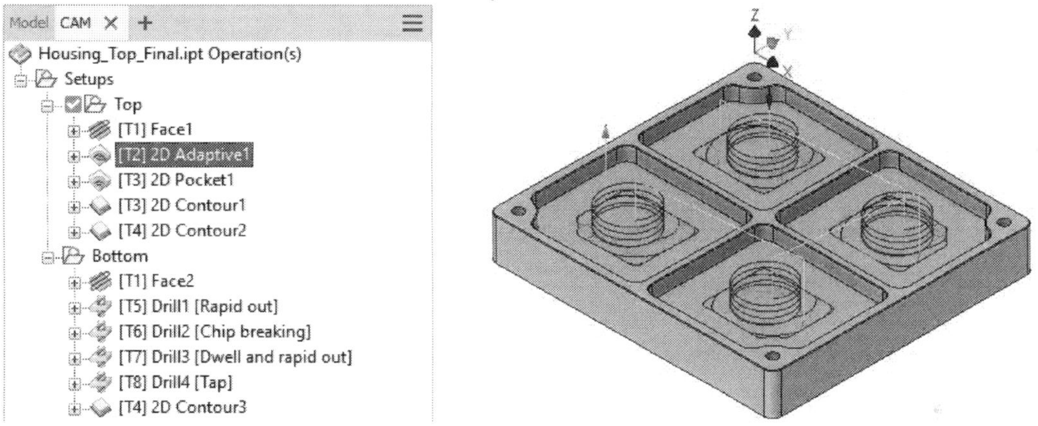

Figure 1–72

8. Press and hold <Ctrl> and select **Face1**, **2D Adaptive1**, and **2D Pocket1** in the CAM browser.

9. In the Toolpath panel, click (Simulate).

10. In the Simulation palette, clear the selection of the **Toolpath** option. This ensures that once the simulation is complete, it will be easier to review the results without all the toolpath lines being displayed.

11. Play the entire simulation.

12. In the Simulation palette, select the (Statistics) tab (as shown in Figure 1–73). Review the machining time of the three selected operations, machining distance, the number of operations, and the number of tools used in the three operations.

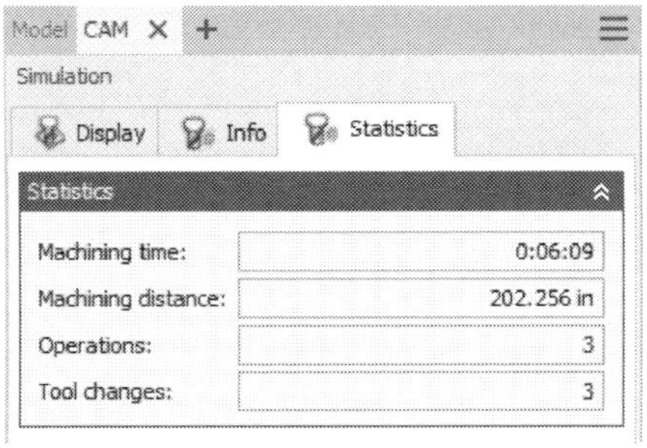

Figure 1–73

13. In the Simulation palette, select the (Info) tab. Review the **Verification** section, as shown in Figure 1–74. Note that initially the *Distance* field indicates a value is unavailable.

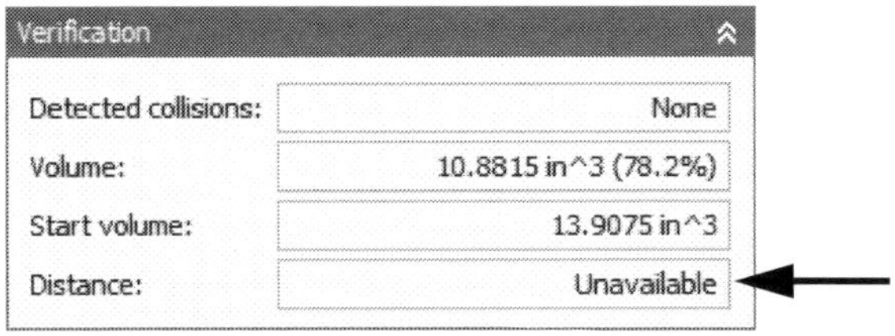

Figure 1–74

14. In the graphics window, hover your cursor over the top of the model as well as the bottom face of the pockets. Note how the *Distance* value updates to **0 in**. This value indicates that there is no stock left on the model. In order for a value to be displayed, the stock must be enabled on the *Display* tab.

15. Hover your cursor over the stock around the outside of the model. This indicates there is **0.04 in**. of stock still shown. This is correct, as only the first three operations were simulated.

16. Click **Close** in the Simulation palette. Close the model without saving. In the following chapters, you will learn to set up the model and add the operations that were created to machine the model. You can access this completed model for reference, as needed.

End of practice

Chapter Review Questions

1. Which of the following are unique interface items in the Inventor CAM environment? (Select all that apply.)
   a. Model browser
   b. CAM browser
   c. ViewCube
   d. Navigation Bar
   e. CAM ribbon tab

2. Multiple setups can be incorporated into a single part in the Inventor CAM environment.
   a. True
   b. False

3. Which of the following are true statements about how the stock is displayed when using the **Simulate** option in Inventor CAM? (Select all that apply.)
   a. The stock is always displayed in a simulation.
   b. The stock can be displayed as transparent during the simulation.
   c. The stock can be displayed as solid during the simulation.
   d. The stock can be set to display in color for each tool used in the simulation.

4. Which of the following are true statements about how the toolpath is displayed when using the **Simulate** option in Inventor CAM? (Select all that apply.)
   a. The toolpath is always displayed in a simulation.
   b. The toolpath can be set to display all paths prior to the simulation.
   c. The toolpath can be set to display paths only after the simulation is run.
   d. The entire toolpath color displays in blue once the simulation is run.

5. Only a single setup can be run at one time in the Simulation environment.
   a. True
   b. False

6. The simulation timeline displays four bands. Which of the following statements cannot be true based on this timeline?
   a. The operation has two setups and each setup has two toolpaths.
   b. The operation has four setups, each with multiple toolpaths.
   c. The operation has one setup and it has four toolpaths.
   d. The operation has four setups and four toolpaths have been selected randomly from within these setups.

7. Which of the following is machining information that can be determined in the Simulation palette when running a toolpath simulation? (Select all that apply.)
   a. Machining time for the currently displayed operation.
   b. Total machining time for all simulated operations.
   c. Amount of stock left to machine at a selected location.
   d. Total number of tool changes required for all simulated operations.

8. Where can you control the speed of the playback for a toolpath's simulation?
   a. CAM browser
   b. Simulation toolpath
   c. Simulation timeline
   d. Simulation player

9. The total machining time for all operations can be displayed by hovering your cursor at the end of the simulation timeline.
   a. True
   b. False

Command Summary

Button	Command	Location
	**Full Navigation Wheel**	• **Ribbon:** *View* tab>Navigate panel • **Navigation Bar**
	**Help**	• **Quick Access Toolbar** • **Keyboard:** < F1>
	**Home View**	• **Ribbon:** *View* tab>Navigate panel • **ViewCube** • **Context Menu: In the graphics window** • **Keyboard:** <F6>
	**Look At**	• **Ribbon:** *View* tab>Navigate panel • **Navigation Bar** • **ViewCube**
	**Open**	• **Quick Access Toolbar** • **File Menu** • **Home tab**
	**Orbit (rotate)**	• **Ribbon:** *View* tab>Navigate panel • **Navigation Bar** • **ViewCube**
	**Pan**	• **Ribbon:** *View* tab>Navigate panel • **Navigation Bar**
Projects...	**Projects**	• **Dialog Box:** Open and New • **Home:** Projects and Settings
	**Save**	• **Quick Access Toolbar** • **File Menu**
	Visual Style	• **Ribbon:** *View* tab>Appearance panel
	**Zoom**	• **Ribbon:** *View* tab>Navigate panel • **Navigation Bar** • **Full Navigation Wheel**
	**Zoom All**	• **Ribbon:** *View* tab>Navigate panel • **Navigation Bar**
	**Zoom Selected**	• **Ribbon:** *View* tab>Navigate panel • **Navigation Bar**
	**Zoom Window**	• **Ribbon:** *View* tab>Navigate panel • **Navigation Bar**

Button	Command	Location
	**Generate**	• **Ribbon:** *CAM* tab>Toolpath panel
	**Simulate**	• **Ribbon:** *CAM* tab>Toolpath panel

Chapter

2

Getting Started with Autodesk Inventor CAM

Prior to creating the first toolpath, you must define the setup parameters for the manufacturing operations that will be done on the Inventor model. This includes defining the machine and operation type, the coordinate system that will define the toolpath directions, and the model and stock size that will be machined. In this chapter, you will learn to define these parameters and will learn to create a Face toolpath to remove the stock on the top and bottom of the model.

Learning Objectives

- Define the required parameters for setting up new manufacturing operations in Inventor CAM.
- Locate, modify, and create tools in the Tool Library.
- Create a Face toolpath in an Inventor CAM model.

2.1 Defining the Setup for Machine Operations

The first step in Inventor CAM, prior to creating any machining toolpaths, is to define the setup for the operations that will machine the model. Multiple setups can exist in each model. The setup defines the following:

- Machine type being used
- Operation type being used to machine the model
- Work coordinate system of the model
- Stock that the model will be machined from
- Post process settings

To create a setup, in the *CAM* tab>Job panel, click (Setup). The Setup palette and model display similarly to that shown in Figure 2–1. The yellow box around the model identifies the default stock.

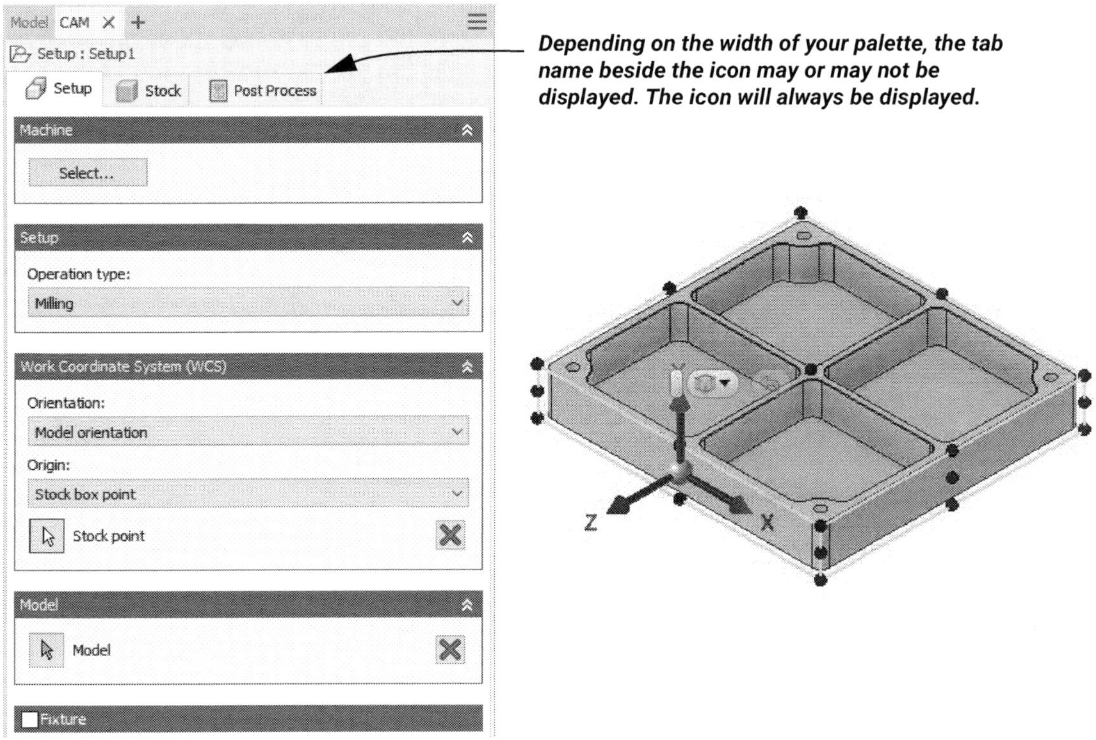

Figure 2–1

The Setup palette has three tabs that are used to fully define the setup.

Setup Tab

The (Setup) tab is the first tab in the palette. It enables you to define the machine, operation type, work coordinate system (WCS), model, and whether a fixture is to be assigned.

- The *Machine* area of the palette enables you to optionally define the type of machine that will be used. The available types include milling, turning, and cutting machines, as shown in Figure 2–2. Select from the list, or if your machine is not available, select a type that closely matches your machine. Click **OK** to assign the machine to the setup. Depending on the machine type chosen, additional parameters may become available in the Setup palette for you to further define your machine's setup.

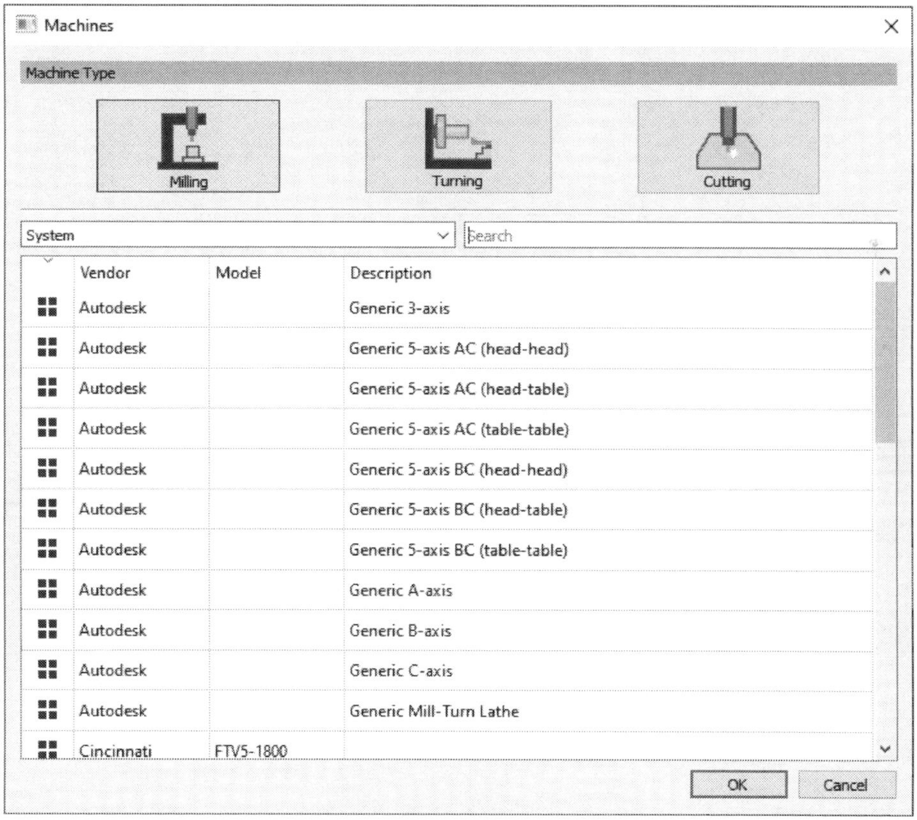

Figure 2–2

- Select the *Operation type* option from the drop-down list. The options include **Milling**, **Turning (or mill/turn)**, or **Cutting**.

- The *Work Coordinate System (WCS)* area of the setup is used to set the orientation for the cutting plane of the machine. By default, the WCS is displayed in the same orientation as the model's coordinate system. For milling machines, the Z-axis should point perpendicular to the surface being machined. For turning, it should be oriented along the centerline of the model.
  - The Orientation drop-down list enables you to define a new orientation for the WCS. You are only required to reorient the WCS if it does not match the orientation required for your machine. The available options are shown in Figure 2–3. Select an option and select edges or vertices in the model to define the WCS's orientation in the X-, Y-, and Z-axis. Use the Flip settings, as needed, to flip the orientation along an axis.

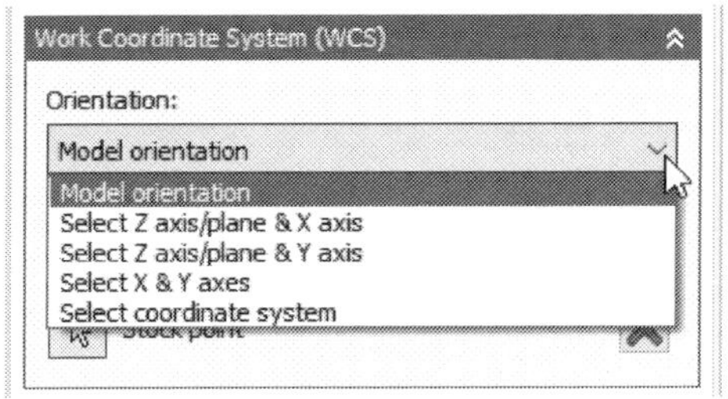

Figure 2–3

  - The Origin drop-down list enables you to define where the WCS is located on the stock. The options enable you to define the WCS on the model origin, at a selected vertex or edge, or on a stock or model point. For example, in Figure 2–4 the WCS is being located on a stock box point.

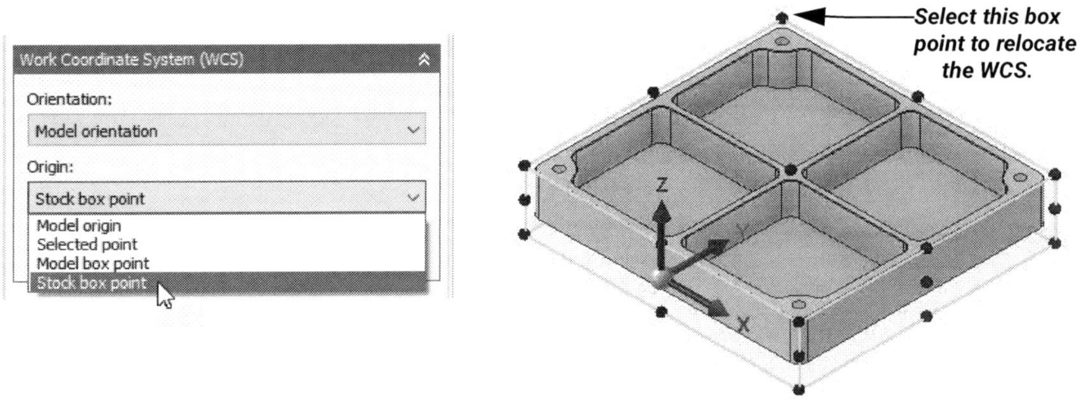

Figure 2–4

Note: *The Origin should be selected such that it will align with the origin of the machine that will be used to cut the model.*

- The *Model* field enables you to select the model being machined. By default, the entire design model is assigned. If the design model is an assembly or multi-body design, where a portion of the model is representing non-machined geometry, use this field to refine the selection. Click to clear the selection and select the geometry to be machined. If the design model is a single part file that represents the model being machined, no changes are required.
- The *Fixture* area at the bottom of the *Setup* tab can be used to assign geometry from the design model as belonging to the machine fixture or its attachment. By default, this field is disabled, but it can be enabled if required. In general, this would be used only if an assembly design model is being used and you want portions of the assembly recognized as fixturing geometry to check toolpaths for collisions.

Hint: Fixtures

A fixture is used to hold and orient the workpiece during manufacturing, similar to that shown in Figure 2–5. Fixture manufacturers generally provide CAD models in the form of Step or IGES data that can be brought into Inventor.

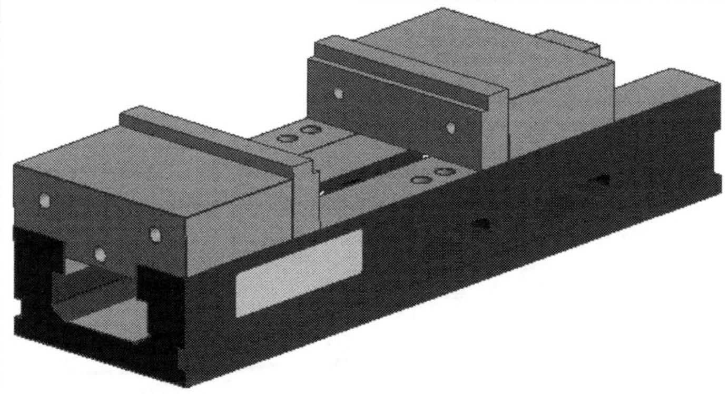

Figure 2–5

Note: *This guide initially focuses on learning the tools to create operations on your models. Fixtures will be briefly introduced at the end of the guide.*

Stock Tab

The toolpaths that are generated are based on the stock that is being removed; therefore, proper stock definition is a key step in setting up your operation. By default, a 0.04 in. (1 mm) side and top offset stock value is assigned. These values can be modified to match your actual stock by selecting the (Stock) tab at the top of the Setup palette. The *Stock* tab is shown in Figure 2–6.

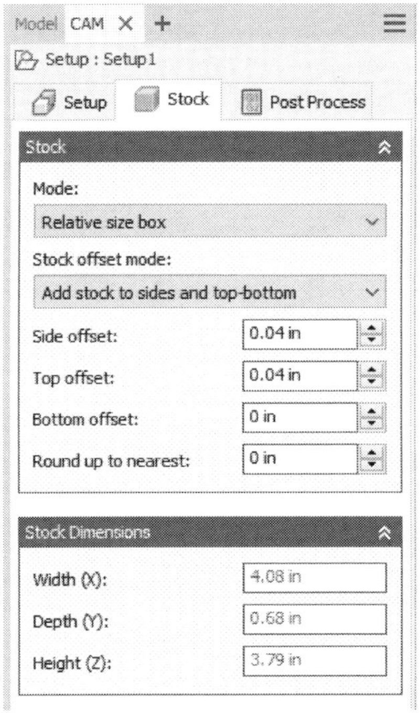

Figure 2–6

- The *Mode* options enable you to define the shape of the stock as either box, cylinder, tube, or a selected solid body from the model. In the case of the box, cylinder, and tube stock shapes, you can define the size as fixed or relative. For fixed, you define the exact size in the x, y, and z directions, whereas for relative you define the size by entering offset values that are measured from the model geometry.
- The *Stock offset mode* options can also be used to refine the offset fields if the stock is being created relative to the model.

  Note: *Ensure that the stock size you use takes into account operations that may be required on the top, bottom, and sides.*

- The *Stock Dimensions* area of the *Stock* tab includes non-editable fields that display the overall size of the stock being used. As changes are made, these values automatically update.

Post Process Tab

The final tab in the Setup palette is the  (Post Process) tab. This tab enables you to define the post processing parameters for the machine. It includes the program number and comments, as well as the WCS offset. Post processing will be discussed in more detail later in this guide.

To complete the setup, click **OK** at the bottom of the Setup palette. Setup1 appears listed in the CAM browser. It is recommended to rename each setup to help identify its intent. To rename, slowly select **Setup1** twice and enter a name. The CAM browser shown in Figure 2–7 shows that a setup called **Top** has been created in the model.

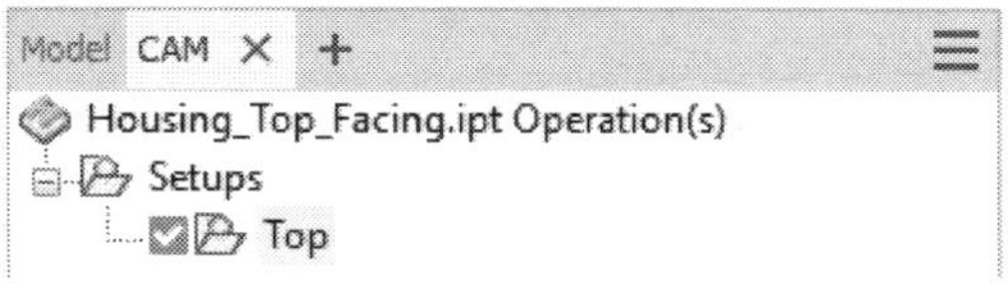

Figure 2–7

2.2 Tool Library

A default tool library is available with the installation of the Inventor CAM add-in. This library provides access to a large database of tools that can be used to cut your toolpaths. Although tools are assigned during toolpath creation, you can also access the Tool Library directly to create and manage your own custom tools. In either situation, the Tool Library functions the same once it is opened.

To open the Tool Library, in the *CAM* tab>Manage panel, click (Tool Library). The open models are all listed in the Open Documents node. For models that already have tools assigned, the Tool Library appears similar to that shown in Figure 2–8; otherwise, the right-hand pane will be empty until a tool is assigned.

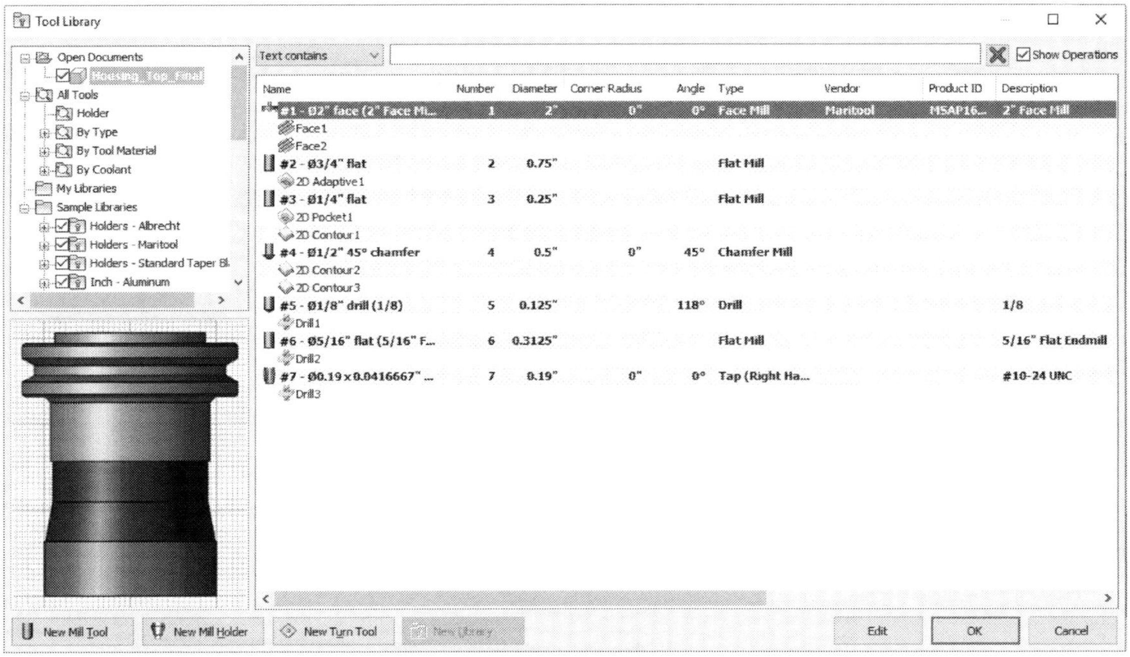

Figure 2–8

Locating Tools in the Tool Library

The default tools are organized by category in the top-left pane of the Tool Library dialog box.

- All tools that have been assigned to an open model are listed in the **Open Documents**>model name categories.
- The **All Tools** and **Sample Libraries** categories list all the default tools that are installed with Inventor CAM.
- The **My Libraries** category lists any custom tool libraries that you create.

To locate a tool, you can simply navigate through the category folder structures or you can use the filter and sorting tools that are available in the dialog box to refine the list. Consider the following (as are shown in Figure 2–9):

- Select a search option from the drop-down list to best describe the tool you are looking for. Enter the supporting text in the search field adjacent to the list.
- Select a column header to sort in ascending/descending order.
- Drag and drop the column headers to reorder the display order of the columns. This can help you more easily see the columns that are important to you.

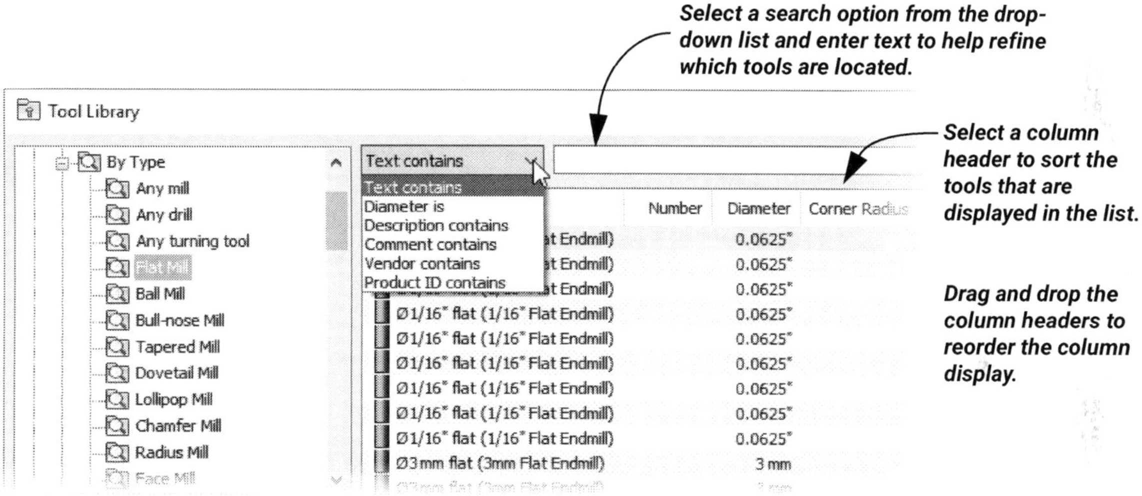

Figure 2–9

- In the **Sample Libraries** and **My Libraries** categories, you can clear the activation boxes adjacent to the tool folders to clear them from the search.

Tool Preview

A preview of the selected tool is located in the lower-left pane. This provides a visual preview as to the shape and size of the tool, as shown in Figure 2–10.

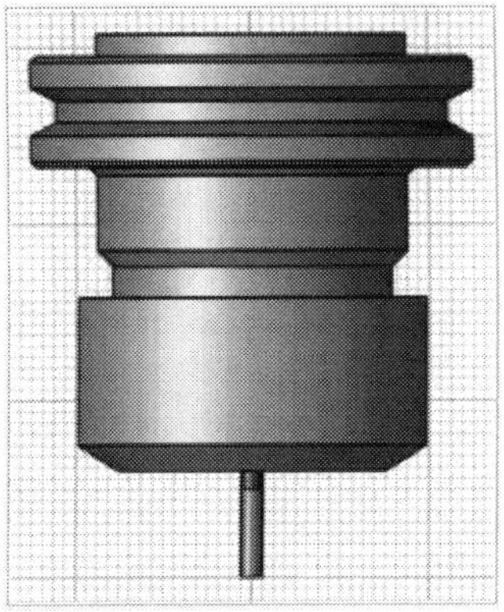

Flat Endmill

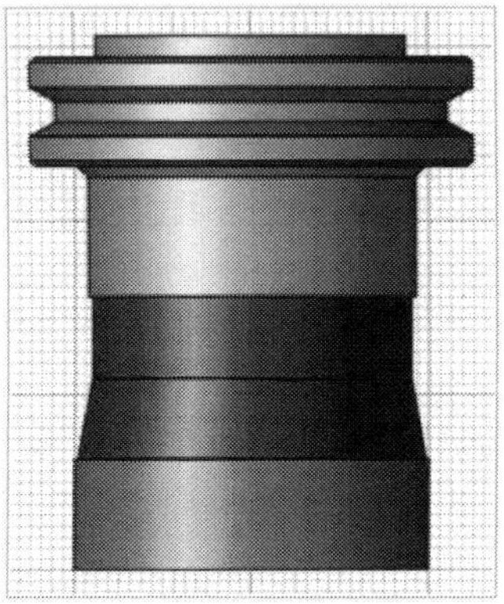

Face Mill

Figure 2–10

Consider the following regarding the tool preview:

- For inch tools, the distance between the thin gridlines is 1/16 in. and the distance between the thick lines is 1 in.
- For metric tools, the distance between the thin gridlines is 1 mm and the distance between the thick lines is 10 mm.
- Hover your cursor over the preview to zoom into the cutting portion of the tool.

Tool Creation

Custom tools are stored in custom libraries in the **My Libraries** category. To populate a custom library, you can copy from the provided standard library or create new tools. To create a library, right-click on the **My Libraries** category and select **New Library** or click **New Library** at the bottom of the dialog box. Enter a descriptive name to accurately describe the new custom library.

Reuse an Existing Standard Tool

The default tools can be used as a reference in creating new tools. This simplifies the creation process because you can locate a similar tool, copy it to your custom library, and edit it as needed. To copy a tool, right-click on the parent tool that will be copied, select **Copy**, then navigate to the custom library folder and right-click in the list and select **Paste**. To edit the tool once copied, select the tool name and click **Edit**.

How To: Create a New Tool

Use the following steps to create a new custom tool.

1. Select a custom library name in the **My Libraries** category.
2. Select a new tool option from the bottom of the dialog box, as shown in Figure 2–11. The options enable you to create a new milling tool, mill holder, and turning tool.

Figure 2–11

3. The Tool dialog box opens, enabling you to define the tool. There are six tabs available for you to define the tool.
   - *General* tab - Enables you to define the general parameters of the tool. These include the tool number, offset values, description, etc., as shown in Figure 2–12.

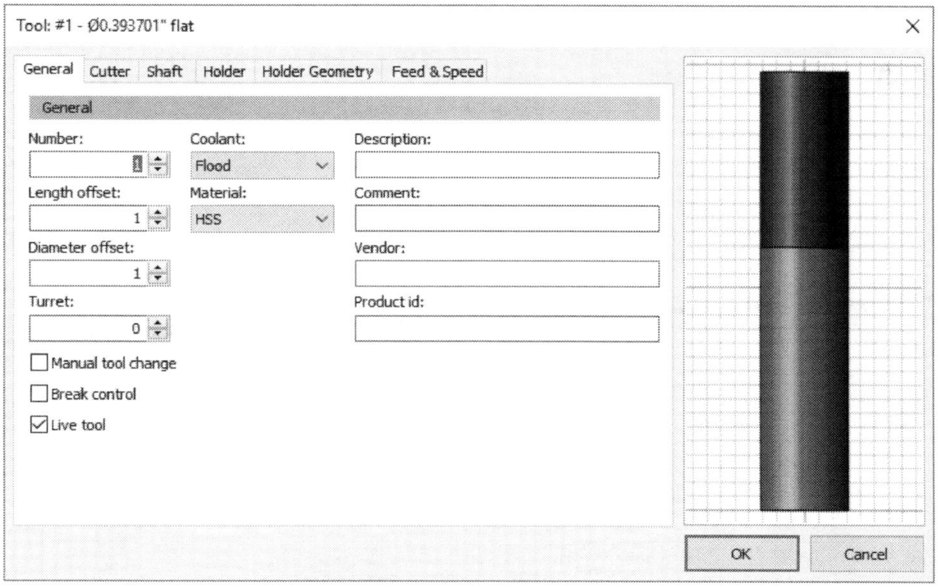

Figure 2–12

- *Cutter* tab - Enables you to select the tool type and define its dimensions. Figure 2–13 shows the dimensions required for a Flat Mill.

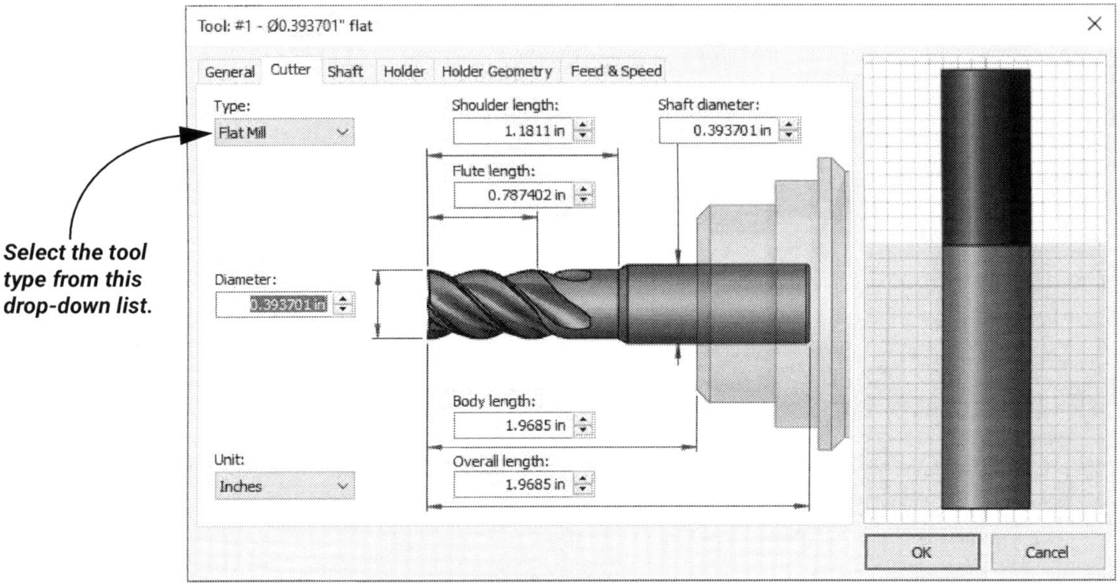

Figure 2–13

- *Shaft* tab - Enables you to define the size and segments of the non-cutting portion of the tool, as shown in Figure 2–14.

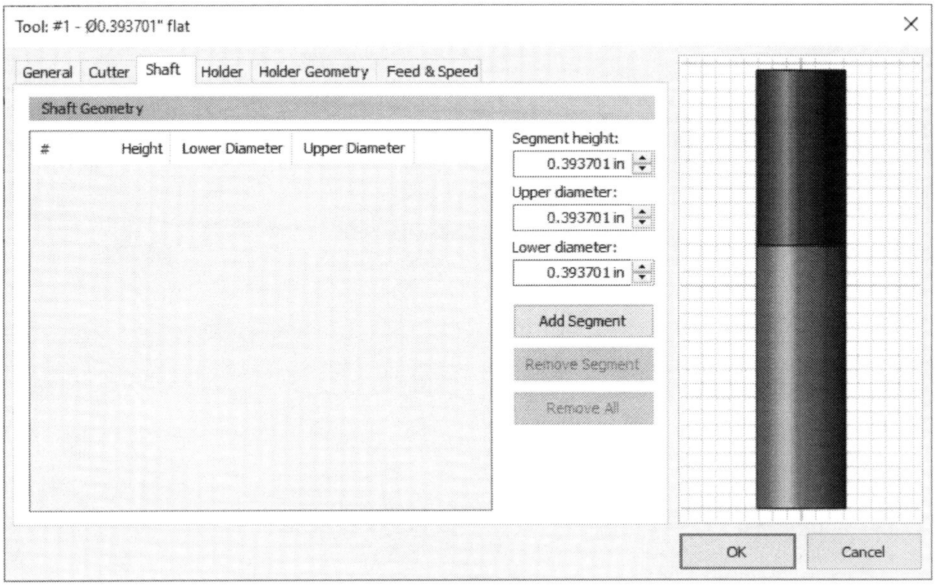

Figure 2–14

- *Holder* and *Holder Geometry* tabs - Enable you to select a holder from the Holder Library and define the holder's dimensions.
- *Feed & Speed* tab - Enables you to assign cutting and non-cutting feedrates and spindle speeds for the cutter, as shown in Figure 2–15. Default values are provided for you; however, these parameters should be modified to match your actual machine values to ensure accurate toolpath data is generated.

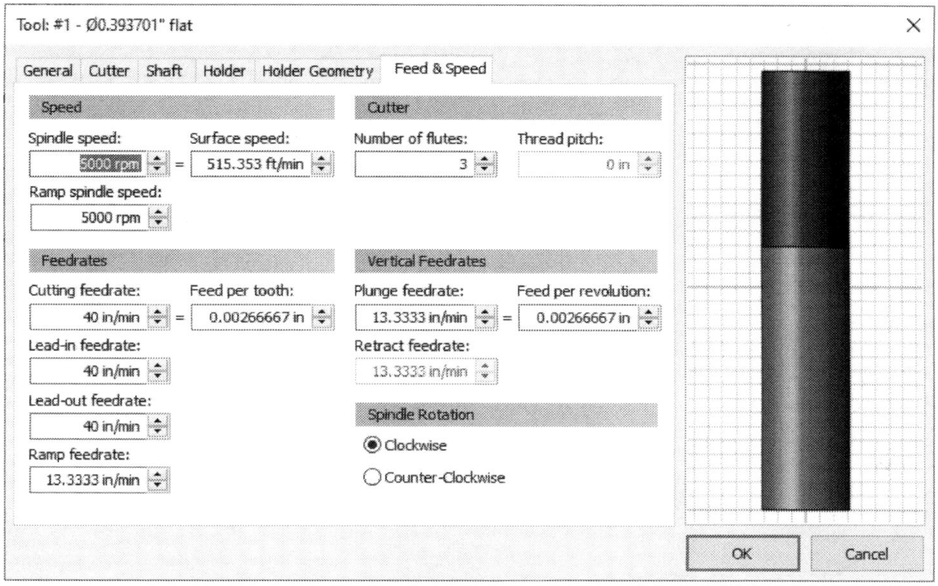

Figure 2–15

4. Click **OK** to complete the tool and add it to the custom library.

Additional Tool Library Commands

The Tool Library has additional context-sensitive commands that can be accessed in the right-click menus, as shown in Figure 2–16. These enable you to do the following:

- Delete tools that are no longer required.
- Cut/copy/paste/duplicate tools that are used as the foundation for new tools.
- Renumber tools to match the requirements for your machine. To access the renumbering settings, right-click in the list and select **Renumber Tools**.
- Remove tools that are no longer used in cutting a toolpath. To purge unused tools from the model, right-click in the list and select **Remove Unused Tools**.

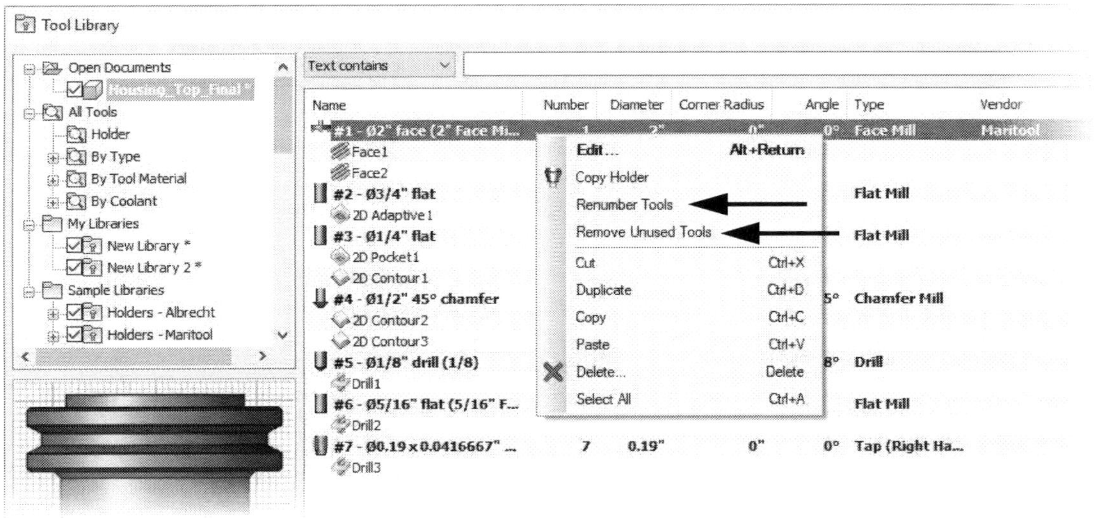

Figure 2–16

Hint: Assigning Tools to a Toolpath

Accessing the Tool Library through its option on the *Manage* tab is used to manage and create tools. All tool assignment is done during toolpath creation. At that time, the same Tool Library dialog box is accessed. All functionality discussed in this topic can also be used while assigning tools to a toolpath.

2.3 Face Toolpath

A Face toolpath enables you to machine large flat areas of raw stock down to a smaller shape without cutting into the reference model. For most applications, face milling is a relatively simple operation, at least in the sense that it usually does not include any special contouring motions. Facing toolpaths are typically added as the first toolpaths on the exterior faces of a model. The tool typically used for facing is a multi-tooth cutter, called a face mill, although end mills can also be used for small areas.

How To: Create a Face toolpath.

1. To add a Face toolpath, in the 2D Milling panel, click (Face). The Face palette opens as shown in Figure 2–17. Each of the tabs along the top of the palette provides access to the options that define the cut.

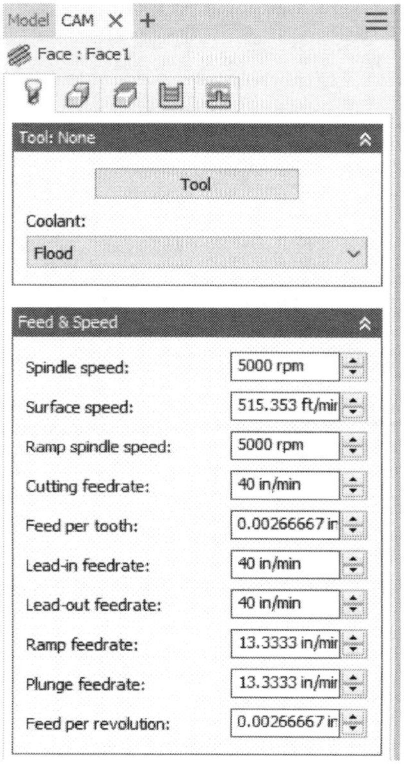

Figure 2–17

Note: *Each toolpath palette has the same tab layout; however, the options within each tab will vary depending on the toolpath type. Hovering your cursor over the fields in a toolpath palette provides access to a descriptive help tooltip. This can be done to help learn more about how the option can be used to control the cutting operation.*

2. In the (Tool) tab, select **Tool** to access the Tool Library to assign the tool. Locate and select the required tool for the toolpath and click **Select**.
   - Once the tool is selected, it is added to the list of tools in the **Open Documents** section of the Tool Library. Each toolpath that uses the tool is listed individually within the tool name. For example, in Figure 2–19, the **#1 - ø2" face (2" Face Mill)** tool was used for both the Face1 and Face2 toolpaths.
   - By default, the **Coolant** field is populated with the option that was assigned to the selected tool. To change the type, select a new option in the Coolant drop-down list. The options are shown in Figure 2–18.

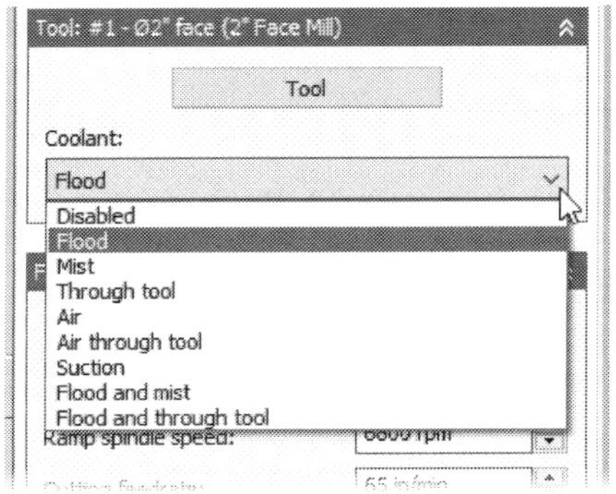

Figure 2–18

   - All of the parameters in the (Tool) tab update to that of the selected tool. Changes to the tool parameters can be made in the palette or you can edit the tool in the Tool Library dialog box. Changes made to the parameters in the *Tool* tab are listed for the toolpath and will not update the parent tool. For example, in Figure 2–19 the parent tool has a *Spindle Speed* of 6500, whereas when used for the Face1 toolpath, its speed was reduced to 6000.

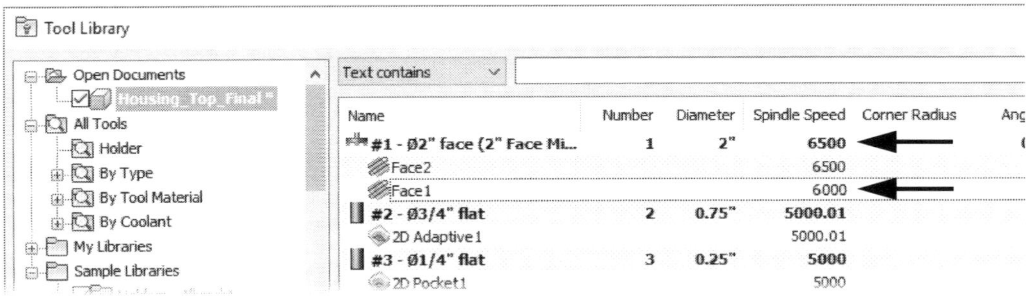

Figure 2–19

3. Select the (Geometry) tab on the palette. The Face palette displays as shown in Figure 2–20. A yellow bounding box is displayed in the graphics window that represents the area of the stock being faced.

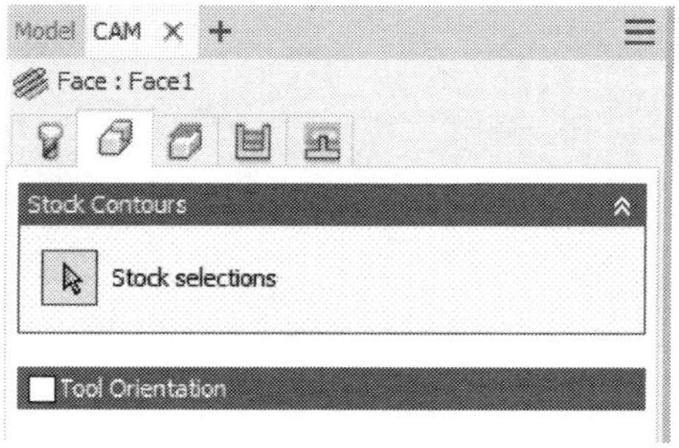

Figure 2–20

- By default, the stock's outside boundary is preselected. If the boundary for the toolpath is not displayed as required, you can select (Stock selections) and select edges or a sketch to define the area. For facing sequences, the geometry does not have to be modified.
- For facing toolpaths, the top of the model is based on how the WCS was set up for the operation. Enable the **Tool Orientation** option to change the face that is being cut. The orientation options are the same as those used to define the WCS orientation during setup.

4. Select the (Heights) tab. The Face palette displays along with the model, which updates to show planes similar to that shown in Figure 2–21. Each plane is color coded based on the categories on the *Heights* tab. This gives you a visual representation of the planes. Edit any of the values, as needed, directly in the palette or in the mini-toolbar.

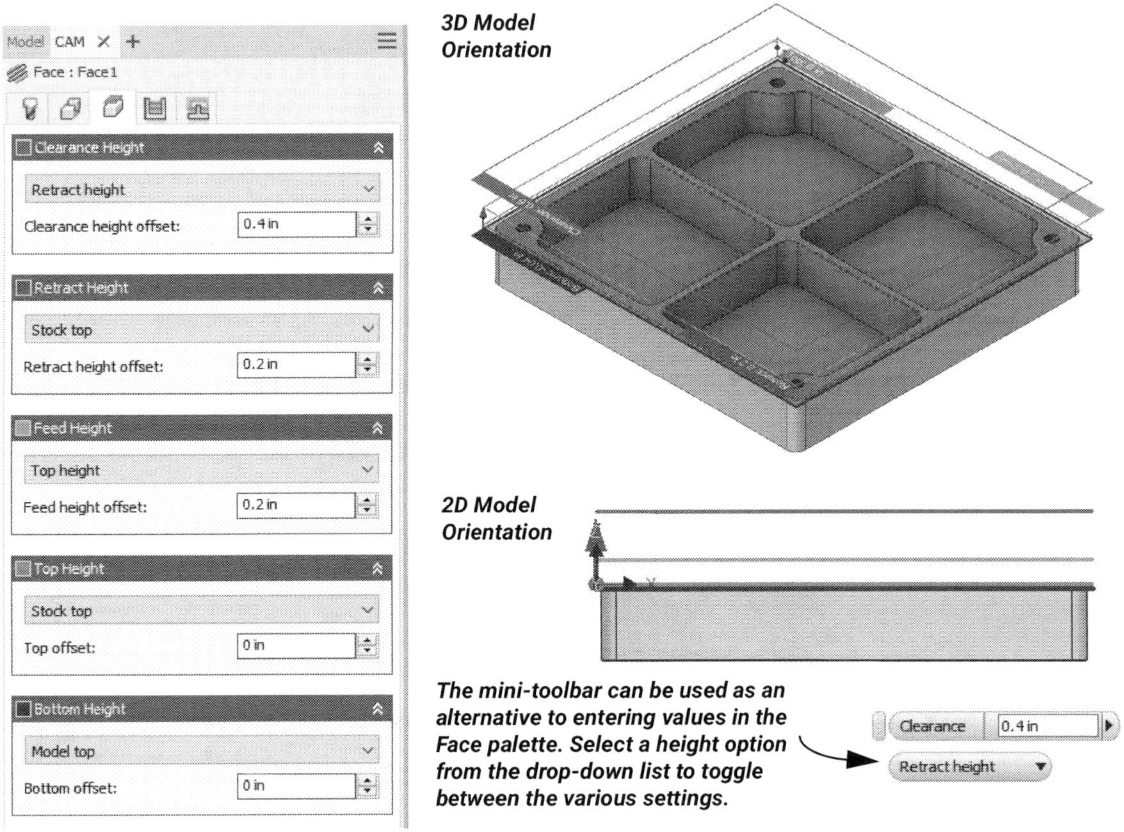

Figure 2–21

- The red plane indicates the *Clearance Height* for the tool.
- The *Retract Height* and *Feed Height* (different shades of green) are at the same height in this model. The *Retract Height* sets the height that the tool will move to before a pass. The *Feed Height* sets the height that the tool rapids to before changing to the cutting rates defined to cut the stock.
- The *Top Height* is set at the top of the stock.This is where cutting begins.
- Because facing is a finishing pass, by default, the *Bottom Height* is set as the **Model top** with no offset value.

5. Select the (Passes) tab. The *Passes* tab displays as shown in Figure 2–22. This tab's options set how the toolpath passes are defined.

The default values assigned in these fields are based on the tool and type of operation. The values can be changed as needed.

Figure 2–22

- In the *Passes* area, the **Tolerance** value defines the tolerance that is used to cut non-linear paths using linear toolpath. Hover your mouse over the value for more in-depth information.
- In the *Passes* area, use the **Pass Direction Reference** field to select a custom direction that the passes should begin from. The default setting, if not changed is the tool's X-axis.
- In the *Passes* area, the **Pass extension** value, by default, is set to 0 in. This enables you to set a distance that the tool should extend past the machining boundary prior to starting a new cut.
- In the *Passes* area, the **Stock offset** value, by default, is set to 0 in. This enables you to set an offset from the stock boundary to define the machining boundary.
- In the *Passes* area, the **Stepover** size is set to 1.9 in. This indicates there is only a 0.1 in. overlap of the cutting path because a 2 in. tool is being used.
- The *Multiple Depths* area is not enabled by default. This indicates that the stock depth (0.04 in.) is being removed in a single pass. If a depth is to remain after the facing toolpath, this option can be enabled and values set.
- The *Stock to Leave* area is not enabled by default. If enabled, you can set values for stock that will remain for future toolpath operations.

6. Select the (Linking) tab. The *Linking* tab displays as shown in Figure 2–23. This tab's options define how each toolpath pass should be linked to the others and how leads and transitions should be generated.

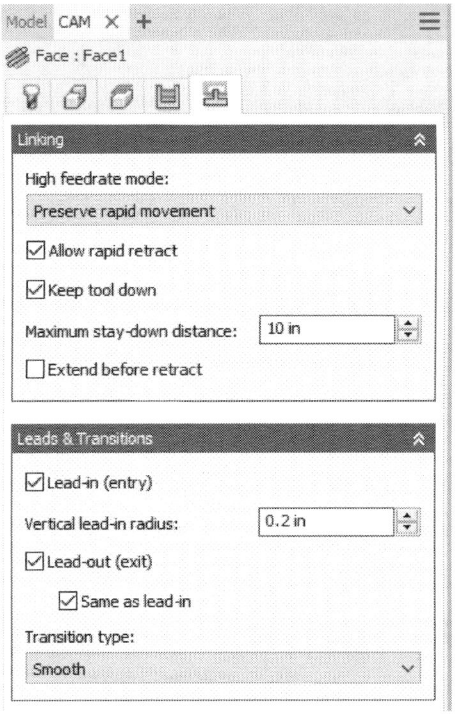

Figure 2–23

- In the *Linking* area, the High feedrate mode drop-down list provides multiple options to determine if rapid movements will be output as G0 (true rapids) or G1 (high feedrate movements). By default, the **Preserve rapid movement** option is set. Additional options in this area enable you to further customize how the path is generated.
- The *Leads & Transitions* area contains options that enable you to define if the leads and transitions are to be generated in the final toolpath and their values, as well as define a transition type (**No Contact**, **Straight line**, **Shortest path**, **Smooth**).

7. Click **OK** at the bottom of the Face palette to complete the toolpath creation.

Once the toolpath is completed, it is added to the active setup and is listed in the CAM browser.

- The icon adjacent to the toolpath name indicates the type of toolpath (e.g., the  icon indicates that it is a Face toolpath).
- The **[T#]** entry indicates the tool number.
- Expanding the toolpath node reveals more details about the toolpath, as shown in Figure 2–24, including the tool name and size, WCS, and toolpath size. You can right-click on these options to quickly gain access to the Tool Library, *Heights* tab, and *Linking* tab, respectively.

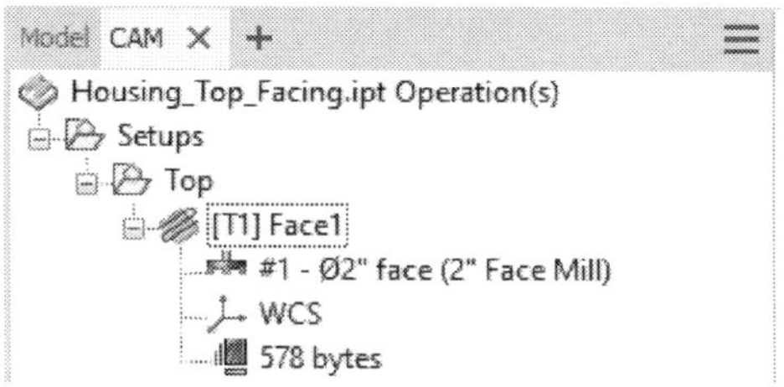

Figure 2–24

- To review the toolpath movements, select the toolpath name in the CAM browser. A colored path is displayed as described in Figure 2–25.

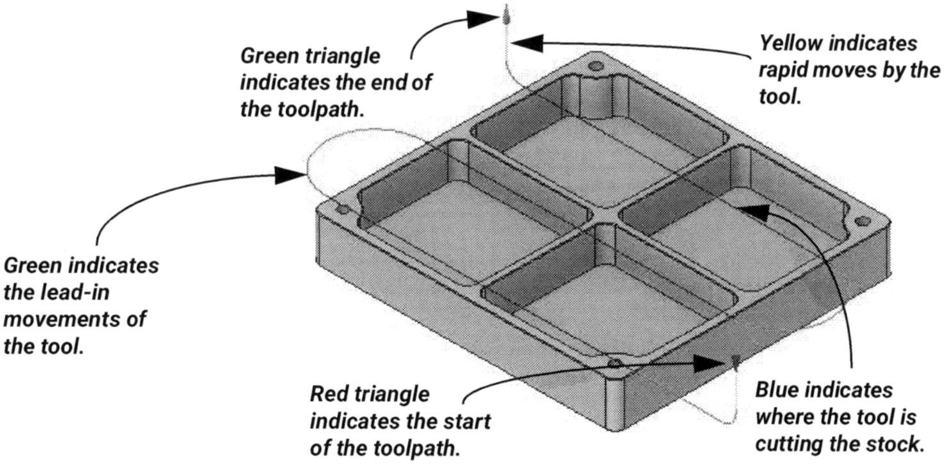

Figure 2–25

- To rename a toolpath, slowly select it twice and enter a new name. Once renamed, the tool number still remains as the prefix in the node to easily identify the tool that is used.

Practice 2a
Setting Up and Facing a Model

Practice Objectives

- Create a setup that includes facing for the top of the model.
- Create a setup that includes facing for the bottom of the model.
- Use the Simulation tools in Inventor CAM to display the newly created facing toolpaths.

In this practice, you will add machining operations to a model. This will be done for both the top and bottom of the model. You will begin by defining the work coordinate system (WCS) and stock requirements for the model, then you will add a facing toolpath for each setup.

Task 1: Open a model and begin the machining setup for the top of the model.

1. Open **Housing_Top_Facing.ipt**. The model and Model browser display as shown in Figure 2–26.

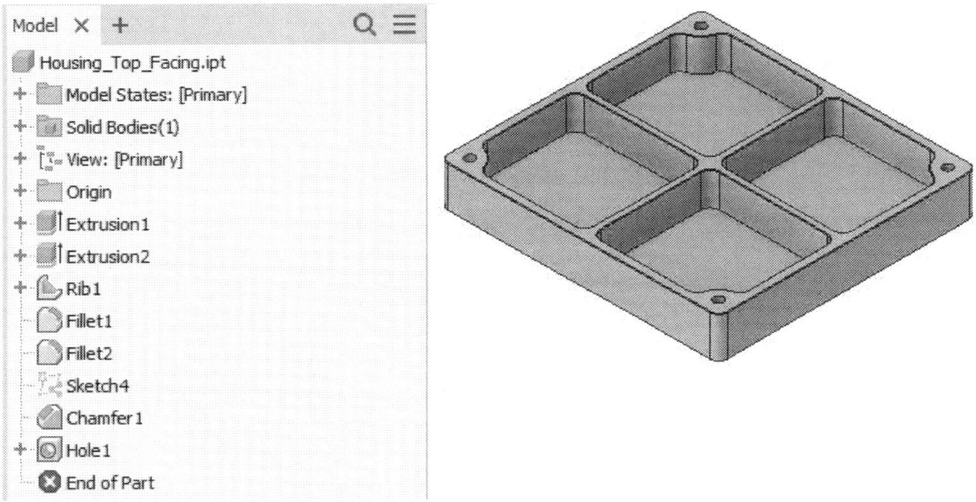

Figure 2–26

2. If the model does not display in the Shaded with Edges display style, in the *View* tab>Appearance panel, expand Visual Style and click **Shaded with Edges**. This display style can be helpful when selecting references and reviewing operations in the CAM environment.
3. Ensure that the model is displayed in its default Home view. This is the top of the model that will be machined in the first setup.

4. In the ribbon, select the *CAM* tab. It appears as shown in Figure 2–27.

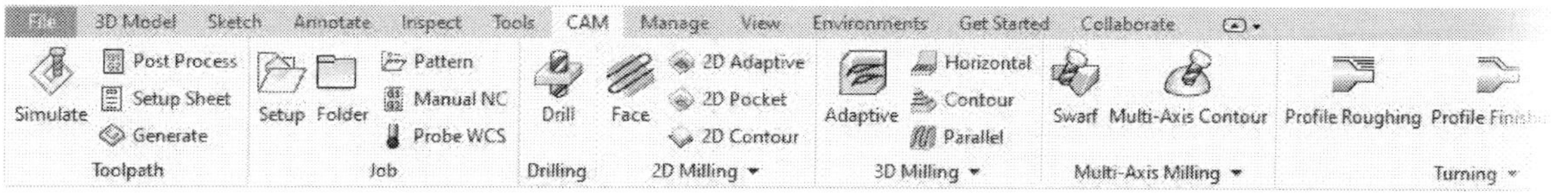

Figure 2–27

5. In the Job panel, click (Setup). The Setup palette and model display as shown in Figure 2–28. The yellow box around the model identifies the default stock. The (Setup) tab is the first tab that is available. This enables you to define the operation type, WCS, and model, as well as whether a fixture is to be assigned.

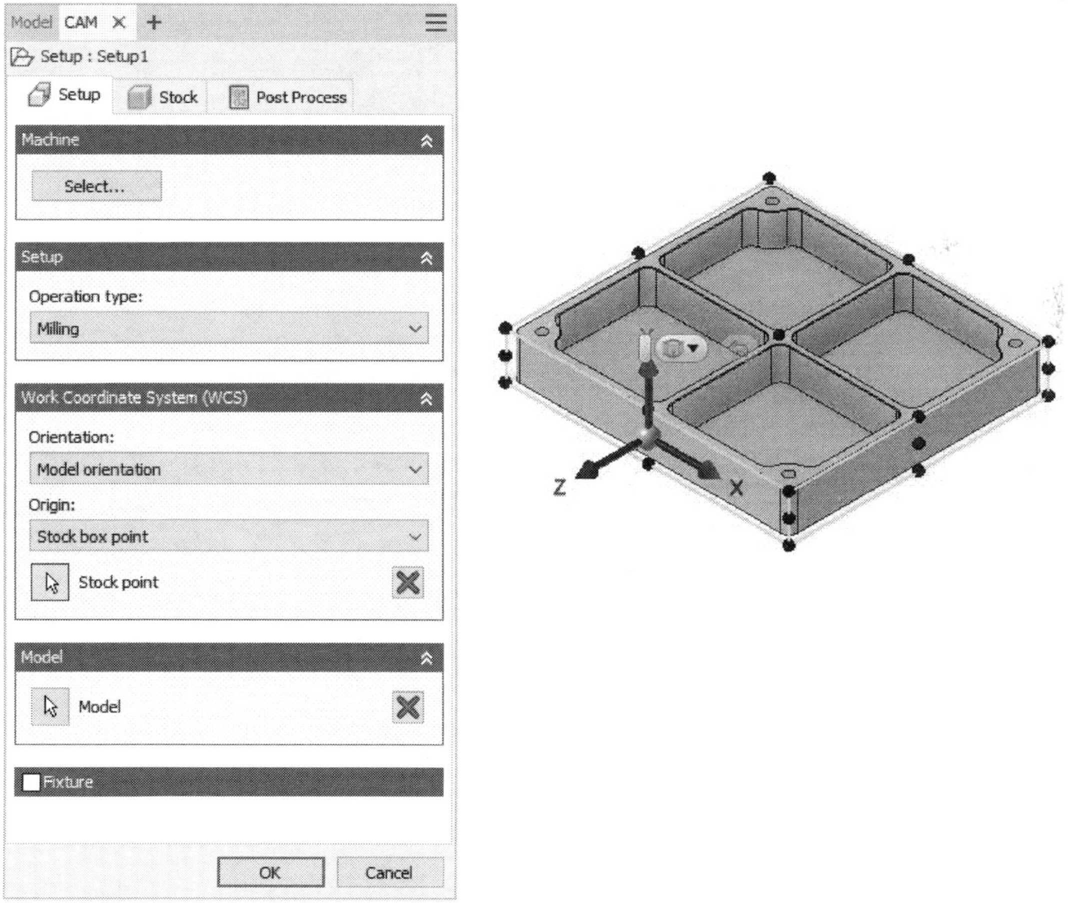

Figure 2–28

6. In the *Machine* area of the palette, click **Select**. Select **Milling** at the top of the Machines dialog box, if not already active. In the list of machines, you would normally select the machine to match what would ultimately be used to machine the model. For this exercise, select **Generic 3-axis** to best define the machine. Select **OK**.
7. Ensure that the *Operation type* option is set as **Milling**.
8. By default, the WCS is displayed in a default location on the stock. In the *Work Coordinate System (WCS)* area, ensure that the *Origin* option is set as **Stock box point**. Select the box point shown in Figure 2–29.

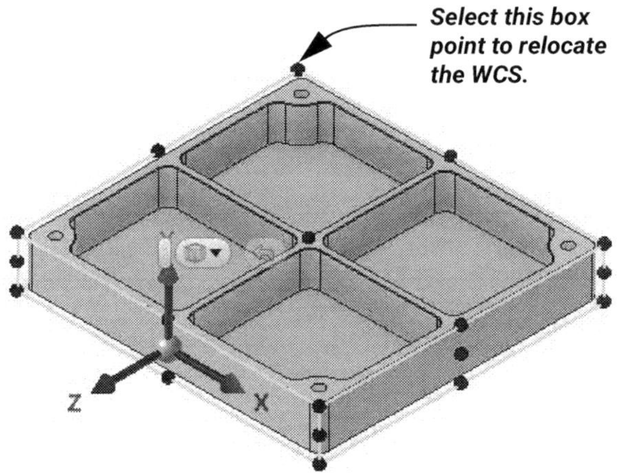

Figure 2–29

Note: *The Origin should be selected such that it will align with the origin of the machine that will be used to cut the model.*

9. In the current WCS orientation, the Y-axis is pointing upwards. This direction must represent the Z-axis of the machine.
10. In the *Work Coordinate System (WCS)* area, set the *Orientation* option to **Select Z axis/plane & X axis**. This enables you to define the orientation of the WCS based on the selection of a Z and X direction. This must be set to match how the stock will be placed in the machine.

11. In the *Orientation* area, ensure that the **Z Axis** selection is active. If not, select it so that the selection box highlights blue. In the model, select one of the edges that run in the current Y-axis, as shown in Figure 2–30.

    Note: *When defining the orientation for the WCS, you can select faces, edges, or displayed axis to define the direction.*

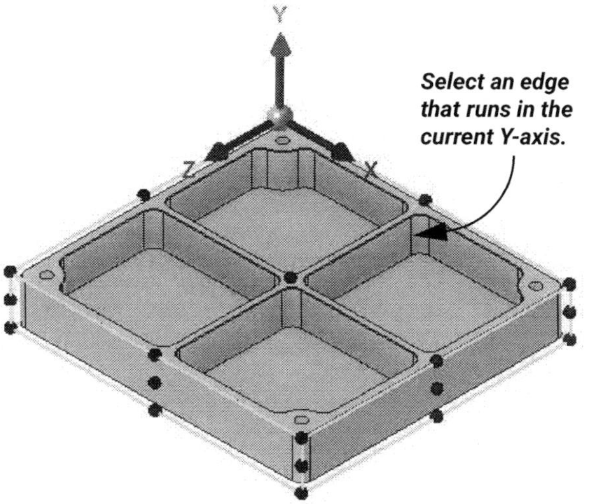

Figure 2–30

12. The WCS reorients as shown in Figure 2–31 with the Z-axis pointing upwards. If it does not update as expected, reselect the edge reference or select the **Flip Z axis** option to flip the direction of the axis along the selected edge. If the stock box point moves, reselect it in the correct location.

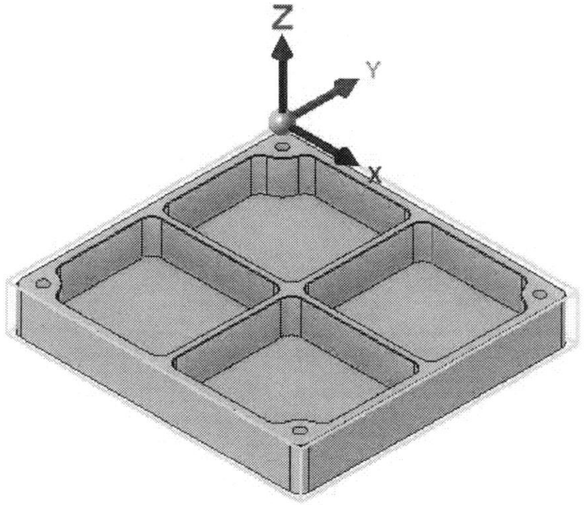

Figure 2–31

13. Depending on the resulting orientation of the WCS once the Z-axis is defined, you may or may not be required to change the X-axis orientation. In the model's default Home view, if the X and Y directions are as shown in Figure 2–31, you do not need to change the X-axis. If the orientation is something other than that shown, you must select an edge to define the X direction or flip it, as needed.
14. Since there is only a single model in the file, Inventor CAM preselects the model. If there were multiple models (i.e., an assembly fixture design), you can use the *Model* field to select only the model being machined.
15. This model does not include fixtures, vices, or clamps that would be required by the CNC machine to hold the model, so leave the **Fixture** option cleared. If the model had these design components included in the file, you could select this option to specify which components the toolpaths must avoid. This guide initially focuses on learning the tools to create operations on your models. Fixtures will be discussed at the end of the guide.
16. At the top of the Setup palette, select the (Stock) tab. The tab displays as shown in Figure 2–32. The stock size is assigned by default and can be changed using the fields on this tab.

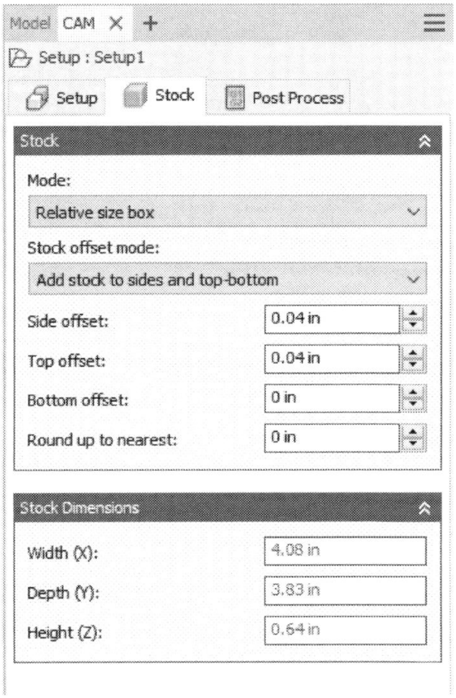

Figure 2–32

17. Maintain the default options for *Mode* (**Relative size box**) and *Stock offset mode* (**Add stock to sides and top-bottom**). These options ensure that the stock is a box that is sized relative to the model's size and that stock will be added to all six faces of the box. If the model size changes, the stock size will automatically adjust.

18. Review the offset values for the sides and top of the stock. A **0.04 in** offset is assigned to both the sides and top. Because of this, operations will be required on both the top and sides to provide a smooth finish. If the stock being used were the exact size, no offsets would be set and no operations added.

19. The *Bottom offset* is currently set as 0 in. Enter **0.25 in** as the new value. This value is required so that stock is included to hold the model in the machine's fixture. Note how the stock size updates (as shown in Figure 2–33) to show the new offset on the bottom of the model.

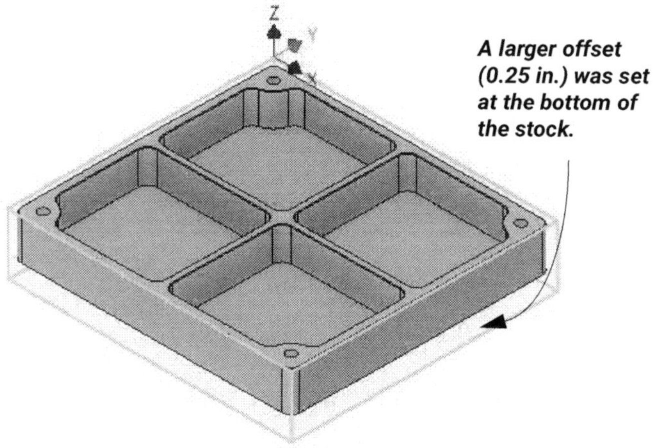

Figure 2–33

Note: *In this situation, the bottom stock has been added to illustrate one possible consideration in determining the stock size. In programming the machining toolpaths, there are often many different methods that can be used. For example, in this case you could also have chosen to add only a small stock offset to the bottom and added toolpaths to both the top and bottom to remove all the outside stock.*

20. The final tab in the Setup palette is the (Post Process) tab. This sets the default program number for the setup. No changes are required.

21. Click **OK** at the bottom of the Setup palette to complete the setup definition. Setup1 appears listed in the CAM browser.

22. Slowly select **Setup1** twice to rename it. Enter **Top** as the name, as shown in Figure 2–34. This indicates the setup will contain all the operations performed on the top of the model.

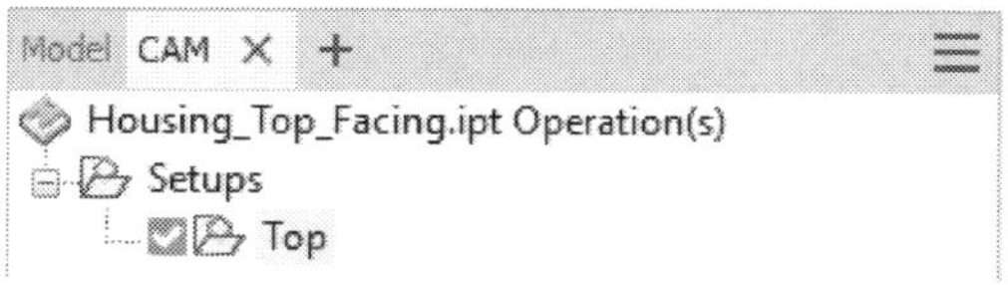

Figure 2–34

Task 2: Create a Face toolpath to machine the top of the stock.

In this task, you will create a Face toolpath. You will learn to define the geometry to be machined, the tool to use, and customize the toolpath, as needed.

1. In the 2D Milling panel, click (Face). The Face palette appears as shown in Figure 2–35.

   The (Tool) tab is initially open, by default. This is consistent with every toolpath type. It indicates that tool selection must be set to start defining the toolpath.

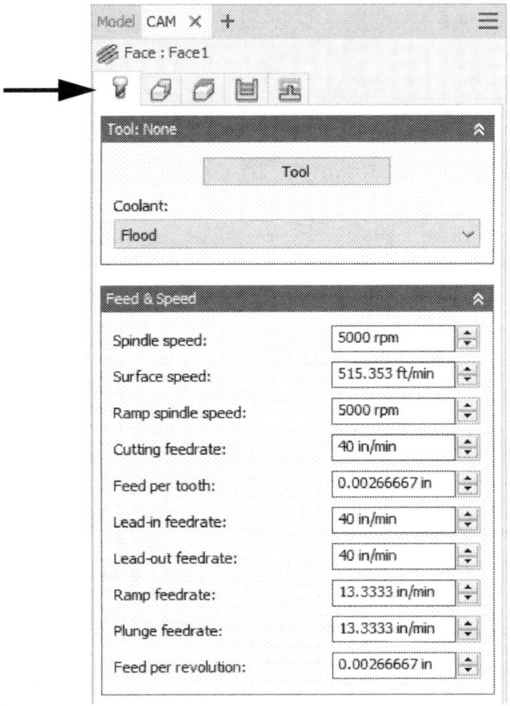

Figure 2–35

2. In the *Tool: None* area, select **Tool**. The Select Tool dialog box opens.
3. The right-hand frame is empty because the **Housing_Top_Facing** model is selected in the *Open Documents* node and there are currently no tools assigned to the model. As tools are selected for toolpaths, this list will be populated.
4. Expand **All Tools>By Type** and select **Face Mill**. All Face Mill tools that are available in the library are listed.

5. Select **#1 - Ø2" face (2" Face Mill)**, as shown in Figure 2–36.

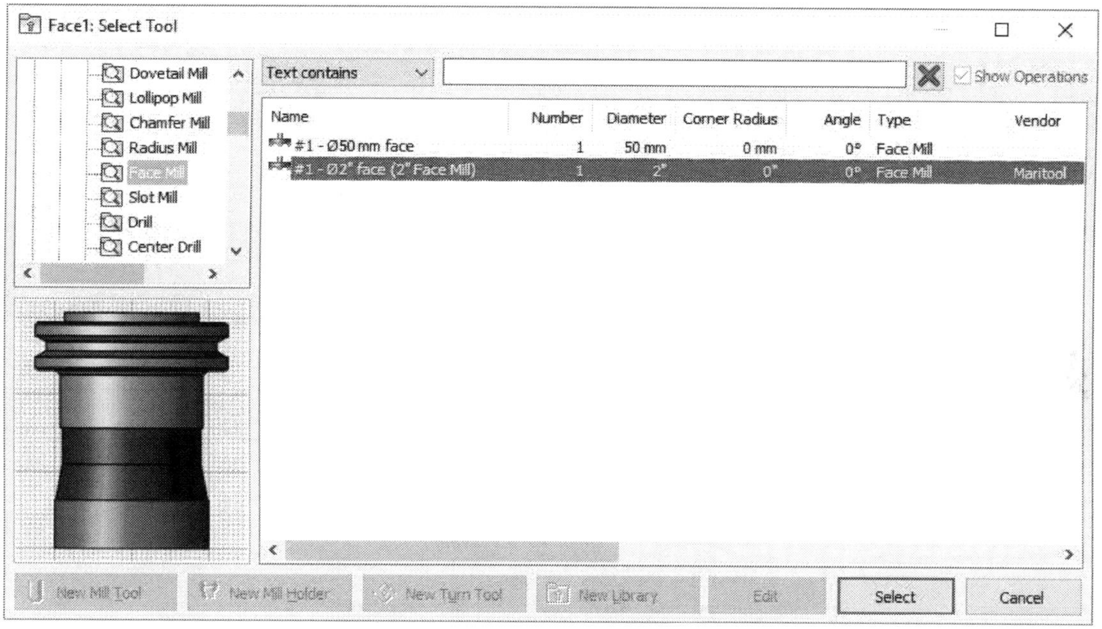

Figure 2–36

6. Right-click **#1 - Ø2" face (2" Face Mill)** and select **Edit**. The Tool dialog box opens, as shown in Figure 2–37.

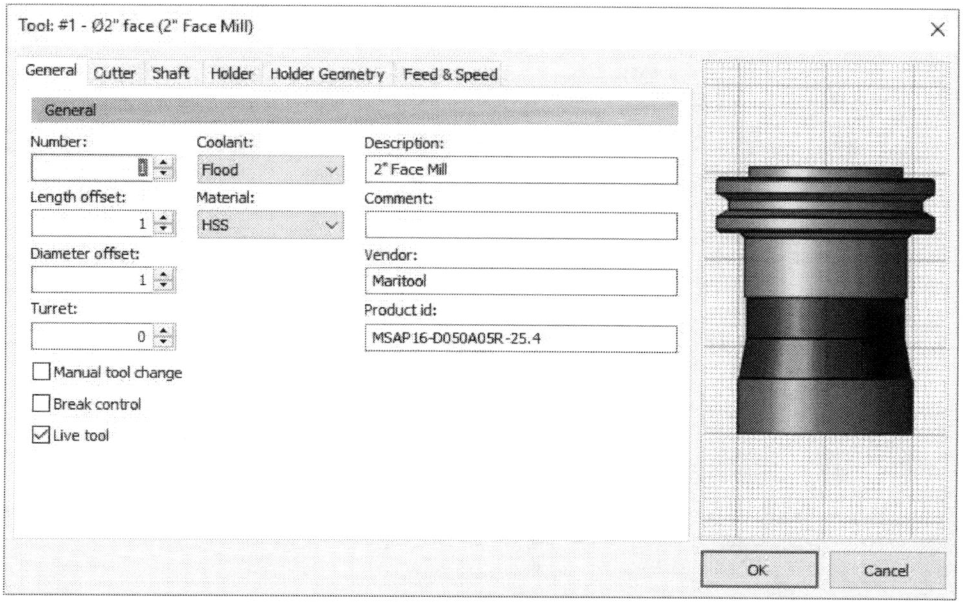

Figure 2–37

7. Review the following in the Tool dialog box.
   - On the *General* tab, the tool number (assigned in the library) is Tool #1. The number should match your machine. For this exercise, you can leave this value.
   - On the *Cutter* tab, note that the type is set as **Face Mill** and the sizes are all defined. Changes can be made to customize the size of tool being used in the toolpath. For this exercise, you can leave these values.
   - On the *Feed & Speed* tab, note that all the speeds and feedrates are specified. These values should all be set to match the tool being used on your machine.
8. Click **OK** to close the Tool dialog box without changes.
9. In the Select Tool dialog box, ensure that the **#1 - ⌀2" face (2" Face Mill)** tool remains selected and click **Select**. The tool is assigned for Face1, as shown in Figure 2–38.

   Note: *The Feed & Speed settings for the tool can be edited in the Tool dialog box or on the Tool tab in the Face1 palette.*

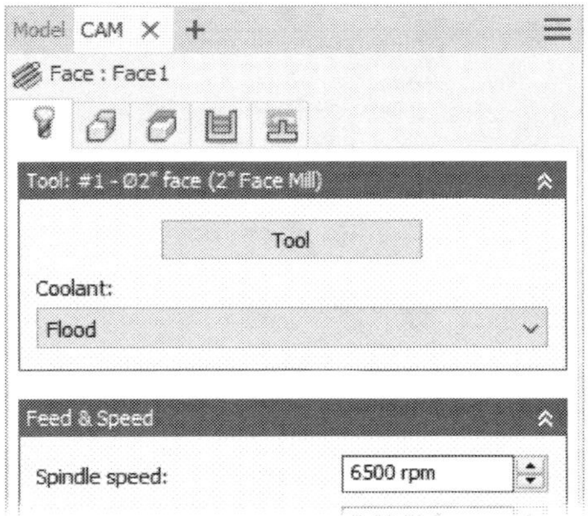

Figure 2–38

10. Select the (Geometry) tab in the Face palette.
11. Reorient the model to the **Front** view using the ViewCube and note that the yellow plane that will be machined is the top of the stock.
12. No changes are required on the *Geometry* tab. Select the (Heights) tab. The Face palette and model display as shown in Figure 2–39. Each plane is color coded based on the categories on the *Heights* tab.
    - The red plane indicates the *Clearance Height* for the tool.
    - The *Retract Height* and *Feed Height* (different shades of green) are at the same height in this model. The *Retract Height* sets the height that the tool will move to before a pass. The *Feed Height* sets the height that the tool rapids to before changing to the cutting rates defined to cut the stock.

- The *Top Height* is set at the top of the stock. This is where cutting begins.
- Because the facing is a finishing pass, the *Bottom Height* is set as the **Model top** with no offset value.

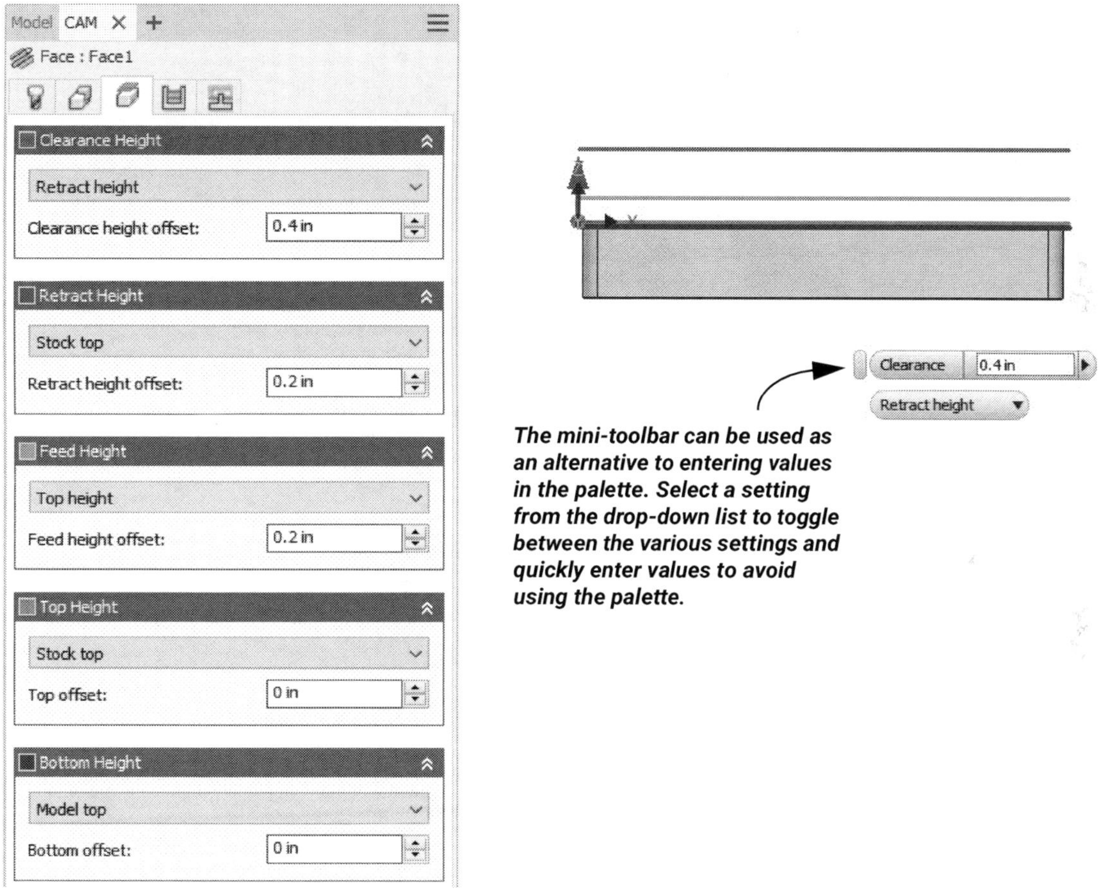

Figure 2–39

13. No changes are required on the *Heights* tab. Select the (Passes) tab. The *Passes* tab displays as shown in Figure 2–40.

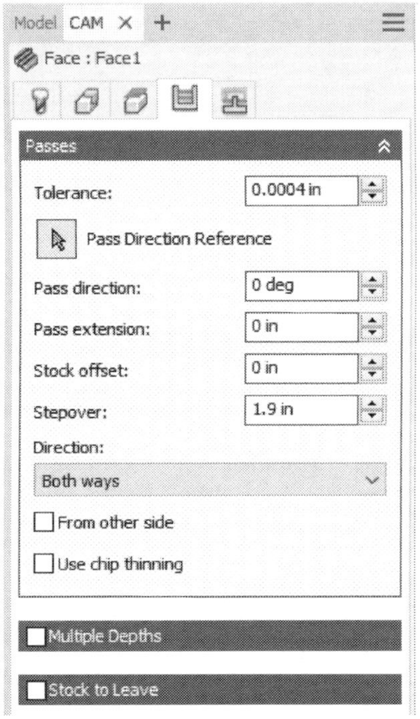

Figure 2–40

14. Review the following settings in the *Passes* tab. The default values assigned in these fields are based on the tool and type of operation. The values can be changed as needed.

    - In the *Passes* area, the **Pass extension** value, by default, is set to 0 in. This means that the tool is constantly cutting the stock. Modifying this value enables you to set a distance that the tool should extend past the machining boundary prior to starting a new cut.
    - In the *Passes* area, the **Stock offset** value, by default, is set to 0 in. This enables you to set an offset from the stock boundary to define the machining boundary. This ensures that all stock is removed in the toolpath.
    - In the *Passes* area, the **Stepover** value is set to 1.9 in. This indicates that there is only a 0.1 in. overlap of the cutting path because a 2 in. tool is being used. This is appropriate for the toolpath.
    - The *Multiple Depths* area is not selected. This indicates that the stock depth (0.04 in.) is being removed in a single pass. This is appropriate for the toolpath.
    - The *Stock to Leave* area is not selected. This is appropriate for the toolpath because the Face toolpath is being done as a finishing pass.

15. No changes are required on the *Passes* tab. Select the (Linking) tab. This tab's options define how each toolpath pass should be linked to the others.
16. In the *Leads & Transitions* area, hover your cursor over the **Lead-in (entry)** field. Notice how a descriptive help tooltip appears to describe the options. This can be done on all options on all tabs in the palette to help you learn more about how each option can be used to control the cutting operation.
17. No changes are required on the *Linking* tab. Click **OK** at the bottom of the Face palette to complete the toolpath.
18. Return the model to its default Home view. The CAM browser and the model update as shown in Figure 2–41.
    - The **[T1] Face1** toolpath is now listed in the CAM browser.
    - The toolpath movements are colored as described in Figure 2–41.

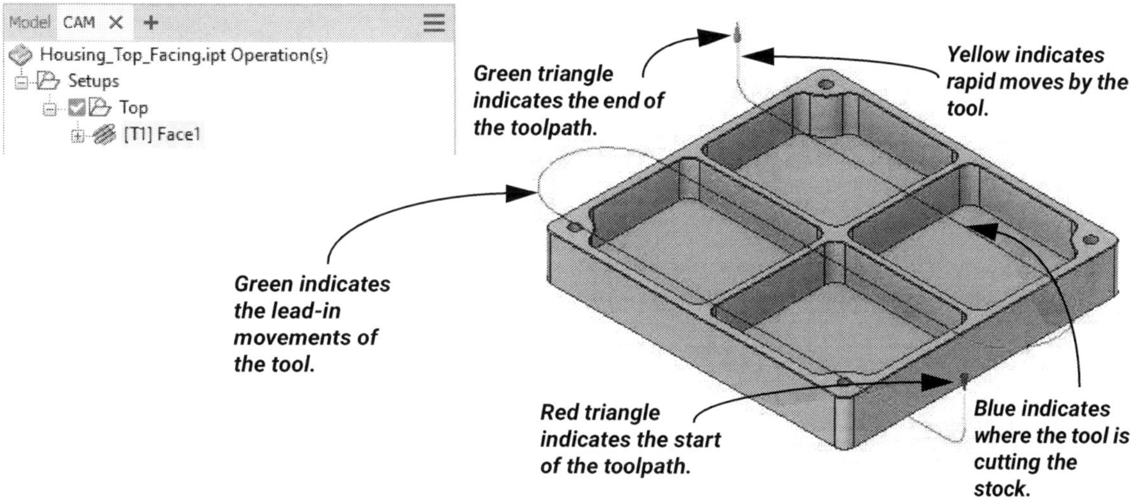

Figure 2–41

19. Save the model.

Task 3: View a simulation of the toolpath.

In this task, you will use the **Simulate** option to visually preview the Face toolpath that you just created.

1. In the CAM browser, ensure that the **[T1] Face1** toolpath is selected.
2. Return to the model's default Home view, if not already set.

3. In the Toolpath panel, click  (Simulate). The Simulation palette opens as shown in Figure 2–42. The *Display* tab is active by default. Review the following:
   - By default, the **Tool** is set to display in the simulation.
   - By default, the **Toolpath** is set to display as the simulation is played.
   - By default, the **Stock** is not set to be displayed.

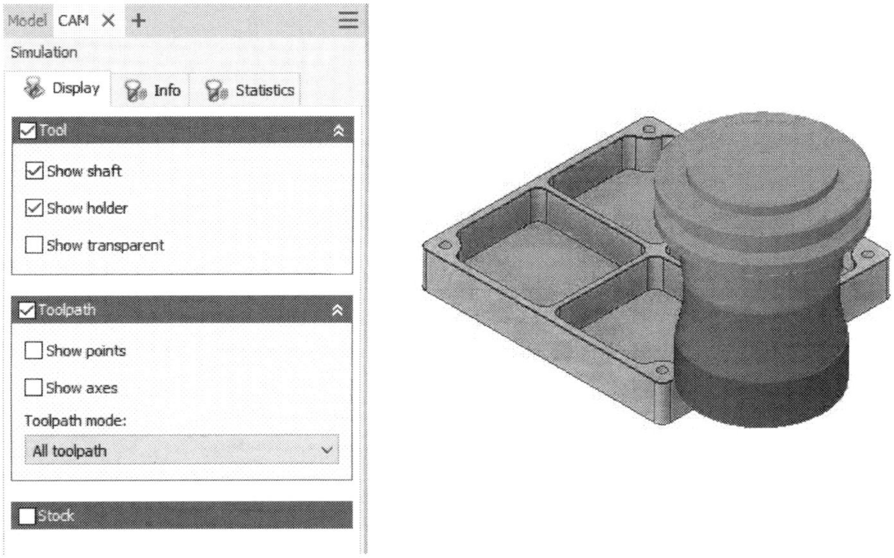

Figure 2–42

__Note:__ If you have previously changed any of the settings in the Simulation palette, the last setting will be maintained. For this exercise, use the settings shown in Figure 2–42.

4. Enable the **Stock** option at the bottom of the Simulation palette. The stock appears as green solid geometry around the model, as shown in Figure 2–43.

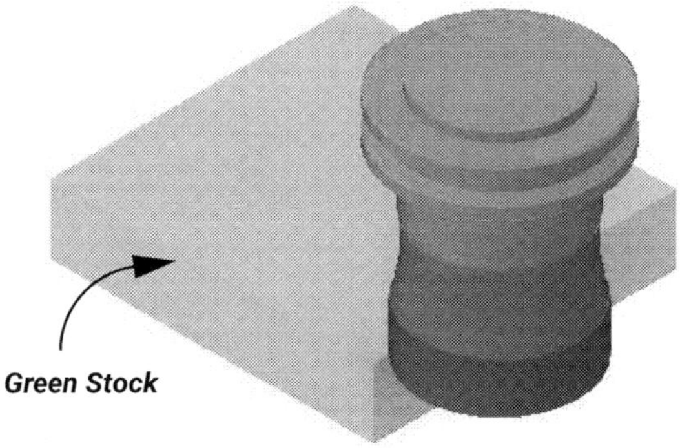

Figure 2–43

5. Click ▷ in the simulation player to play the Face toolpath.
6. Once the simulation has been reviewed, click **Close** at the bottom of the Simulation palette.

Task 4: Set up a second toolpath to face the bottom of the model.

In this task, you will create a second setup and add a Face toolpath to machine the bottom of the stock. A new setup is required because the model would be manually flipped prior to the paths in this setup being run.

1. In the Job panel, click (Setup). The Setup palette opens.
2. Rotate the model to a view similar to that shown in Figure 2–44. Note how the stock displayed around the model does not take into account the size that was defined for the Top setup. Each setup is unique and must be defined accordingly. The only option that does not need to be selected a second time is the Machine setting.

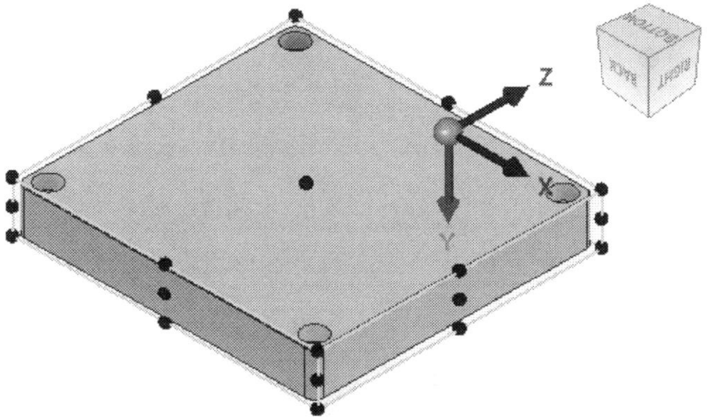

Figure 2–44

3. On the (Setup) tab, ensure that the *Operation type* option is set as **Milling**.

4. Use the options in the *Work Coordinate System (WCS)* area (as previously described in Task 1) to relocate and reorient the WCS as shown in Figure 2–45.

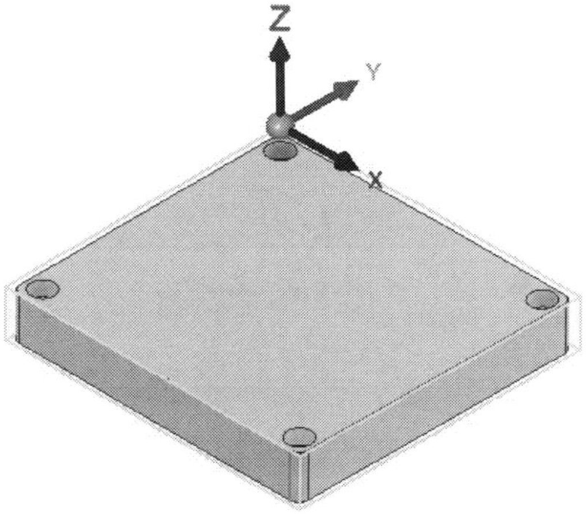

Figure 2–45

Note: *The Origin should be selected such that it will align with the origin of the machine that will be used to cut the model.*

5. Select the  (Stock) tab. Because this is a second setup for the model, you must manually assign the stock values to adjust for the new orientation so that it is consistent with the stock assigned in the Top setup. Assign the values as shown in Figure 2–46.
   - Maintain **0.04 in** as the *Side offset* value.
   - Enter **0.25 in** as the *Top offset* value. This was the value that was assigned to the bottom for the Top setup. Now that the model has been flipped, this stock must be machined off the top.
   - Maintain **0 in** as the *Bottom offset* value.

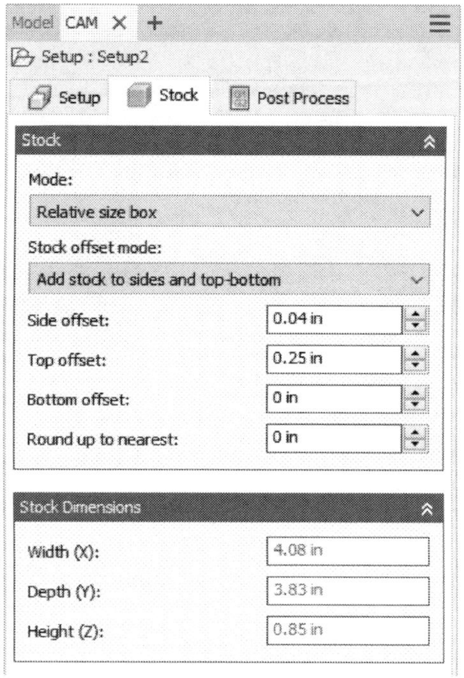

Figure 2–46

6. Click **OK** at the bottom of the Setup palette to complete the setup. Setup2 appears listed in the CAM browser.
7. Slowly select **Setup2** twice to rename it. Enter **Bottom** as the name, as shown in Figure 2–47.

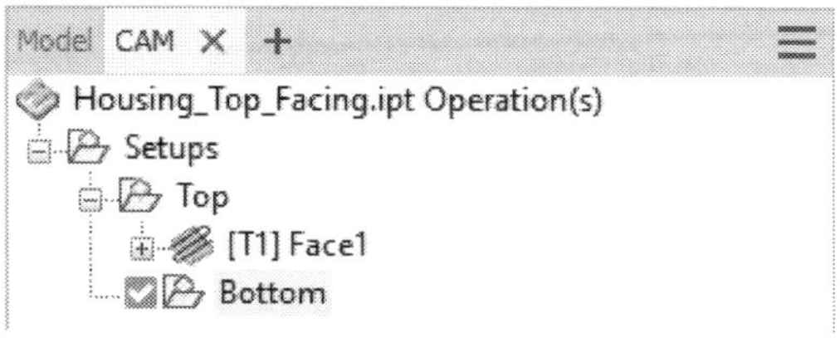

Figure 2–47

8. Ensure that Bottom has a checkmark adjacent to it indicating it is the active setup. If not, right-click on the **Bottom** setup and select **Default Folder** to activate it.
9. In the 2D Milling panel, click (Face). The Face palette appears. Use the tabs to define the Face toolpath for the Bottom (Setup2). Maintain the same tool that was used for the first facing toolpath and maintain the defaults.This tool was set as default because it is currently the only tool in the model's tool list.

10. Select the (Passes) tab and select the **Multiple Depths** option to enable the area. Currently there is 0.25 in. of stock on the model that is required to be machined. Enter **0.15 in** as the Maximum stepdown value so that the facing is completed in two passes. Also enable **Use even stepdowns** so that the two passes are 0.125 in. each.

11. Click **OK** at the bottom of the Face palette to complete the toolpath. The CAM browser should appear as shown in Figure 2–48.

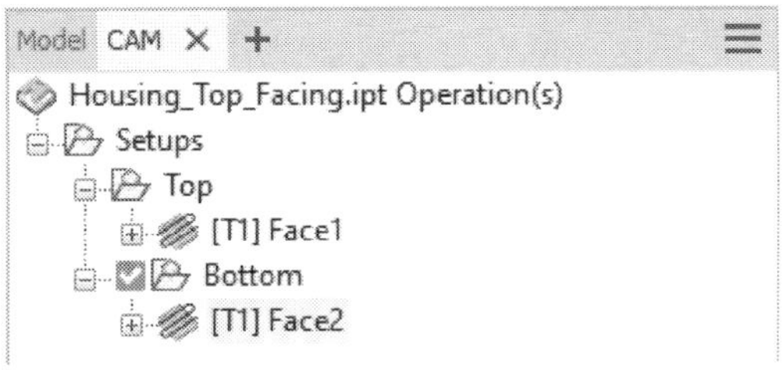

Figure 2–48

Task 5: View a simulation of the two facing toolpaths.

In this task, you will use the **Simulate** option to visually preview the two facing toolpaths that you just created.

1. Return the model to its default Home view.
2. Activate the Simulation palette.

   Note: *For 2D Milling, the two setups will not be run at once. The machine must be stopped, stock flipped, and the second setup started. The simulation is for review purposes only.*

3. Ensure that the stock is displayed and run a simulation that shows both facing toolpaths. (Hint: Ensure that **Housing_Top_Facing.ipt Operation(s)** is selected at the top of the CAM browser to play both toolpaths together.)
4. Play the simulation.
5. Close the Simulation palette and ensure that the facing toolpaths display as required.
6. Save the model.

End of practice

Chapter Review Questions

1. Which of the following are defined in the initial setup of an operation? (Select all that apply.)
   a. Tool type
   b. Operation type
   c. Work coordinate system
   d. Stock size

2. Which of the following are valid methods for defining the stock that will be used in an operation? (Select all that apply.)
   a. Box with a fixed size.
   b. Box with values entered for stock offsets on sides, top, and bottom.
   c. Cylinder with a fixed size.
   d. Cylinder with values entered for stock offsets radially, front, and back.
   e. Rectangle with values entered for stock offsets on x- and y-sides, top, and bottom.
   f. Selected solid model geometry.
   g. Selected surface geometry.

3. Based on Figure 2–49, which of the following statements are true? (Select all that apply.)

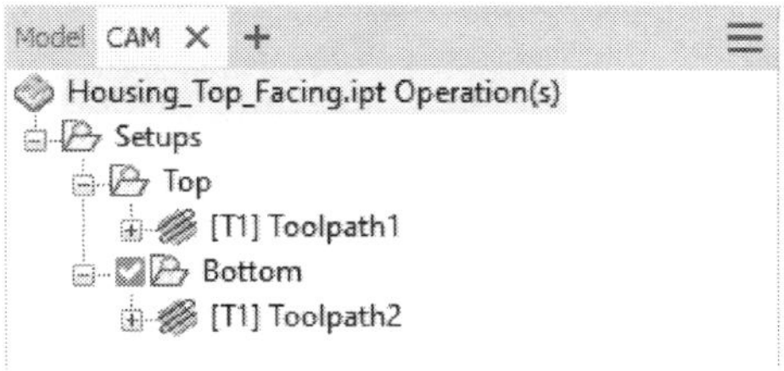

Figure 2–49

   a. There are two setups assigned to the model.
   b. There are two toolpaths assigned to the model.
   c. There are two different tools used in the model.
   d. Any new toolpath that is added to the model will be added to the Top setup.
   e. The toolpath names are currently displayed with their default naming convention.

4. Any changes that are made to a selected tool's parameter values are reflected in the parent tool for future use.
    a. True
    b. False

5. In which of the following Tool Library categories do you find the list of tools used to machine a model?
    a. Open Documents
    b. All Tools
    c. My Libraries
    d. Sample Libraries

6. The **Remove Unused Tool** option enables you to purge custom tools that have been created and are not being used from your library of tools.
    a. True
    b. False

7. Which of the following are defined in the creation of a Face toolpath? (Select all that apply.)
    a. Tool to be used
    b. Geometry to be faced
    c. Work coordinate system
    d. Stock size
    e. Tool heights

8. Which of the following heights is not defined in the *Heights* tab when defining a Face toolpath?
    a. Stock Height
    b. Clearance Height
    c. Retract Height
    d. Bottom Height

9. A 2-inch tool is being used in a Face toolpath. The stepover size is set as 1.9 inches. There is an overlap of 0.1 inches in the resulting cutting path.

a. True

b. False

10. A facing toolpath is being used as a roughing pass and it has been set to leave 0.05 inches of stock on the top of the model. Which of the following settings allow for this? (Select all that apply.)

a. In the Heights tab, set the Bottom Height as Model top and enter a Bottom offset value of 0.05 in.

b. In the Heights tab, set the Feed Height to Model top and enter a Feed height offset value of 0.05 in.

c. In the Passes tab, set a Stock offset value of 0.05 in.

d. In the Passes tab, select Stock to Leave and enter 0.05 in as the axial stock to leave.

Command Summary

Button	Command	Location
	**Face (toolpath)**	• **Ribbon:** *CAM* tab>2D Milling panel
	**Setup**	• **Ribbon:** *CAM* tab>Job panel
	**Tool Library**	• **Ribbon:** *CAM* tab>Manage panel

Chapter 3

2D Roughing and Finishing

Once a facing toolpath has been added to an Inventor CAM model to remove the top of stock, you can begin to incorporate roughing and finishing toolpaths to design the manufacturing code that can be used to machine the final model. The next toolpath that should be incorporated is one that quickly removes large amounts of stock from the model. These are called roughing toolpaths. For 2D milling, roughing toolpaths can be added as either a 2D Adaptive or 2D Pocket sequence. In this chapter, you will learn how to create both of these toolpaths. To complete the chapter, you will learn how to create a 2D Contour toolpath that can be used as a finishing operation on your model.

Learning Objectives

- Add 2D Adaptive toolpaths to an Inventor CAM model.
- Add 2D Pocket toolpaths to an Inventor CAM model.
- Add 2D Contour toolpaths to an Inventor CAM model.

3.1 2D Adaptive Toolpath

A 2D Adaptive toolpath is a clearing/roughing sequence that is used to remove large amounts of material from your model quickly and easily (e.g., cavities, pockets, areas around bosses, etc.). As compared to traditional CAM roughing toolpaths, where the focus is on maximum stepover distance, an Adaptive toolpath allows you to specify the optimal load of the cutter. This sets the maximum amount of engagement that the tool should maintain during the cutting path. This is considered a high-speed machining strategy that results in faster material removal while at the same time increasing the life of your tool.

When creating a 2D Adaptive toolpath using Inventor CAM, the cutting area is defined by selecting edges, solid faces, or a pre-existing sketch. The toolpath that is generated is optimized automatically to provide the uniform and even tool load that is specified. In the example shown in Figure 3–1, two 2D Adaptive toolpaths were created to quickly remove large portions of interior stock.

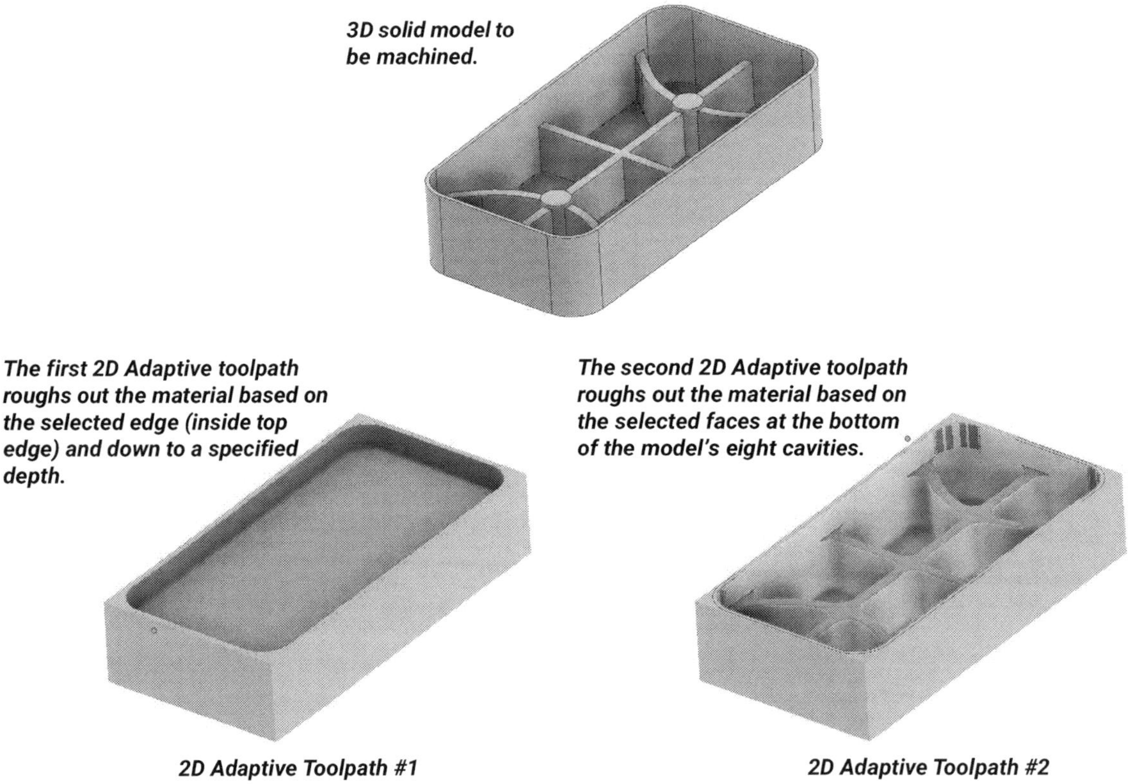

Figure 3–1

How To: Create a 2D Adaptive toolpath.

1. In the 2D Milling panel, click (2D Adaptive). The 2D Adaptive palette opens similarly to that shown in Figure 3–2. Each of the tabs along the top of the palette provide access to the options that define the cut.

   ***Note:** As you progress through this guide, the instructions for how to create each toolpath will focus on the high-level tasks that vary from previously discussed toolpaths. Refer to content in Chapter 2 for more details on each tab.*

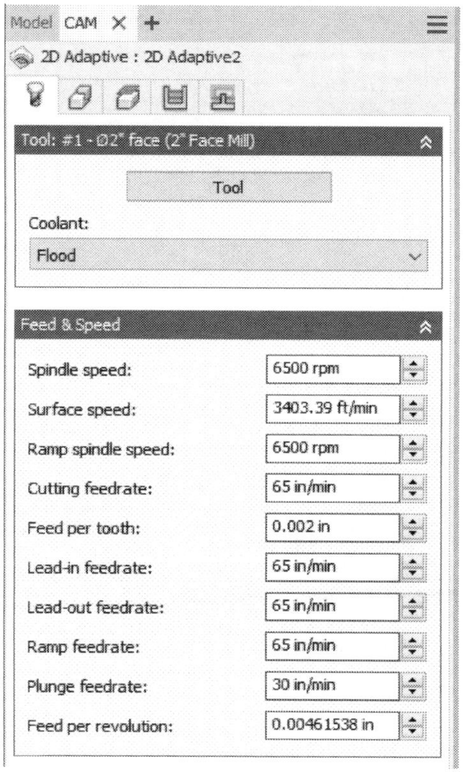

Figure 3–2

2. If a 2D Adaptive toolpath is not the first toolpath in the model, the tool used in the previous toolpath is automatically assigned. To assign or change a pre-assigned tool, in the (Tool) tab, select **Tool** to access the Tool Library. Locate and select the required tool, then click **Select**.

   ***Note:** The Tool Library is used in the same way for all toolpaths. Refer to the Tool Library topic or the description for creating a Face toolpath in Chapter 2 for more details on the Tool Library.*

3. Select the (Geometry) tab. The palette updates as shown in Figure 3–3. Unlike a Face toolpath, the geometry for a 2D Adaptive toolpath is not automatically selected.

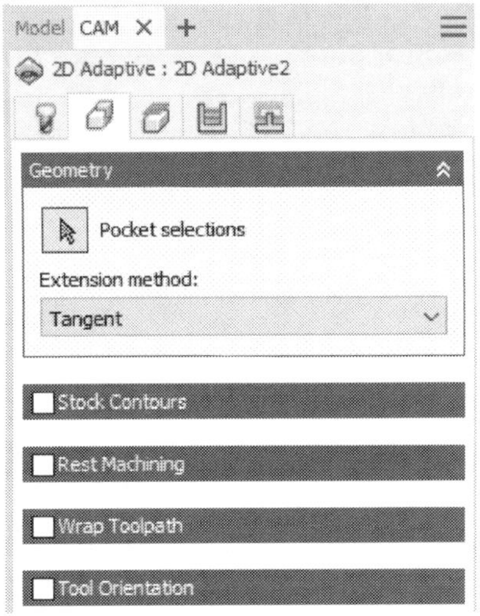

Figure 3–3

- By default, the (Pocket selections) option is active to select the references that will define the cutting area. For a 2D Adaptive toolpath, you define the geometry by selecting edges, solid faces, or a pre-existing sketch from the model, as shown in Figure 3–4.

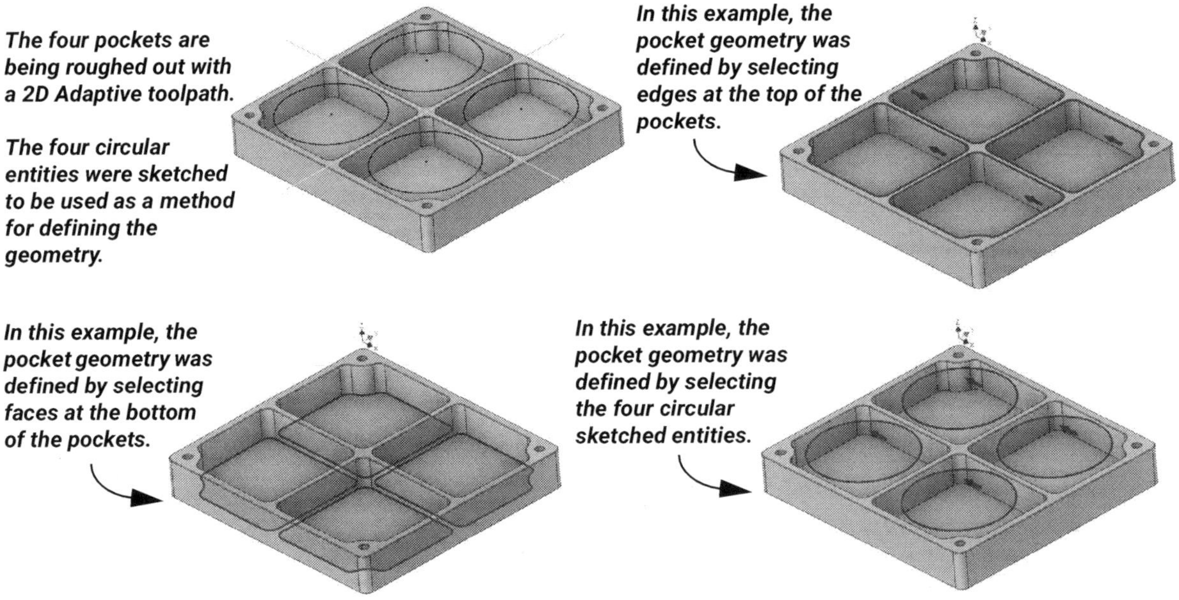

Figure 3–4

- If an edge or a sketch is selected as the pocket reference, a red arrow appears indicating the side on which machining will be conducted. Ensure that the default direction is set properly before continuing. To flip the side, select the arrow. Figure 3–5 shows an example of the two directions that are available for the selected pocket reference.

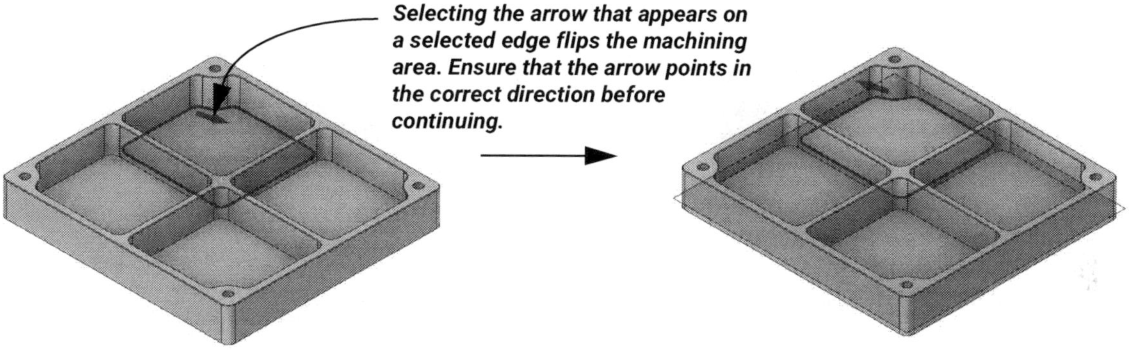

Figure 3–5

- For open pockets (i.e., edges that don't have a closed boundary), you can set an *Extension Method* that defines a closed contour for the tools path. Hover your mouse over the option to review images of each option.
- The *Stock Contours* area is disabled by default; however, for situations where a non-enclosed pocket is being cut, it can be enabled to define the stock machining area for toolpath calculations. For closed pockets, leave this option cleared.
- The *Rest Machining* area (**RE**maining **ST**ock) is disabled by default; however, it can be enabled to limit the toolpath to only removing material that was not removed in a previous toolpath (i.e., where a previous tool was too large).
- The *Wrap Toolpath* area enables you to wrap a toolpath around a selected cylinder. When enabled, the tool orientation cannot be changed because the axis of the cylinder defines the orientation.
- By default, the tool orientation is based on the work coordinate system (WCS) that was set up for the operation. Enable the **Tool Orientation** option to change the face that is being cut. The orientation options are the same as those used to define the WCS orientation during setup.

Note: *Hover your cursor over each of the areas and options in the palette to obtain tooltip information about the options. These are available in all tabs.*

4. Select the (Heights) tab. The palette displays the available plane height options (Clearance, Retract, Top, and Bottom) and they are visually represented on the model geometry. Edit any of the values, as needed, directly in the palette or in the mini-toolbar.

Note: *A Feed Height plane is not available for 2D Adaptive toolpaths because this toolpath calculates the height on its own to optimize tool movements.*

5. Select the (Passes) tab to define how the passes for the toolpath are defined, as shown in Figure 3–6. The options that are available in this tab vary from those used in the Face toolpath that was previously discussed.

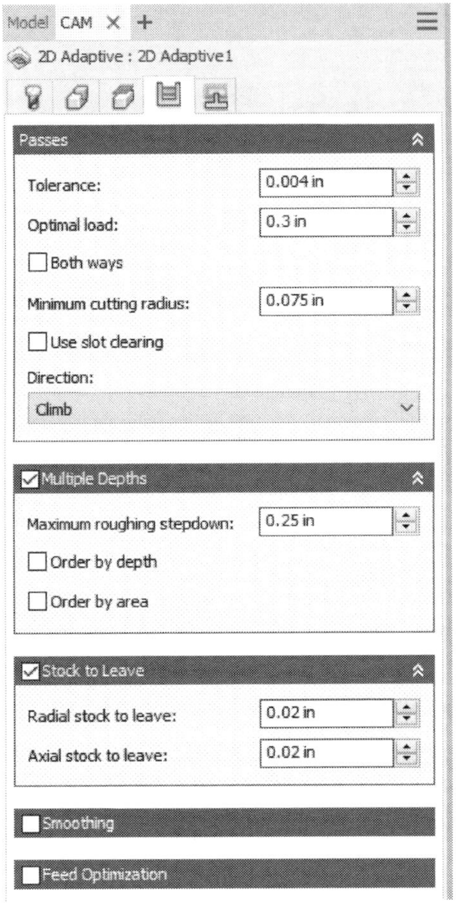

The default values assigned in these fields are based on the tool and type of operation. The values can be changed as needed.

Figure 3–6

- In the *Passes* area, the options enable control over the cutting tolerance, optimal load for the tool, minimum cutting radius, and the cutting direction (conventional milling or climb milling).
- The *Multiple Depths* area is enabled by default. This indicates the stepdown for stock removal in a single pass. The **Order by depth** and **Order by area** options can be used, if required, to change the toolpath order based on cavity depth and area. By default, these options are disabled and the cutting order is based on order the geometry was selected in.

- The *Stock to Leave* area is enabled by default because 2D Adaptive is meant as a roughing toolpath. Set the radial and axial values to define how much stock should remain for future toolpaths.
- The *Smoothing* area is disabled by default; however, it can be enabled to reduce the cutting tolerance control for curved areas. When enabled, it replaces the collinear lines and multiple line segments that are used to define a curved area with a single line and tangent arc, respectively. Using this option helps reduce the code size for the 2D Adaptive toolpath.
- By default, feed speeds are constant for an entire toolpath. The *Feed Optimization* area (disabled by default) can be enabled and its values set in order to control the tool feedrate in corners.

6. Select the  (Linking) tab. The *Linking* tab displays as shown in Figure 3–7. This tab provides many additional options than those available for the Face toolpath.

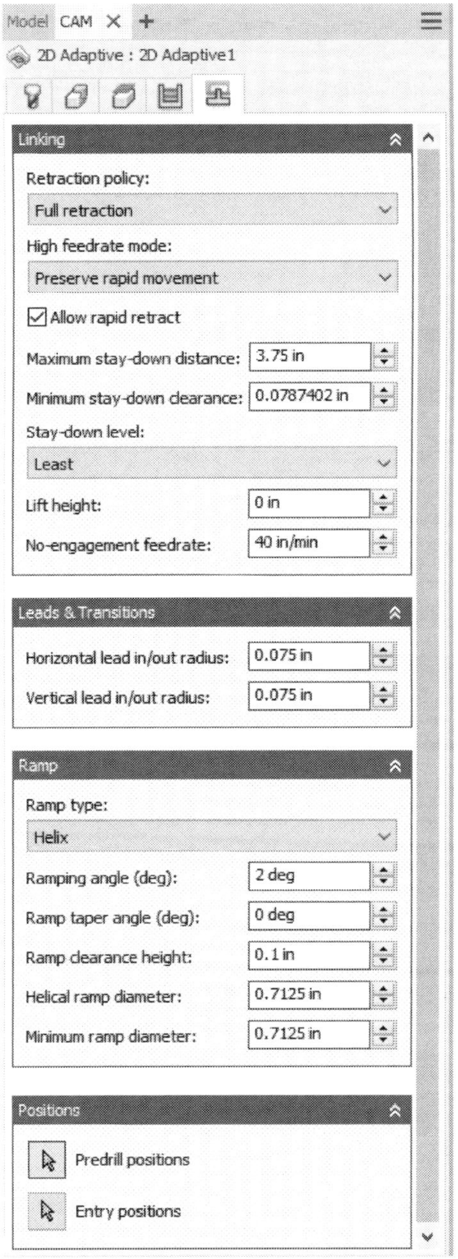

Figure 3–7

- In the *Linking* area, there are some options that are the same as those for the Face toolpath; however, there are also additional options that provide more control over the stay-down clearance, level, height, and feedrate for the tool when it is not cutting. Additionally, you can set a retraction policy that defines how the tool moves between cutting passes.
- The *Leads & Transitions* area for the 2D Adaptive toolpath enables you to define exact values for the horizontal/vertical lead in/out radius values to control the path generation.
- The *Ramp* area enables you to define how the tool moves down into position for each cut depth. You can define the ramp type (e.g., predrill, plunge, helix) and then define the values that are associated with the ramp approach.
- The *Positions* area enables you to modify the location the tool begins cutting in. You can define both predrill positions where holes are drilled to provide clearance and entry points where the tool should enter the model.

7. Click **OK** at the bottom of the 2D Adaptive palette to complete the toolpath creation.

3.2 2D Pocket Toolpath

Similar to a 2D Adaptive toolpath, a 2D Pocket toolpath can also be used as a roughing sequence to remove material from closed curve cavities and pockets in a model. However, it can also be used as a finishing pass after the material has been roughed out. Its cutting path starts at the center of the pocket and gradually works outwards. The cutting area is defined by selecting edges, solid faces, or a pre-existing sketch. Because the 2D Adaptive toolpath is optimized for roughing, it is generally more efficient to use the 2D Pocket toolpath as the finishing path.

In the example shown in Figure 3–8, the pocket is fully machined with two toolpaths. A 2D Adaptive toolpath is used for roughing and a 2D Pocket toolpath for the finishing pass.

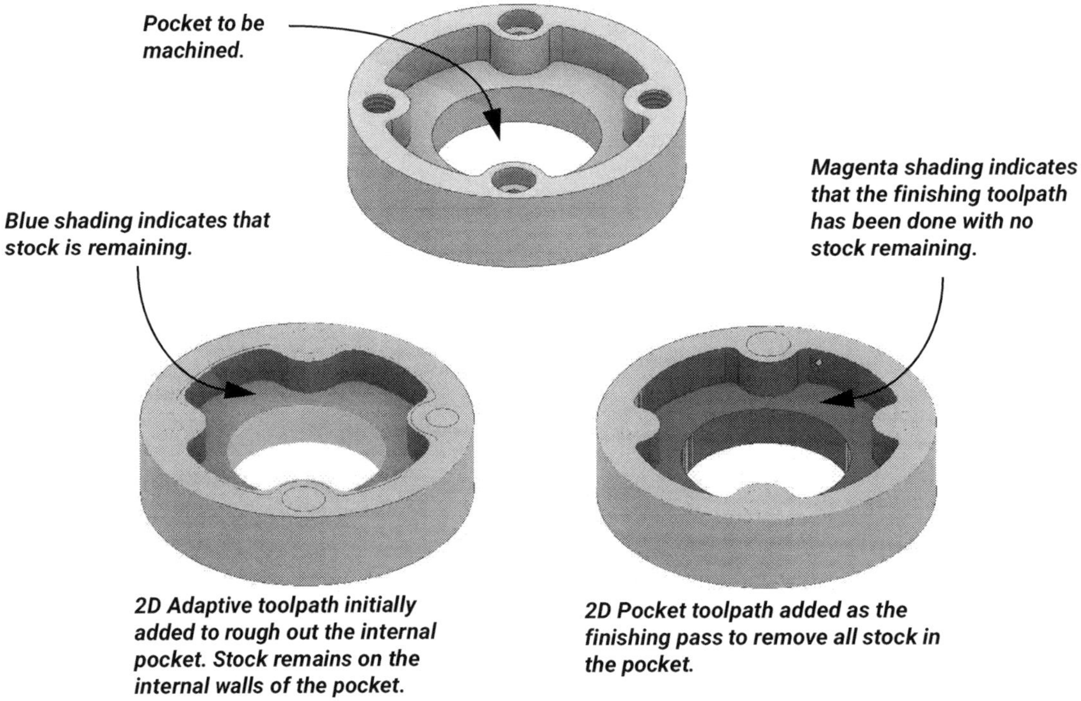

Figure 3–8

Note: *As you progress through this guide, the instructions for how to create each toolpath will focus on the high-level tasks that vary from previously discussed toolpaths. Refer to the previous discussions or hover your cursor over the options to access tooltips for the options in the palette.*

How To: Create a 2D Pocket toolpath.

1. In the 2D Milling panel, click (2D Pocket). The 2D Pocket palette opens similarly to that shown in Figure 3–9. Each of the tabs along the top of the palette provides access to the options that define the cut.

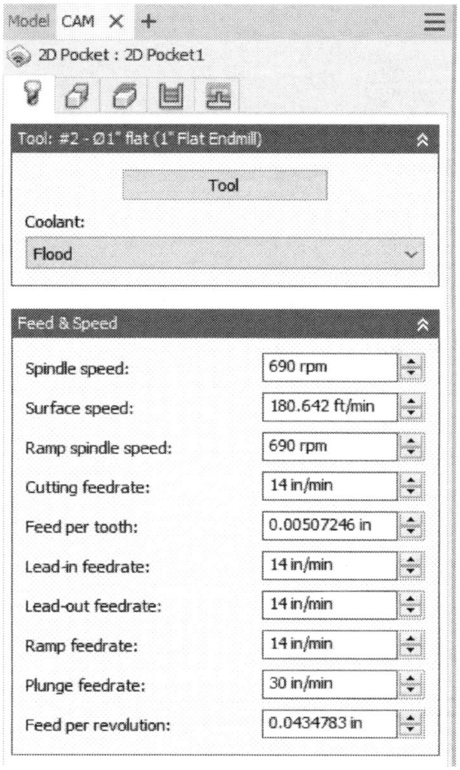

Figure 3–9

2. If a 2D Pocket toolpath is not the first toolpath in the model, the tool used in the previous toolpath is automatically assigned. To assign or change a pre-assigned tool, in the (Tool) tab, select **Tool** to access the Tool Library. Locate and select the required tool, then click **Select**.

   Note: *The Tool Library is used in the same way for all toolpaths. Refer to the Tool Library topic or the description for creating a Face toolpath in Chapter 2 for more details.*

3. Select the (Geometry) tab on the palette. The palette options for 2D Pockets are the same as those available for a 2D Adaptive toolpath. Define the geometry by selecting edges, solid faces, or a pre-existing sketch from the model. Ensure that the machining direction is correct if you define the geometry using a sketch or an edge.

4. Select the (Heights) tab. The palette displays the available plane height options (Clearance, Retract, Feed, Top, and Bottom) and they are visually represented on the model geometry. Edit any of the values, as needed, directly in the palette or in the mini-toolbar.

5. Select the (Passes) tab to set the options for how the toolpath passes are defined. The options in this tab vary from those discussed for the Face and 2D Adaptive toolpaths. In addition, they also vary depending on if the **Finishing passes** option is enabled or not, as shown in Figure 3–10.

For more information on any of the options that are not discussed here, refer to the 2D Adaptive toolpath descriptions or hover your cursor over the option to display a tooltip for that option.

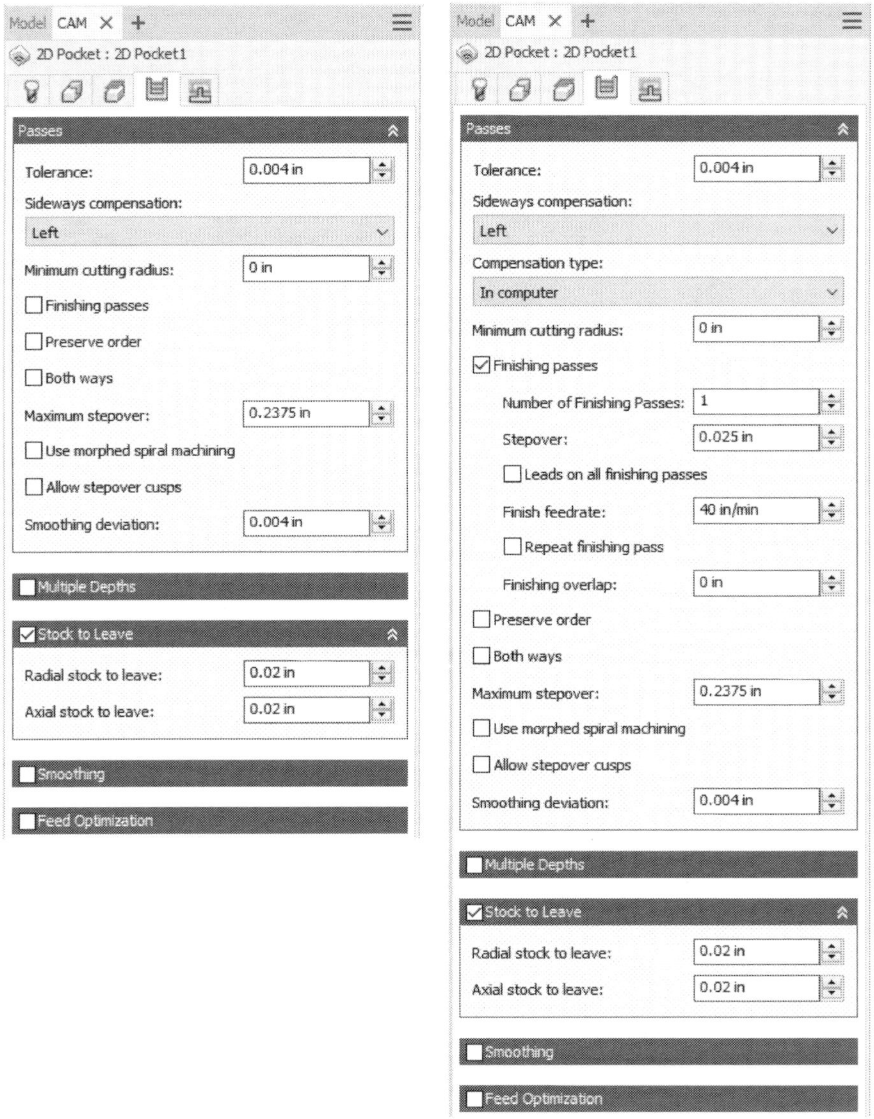

Figure 3–10

- The *Passes* area controls the cutting tolerance, compensation setting, type of passes, minimum cutting radius, etc. and controls how the toolpath is generated. Ensure that **Finishing passes** is enabled if you are using a 2D Pocket as a finishing toolpath.
- The *Multiple Depths* area enables you to set stepdown values for roughing and finishing.

6. Select the (Linking) tab. The *Linking* tab displays as shown in Figure 3–11.

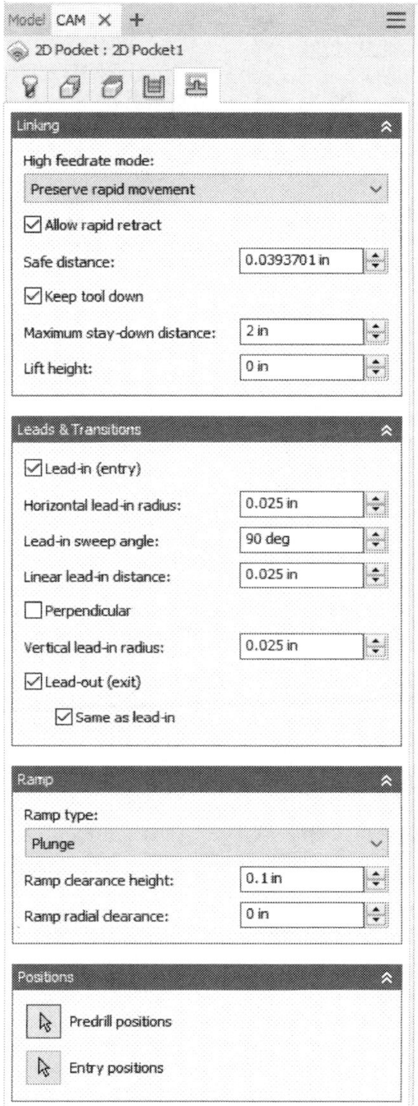

Figure 3–11

- In the *Linking* area, there are options that are the same as those for the 2D Adaptive toolpath; however, there are fewer linking options for a 2D Pocket toolpath.

- The *Leads & Transitions* area for the 2D Pocket toolpath provides further control over the lead in and transitions versus the 2D Adaptive toolpath (where you can only set the horizontal/vertical lead in/out radius values). For a 2D Pocket toolpath, you can set lead in/out values as equal or unique, as well as define a lead in/out sweep value or set the move as perpendicular to an arc for tangential extensions.

7. Click **OK** at the bottom of the 2D Pocket palette to complete the toolpath creation.

Hint: Adaptive vs. Pocket Toolpaths

The goal with an Adaptive toolpath is to maintain a constant load on the cutter. Since this is generally a roughing operation, it is assumed that a large portion of the cutting tool's length is used with tight passes. A Pocket toolpath is generally the finishing pass and therefore smaller depths of stock are being removed, so the focus is on controlling the stepover distance.

3.3 2D Contour Toolpath

A 2D Contour toolpath is typically a finishing sequence that is used to remove material around a profile. Its cutting area is defined by selecting either edges or a pre-existing sketch. In the example shown in Figure 3–12, two chamfered edges were selected as the references for a 2D Contour toolpath that removed the sharp edges around the top of the model.

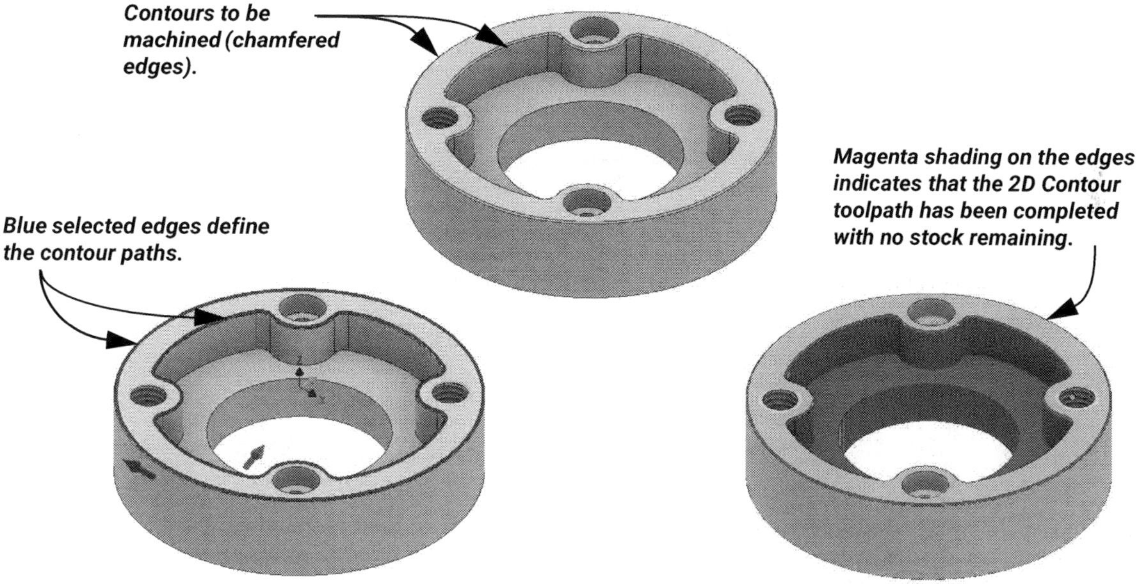

Figure 3–12

A 2D Contour toolpath can also be used to machine the stock around the outer faces of a model, as shown in Figure 3–13.

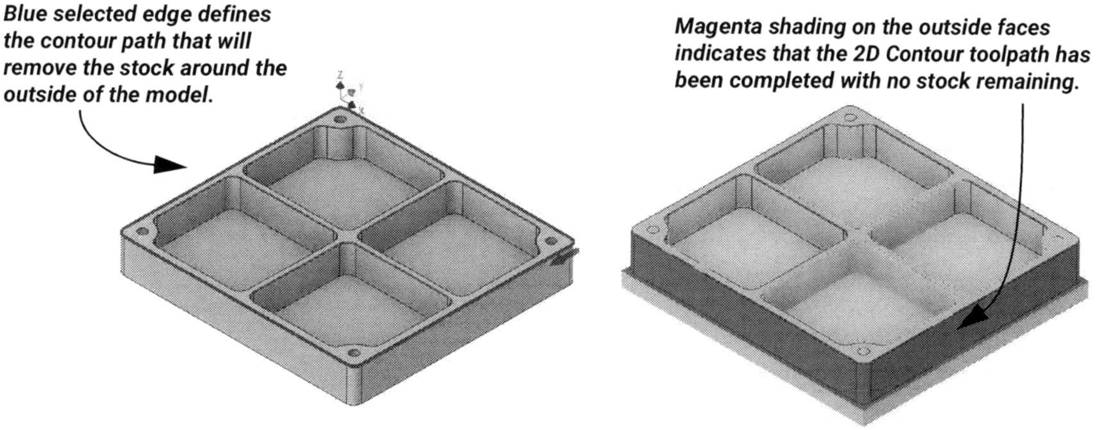

Figure 3–13

How To: Create a 2D Contour toolpath.

1. In the 2D Milling panel, click (2D Contour). The 2D Contour palette opens similarly to all of the other 2D milling toolpaths. Each of the tabs along the top of the palette provides access to the options that define the cut.

   ***Note:** Refer to the previously discussed toolpaths or hover your cursor over the options to access tooltips. The Tool Library is used in the same way for all toolpaths. Refer to the Face toolpath in Chapter 2 for more details.*

2. The tool used in the previous toolpath is automatically assigned. To change a pre-assigned tool, in the (Tool) tab, select **Tool** to access the Tool Library. Locate and select the required tool, then click **Select**.

3. Select the (Geometry) tab. The palette options are similar to the previously discussed toolpaths, but there are a few differences (as shown in Figure 3–14).

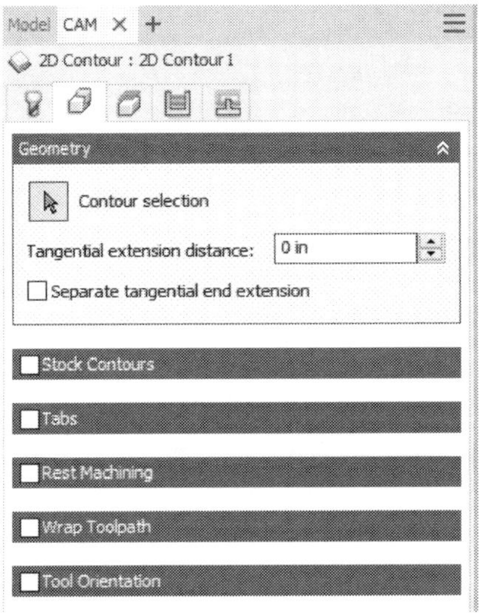

Figure 3–14

- The contour geometry is selected based on edges or a pre-existing sketch. Selecting the lower edge in a cavity/pocket automatically sets the cutting depth. Ensure that the machining direction is correct by selecting the red arrow to toggle it.
- For open contours, consider setting tangential extension distances to extend the toolpath past the boundary of the open contour.
- Consider using the *Tabs* area to incorporate the addition of tabs to your model to help hold the part when cutting its profile. Using the options in this area, you can define the shape and size of the tab and eliminate having to explicitly model this geometry.

4. Select the (Heights) tab. The palette displays the available plane height options (Clearance, Retract, Feed, Top, and Bottom), and they are visually represented on the model geometry. Edit any of the values, as needed, directly in the palette or in the mini-toolbar.

5. Select the (Passes) tab to set the options for how the toolpath passes are defined. The options that are available in this tab vary from those discussed for the previous toolpaths as the 2D Contour toolpath is most often used as a finishing operation. The options are shown in Figure 3–15.

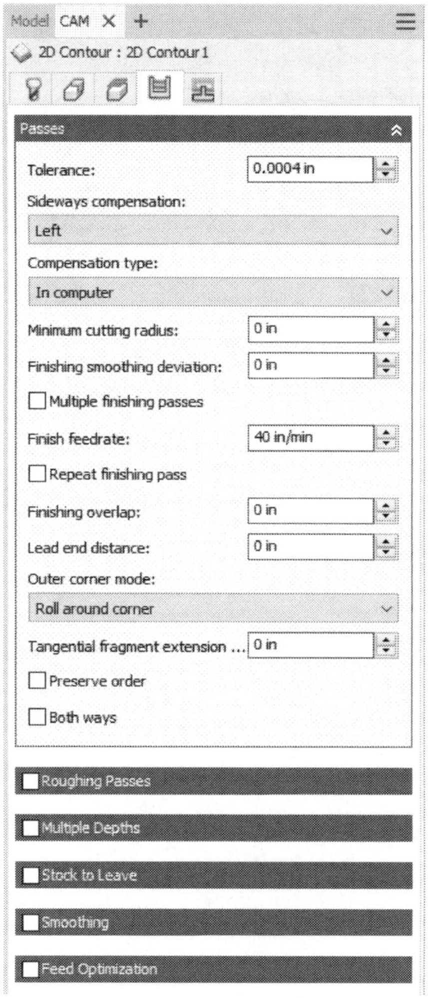

Figure 3–15

- The *Passes* area controls the finishing passes for the 2D Contour toolpath.
- If the 2D Contour toolpath is being used as a roughing operation, consider enabling the *Roughing Passes* and *Stock to Leave* areas and setting their values appropriately.

- A 2D Contour path is generally cut at a single depth. If required, enable the *Multiple Depths* area and set the stepdown values, as needed.

6. Select the (Linking) tab. The *Linking* tab options are similar to those available for a 2D Pocket toolpath.
   - An optional *Ramp* area is available for a 2D Contour toolpath and can be enabled if needed (unlike the 2D Adaptive and 2D Pocket toolpaths where this *Ramp* area is not optional and must be defined). The options, as shown in Figure 3–16, can be used as an alternative to setting multiple depths.

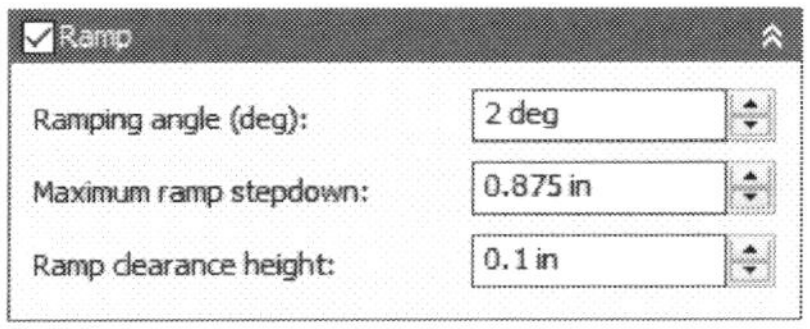

Figure 3–16

7. Click **OK** at the bottom of the 2D Contour palette to complete the toolpath creation.

Hint: Reasons for using 2D Contour toolpaths

The 2D Contour toolpath is typically used to remove excess stock from the external face of the model. However, a 2D Contour toolpath can also be used in conjunction with a chamfer cutting tool to machine chamfered edges. However, you can also consider using a 2D Chamfer toolpath to machine chamfers. With a 2D Chamfer toolpath, you can select an edge to define the path and enter the chamfer width in order to define the cut.

Practice 3a
Roughing and Finishing Pockets in a Model

Practice Objectives

- Create a 2D Adaptive toolpath to rough out the stock within the four pockets on the model.
- Create a 2D Pocket toolpath to create a finishing pass on the four pockets on the model.
- Use the Simulation tools in Inventor CAM to display the operations.

In this practice, you will create two more toolpaths that will remove stock in the four pockets on the top of the model. First you will create a roughing toolpath that will remove the initial portion of the stock. The final toolpath will finish the pocket by removing all remaining stock.

Task 1: Open a model and add a 2D Adaptive toolpath to rough out pockets in the model.

1. Open **Housing_Top_Pockets.ipt**. This model has the previously created Face toolpaths completed for you. Alternatively, you can work with the model you completed in the previous exercise. The CAM browser and model are shown in Figure 3–17.

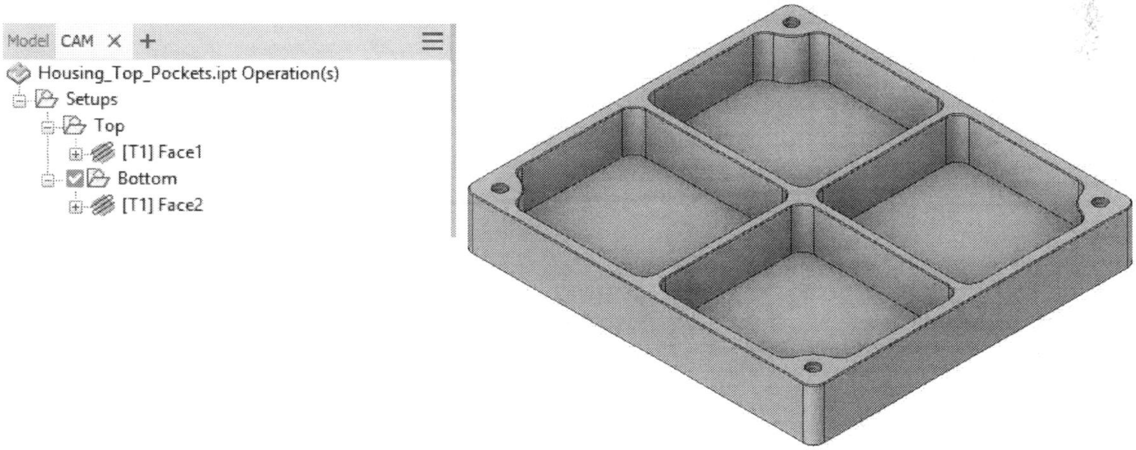

Figure 3–17

2. Ensure that the model is displayed in its default Home view. This is the top of the model and will be where the roughing toolpath will be added to remove the stock from the pockets.
3. Review the CAM browser and note that, because the last toolpath that was added to the model was a facing toolpath in the Bottom setup, **Bottom** is active.

4. Right-click the **Top** setup and select **Default Folder**. The checkmark should now appear adjacent to **Top**, indicating it is the active setup. This ensures that new toolpaths are added to this setup.

   Note: *Toolpaths can be added to a non-active setup by right-clicking on it and selecting the* ***New Operation*** *option to add the toolpath, instead of using the ribbon.*

5. In the 2D Milling panel, click (2D Adaptive). The 2D Adaptive palette opens. The (Tool) tab is initially open and the same tool that was used in the facing toolpaths has been assigned by default.
6. By visually reviewing the display of the tool in the graphics window, it is obvious that the tool is not the correct size to rough out the pockets of the model.
7. In the *Tool* area, select **Tool**.
8. Expand **All Tools>By Type** and select **Flat Mill**. All Flat Mill tools that are available in the library are listed.
9. To filter the list to a specific size, select **Diameter is** in the filter list, if not already set, and enter **.75** in the filter field, as shown in Figure 3–18.
10. Select the **#2 - Ø3/4" flat** tool, as shown in Figure 3–18.

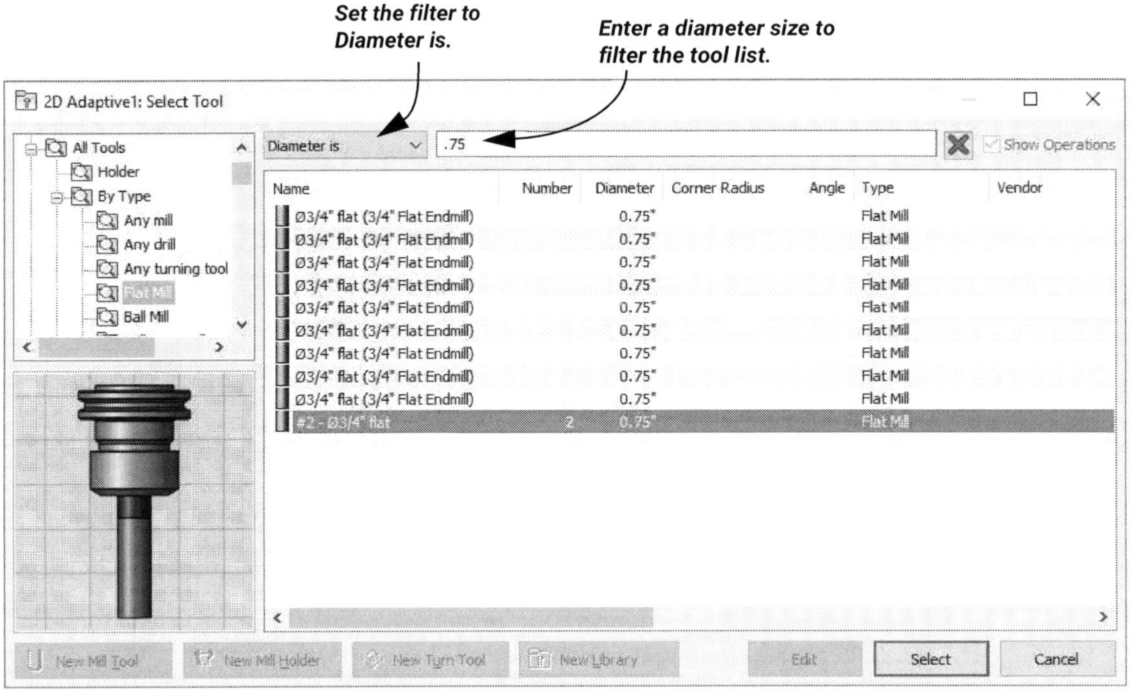

Figure 3–18

11. Click **Select** at the bottom of the Select Tool dialog box to assign the tool.

12. Select the (Geometry) tab.
13. With the *Pocket selections* field active, select the bottom faces of the four pockets shown in Figure 3–19. Note that, unlike with Face toolpaths, for a 2D Adaptive toolpath you must select the geometry.

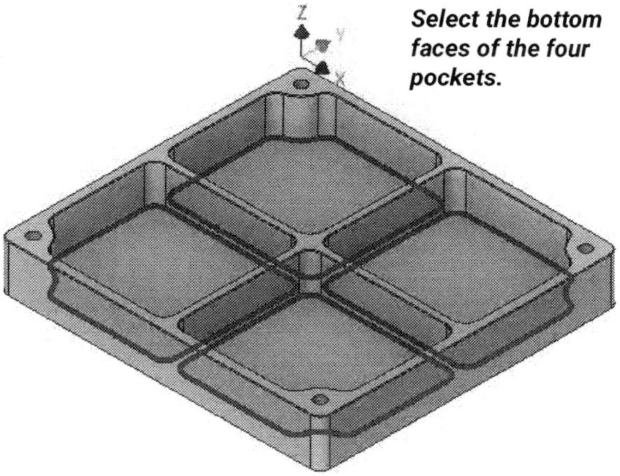

Figure 3–19

Note: *Edges can also be selected to define the geometry. If selecting edges, ensure that the direction of the red arrow is pointing in the required machining direction.*

14. Select the (Heights) tab. Reorient the model to its FRONT view and review the planes. Since a Face sequence was previously added to remove stock down to the top of the model, you must adjust the **Top Height** setting so that the new 2D Adaptive toolpath starts at the top of the model.
15. In the *Top Height* area, select **Model top** from the drop-down list. Note how the blue plane is now located on the top of the model.
16. Return the model to its default Home view.
17. Select the (Passes) tab. The **Stock to Leave** option is selected, indicating the toolpath will be a roughing pass and 0.02 in. of stock will remain radially and axially in the pockets. This is appropriate and no further changes are required.

18. Click **OK** to complete the toolpath. The path generates and displays as shown in Figure 3–20. Review the order that the pockets will be roughed. The order in which you selected the geometry determines the order of machining. The red arrow is the starting location and the green arrow is the end location. The yellow lines show the tool rapids between pockets.

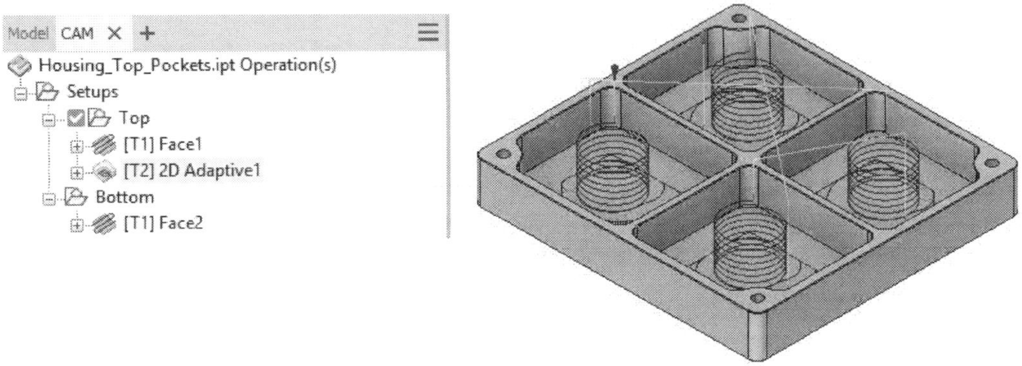

Figure 3–20

19. To edit the toolpath to specify the machining order, right-click **[T2] 2D Adaptive1** and select **Edit**.

20. Select the (Geometry) tab and select to clear the selection of all pockets.

21. Select the pockets a second time in the order that is specified in Figure 3–21.

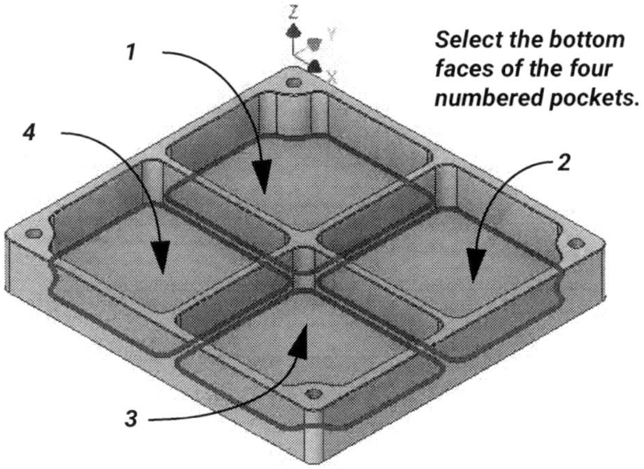

Figure 3–21

22. Click **OK** to complete the toolpath. The path generates and displays as shown in Figure 3–22. Verify the change to the machining order.

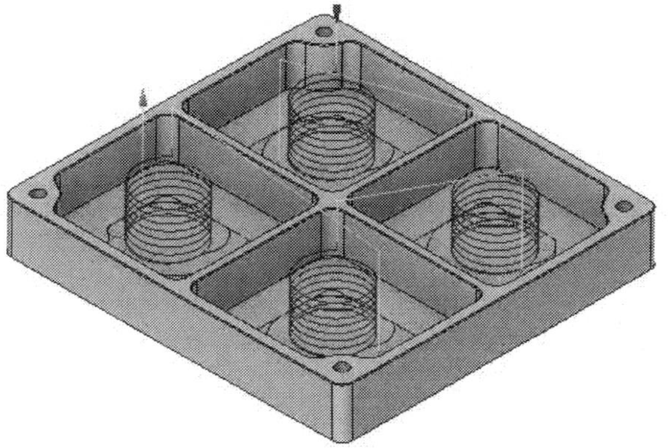

Figure 3–22

Task 2: View simulations of the toolpaths in the Top setup.

1. In the CAM browser, ensure that the **[T2] 2D Adaptive1** toolpath is selected.

2. In the Toolpath panel, click (Simulate). Turn on the display of the stock, if not already displayed.

3. Click in the simulation player to play the toolpath. Note that in this view, it is difficult to see how much stock remains in the pockets (as shown in Figure 3–23). This is because the top facing toolpath was not played and the stock remains on the top of the model.

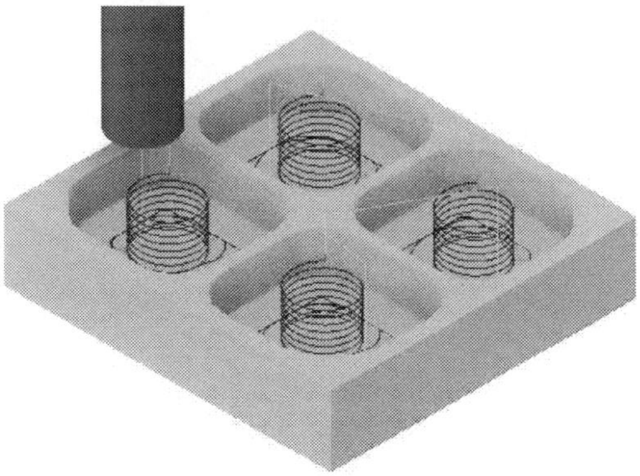

Figure 3–23

4. Click **Close** to close the Simulation palette.

5. Press and hold <Ctrl> and select the two toolpaths in the **Top** setup. Open the Simulation palette and play both toolpaths. By playing both toolpaths together, you have a better view of the material that remains in the pockets (as shown in Figure 3–24).

Figure 3–24

6. Close the Simulation palette.

Task 3: Edit the 2D Adaptive toolpath.

In this task, you will edit the 2D Adaptive toolpath so that the roughing pass is done with a multi-depth cut instead of the default where the tool plunges using a helical movement to the bottom and removes all material at once.

1. Right-click **[T2] 2D Adaptive1** and select **Edit**. The options on the *Tool*, *Geometry*, and *Heights* tabs do not require editing.

2. Select the (Passes) tab.

3. Select the **Multiple Depths** option to enable it. Its options become available in the tab, as shown in Figure 3–25.

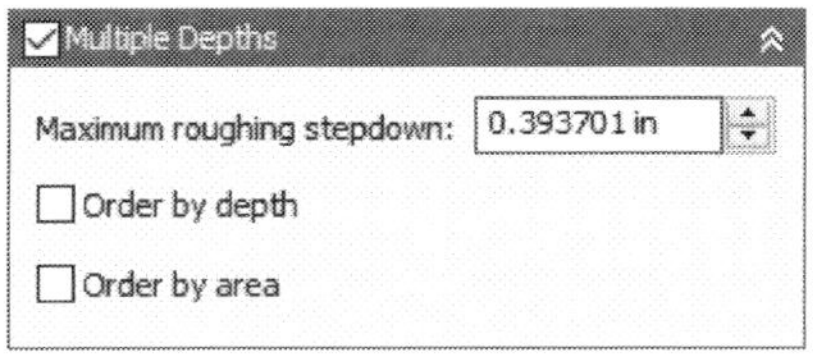

Figure 3–25

4. The depth of the pockets in the model are 0.475 in. Enter **0.25 in** as the *Maximum roughing stepdown* value.

5. Select the (Linking) tab. Note that **Helix** is the type that is currently assigned as the *Ramp type*. This is the movement that is used to rapid into the model. Hover your cursor over the **Helix** option and review the other options that can be selected. Maintain the **Helix** option as the *Ramp type*.
6. Click **OK** to complete the edit. The toolpath updates to show that it is cutting at two depths, as shown in Figure 3–26.

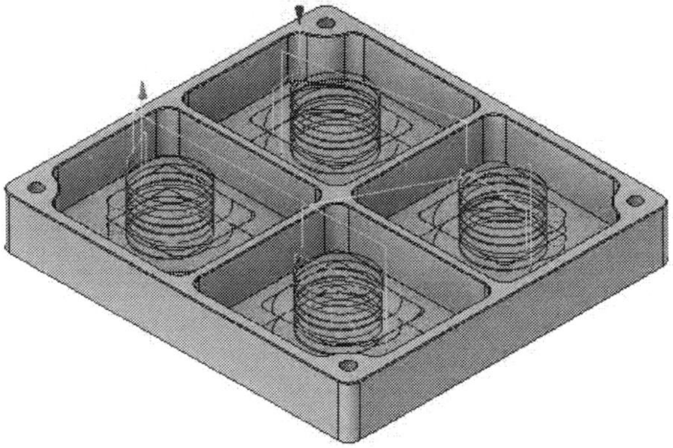

Figure 3–26

Task 4: Create a 2D Pocket toolpath to finish the pockets in the model.

In this task, you will create a 2D Pocket toolpath to finish the four pockets in the model.

1. In the 2D Milling panel, click (2D Pocket). The 2D Pocket palette opens. The (Tool) tab is initially open and the same tool that was used in the last toolpath has been assigned by default. The tool used in the roughing pass was used to remove the majority of material quickly; however, it is too big to cut the corners of the pockets.
2. In the *Tool* area, select **Tool**.
3. Expand **All Tools>By Type** and select **Flat Mill**. All Flat Mill tools that are available in the library are listed.
4. To filter the list to a specific size, enter **.25** in the filter field adjacent to the **Diameter is** option.
5. Select the **#4 - Ø1/4" flat** tool that is listed in the library.
6. Click **Select** at the bottom of the Select Tool dialog box to assign the tool.

7. Select the (Geometry) tab.
8. With the *Pocket selections* field active, select the bottom faces of the four pockets, in order, as shown in Figure 3–27.

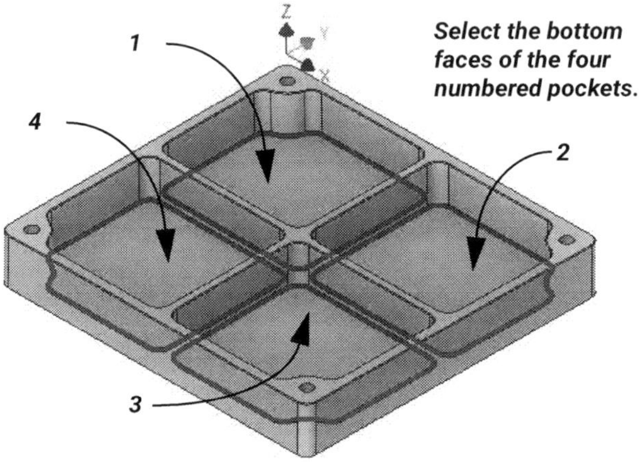

Figure 3–27

9. Select the (Heights) tab and review the planes. Similarly to the previous toolpath, you must adjust the **Top Height** setting so that the new 2D Pocket toolpath starts at the top of the model. In the *Top Height* area, select **Model top** from the drop-down list. The blue plane is repositioned on the top of the model.

10. Select the (Passes) tab and complete the following (as shown in Figure 3–28).

- Clear the **Stock to Leave** option so that the toolpath removes all stock (finishing pass).
- In the *Passes* area, select **Finishing passes** and ensure that there is 1 pass and the stepover is set as **0.025 in**.

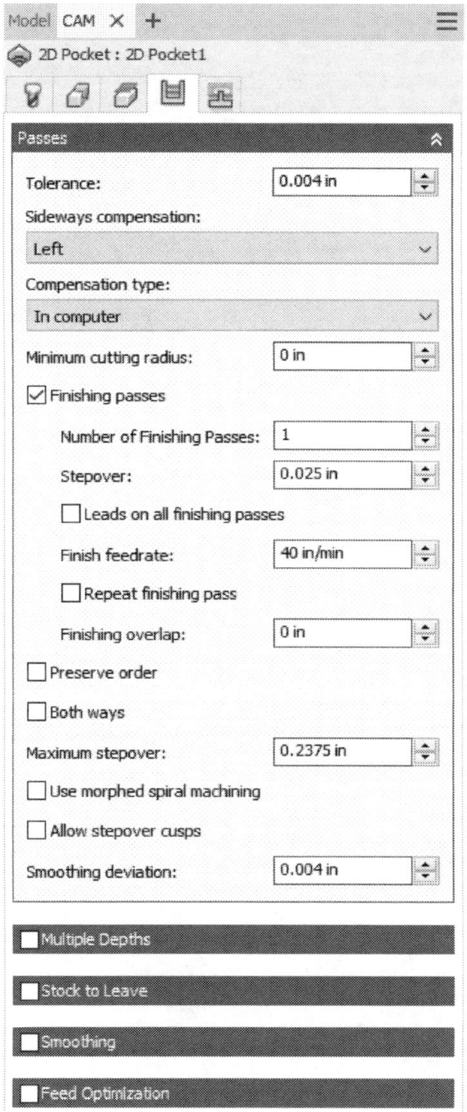

Figure 3–28

11. Select the (Linking) tab. In the *Ramp* area, select **Plunge** as the *Ramp type* and accept the default clearance values.

12. Click **OK** to complete the toolpath. The toolpath updates to show its path, as shown in Figure 3–29.

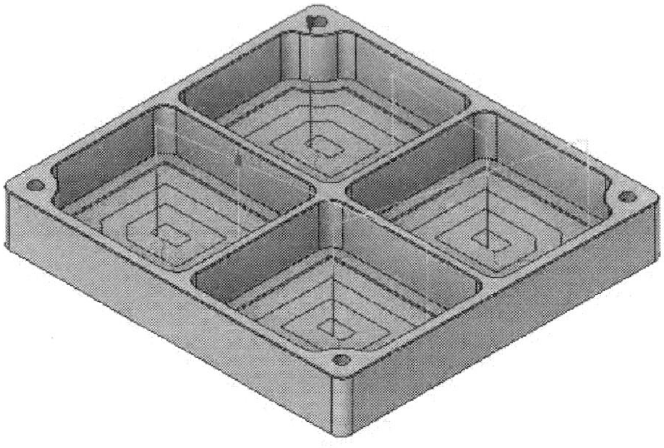

Figure 3–29

Task 5: View a simulation of the Top setup.

In this task, you will simulate the facing, roughing, and finishing toolpaths for the pockets.

1. In the CAM browser, select **Top** to ensure that all toolpaths in the setup will be played in the simulation. Access the Simulation palette and play the toolpaths. Consider turning off the Toolpath display to clearly view the machined stock (as shown in Figure 3–30).

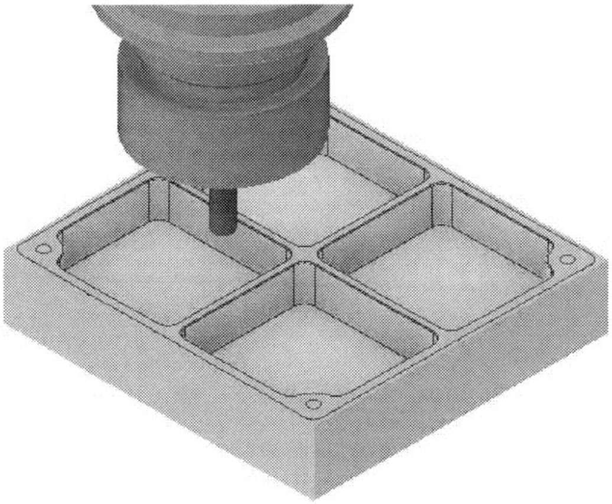

Figure 3–30

2. Once the simulation has been reviewed, select the (Info) tab.
3. In the graphics window, hover your cursor over both the top of the model and the bottom faces of the pockets. Note how in the *Verification* area, the *Distance* value updates to **0 in**. This value indicates that there is no stock left on the top of the model.
4. Hover your cursor over the inside corners of the pockets. Note that a small *Distance* value is specified. This tolerance is acceptable so changes are not required. To be more precise, a smaller tool would be required.
5. Close the Simulation palette.
6. Save and close the model.

End of practice

Practice 3b
Contouring the Model

Practice Objectives

- Create a 2D Contour toolpath to remove stock around the outside of the model.
- Create a 2D Contour toolpath to remove the sharp edges around the top of the model.
- Use the Simulation tools in Inventor CAM to display the toolpaths.

In this practice, you will create two more toolpaths that will remove the stock around the outside of the model. The final toolpath will add the chamfer that was designed to remove the sharp edges at the top of the model.

Task 1: Open a model and add a 2D Contour toolpath to machine the exterior.

1. Open **Housing_Top_Contours.ipt**. This model has all the toolpaths that were created in previous practices completed for you. Alternatively, you can work with the model you completed in the previous exercise. The CAM browser and model are shown in Figure 3–31.

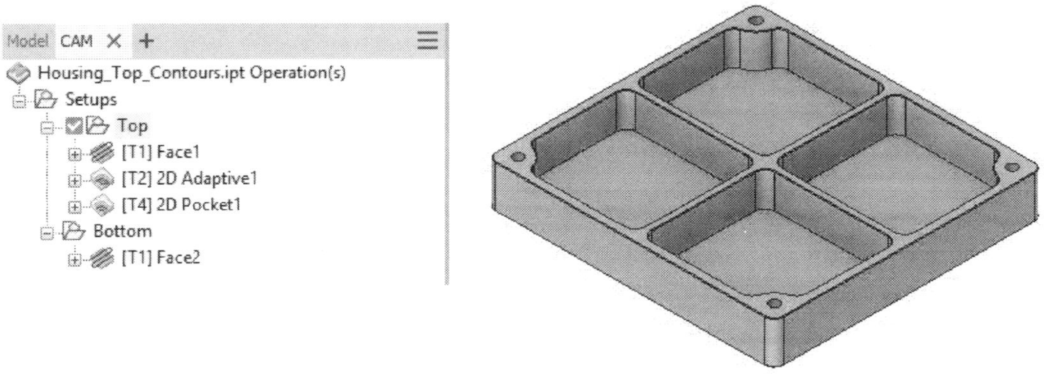

Figure 3–31

2. Review the CAM browser and note that the **Top** setup is still the active folder so all new toolpaths will be added to this setup.

3. In the 2D Milling panel, click (2D Contour). The 2D Contour palette opens.

4. Review the (Tool) tab and note that the same tool that was used in the 2D Pocket toolpath has been assigned by default. This tool can also be used for this next toolpath so no changes are required on this tab.

5. Select the (Geometry) tab.
6. With the *Contour selection* field active, select the chamfer edge that lies on the outside face of the model, as shown in Figure 3–32. Consider zooming in on the model to ensure that you are selecting the correct edge. This edge defines the outside face that is being machined.

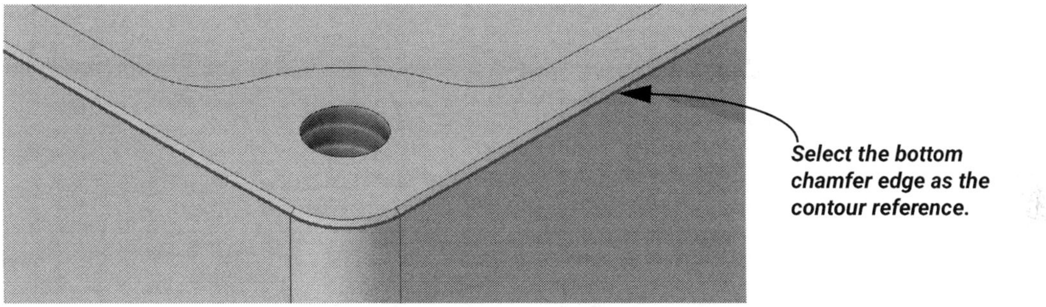

Figure 3–32

7. Once selected, the edge displays in blue and a red direction arrow appears. The direction arrow indicates the side of the edge on which machining will occur. You can select the arrow directly in the graphics window to reverse it, if needed. In this case, the machining direction is on the outside of the model to cut away the side stock so no changes are required.

   Note: *To understand how the direction can affect the toolpath, you can flip it, complete the toolpath, and play a simulation to see how the side affects the cutting path. Be sure to edit the toolpath again to continue the exercise.*

8. Select the (Heights) tab and review the planes. Note that the *Bottom Height* is set to **Selected contour(s)**. Since the contour was selected at the top of the model, this means that the cutter will only machine up to the selected edge.
9. In the *Bottom Height* area, select **Model bottom** as the option and enter **-0.01 in** as the *Bottom offset* value, as shown in Figure 3–33. This ensures that the toolpath removes all stock from the sides and extends past the bottom of the model by a small amount.

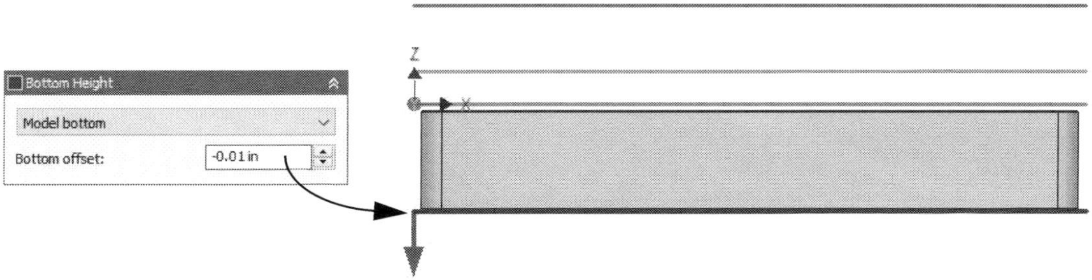

Figure 3–33

10. Select the (Passes) tab and review the options. No changes are required on this tab.
11. Select the (Linking) tab and review the options. No changes are currently required on this tab.
12. Click **OK** to complete the toolpath. The path generates and displays as shown in Figure 3–34. Note how the lead-in and lead-out paths are very short.

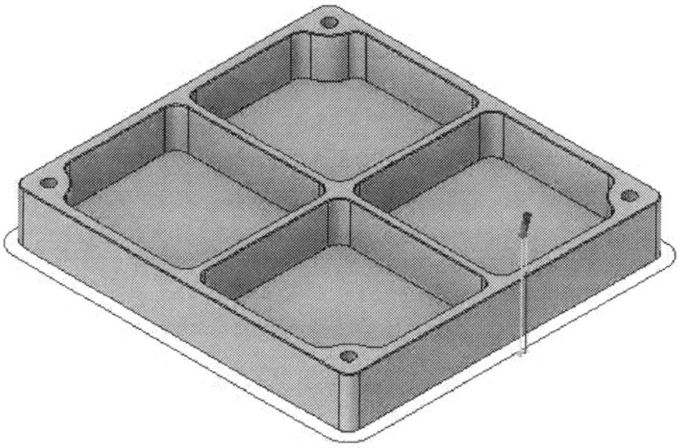

Figure 3–34

13. Right-click **[T4] 2D Contour1** and select **Edit**.
14. Select the (Linking) tab.
15. In the *Linear lead-in distance* field, enter **0.2 in** as the new value.
16. Ensure that the **Lead-out (exit)** and **Same as lead-in** options are enabled. This ensures that both lead-in and lead-out distances will be 0.2 in.
17. The tool is currently approaching at 90 deg to the face of the model. To prevent the tool from leaving a mark, you can change its approach angle. In the *Lead-in sweep angle* field, enter **30 deg**.
18. If the lead-in/lead-out location was not appropriate, you can activate the **Entry positions** field in the *Positions* area and select a new location. In this case, the center of the edge is satisfactory so no changes are required.

    Note: *Entry positions are defined by selecting workpoints or vertices that exist in the model.*

19. Click **OK** to complete the toolpath. The path generates and displays as shown in Figure 3–35.

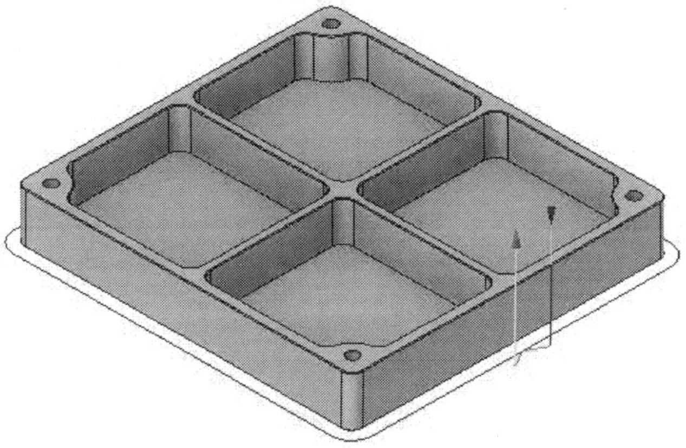

Figure 3–35

20. In the CAM browser, select **[T4] 2D Contour1** to ensure that this toolpath alone will be played in the simulation. Access the Simulation palette. Review the simulation player timeline and note that there are red lines in the timeline. Hover your cursor over the first red line. The tooltip that displays indicates there is a collision between the shaft and stock, as shown in Figure 3–36.

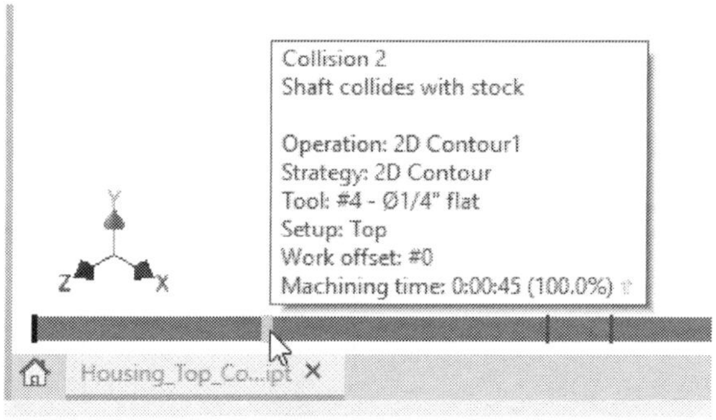

Figure 3–36

21. To review the collision, reorient the model to the FRONT view using the ViewCube, and use the button in the simulation playback control bar to slowly advance through the simulation. Just before the collision occurs (as shown in Figure 3–37), the tool has moved down to its cutting depth and it begins to cut into the stock. The tool that is being used has a Shoulder length value of only **0.6 in**. The collision is occurring because the cutting length of the tool is not long enough for the operation. The tool size must be edited.

Figure 3–37

22. Close the Simulation palette.
23. Use the **Measure** tool in the *Inspect* tab to measure the overall height of the model. With this value and the distance that the cut will extend beyond the bottom of the model (0.01 in.), the tool must be longer than 0.61 in.
24. Return to the *CAM* tab. In the Manage panel, select (Tool Library) to open the Tool Library.
25. In the list of tools for the model, select the **#4 - Ø1/4" flat** tool and select **Edit**.
26. In the Tool dialog box, select the *General* tab and enter **3** as the new tool *Number*.
27. In the Tool dialog box, select the *Cutter* tab. Modify the following values for the tool size (as shown in Figure 3–38).
    - *Shoulder length* = **0.9 in**
    - *Flute length* = **0.7 in**
    - *Body length* = **1.25 in**
    - *Overall length* = **1.75 in**

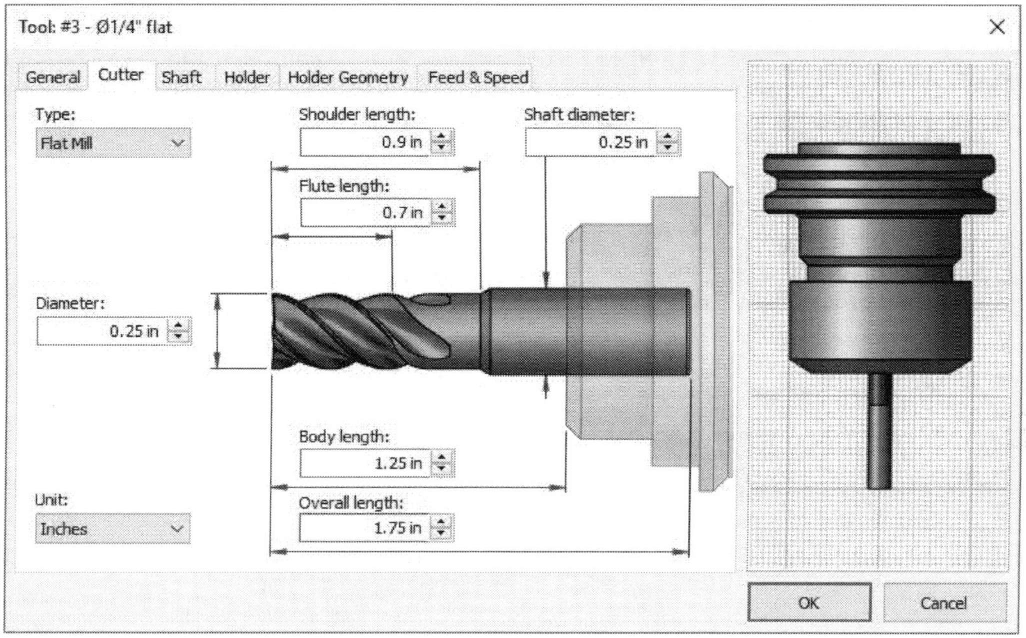

Figure 3–38

Note: *As an alternative to editing the sizes for the same tool that was used in both toolpaths, you could have copied the tool and made changes to only one.*

28. Click **OK** and confirm the tool changes. Note in the CAM browser (as shown in Figure 3–39) that the tool number has updated to T3 and the two toolpaths that use this tool are showing as out of date and must be generated again.

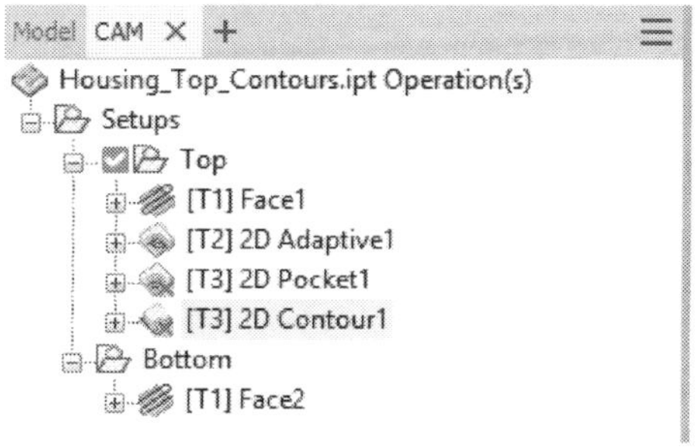

Figure 3–39

29. Click **OK** to close the Tool Library.

30. In the Toolpath panel, click (Generate). Note that if you still have the **[T3] 2D Contour1** toolpath selected, only it is generated. To generate both toolpaths at the same time, you can use <Ctrl> to multi-select them prior to generating, or you can select the **Top** setup to generate all toolpaths at once.
31. Generate the **[T3] 2D Pocket1** toolpath if not already updated. The changes in length of the tool do not affect this toolpath.
32. Use the Simulation tool to play all the toolpaths in the Top setup. Note that there are no longer any collisions occurring. The model displays as shown in Figure 3–40 once the simulation is complete.

Figure 3–40

33. Close the Simulation palette.
34. Save the model.

Task 2: Create a 2D Contour toolpath to chamfer the sharp edges around the top of the model.

In this task, you will create a second 2D Contour toolpath to machine the chamfered edge around all the sharp edges at the top of the model.

1. In the 2D Milling panel, click (2D Contour). The 2D Contour palette opens.
2. Use the (Tool) tab and open the Tool Library. Search for and select the **Ø1/2" 45°** **chamfer** tool in the Chamfer Mill type category.

3. Edit the **Ø1/2" 45° chamfer** tool so that it is identified as tool #4. Complete the edit and close the dialog box by selecting the tool for use with the toolpath.

4. Select the (Geometry) tab. Ensure the *Contour selection* field is active and select the five loops of edges that define the top edge of the chamfer features (the edges lying on the top face of the model), as shown in Figure 3–41.

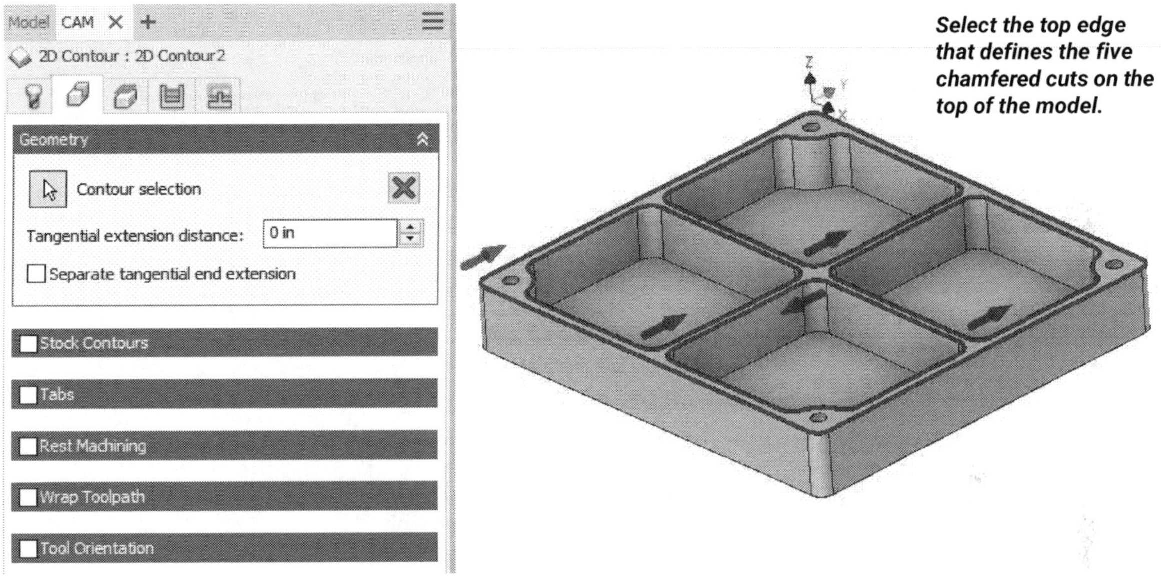

Figure 3–41

5. Select the (Heights) tab and review the planes. Adjust the **Top Height** setting so that the new 2D Contour toolpath starts at the top of the model. In the *Top Height* area, select **Model top** from the drop-down list. The blue plane is repositioned on the top of the model.

6. Select the (Passes) tab. Enable the **Chamfer** option, if not already selected. Enter **0.02 in** as the *Chamfer tip offset* value, as shown in Figure 3–42. The use of this option ensures that the tool remains in contact with the selected edges being contoured and cuts below the edge, preventing you from cutting with the bottom tool edge.

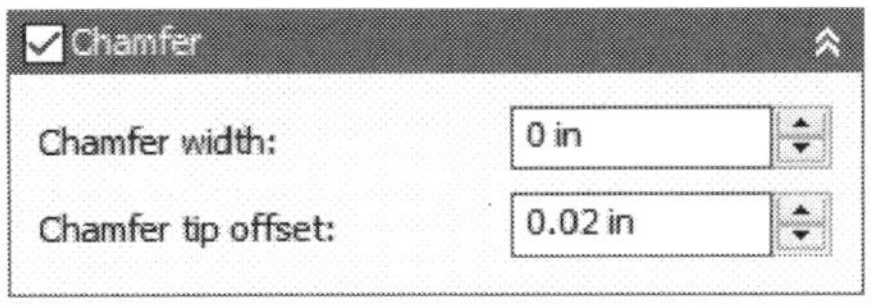

Figure 3–42

7. Ensure the **Stock to Leave** option is cleared so that the toolpath removes all stock (finishing pass).

8. Select the (Linking) tab. In the *Leads & Transitions* area, edit the following (as was done in the previous contouring toolpath).
   - In the *Linear lead-in distance* field, enter **0.1 in** as the new value.
   - Ensure that the **Lead-out (exit)** and **Same as lead-in** options are enabled. This ensures that both lead-in and lead-out distances will be 0.1 in.
   - In the *Lead-in sweep angle* field, enter **30 deg** to change the approach angle to prevent the tool from leaving a mark.
9. Click **OK** to complete the toolpath.
10. Use the Simulation tool to review all toolpaths that are required for the top of the model. Clear the display of the Tool from the display. Note how when the tool display is cleared, the tip of the tool is displayed as a green dot, as shown in Figure 3–43.

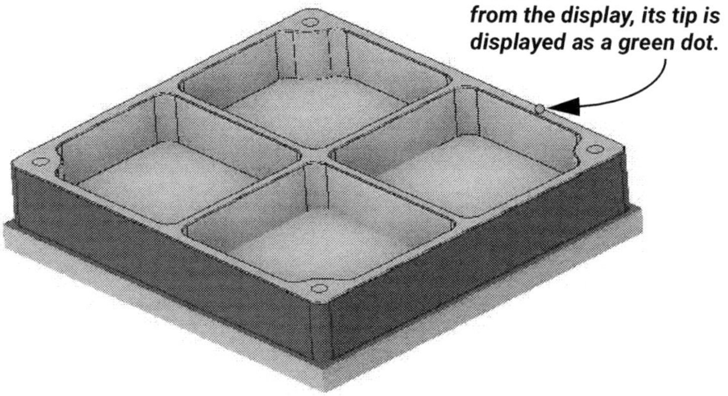

Figure 3–43

11. Close the Simulation palette.
12. Save the model.

Task 3: Create a contouring toolpath to chamfer the sharp edges around the bottom of the model.

In this task, you will create a toolpath that will chamfer the outside edge in the Bottom setup. Only high-level steps will be provided for this task, but you can refer to the steps provided in Task 2 to successfully create the toolpath.

1. Right-click the **Bottom** setup and select **Default Folder** to set it as the active setup.
2. Rotate the view to easily identify the geometry on the bottom of the model.
3. As an alternative to creating a new 2D Contour toolpath and setting all the options that were previously set up in the other toolpath, you can copy and paste toolpaths. Right-click **[T4] 2D Contour2** and select **Copy**.

4. Right-click on the Bottom setup header and select **Paste**. The **[T4] 2D Contour2** toolpath is copied as shown in Figure 3–44. Once pasted, you can see that it is out of date.

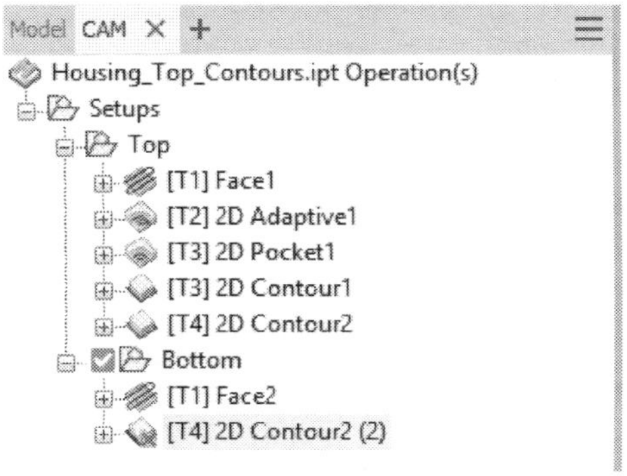

Figure 3–44

5. Slowly select the pasted toolpath twice and rename it as **[T4] 2D Contour3**.
6. Generate the toolpath and note that the contour references are still on the top of the model; however, the Bottom UCS is referenced for direction. Right-click the toolpath and select **Edit**.
7. Select the (Geometry) tab and in the *Geometry* area, select to clear the selection of the references.
8. Ensure the *Contour Selection* field is active and select the edge loop (i.e., the edges lying on the bottom face of the model) as shown in Figure 3–45.

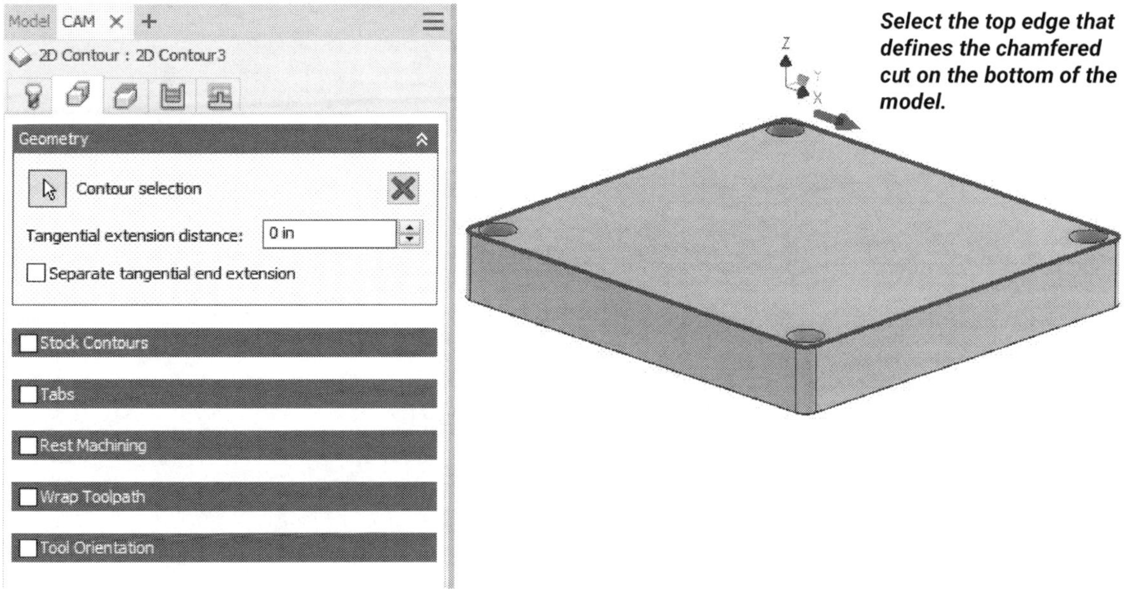

Figure 3–45

9. Review the *Heights*, *Passes*, and *Linking* tabs. Because the toolpath was copied, all the settings that were previously set are maintained in this toolpath. Click **OK** to complete the toolpath.
10. Use the Simulation tool to review all toolpaths that are required for the bottom of the model. Note that the display settings are maintained based on the setting used when the previous simulation was run. Set the display settings for the simulation as desired.
11. Close the Simulation palette.
12. Save and close the model.

End of practice

Chapter Review Questions

1. Which of the following toolpaths can be used for both roughing and finishing? (Select all that apply.)
   a. 2D Adaptive
   b. 2D Pocket
   c. 2D Contour

2. A 2D Adaptive toolpath's focus is on the maximum stepover distance.
   a. True
   b. False

3. For the 2D Adaptive, 2D Pocket, or 2D Contour toolpaths, the default Bottom Height reference is the same. Which of the following is the default value?
   a. Stock top
   b. Model top
   c. Model bottom
   d. Selected contour(s)
   e. Selection

4. Which of the following toolpaths' references can be defined by selecting either an edge, face, or pre-existing sketch? (Select all that apply.)
   a. 2D Adaptive
   b. 2D Pocket
   c. 2D Contour

5. For a roughing 2D Pocket or 2D Adaptive toolpath, you can specify to leave stock both radially and axially as separate values.
   a. True
   b. False

6. Which of the following toolpaths contain options that can be used to control the order in which selected areas are machined, as opposed to selection order dictating the order?

a. 2D Adaptive

b. 2D Pocket

c. 2D Contour

d. None of the above

Command Summary

Button	Command	Location
	**2D Adaptive (toolpath)**	• **Ribbon:** *CAM* tab>2D Milling panel
	**2D Contour (toolpath)**	• **Ribbon:** *CAM* tab>2D Milling panel
	**2D Pocket (toolpath)**	• **Ribbon:** *CAM* tab>2D Milling panel
	**Generate**	• **Ribbon:** *CAM* tab>Toolpath panel
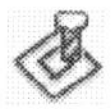	**Simulate**	• **Ribbon:** *CAM* tab>Toolpath panel

Chapter 4

Drilling

A Drill toolpath is used in Inventor CAM to define holemaking sequences. The holes that are to be machined can be selected by explicitly selecting faces or points on the model, or you can define a diameter range within a specified containment area to automatically have the software select the holes for you. In this chapter, you will learn how to create these holemaking sequences and use the Drill toolpath to customize the cycle type that will be used (e.g., drilling, counterbore, chip breaking, etc.).

Learning Objective

- Add Drill toolpaths to an Inventor CAM model.

4.1 Drill Toolpath

The Drill toolpath in Inventor CAM can be used to generate many different types of drilling operations to machine holes. These include drilling, tapping, boring, and reaming. The cutting strategy is defined in the *Cycle* tab.

In the examples shown in Figure 4–1, a separate Drill toolpath can be created to machine each type of hole.

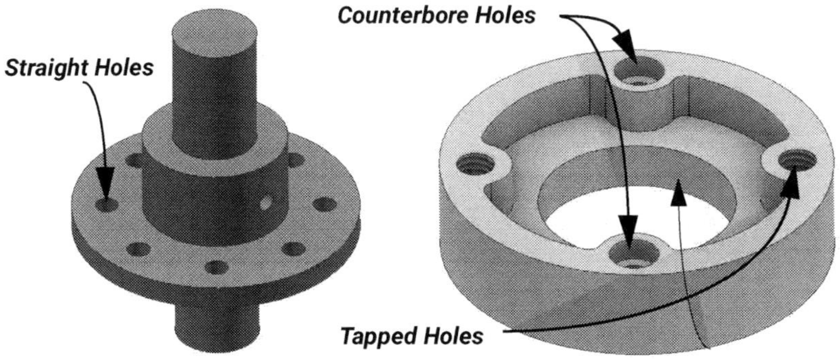

Figure 4–1

> **Note:** *The Drill toolpath can also be used to mill cylindrical pockets and islands using the Circular pocket milling cycle strategy.*

Hint: Drilling vs. Boring a Counterbore

Counterbores can be machined using a Drill toolpath or a Bore toolpath. In general, a Bore toolpath can be a more accurate toolpath to use to create the counterbore for a hole, so if there is a high tolerance requirement, it may be the better choice of toolpath to use. If tolerance is not an issue, consideration on when a Drill toolpath is used versus a Bore toolpath might be simply whether an exact tool size is available or not for drilling. If an exact tool size is available, a Drill toolpath can be used. In the next chapter, you will complete an exercise that uses the Bore toolpath to cut a counterbore.

How To: Create a Drill toolpath:

1. In the Drilling panel, click (Drill). The Drill palette opens similarly to that shown in Figure 4–2. Each of the tabs along the top of the palette provide access to the options that define the hole.

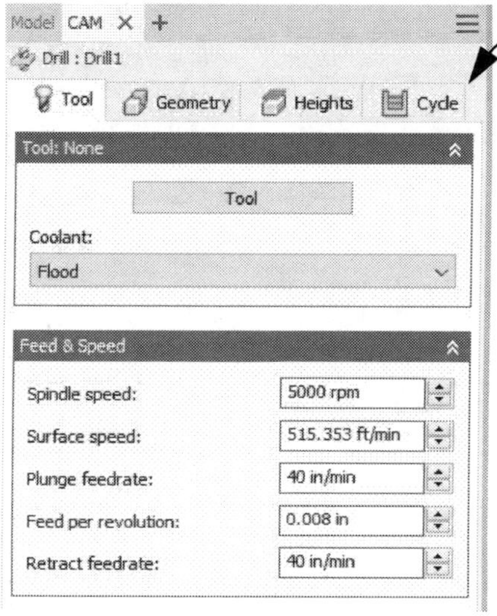

A reduced set of tabs are available to define a Drill toolpath, as compared to the toolpaths previously discussed in the 2D Milling panel.

Figure 4–2

Note: *Hover your cursor over each of the areas and options in the palette to obtain tooltip information about the options. These are available in all tabs.*

2. If a Drill toolpath is not the first toolpath in the model, the tool used in the previous toolpath is automatically assigned. To assign or change a pre-assigned tool, in the (Tool) tab, select **Tool** to access the Tool Library. Locate and select the required tool and click **Select**.

Note: *The Tool Library is used in the same way for all toolpaths. Refer to the Tool Library topic or the description for creating a Facing toolpath in Chapter 2 for more details on the Tool Library.*

3. Select the (Geometry) tab on the palette. The hole geometry that is to be drilled can be defined by selecting a cylindrical face, selecting points, or defining a diameter range within a boundary. The palette updates depending on which of these options is selected in the Hole mode drop-down list. Figure 4–3 shows the palette when each option is selected.

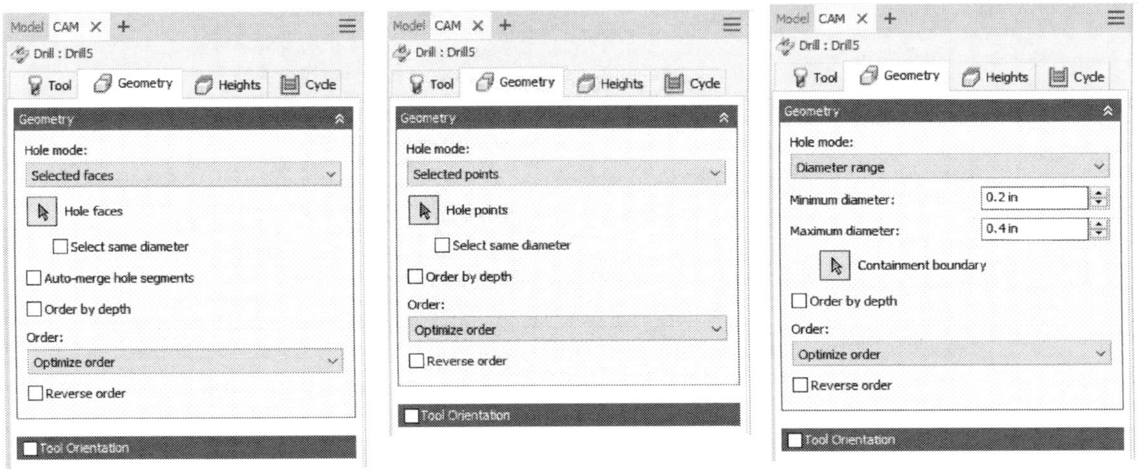

Figure 4–3

- With the **Selected faces** *Hole mode* set, you can select cylindrical faces on the model to define the geometry to drill. Consider enabling the **Select same diameter** option to have Inventor auto-select any remaining holes that have the same diameter.

Note: *The **Select same diameter** option is associative. If additional holes of the same diameter are added to the model, the toolpath will recognize this and they will be automatically included once the toolpath is regenerated.*

- With the **Selected points** *Hole mode* set, you can select sketched points, work points, projected sketch points, a circular edge (selects the centerpoint), or endpoints of linear or arc-shaped sketched entities.
- With the **Diameter range** *Hole mode* set, you can enter a minimum and maximum size range for the diameter, as well as define the containment boundary. Any hole that is within the defined size and lies within the boundary will be auto-selected for drilling. The containment boundary can be a closed loop of edges or a sketch.
- The remaining options in the palette can be used to control the order the holes are drilled if multiple holes are being machined. By default, the **Optimize order** option is enabled to reduce cycle time by defining the path based on the shortest distance between holes. The remaining options can be selected to customize the order.
- By default, the tool orientation is based on the work coordinate system (WCS) that was set up for the operation. Enable the **Tool Orientation** option to change the tool orientation for the toolpath. The orientation options are the same as those used to define the WCS orientation during setup.

4. Select the (Heights) tab. The palette displays the available plane height options (Clearance, Retract, Feed, Top, and Bottom), and they are visually represented on the model geometry. Edit any of the values, as needed, directly in the palette or in the mini-toolbar.

    - For Drill toolpaths, an additional option (**Drill tip through bottom**) is available in the *Bottom Height* area that forces the tool to cut through the full length of the hole. Examples of this option both disabled and enabled are shown in Figure 4–4.

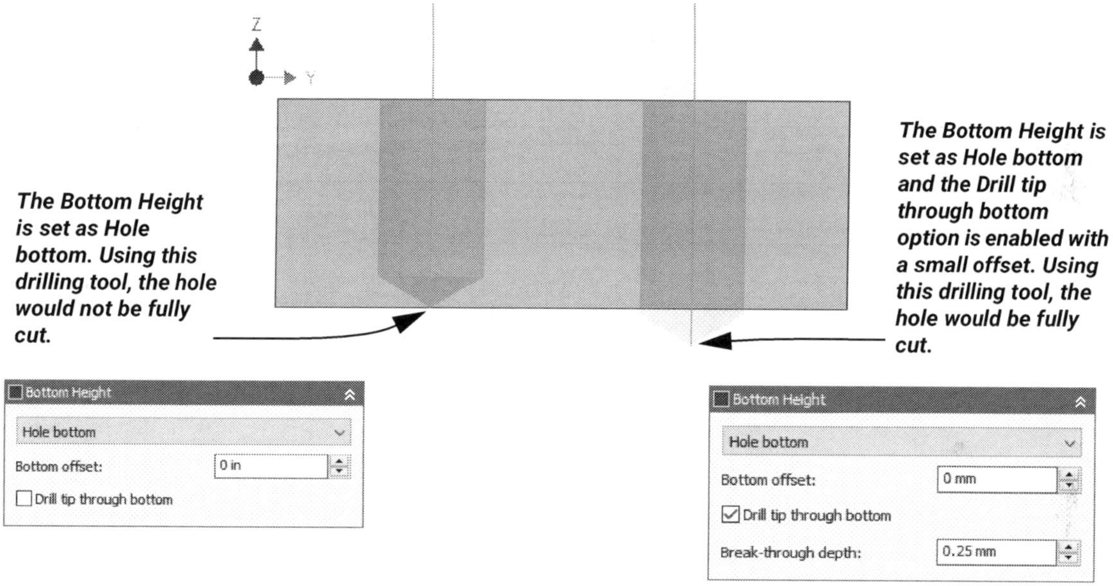

Figure 4–4

5. Select the (Cycle) tab. The options available in the Cycle type drop-down list define the cutting strategy that will be used. By default, the value is set as **Drilling - rapid out**. The list of strategies is shown in Figure 4–5. Depending on the strategy selected, additional options/values may be required.

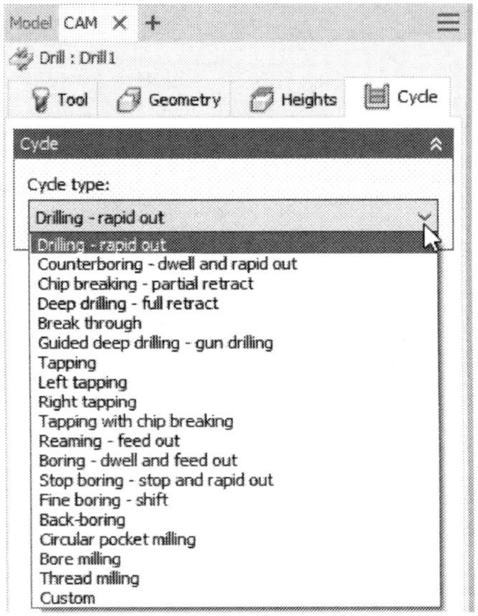

Figure 4–5

- To review each strategy and its G-code, hover your cursor over the drop-down list to reveal a tooltip. Figure 4–6 shows a subset of these descriptions.

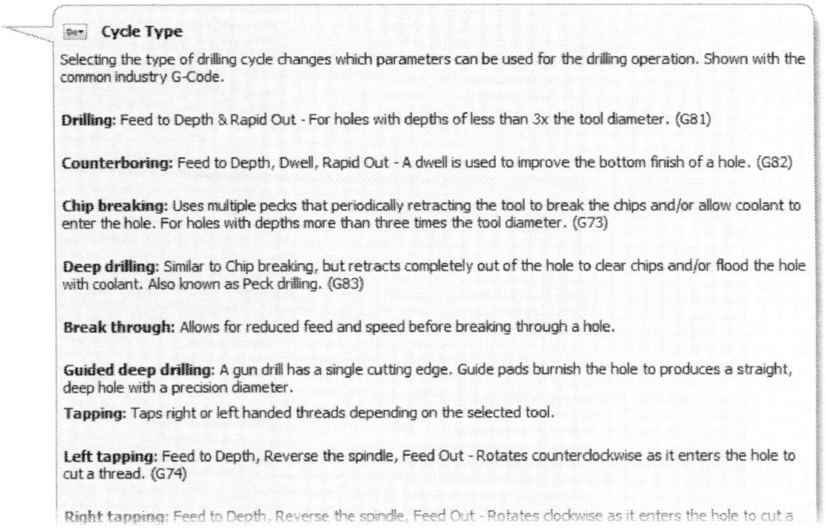

Figure 4–6

6. Click **OK** at the bottom of the Drill palette to complete the toolpath creation.

Hint: for Drilling Toolpaths

Prior to drilling a hole in metal, first use a spot drill (or center drill) to make a starter hole. This will help prevent the bit from sliding off center. The depth of the starter hole should be equal to half the hole diameter (or smaller).

If the depth to diameter ratio is greater than three, the hole must be drilled using a special drilling cycle called **Deep drilling - full retract** (or peck drilling). This prevents the drill from breaking by drilling only a fraction of the hole depth at a time and fully retracting the drill to remove chips.

Practice 4a
Drilling Holes in a Model

Practice Objectives

- Create Drill toolpaths that drill holes, tap the holes, and add the counterbore.
- Use the Simulation tools in Inventor CAM to display the operations.

In this practice, you will create three different drilling toolpaths that will machine the four 10-24 UNC counterbore holes located on the four corners of the housing.

Task 1: Open a model and review the hole geometry.

1. Open **Housing_Top_Drilling.ipt**. This model has all the toolpaths that were created in previous practices completed for you. Alternatively, you can work with the model you completed in the previous exercise. The CAM browser and model (rotated to view the bottom) are shown in Figure 4–7.

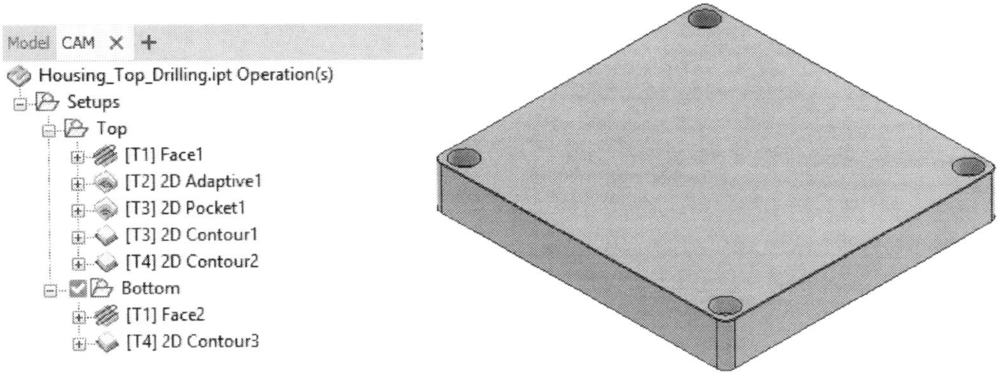

Figure 4–7

2. Ensure that the **Bottom** setup is active. If not, set it as the default folder so that all new toolpaths are added to its setup.
3. Open the Model browser and double-click on **Hole1** to open its feature creation palette. Note that it was created using a 10-24 UNC counterbore hole. The Hole palette is shown in Figure 4–8. You can also use standard Inventor measuring tools to measure the diameters of the holes in your model.

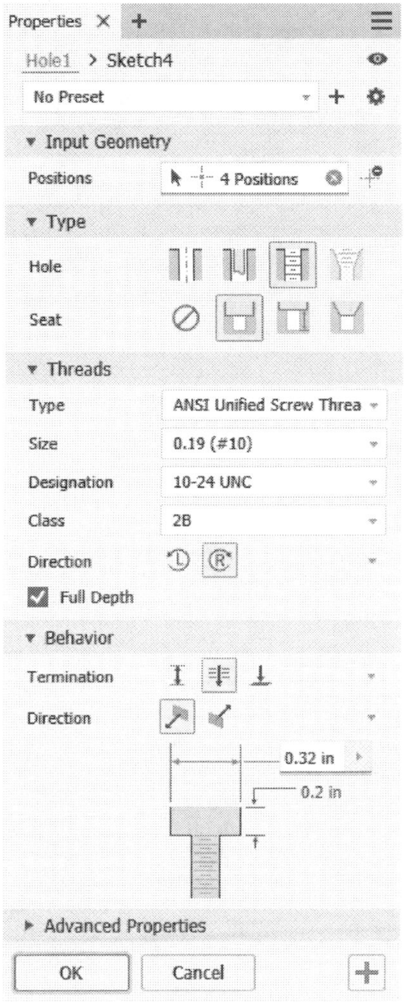

Figure 4–8

Based on the hole information, you know the size of the hole and counterbore so that proper tools can be selected for the machine operations. Click **Cancel** to close the palette and return to the CAM browser. If you click **OK** to close the Hole palette, Inventor will identify the model as having changed and you will have to Generate the existing toolpaths in the model.

Note: *Four drilling toolpaths will be added to this model. They are intended to showcase the different types of cycles that can be created in Inventor CAM. In your environment, you may choose many different strategies to create your toolpaths. Our aim is to show you the different tools and options that you can use.*

Task 2: Add a Drill toolpath to spot drill the holes on the four corners.

In this task, you will spot drill the four corners to learn how you can use the Drill toolpath for this type of drilling cycle.

1. In the Drilling panel, click (Drill). The Drill palette opens.
2. In the (Tool) tab, open the Tool Library and search for the **⌀3/16" drill** tools. In the list, locate and select the tool that has a *Spindle Speed* value of **2550**. (Hint: Set the filter field to **Diameter is** and enter 0.1875" as the search value, or **Text contains** and enter **3/16"**.)
3. Edit the selected tool and assign it as the next tool number in the sequence (#5), if it does not update automatically. Complete the edit and click **Select** to assign it to the toolpath.
4. Select the (Geometry) tab.
5. With the *Hole faces* field active, select the larger diameter hole face for the counterbore, as shown in Figure 4–9.

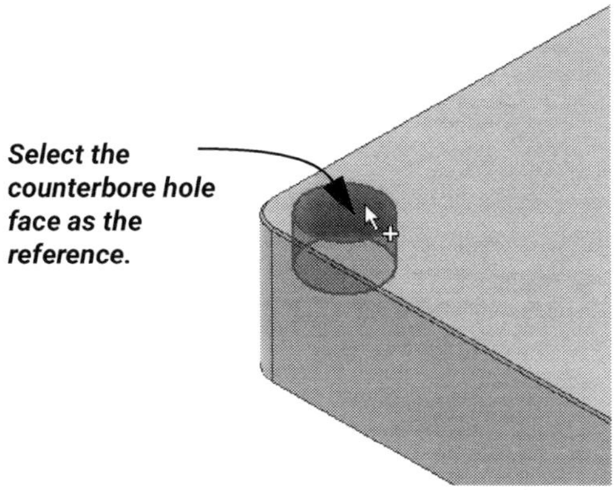

Figure 4–9

6. Enable the **Select same diameter** option to ensure that all four holes are automatically selected. In this model, the four holes have the same diameter and depth so the additional sub-options are not required. As an alternative, you also could have selected each cylindrical face separately.

7. Review the remaining options in the list (as shown in Figure 4–10). These options enable you to customize how the holes will be machined. Ensure that **Optimize order** is selected in the Order drop-down list.

   Note: *To control the order of selection, it is recommended that you manually select the faces and set the required option in the Order drop-down list.*

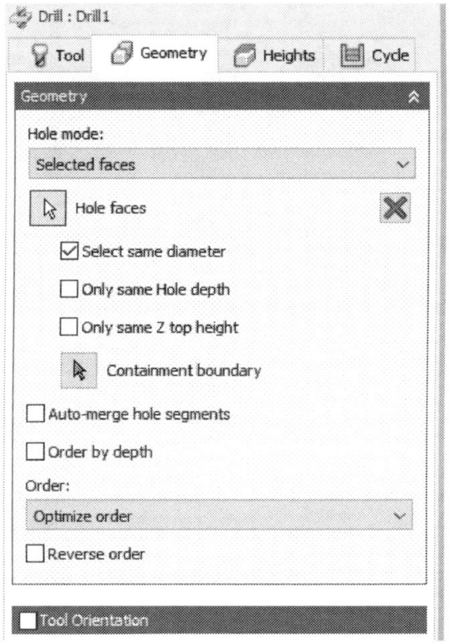

Figure 4–10

8. Select the (Heights) tab and review the planes. Note that the *Bottom Height* option is set as **Hole bottom**. This drilling cycle is only spot drilling so it only needs to drill into the top of the model slightly. Change the *Bottom Height* option to **Hole top** and set the *Bottom offset* value to **-0.05 in**.

9. Select the (Cycle) tab. Maintain the default *Cycle type* option as **Drilling - rapid out**.

10. Click **OK** to complete the toolpath.

11. View a simulation of the new Drill toolpath and ensure that the spot drill removes material at the center of each hole to a depth of 0.05 in.

Task 3: Add a Drill toolpath to drill the holes on the four corners.

1. In the Drilling panel, click (Drill). The Drill palette opens.

2. In the (Tool) tab, open the Tool Library and search for the **⌀5/32" drill** tools. In the list, locate and select the tool that has a *Spindle Speed* value of **1100**. (Hint: Set the filter field to **Diameter is** and enter 0.15625" as the search value, or **Text contains** and enter **5/32"**.)
3. Edit the selected tool and assign it as the next tool number in the sequence (#6), if it does not update automatically. Complete the edit and click **Select** to assign it to the toolpath.
4. Select the (Geometry) tab.
5. With the *Hole faces* field active, select the smaller diameter hole face and enable the **Select same diameter** option to ensure that all four holes are automatically selected, as shown in Figure 4–11.

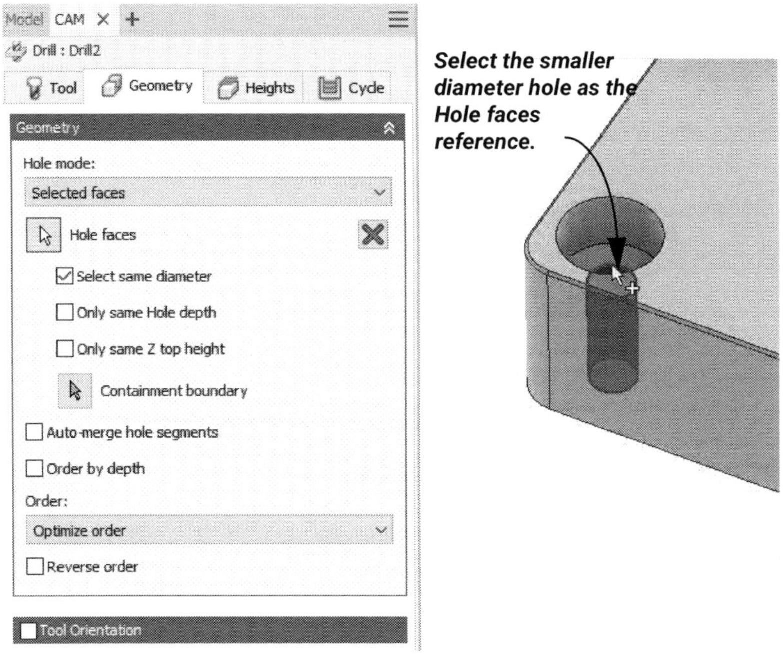

Figure 4–11

6. Review the remaining options in the list. These options enable you to customize how the holes will be machined. Ensure that **Optimize order** is selected in the Order drop-down list.
7. Select the (Heights) tab and review the planes. Note that the *Bottom Height* option is set as **Hole bottom**. Select the **Drill tip through bottom** option and enter **0.05 in** as the *Break-through depth* value. This ensures that the drilling cycle completely breaks through the hole.

8. Note that the *Top Height* option is set, by default, as **Hole top**. This option is not appropriate because the smaller diameter hole is being drilled first, prior to the countersink, so it must cut from the top of the model. As an alternative to modifying the *Top Height* setting, return to the (Geometry) tab and select **Auto-merge hole segments**. This option automatically includes the countersink in the toolpath. Note how the preview now extends to the top of the model.

9. Select the (Cycle) tab. Set the *Cycle type* option as **Chip breaking - partial retract**. Maintain the default options that are provided to define the chip breaking cycle.

10. Click **OK** to complete the toolpath. The path generates and displays as shown in Figure 4–12. Review the order that the holes will be drilled. The red arrow is the starting location and the green arrow is the end location. The yellow lines show the tool rapids between pockets.

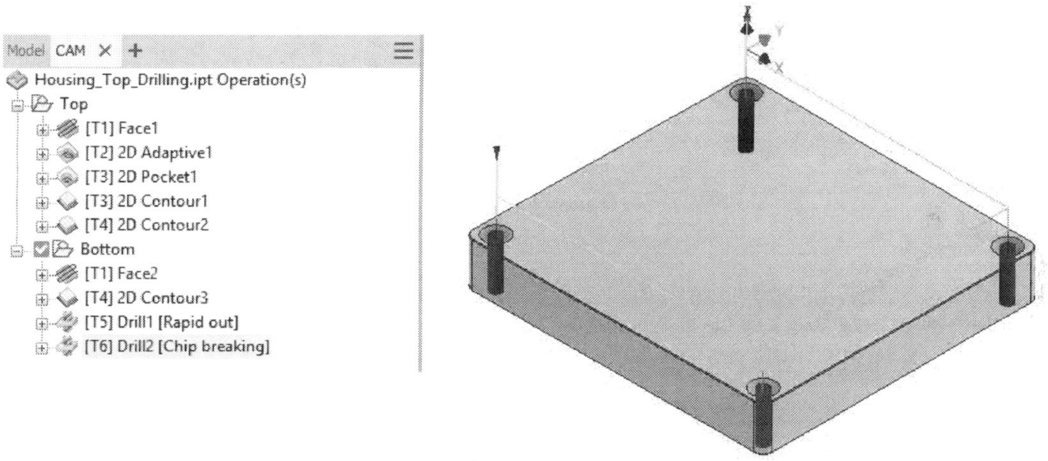

Figure 4–12

Task 4: Drill the four countersink holes.

1. In the Drilling panel, click (Drill).

2. In the (Tool) tab, search for and select a **⌀5/16" Flat Endmill** tool with a *Spindle Speed* of **3670** for this toolpath. Edit the tool and assign it as the next tool number in the sequence (#7), if it does not update automatically.

3. Select the (Geometry) tab.
4. With the *Hole faces* field active, select the larger diameter hole face as shown in Figure 4–13.

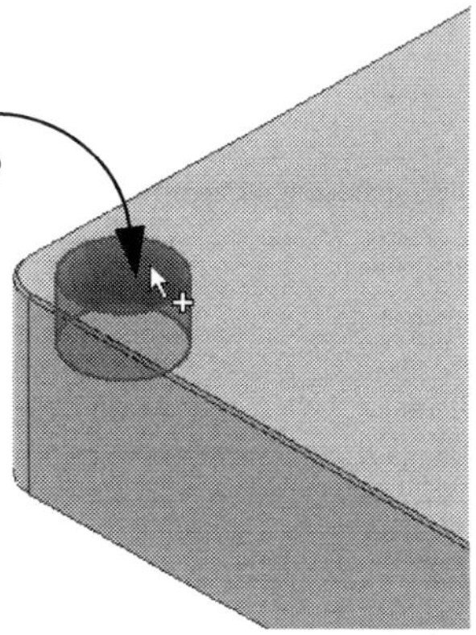

Figure 4–13

5. Enable the **Select same diameter** option to ensure that all four counterbores are automatically selected. Ensure that the only option selected in the list is the **Optimize order** option.
6. Select the (Heights) tab and review the planes. Note that the *Bottom Height* option is set as **Hole bottom**. In this case, the drill should not cut through the bottom of the hole, only up to it, so this option must remain selected.
7. Select the (Cycle) tab. Set the *Cycle type* option as **Counterboring - dwell and rapid out** and set the *Dwelling period* value to **0.5 s**.
8. Click **OK** to complete the toolpath.

Task 5: Add a final tapping toolpath to tap the four 10-24 UNC holes.

1. In the Drilling panel, click (Drill).
2. In the (Tool) tab, search for 10-24 UNC tools using the Text Contains filter. Select the **Ø0.19 x 0.0416667" right tap (#10-24 UNC)** tool for this toolpath. Edit the tool and assign it as the next tool number in the sequence (#8), if it does not update automatically.
3. Select the (Geometry) tab. Using the same technique that was described in the last two tasks, select one of the smaller diameter hole faces and ensure that the remaining holes are automatically selected and that the order of machining is optimized.

4. In the (Heights) tab, ensure that the hole is tapped through to the bottom with the drill tip cutting through the bottom of the hole by 0.01 in.

5. In the (Cycle) tab, note that the *Cycle type* option is already set as **Tapping**. This is because a tapping tool was selected, and Inventor CAM recognizes this and properly assigns the cycle type.

6. Click **OK** to complete the toolpath.

Task 6: Reorder the toolpaths.

1. In the CAM browser, press and hold the left mouse button on the **2D Contour3** toolpath. Drag the toolpath below the last Drill toolpath (as shown in Figure 4–14). Once the line appears identifying the toolpath's new placement location, release the mouse button to relocate it. This reorders the contouring toolpath that machined the sharp edge around the outside of the bottom of the model so that it is after all of the drilling toolpaths.

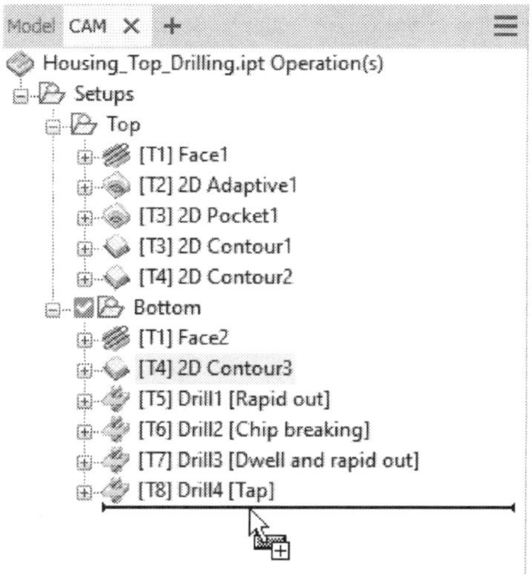

Figure 4–14

2. Use the Simulation tool to play the toolpaths created on the Bottom setup (as shown in Figure 4–15). Note that all the stock is not removed from the outside of the model. This is because the Top and Bottom setups work in combination with one another to fully machine the model.

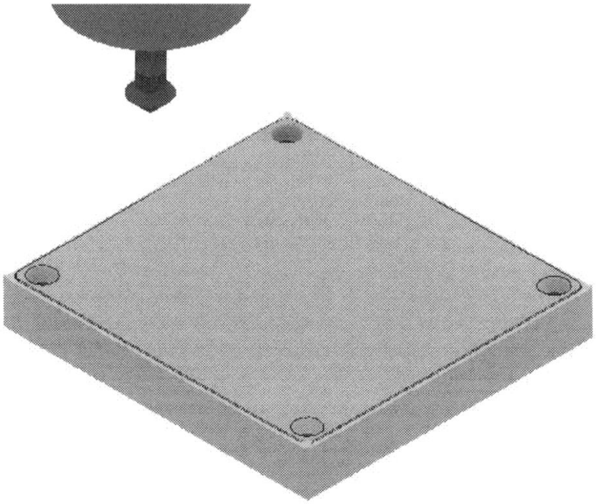

Figure 4–15

3. Play the Top and Bottom setups together and review the final geometry. Reviewing the final simulations without the tool displayed can help you easily visualize the final geometry, as shown in Figure 4–16.

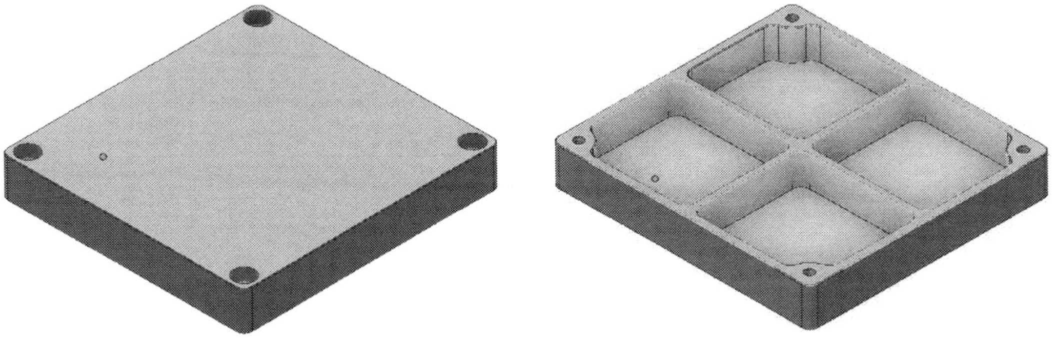

Figure 4–16

4. Close the Simulation palette.
5. Save and close the model.

End of practice

Chapter Review Questions

1. Which of the following are valid selection options for selecting which holes are to be drilled in the model? (Select all that apply.)
   a. Selected edges
   b. Selected faces
   c. Selected points
   d. Diameter range

2. A containment area must be selected to define a boundary in which all holes can be selected.
   a. True
   b. False

3. The tool orientation that was defined during setup can be overwritten when creating a Drill toolpath.
   a. True
   b. False

4. Which of the following options can be enabled to ensure that the drill cuts through the bottom of the hole when creating a **Drilling - rapid out** cycle?
   a. Break through
   b. Drill tip through bottom
   c. Offset from edge
   d. Offset from bottom

5. A model includes two identical straight holes. Both holes require a spot drill to locate them. What is the minimum number of toolpaths needed to machine these holes?
   a. 1
   b. 2
   c. 3
   d. 4

Command Summary

Button	Command	Location
	**Drill**	• **Ribbon:** *CAM* tab>Drilling panel

Chapter 5

Project Exercises I

In this chapter, you will be provided with two project exercises that allow you to practice setting up and defining the 2D milling toolpaths needed to machine solid part models. These project exercises assume that you have completed the previous exercises and understand the general Inventor CAM workflow for both setting up milling operations and adding 2D toolpaths. Detailed instructions will not be provided. For more detailed instructions, refer to the steps in the previous exercises. For topics that have not been previously discussed (i.e., fixtures, importing tool libraries, post processing, and tool templates), more detailed explanation will be included in the tasks.

Learning Objectives

- Import a tool library.
- Create a setup that includes toolpaths and a fixture to fully machine a model.
- Post process an Inventor CAM setup to output the CNC code required to machine the model.
- Save selected toolpaths as templates.

Practice 5a
Generating Toolpaths I

Practice Objectives

- Import a tool library.
- Create a setup that includes toolpaths to machine the top and bottom of the model.
- Post process an Inventor CAM setup to output the CNC code required to machine the model.

In this practice, you will add machining toolpaths to both the top and bottom of a model that is assembled in a fixture. To complete the project, you will post process the CAM data to create the CNC code required to machine the model.

Task 1: Open the assembly model and review the model and fixture.

1. Open **2D_Roughing_Fixture.iam** from the *2D Milling Assembly Fixture* folder. Switch to the Model browser, if not already active. The assembly and Model browser display as shown in Figure 5–1.

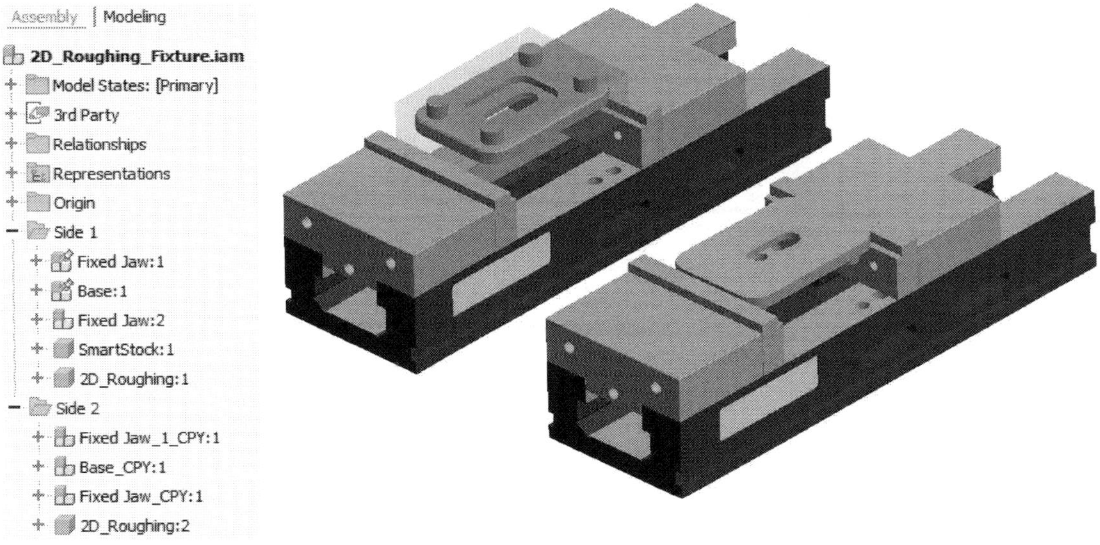

Figure 5–1

Note: *A completed assembly (**FINAL_2D_Roughing_Fixture.iam**) has been provided in the 2D Milling Assembly Fixture folder. This model contains all completed setups and toolpaths that will be created in this project.*

In previous exercises, all toolpaths were added directly in part models. In this exercise, multiple components have been assembled for you using standard Inventor constraint functionality. The components in the assembly represent the model to be machined, the stock, and the machine's fixture. Consider the following:

- **Side 1** and **Side 2** are folders that have been set up in the assembly to help organize the two Fixture assemblies. Expand these folders, if not already expanded.
- **2D_roughing.ipt** is the model that is to be machined. Two instances of it have been assembled, one in each fixture assembly. This allows you to define the two required setups needed to machine the top and bottom of the model.
- The **Side 1** folder contains the initial instance of the fixture's components along with an Inventor model (**SmartStock**) that will be used as the stock model. Side 1 instances will be used to machine the top of the model.
- The **SmartStock.ipt** solid model was designed with user parameters. These parameters are populated with the overall size of the design model and the stock model updates to add stock to the top, bottom, and sides. No changes are required for this.
- The **Side 2** folder contains copies of the fixture's components along with the model being machined. Side 2 instances will be used to machine the bottom of the model.

2. Right-click on **SmartStock:1** and select **Transparent**. This allows you to clearly see that the design model is assembled within it.
3. Open **2D_roughing.ipt** and review the model geometry that will be machined. Close the model and return to the assembly. All CAM operations and toolpaths will be added at the assembly level.

Task 2: Import a tool library.

In previous exercises, all of the required tools were selected from the Tool Library that was installed with Inventor CAM. To help simplify the tool selection process, you can also import a tool library that would include the tools that you have available for your machine.

1. Open the Tool Library.
2. To import a library into the model, right-click on the **2D_Roughing_Fixture** name in the *Open Documents* area and select **Import Tools from Library**.
3. Locate, select, and open the **2D_Roughing_Fixture.hsmlib** file from the *2D Milling Assembly Fixture* folder in your practice files folder. Four tools are added to your tool library. These will be used throughout this project as an alternative to searching and assigning tools from the Autodesk Tool Library.
4. Click **OK** to close the Tool Library.

Hint: Exporting a Tool Library

To create a tool library, simply add all the tools required into a single model. The model can already exist and contain solid geometry and CAM toolpaths or it can be an empty model that is simply being used to generate the tool library. Activate the CAM environment and open the Tool Library. In the Tool Library, add and modify the tools and their parameters. Once all the tools required for your custom library have been confirmed, right-click on the document name in the *Open Documents* area and select **Export**. Enter a new descriptive name and save the .HSMLIB file to your local computer or a network location. The location should be one that is easily accessible.

Task 3: Define the setup for the top of the model and its toolpaths.

1. Activate the Inventor CAM environment and begin the setup for the top of the model. This will be completed on the files in the **Side 1** folder. To define the setup, consider the following:
   - By default, all of the models in the assembly are preselected as the Model references for machining. Redefine the reference so that only the **2D_roughing.ipt** model for Side 1 is selected.
   - On the *Stock* tab, change the stock mode to **From solid** and select the **SmartStock.ipt** model. This should be done once the model is selected so that the work coordinate system (WCS) can be properly defined on the solid stock model.
   - Return to the *Setup* tab and define the operation type and WCS so that it appears as shown in Figure 5–2.

   Note: *For image clarity, the components in Side 2 are not displayed in images for this task.*

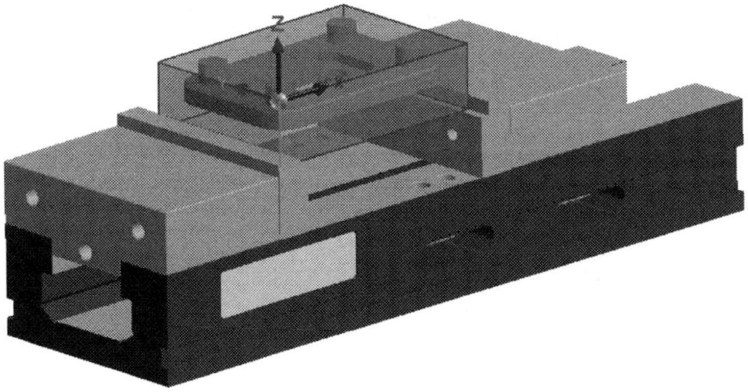

Figure 5–2

- Enable the *Fixture* area and define the remaining components in the Side 1 folder (seven components) as the Fixture geometry, as shown selected in Figure 5–3.

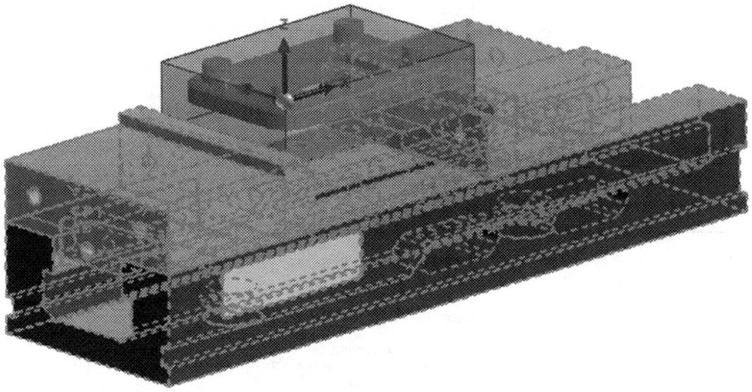

Figure 5–3

- Define a generic 3-axis machine and Milling operation.
- Complete the setup and rename the setup **Side 1**.

2. Add a Face toolpath to machine the top of the stock.
   - Assign the **#1 1 3/4" Face Mill** tool that was imported as one of the provided library tools. No changes to the parameters are required.
   - Ensure that the top outside edge of the solid stock model is preselected as the geometry reference.
   - Ensure that the Bottom Height for the cut is set to **Model top**. The model was assembled offset from the top to ensure that a cutting pass was required to machine the top of the stock and clear it of any irregularities.
   - Set the *Pass extension* value to **1.0 in** to ensure that the tool clears the stock before turning for the next cutting pass.
   - Accept the remaining defaults and complete the toolpath.
   - Play the simulation and verify that there is no stock remaining at the top of the four posts. (Hint: Use the *Info* tab and the *Verification* area to verify this. The stock must be displayed to obtain a value; however, you can set the stock to display as transparent to easily locate the top of the posts.)
3. Prior to defining the remaining toolpaths, it is recommended that you disable the solid stock model. This will allow you to visually see the model, but will avoid its selection during toolpath definition. To disable the model, select it in the graphics window or in the Model browser, right-click, and clear the **Enabled** option in the menu. Hover over the model in the graphics window to verify that you can no longer select it.

   Note: *To enable a component once it is disabled, you must select it in the Model browser and select* ***Enabled****. A disabled component cannot be enabled in the graphics window because it cannot be selected while it is disabled.*

4. Add a 2D Adaptive toolpath to clear the stock around the outside of the model.
   - Assign the **#2 1/2" Flat Endmill** tool that was imported as one of the provided library tools. No changes to the parameters are required. Assign the bottom edge of the model being machined as the geometry reference for the toolpath, as shown in Figure 5–4.

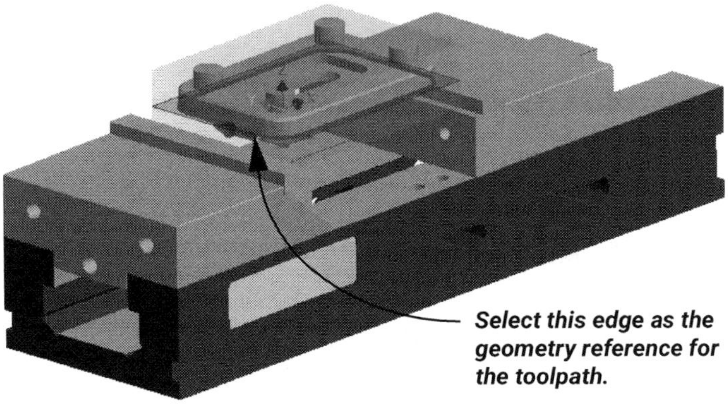

Figure 5–4

   - Set the toolpath to cut with multiple depths and set the *Maximum roughing stepdown* to **0.5 in**.
   - The cut should remove all material down to the bottom of the part (axially) and leave **0.05 in** of stock around the outer face (radially) so that a finishing toolpath, that is run at a slower feedrate, can be assigned to finish the outside of the model.
   - Change the *Retraction Policy* to **Minimum retraction**. This sets the retract so that on each cutting motion, the tool is prevented from a full retraction and simply retracts to clear the stock. This helps reduce cutting time, especially on larger models.
   - Play the simulation and verify that there is 0.05 in. of stock remaining on the outside faces. Note that along the flat portions of the wall, the remaining stock is 0.05 in., while on the corners the value varies a little. This difference is based on the Tolerance value that is set in the *Passes* tab. For finishing passes, this tolerance value could be tighter.
5. As an alternative to creating and setting similar settings to the previous Adaptive toolpath, you can derive a new toolpath from an existing one to more efficiently work with the model. This will be done to clear the stock inside the model. Right-click on the **2D Adaptive1** toolpath that was previously created and select **Create Derived Operation>2D Milling> 2D Adaptive**.

- A duplicate of the selected toolpath is created. Redefine the geometry that will be machined such that only the circular edges of the four posts are selected, as shown in Figure 5–5.

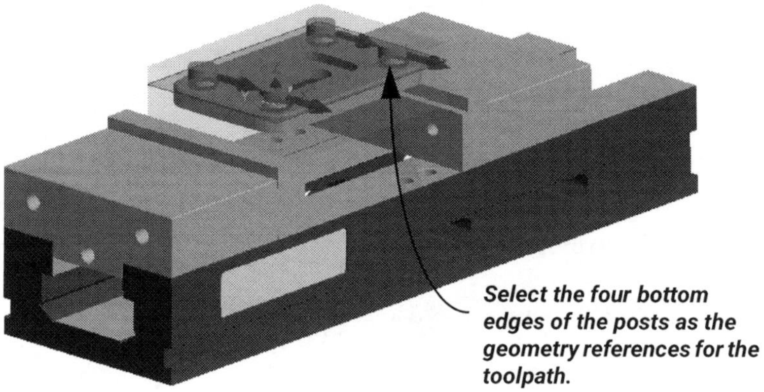

Figure 5–5

- Enable the *Stock Contours* area to further define the area being machined. This enables the toolpath calculation to also consider a selected boundary versus the actual stock boundary that was previously roughed out.
- Select the outer edge of the model, as shown in Figure 5–6, as the stock contour selection reference. Once selected, it appears as an orange dashed line.

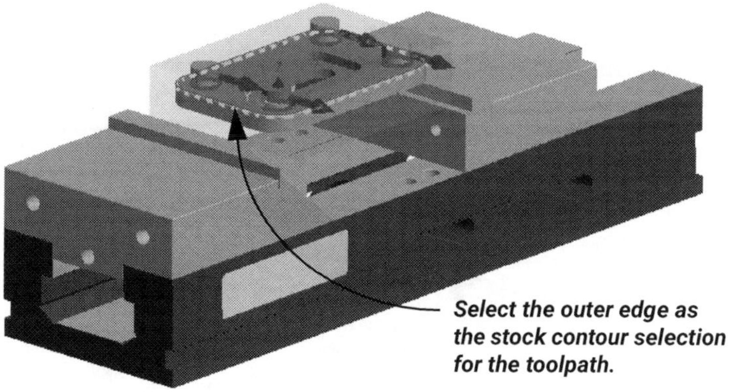

Figure 5–6

- Clear the Multiple Depths setting for this toolpath.
- Modify the *Radial stock to leave* to **0.02 in**.
- Play the simulation and verify that there is stock remaining on the outside faces of the posts.

6. Add a 2D Pocket toolpath to clear the stock from the internal pocket.
   - Use the **Create Derived Operation** command on the 2D Adaptive2 toolpath that was just created to create a new **2D Pocket** toolpath.
   - Clear the current Pocket selection option and select the bottom edge of the pocket, as shown in Figure 5–7. Maintain the stock contour reference selection.

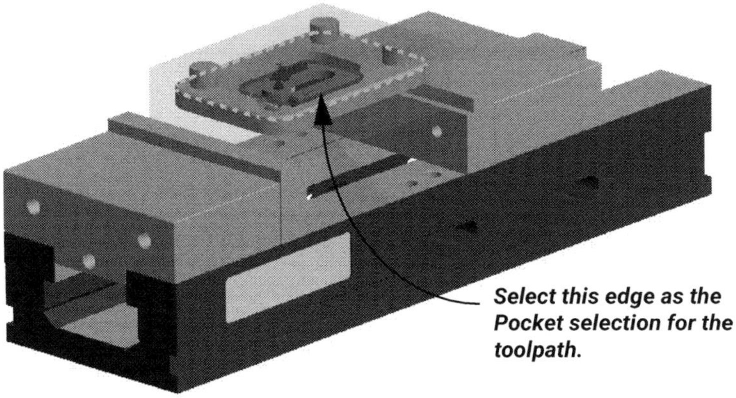

Figure 5–7

   - Change the *Top Height* reference option to **Selection** (previously set as Stock top) and select the top face of the model that is being machined as the reference, as shown in Figure 5–8. No offset value is required. (Hint: You may have to rotate and zoom in on the model to ensure that you are selecting the face and not activating one of the other Height planes.)

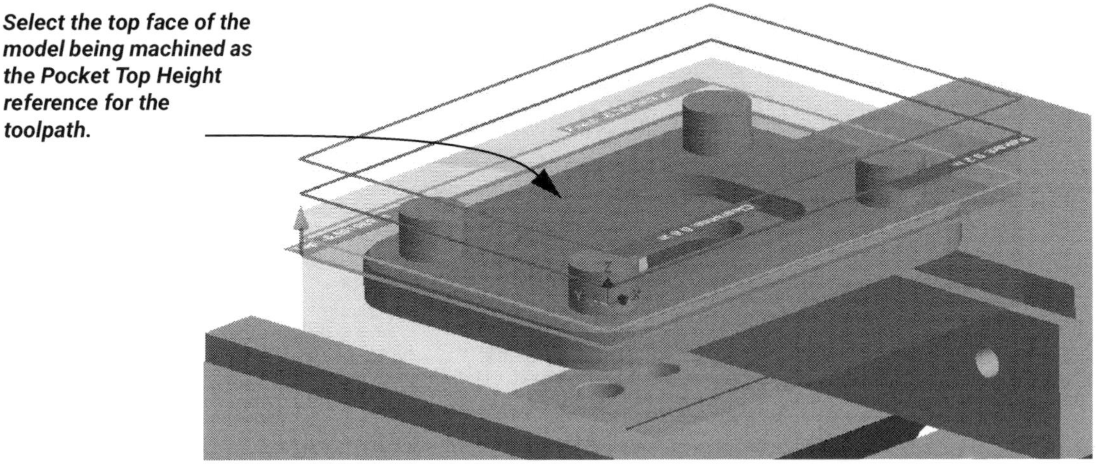

Figure 5–8

- Although this toolpath was derived from a roughing toolpath, this one will be completed as a finishing toolpath. Enable the **Finishing Passes** option and reduce the *Maximum stepover* value to **0.2 in**.
- Since this is a finishing toolpath, also clear the *Stock to Leave* area to ensure that the toolpath removes all stock.
- Play the simulation and verify that all stock has been removed within the pocket.

7. Add a Slot toolpath to clear the stock in the remaining pocket/slot. Additional toolpaths, such as Slot, are available in the 2D Milling drop-down list.
   - Assign the **#3 3/4" Flat Endmill** tool.
   - Assign the bottom edge of the slot as the geometry reference for the toolpath, as shown in Figure 5–9.

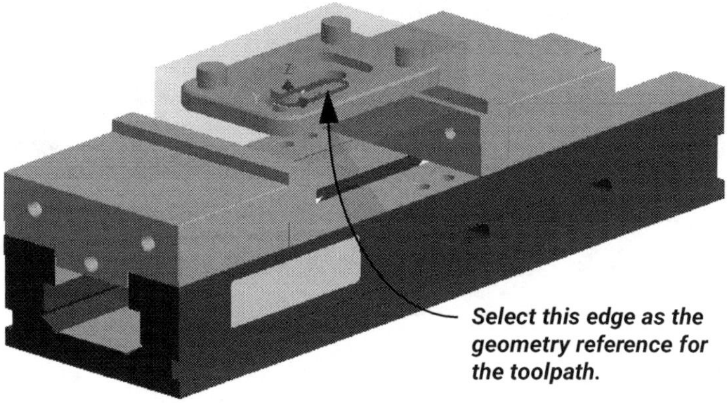

Figure 5–9

- Change the *Top Height* reference option to **Selection** and select the bottom face of the pocket as the reference, as shown in Figure 5–10. No offset value is required.

Note: *You may have to rotate and zoom in on the model to ensure that you are selecting the face and not activating one of the other Height planes.*

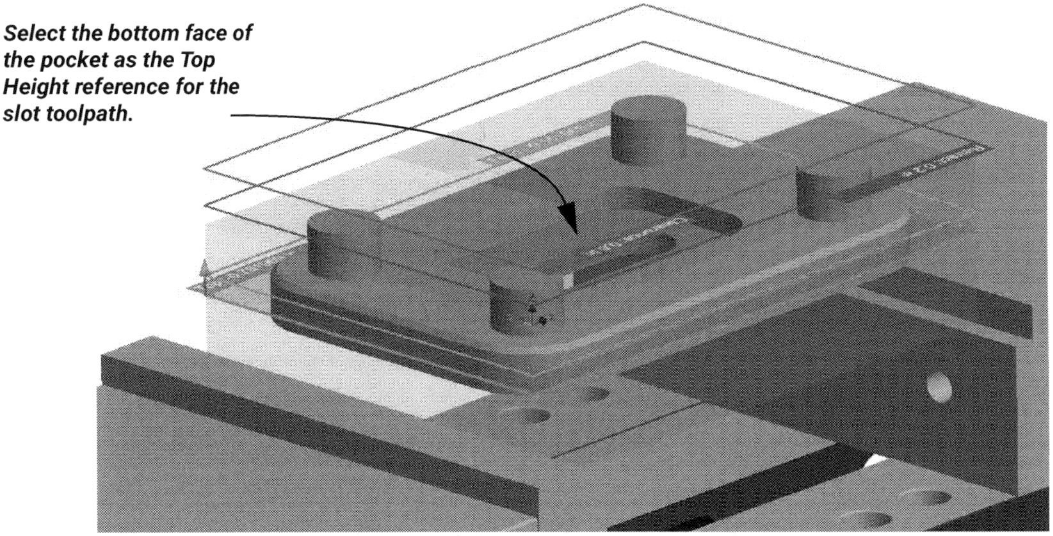

Figure 5–10

- To ensure that there are no slivers/cusps left at the bottom of the slot after facing is completed on the other side of the model, set a **-0.05 in** *Bottom offset* value.
- To finalize the toolpath, set the *Backoff Distance* value to **0.25 in**. This sets the distance to move away from the last cut before retracting the tool. Also enable **Repeat finishing pass** to run an additional pass for finishing.
- Play the simulation and verify that there is stock removed from below the model within the slot.

Note: *You will need to turn off the display of the stock or set it as Transparent and reorient the model to the RIGHT view to see the toolpath extend below the bottom of the model.*

8. Add a 2D Contour toolpath to define the finishing pass for the four posts and the exterior of the model.
   - Ensure the **#3 3/4" Flat Endmill** is set as the tool.
   - Assign the four bottom circular edges of the posts and the bottom outside edge of the model as the geometry references for the toolpath, as shown in Figure 5–11.

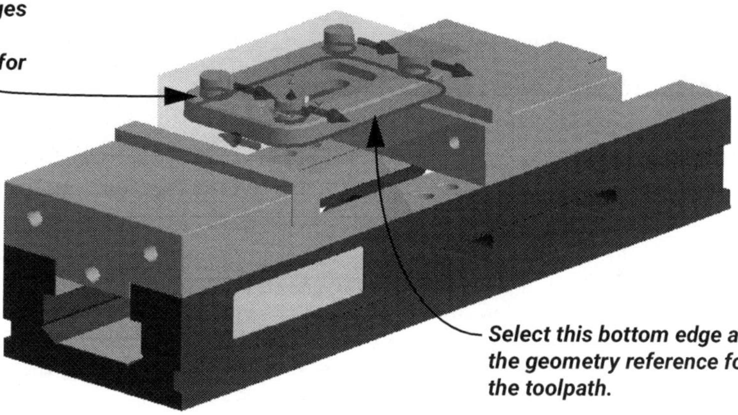

Figure 5–11

   - No additional changes are required.
   - Play the simulation and review.

Hint: Preserving Cut Order

By default, the first reference selected defines where the tool will begin cutting. The order in which the remaining reference geometry is cut is dependent on the system. Inventor CAM optimizes this order for you. To set the cutting order to maintain the order in which you made selections, you can enable the **Preserve order** option in the *Passes* tab.

Hint: Controlling the Tool Entry Location

The tool entry location for a cut is randomly defined. This location may not be ideal for a finishing toolpath as it could leave marks or gouges on your machined model. To control the entry point, you can select a workpoint or vertex on the model to specify an entry position. For Contour toolpaths, the entry position is defined on the *Linking* tab in the *Positions* area. Each Contour toolpath can only have one manually assigned entry point. It is recommended that, for cases such as the four posts in our model, you define four different 2D Contour toolpaths if you want to control the entry points for each path.

9. Add a 2D Contour toolpath to add the chamfer to the top edge of the model.
   - Assign the **#4 1/4" 45° Chamfer** tool for the cut.
   - Select the bottom edge of the chamfer that cuts the top edge of the model.
   - To ensure that the cut cleanly removes all the stock, set the *Chamfer tip offset* to **0.02 in**. This sets the tip of the stock below the selected edge and ensures the full use of the cutting tool.
   - Play the simulation and review the cutting path. (Hint: Change to side view while playing to notice the tool offset.)
10. Save the assembly.

Task 4: Set up a second setup to machine the bottom of the model.

In this task, you will create a second setup and add toolpaths to machine the bottom of the stock. A new setup is required because the model would be manually flipped prior to the paths in this setup being run. Consider the following:

- The **Side 2** folder contains copies of the fixture's components along with the model being machined.
- In this setup, stock will be defined during the operation's setup. The **SmartStock.ipt** model is not being used to represent the stock because the top of the stock has already been machined, so the fixture would be directly holding the model. By representing the stock in the Setup, you can accurately define it and properly identify if collisions will occur with the fixture.

1. Prior to beginning the setup, you should review the stock that is remaining after the Side 1 operation is complete. This will provide you with the proper size settings for the stock in the Side 2 setup. To determine these values, consider the following:
   - Return to the Model browser, right-click on the **SmartStock** model, and click **Enabled**. This activates the model so that it can be selected again.
   - Use the **Measure** tool on the *Tools* tab to measure the stock offsets from the sides of the model and the offset from the bottom of the stock to the bottom face. These values are **0.25 in** and **0.748 in**, respectively.

2. Initiate the setup for the bottom of the model. This will be completed on the files in the **Side 2** folder. To define the setup, consider the following:

   - Ensure the machine and operation type are assigned.
   - Redefine the Model references so that only the **2D_roughing.ipt** model for Side 2 is selected.
   - Similarly to the Side 1 setup, enable the *Fixture* area and define the remaining components in the Side 2 folder (seven components) as the Fixture geometry.
   - Modify the WCS so that it appears as shown in Figure 5–12.

   Note: *For image clarity, the components in Side 1 are not displayed in the images for this task.*

   - On the *Stock* tab, define the size of the remaining stock that must be removed. The values should be based on the remaining stock after the Side 1 toolpaths are complete. Based on the measurements made in the previous step, consider using the values shown in Figure 5–12.

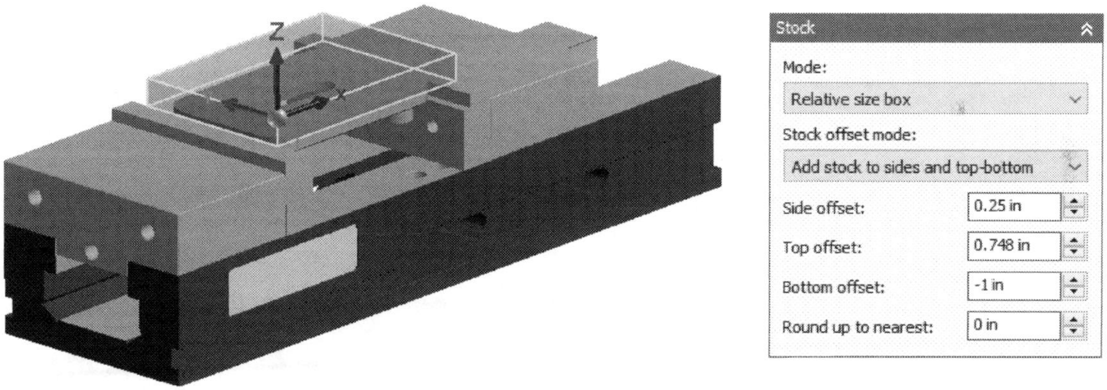

Figure 5–12

   - Complete the setup and rename the setup **Side 2**.

3. Add a Face toolpath to clean up the stock and ensure that the stock is flat and free of irregularities.

   - Assign the **#1 1 3/4" Face Mill** tool for the toolpath.
   - Ensure that the top outside edge of the solid stock model is preselected as the geometry reference.
   - By default, the *Bottom Height* setting for the cut is set to Model top; change this option to **Stock top**. This sets the cut so that the toolpath cuts only up to the top plane for the stock.
   - Set the *Pass extension* value to **1.0 in** to ensure the tool clears the stock before turning for the next cutting pass.

4. Add a 2D Pocket toolpath to clear all remaining stock.
   - Assign the **#3 3/4" Flat Endmill** tool for the toolpath.
   - Select the bottom face of the model as the Pocket geometry selection. Also enable the *Stock Contours* area so that the boundary of the existing stock is also considered in the toolpath calculations. The references highlight in the model, as shown in Figure 5–13.

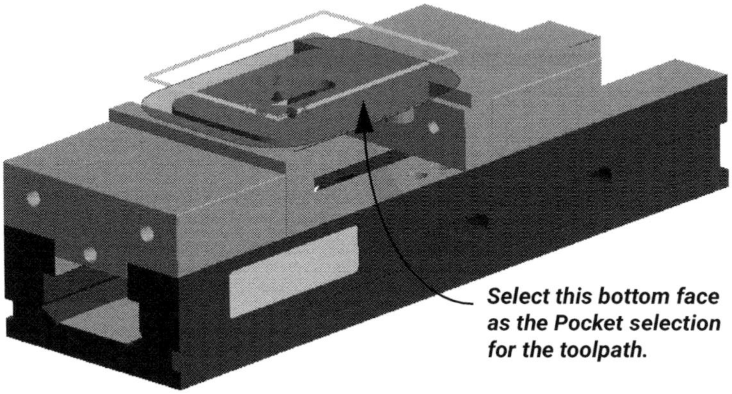

Figure 5–13

   - Set the *Maximum stepover* value to **0.2 in**. This value is small enough that the material removal will be done at one depth so multiple depth settings are not required.
   - Since this is a finishing toolpath, clear the *Stock to Leave* area to ensure that the toolpath removes all stock.
   - Change the *Ramp type* setting to **Plunge**.
   - Play the Side 2 toolpaths and verify that all stock has been removed.
5. Save the assembly.

Hint: Toolpath Selection

There are many different toolpaths that can be used to define the same cutting path. For example, the final toolpath in this exercise could have been a 2D Adaptive toolpath. The choice of toolpath is dependent on many factors, including personal preference, machine/ tool capabilities, machining time, etc. In this guide, you were presented with different toolpaths to show you how to use them and how to define their parameters. Ultimately, it will be up to you to decide which toolpaths you use and when.

Task 5: Generate the CNC code required to machine the model.

In this task, you will post process the Side 1 toolpaths to create the code required by the CNC machine to cut the top side of the model. This task does not teach you how to edit the file as that is considered advanced functionality that is outside the scope of this learning content.

1. Set the **Side 1** setup as the default folder so that post processing is run on these toolpaths.

2. In the Toolpath panel, click (Post Process). The Post Process dialog box opens. Define the following settings (as shown in Figure 5–14):

   - Select **HAAS (pre-NGC) / haas** as the post process configurator to be used. This can be selected from the configuration drop-down list.
   - Change the *Output folder* to your practice files folder.
   - Note that the *Program name or number* is set by default to **1001**. This was the value that was assigned by default when the Side 1 setup was created.

   ***Note:** To change the default Program name or number, you could have entered an alternate value on the (Post Process) tab during setup. You can also modify the value during post processing.*

   - Enter **Project Exercise Side 1** as the *Program comment* to help identify the program.
   - Ensure that **Open NC file in editor** is selected so that once the *.nc file is created, it will be displayed in the editor.

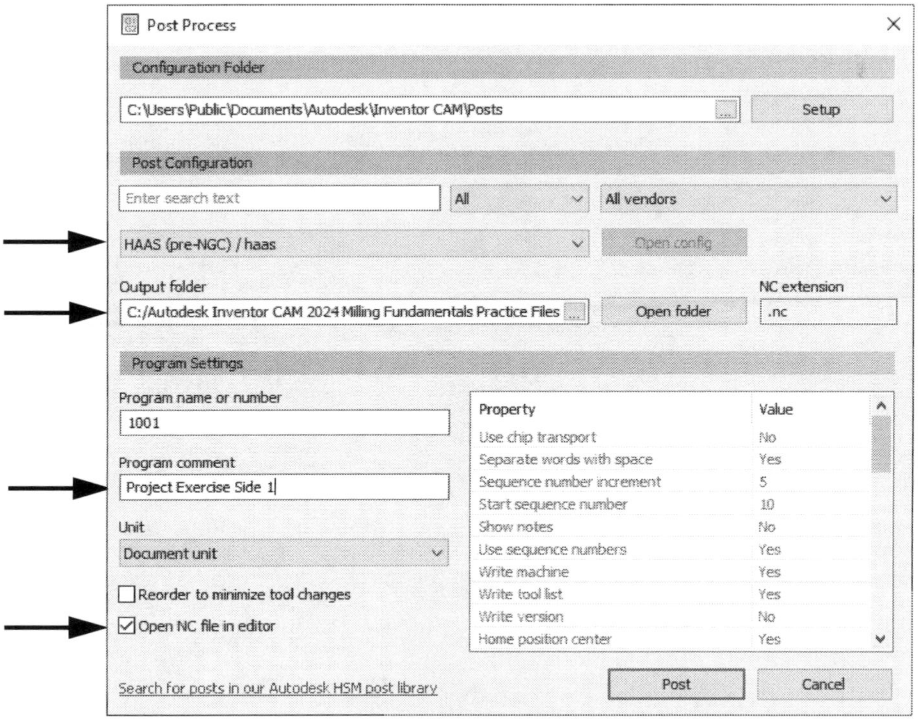

Figure 5–14

3. Click **Post**, then click **Save** to accept the default **1001.nc** file name and begin post processing. Verify the path is set to the Output folder location.

4. Once complete, the post processed machine code will open in an editor, as shown in Figure 5–15. In this case, the resulting code is N-code that is readable by a **HAAS (pre-NGC) / haas** machine. Scroll through the N-code to review it.

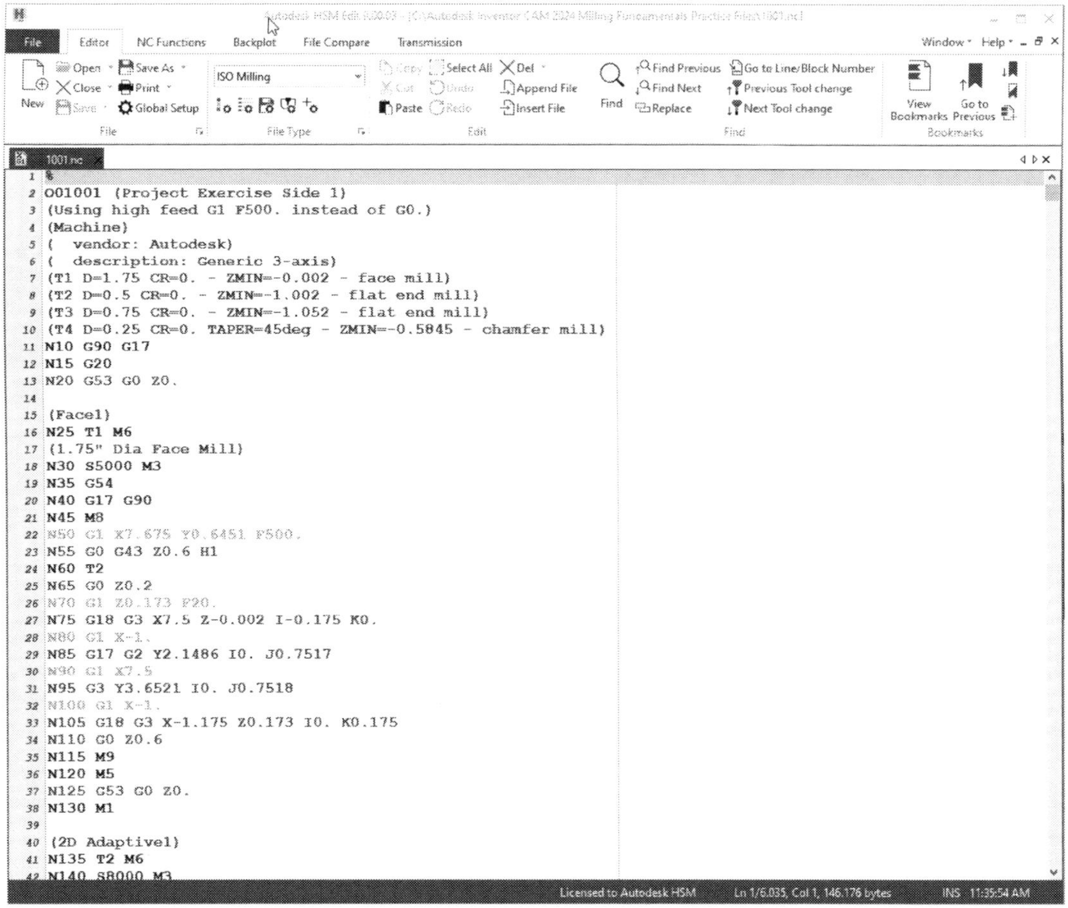

Figure 5–15

5. Close the file without making changes.
6. Return to the Inventor software. If time allows, consider completing the following:
    - Post process the Side 2 setup using the same CNC machine.
    - Suppress the 2D Pocket2 toolpath and remove the same material using a 2D Adaptive toolpath. Compare the two, considering their size and the N-code that is generated for each. These comparisons can help determine which toolpath is best for your machine.
7. Save the assembly file and close all files.

End of practice

Practice 5b
Generating Toolpaths II

Practice Objectives

- Import a tool library.
- Create a setup that includes toolpaths to machine the top of the model.
- Post process an Inventor CAM setup to output the CNC code required to machine the model.
- Save selected toolpaths as templates.

In this practice, you will add a setup that will generate the required CNC code to machine the top of the model. To complete the project, you will also learn to save toolpaths for use as templates.

Task 1: Open the model and review its geometry.

1. Open **Collar.ipt** from the top-level practice files folder. Switch to the Model browser, if not already active. The model and Model browser display as shown in Figure 5–16. Review the model geometry that will be machined.

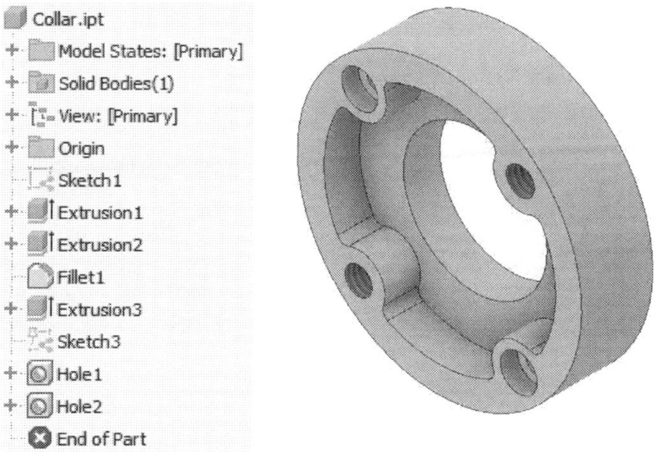

Figure 5–16

__Note:__ A completed model (__Collar_Final.ipt__) has been provided in the practice files folder. This model contains all completed setups and toolpaths that will be created in this project.

Task 2: Import a tool library.

To help simplify the tool selection process, you can import a tool library that has been provided.

1. Open the Tool Library.
2. To import a library into the model, right-click on the **Collar** name in the *Open Documents* area and select **Import Tools from Library**.
3. Locate, select, and open the **Collar.hsmlib** file from the top-level practice files folder. Ten tools are added to your tool library. These will be used throughout this project.

   ***Note:** You can export a library from an open document. Right-click on the document name in the Open Documents area and select **Export**.*

Task 3: Define the setup and toolpaths for the top of the model.

1. Activate the Inventor CAM environment and begin the setup for the top of the model. Consider the following:
   - On the *Stock* tab, change the stock mode to **Relative size cylinder**. Assume the stock is the exact diameter of the finished model and that no toolpaths will be run on the outside. Include a **0.05 in** offset of stock on the top of the model (*Frontside offset*). This stock will be machined in the first toolpath to ensure that the stock is flat and free of irregularities.
   - On the *Setup* tab, assign the **Generic 3-axis** machine and set **Milling** as the operation type. Ensure the WCS is set at the center of the stock, as shown in Figure 5–17.

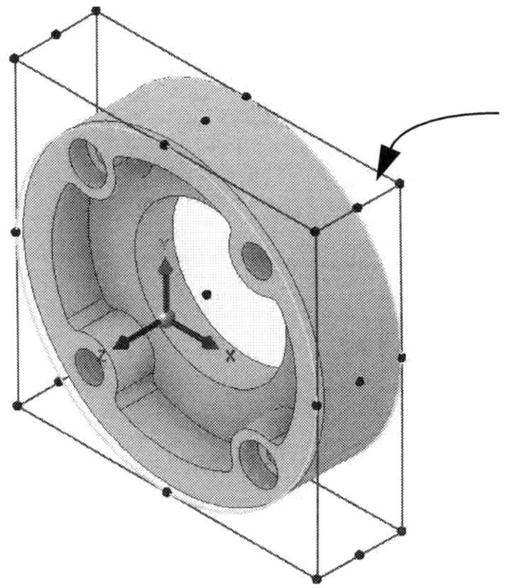

Figure 5–17

   - Complete the setup and rename the setup **Top**.

2. Add a Face toolpath to machine the top of the stock.
   - Assign the **#1 1 3/4" Face Mill** tool that was imported as one of the provided library tools.
   - Ensure that the top outside edge of the solid stock model is preselected as the geometry reference.
   - Ensure that the *Bottom Height* for the cut is set to **Model top**. The stock was designed offset from the top to ensure that a cutting pass was required to machine the top of the stock and clear it of any irregularities.
   - Set the *Stock offset* value to **0.25 in** to ensure that the tool clears the stock before turning for the next cutting pass.
   - Accept the remaining defaults and complete the toolpath.
   - Play the simulation and verify that there is no stock remaining at the top of the model.

   Note: *Rotate the model to the FRONT orientation using the ViewCube to easily recognize whether the toolpath removes the material as required. Additionally, turn off the display of the tool's shaft in the 2D orientation to view only the cutting tool's diameter, as shown in Figure 5–18.*

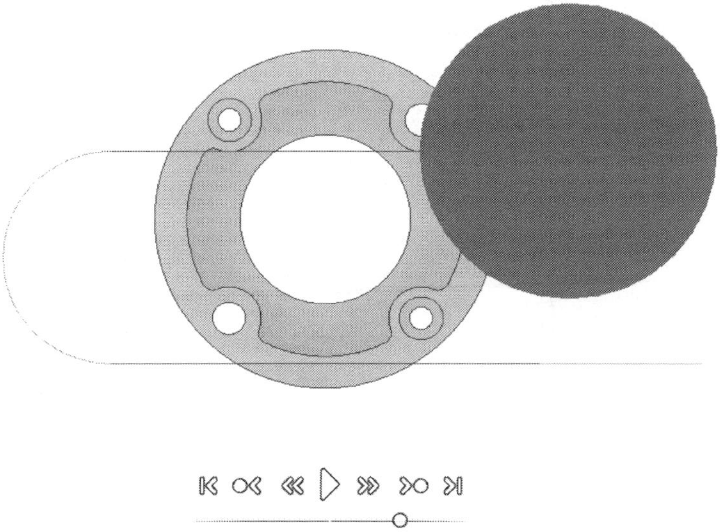

Figure 5–18

3. Return to the model's default orientation. Note how in this view, the simulation is not conveniently displayed. Using the ViewCube or standard Inventor orientation tools, rotate the model to a view similar to that shown in Figure 5–19.

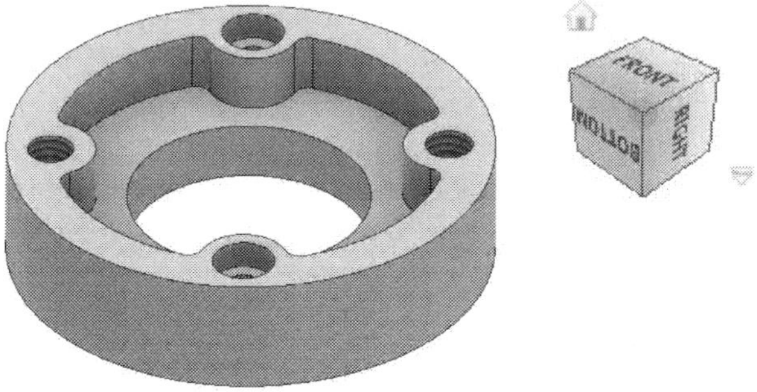

Figure 5–19

4. This view can be set as the Home view. Hover your cursor over the ViewCube and select  to expand a menu of options. Click **Set Current View as Home>Fixed Distance**.
5. Rotate the model again and return it to its new default Home view to ensure that it has been set properly. This is an orientation change only. It has no impact on the toolpaths or the CNC code that will be generated to machine the model.
6. Add a 2D Adaptive toolpath to clear the stock from inside the model.
   - Assign the **#2 1/4" Flat Endmill** tool for the toolpath.
   - Select the two edges shown in Figure 5–20 as the Pocket selection geometry references for the toolpath.

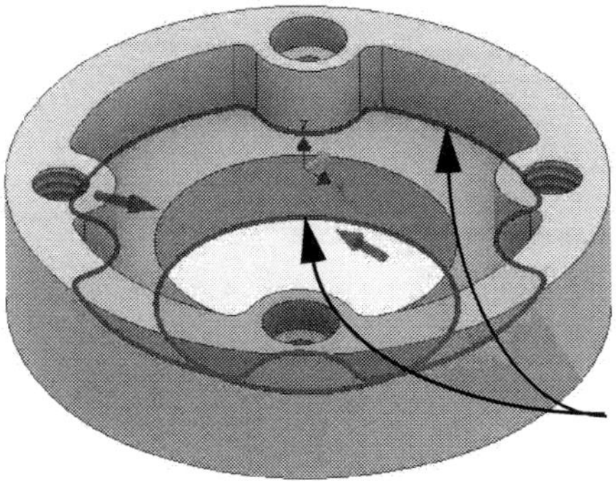

Figure 5–20

   - By default, the *Top Height* setting for the cut is set to Stock top; change this option to **Model top**. This sets the cut so that the toolpath starts at the top of the model because the previous facing toolpath has already removed the excess stock between the top of the stock and the top of the model.

- This roughing cut should remove all but **0.02 in** of stock both radially and axially. A finishing toolpath will be added later to finish the inside of the model.
- Change the *Retraction Policy* to **Minimum retraction**. This sets the retract so that on each cutting motion, the tool is prevented from a full retraction and simply retracts to clear the stock. This helps reduce cutting time, especially on larger models.
- This is an internal pocket so ensure the **Helix** *Ramp type* is used.
- Complete the toolpath and rename it as **2D Adaptive Rough 1**.
- Play the simulation. Notice how in the simulation, the tool retracts between the cuts for each edge. Because the *Top Height* was set to **Model top**, this is where the tool will begin its movement (helical) into the model. To be more efficient with this toolpath, you can create both cuts as separate paths.

7. Right-click on the **2D Adaptive Rough 1** toolpath and select **Create Derived Operation>2D Milling>2D Adaptive**. A duplicate of the selected toolpath is created.
   - Redefine the geometry that will be machined such that only the bottom circular edge is selected, as shown in Figure 5–21.
   - Change the *Top Height* setting for the cut to **Selection** and select the inside lower face, as shown in Figure 5–21.

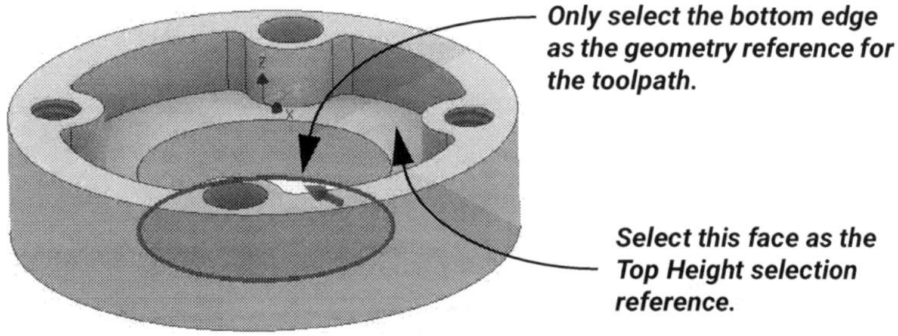

Figure 5–21

   - Leave the remaining defaults that were copied from the previous toolpath.
   - Complete the toolpath and rename it as **2D Adaptive Rough 2**.

8. Double-click on the **2D Adaptive Rough 1** toolpath to edit it.

   - Return to the (Geometry) tab and click to clear the pocket selections. Select the edge shown in Figure 5–22.

Note: *As an alternative to clearing all geometry selections, you can also press and hold <Ctrl> and select the bottom edge again to deselect it.*

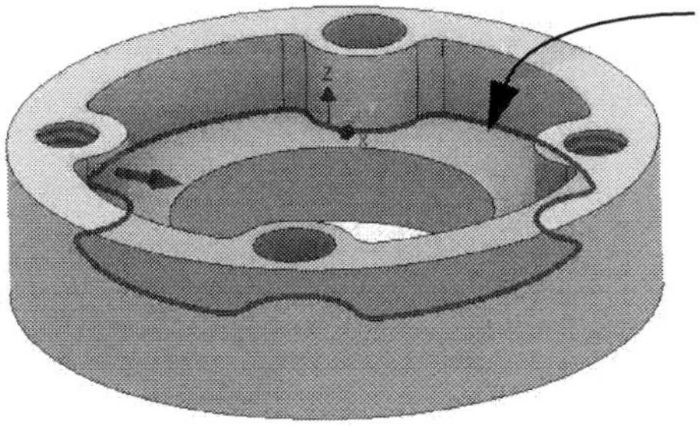

Figure 5–22

   - Click **OK** to complete the toolpath without making any further changes.

9. Play the entire simulation and verify there is at least 0.02 in. of stock remaining on the inside faces of the model. Note as well that there is stock at the bottom of the model, as shown in Figure 5–23.

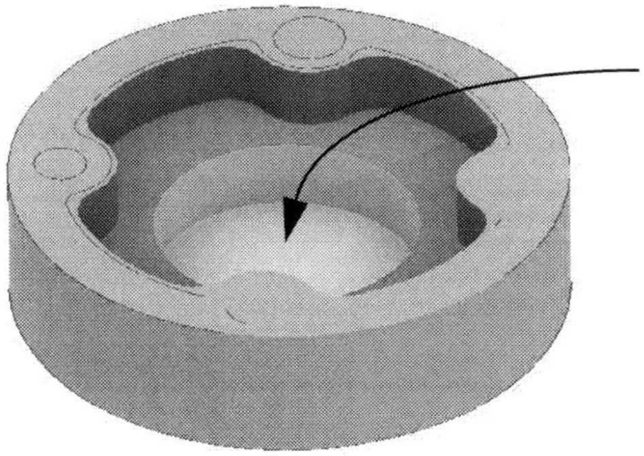

Figure 5–23

   - This leftover stock is not required. The toolpath this was derived from was set to leave stock axially because it was a roughing pass. This is not required for the second adaptive roughing toolpath, so it must be edited.

- Edit the toolpath and set it so that no stock is left axially and that the roughing pass cuts **0.02 in** below the selected edge, as shown in Figure 5–24.

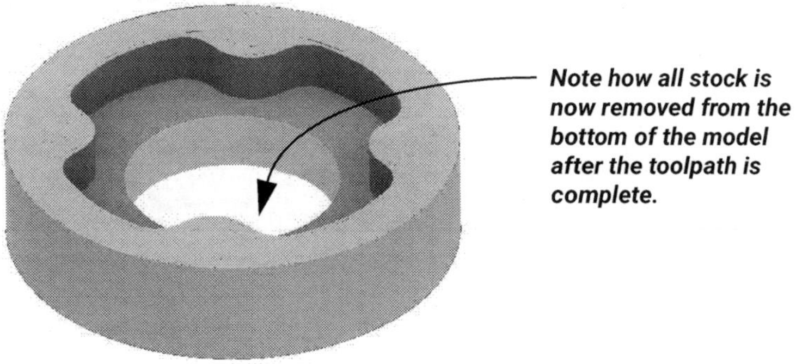

Figure 5–24

10. Add a 2D Pocket toolpath to clear all of the remaining stock from the internal pocket.

- Assign the **#3 1/8" Flat Endmill** tool for the toolpath.
- Define the geometry for this finishing pass in a similar way to what you did for the adaptive roughing passes. Begin by adding both edges.
- Change the *Top Height* reference to the top of the model.
- Ensure that **Finishing passes** is enabled and that the *Stepover* is set as **0.025 in**.
- Since this is a finishing toolpath, ensure that no stock is left axially or radially once this toolpath is complete.
- Set the *Ramp type* to **Plunge**.
- Complete the toolpath and rename it as **2D Pocket Finish**.
- Play the simulation and verify that all stock has been removed within the pocket.

Note: *The following two toolpaths (Spot Drill and Bore) normally may not both be added to machine a model. They have been included here to allow you to practice adding toolpaths.*

11. Spot drill the four holes on the top of the model.

- Assign the **#4 1/4" Spot Drill** tool for the toolpath.
- Select the four cylindrical faces shown in Figure 5–25 to define the spot drill.

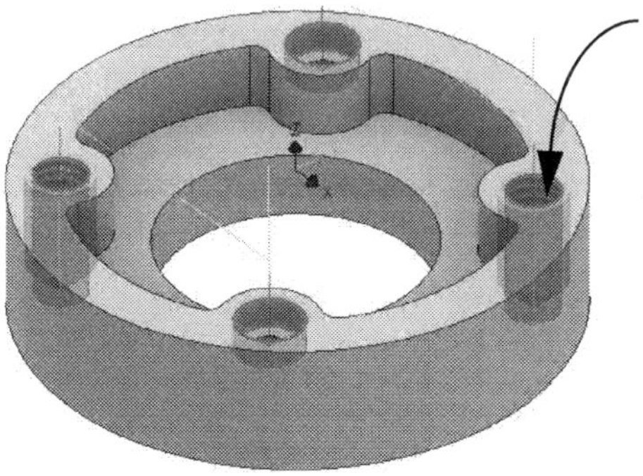

Figure 5–25

- The purpose of this toolpath is to spot drill the four holes to a depth of 0.03 in. Edit the *Bottom Height* option so that the depth of the hole is measured from the **Hole top** and is **0.03 in** depth.
- The cycle type should be **Drilling - rapid out**.
- Complete the toolpath and rename it **Spot Drill**.
- Play the simulation and verify that it removes material to begin further hole creation.

12. Create a Bore toolpath to create the counterbores for the holes on the top of the model. Counterbores can be machined using a Drill toolpath or a Bore toolpath. The Bore toolpath is used in this exercise to introduce it. A consideration on when a Bore toolpath is used versus a Drill toolpath would be whether the exact tool size is available or not. If an exact tool size is available, a Drill toolpath can be used.

- Assign the **#3 1/8" Flat Endmill** tool for the toolpath.
- Select the two cylindrical faces shown in Figure 5–26 to define the Bore toolpath.

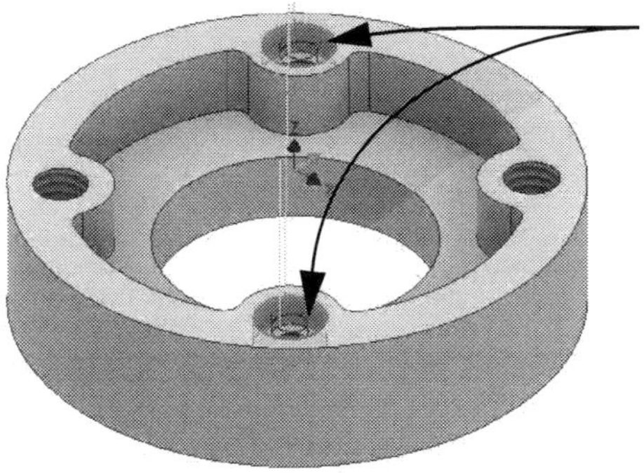

Figure 5–26

- No changes are required to define the heights for this toolpath.
- This toolpath will be a finishing cut. Enable the **Finishing passes** and set the *Stepover* value to **0.01 in**. No stock should be left after this toolpath is complete.
- The cycle type should be set as the default (**Preserve rapid movement**). Leave the values for this cycle type at their default values.
- Complete the toolpath and rename it **Counterbore**.
- Play the simulation and verify that it removes all material for the counterbore.

Note: *In this Bore toolpath, we did not have a metric tool to fit the counterbore size so the 1/8" Flat Endmill tool was used. In general, a Bore toolpath can be more accurate, so if the counterbore hole has a high tolerance requirement it may be the better choice of toolpath to use.*

13. Create a Drill toolpath to finish the two counterbore holes. The hardware that will be used for these holes, when it is assembled, is metric, so a metric drilling tool will be selected. Note that you can use a combination of imperial and metric tools as long as they are all available for your CNC machine.

- Assign the **#8 3mm Drill** tool for the toolpath.
- Select the two cylindrical faces shown in Figure 5–27.

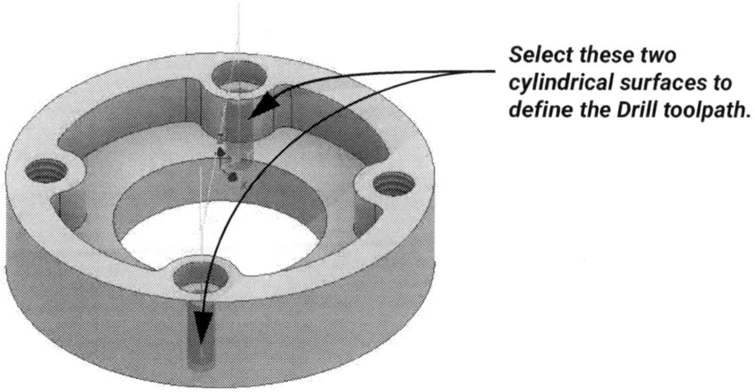

Figure 5–27

- To ensure the tip of the tool cuts through the entire model, select **Drill tip through bottom** in the *Bottom Height* area and set the *Break-through depth* to **0.02 in**.
- The cycle type should be **Chip breaking - partial retract**. Leave the values for this cycle type at their default values.
- Complete the toolpath and rename it as **3mm Drill**.
- Play a simulation for the last three hole toolpaths and verify that they remove all material through the bottom of the model.

Hint: Displaying a Simulation

To obtain a clearer picture of how a hole toolpath is cut, consider using the following view display settings prior to running a simulation:

- Set the View Display as **Shaded with Edges**.
- Create a Work Plane through the hole you would like to review. Use the created Work Plane as the reference for a **Half Section View**.
- Rotate the model parallel to the Work Plane.
- In the simulation, set the stock as **Transparent**.

In the example shown in Figure 5–28, the machining simulation is easily identified for the counterbore holes by manipulating the view display as described above.

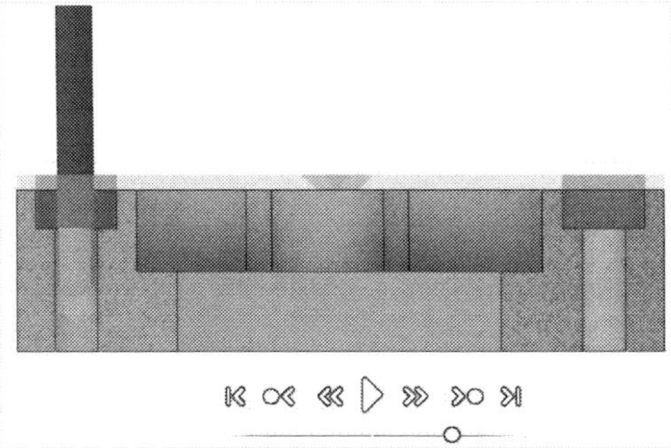

Figure 5–28

14. Derive a new Drill toolpath using the **3mm Drill** toolpath that was just created.

- Assign the **#9 5.2mm Drill** tool.
- Clear the previous hole selection and select the two cylindrical faces for the remaining tapped holes, as shown in Figure 5–29.

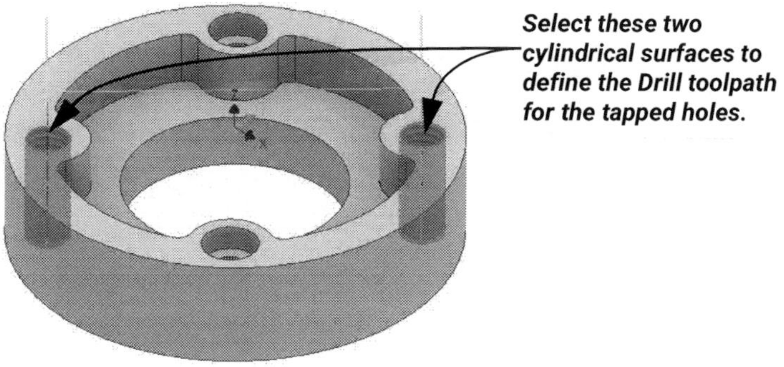

Figure 5–29

- The remaining settings from the derived drilling cycle are appropriate for these holes so no further changes are required.
- Complete the toolpath and rename it as **5.2mm Drill**.

15. Derive an additional Drill toolpath using the new **5.2mm Drill** toolpath that was just created. This will be modified to a tapping cycle.

- Assign the **#10 6 x 1mm right tap (M6)** tool.
- Set the cycle type to **Tapping**.
- Complete the toolpath and rename it as **6mm Tap**.

16. Play a simulation of the completed Top setup. Verify that it removes all material as required.

17. Save the model.

Task 4: Generate the CNC code required to machine the model.

In this task, you will post process the Top toolpaths to create the code required by the CNC machine. This task does not teach you how to edit the file as that is considered an advanced functionality that is outside the scope of this learning content.

1. In the Toolpath panel, click (Post Process). The Post Process dialog box opens. Define the following settings (as shown in Figure 5–30):
   - Select **HAAS (pre-NGC) / haas** as the post process configurator to be used.
   - Change the *Output folder* to your practice files folder, if not already set.
   - Note that the *Program name or number* is set by default to 1001. This was the value that was assigned by default when the Top setup was created.
   - Enter **Project Exercise Top** as the *Program comment* value to help identify the program.

   Note: *When post processing, Inventor CAM maintains the previously selected options for the fields in the Post Process dialog box.*

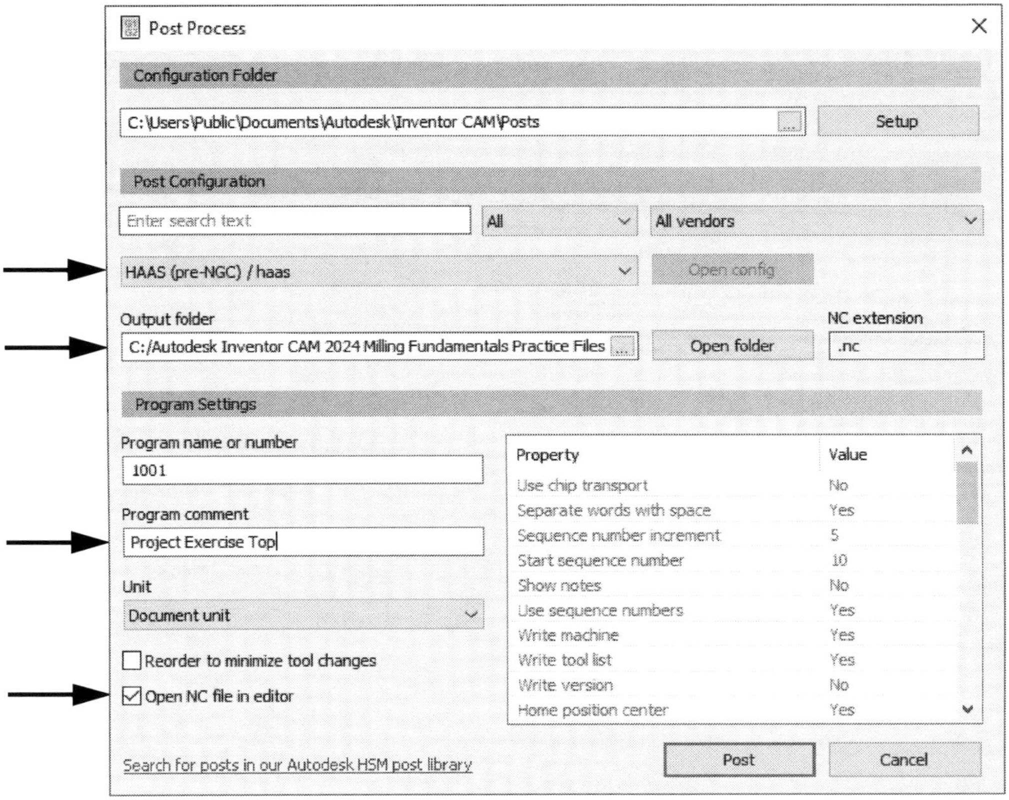

Figure 5–30

2. Click **Post**, then click **Save** to accept the default **1001.nc** file name. If you post processed the previous project, you will be prompted to overwrite the existing file. Rename it or overwrite it, as needed.
3. Once complete, the post processed machine code will open in an editor. Scroll through the N-code to review it. Close the file without making changes.
4. Return to Inventor and save the model.

Task 5: Create a toolpath template.

A toolpath template enables you to combine multiple toolpaths together such that they can be retrieved as a group into the same or different models. This is recommended for sets of toolpaths, like holes, that are routinely used in models. In this task, you will learn to create a template for a counterbore hole and import it for use in a new model.

1. To begin the template creation for a counterbore hole toolpath, complete the following such that the CAM browser appears as shown in Figure 5–31.
   - Create a new setup using the default settings. This is temporary so you can use the default values. Assign a name that helps you identify its purpose (e.g., Template Creation).
   - Copy the toolpaths that are to be included in the template to the new setup. In this case, copy **Spot Drill**, **Counterbore**, and **3mm Drill**.

   Note: *This is a recommended procedure to ensure that you do not make changes to the original toolpaths in the model. The new setup that is created is temporary and can be deleted once the template is created.*

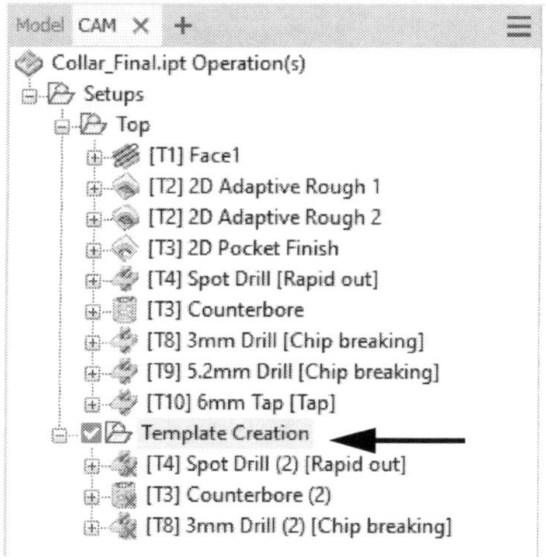

Figure 5–31

2. When defining any drilling toolpath, the cylindrical hole geometry must be selected. In these three toolpaths, the geometry was defined manually by selecting geometry on the model. To improve efficiency with geometry selection when a toolpath template is used, consider the other selection options on the (Geometry) tab.

   - Double-click on the **Spot Drill (2)** toolpath in the new setup to open and review its settings. Select the (Geometry) tab. Note that it still references the hole geometry. To make geometry selection more useful for a template, click to delete the existing reference selections. In the Hole mode drop-down list, select **Diameter range** and enter the minimum and maximum diameter values as shown in Figure 5–32. This enables you to define a size range so that when the counterbore hole template is used, holes will be preselected for you.

   Note: *Entering a smaller range helps to ensure that the exact holes are preselected in the model.*

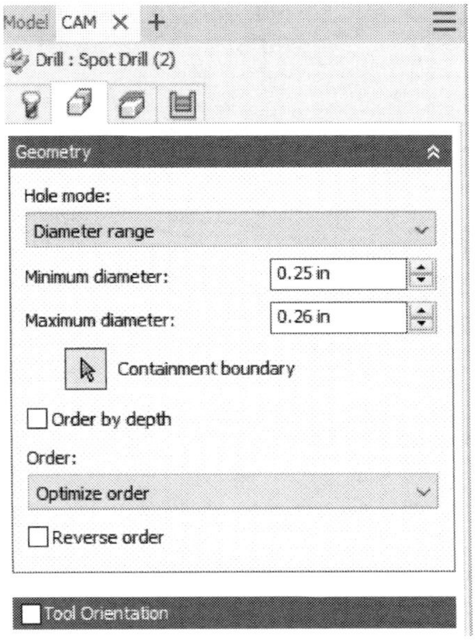

Figure 5–32

   - Modify the **Counterbore (2)** toolpath.Select the (Geometry) tab. It also references the hole geometry. To make geometry selection more useful for a template, click to delete the existing reference selections. In the Selection mode drop-down list, select **Diameter range**. Also ensure that **Holes only** is set for the *Feature type*. Enter the minimum and maximum diameter values as shown in Figure 5–33.

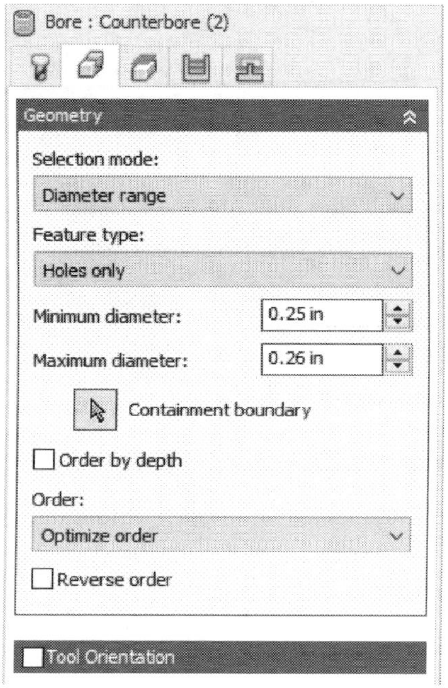

Figure 5–33

- Modify the **3mm Drill (2)** toolpath in a similar way to the Spot Drill so that its selection is based on a range of values. Enter **0.12 in** as the *Minimum diameter* value and **0.15 in** as the *Maximum diameter* value.
- Simulate the three modified toolpaths to ensure that the counterbore holes are machined properly.

3. Press and hold <Ctrl> and select the three modified toolpaths in the new setup. Right-click and select **Store as Template**, as shown in Figure 5–34.

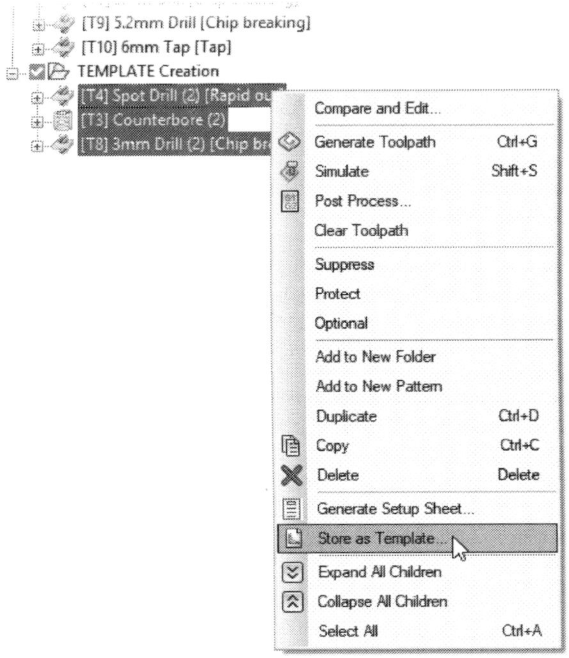

Figure 5–34

4. Navigate to your practice files folder and name the template as **3mm Counterbore.invhsm-template**. Click **Save**.
5. Open **Template Practice.ipt** from your practice files folder. This model has been provided for you to test the use of your new template. A setup has been created for you.
6. Right-click on **Setup1** and select **Create From Template**> **Select Template**. The Select Template dialog box opens. Navigate to your practice files folder, where you saved the template, and select **3mm Counterbore.invhsm-template**. Click **Open**.
7. All three toolpaths are added to the model. On the Toolpath panel, click (Generate).
8. Simulate the setup to ensure that the counterbore holes are machined properly.
9. Save the model and return to the Collar.ipt model.
10. Delete the temporary setup that was used to create the template.
11. Save the model.

Task 6: Optional tasks.

1. If time allows, consider completing the following:
   - Return to the Model browser and modify the diameter of the internal hole at the bottom of the model (Extrusion3) from 1.0 in. to **0.5 in**. Additionally, modify the overall diameter (Extrusion1) from 2.0 in. to **2.5 in**. Update the model geometry and the toolpaths to reflect this change. Simulate the Top setup and verify the toolpaths. Note how the stock size also updated to reflect the new size of the model.
   - Create a toolpath template to combine the drill and tapping toolpaths on the remaining two holes in the model. Test the template in the **Template Practice.ipt** model.
   - Create a Bottom setup, as necessary, to complete the CAM programming.
   - Post process the Bottom setup using the same CNC machine.
2. Save the models and close all windows.

End of practice

Chapter 6

3D Milling

The Inventor 3D Milling toolpath options allow you to generate the CNC code to machine models that have curved or contoured surfaces, thus requiring a third axis. In this chapter, you will learn about the more common of the 3D Milling toolpaths, including 3D Adaptive, 3D Pocket, Contour, Horizontal, Parallel, Pencil, and Scallop. Many of the remaining 3D toolpaths are created in a similar way using the standard palette to define all of the options.

Learning Objectives

- Add 3D Adaptive toolpaths to an Inventor CAM model.
- Add 3D Pocket toolpaths to an Inventor CAM model.
- Add Contour toolpaths to an Inventor CAM model.
- Add Horizontal toolpaths to an Inventor CAM model.
- Add Parallel toolpaths to an Inventor CAM model.
- Add Pencil toolpaths to an Inventor CAM model.
- Add Scallop toolpaths to an Inventor CAM model.

6.1 3D Milling Toolpaths

In general, 2D toolpaths are used to machine models that have vertical and horizontal surfaces. In 2D Milling, the tool moves in the Z axis, cutting is done parallel to the XY plane and is feature based. 3D Milling allows for machining models that have curvature (i.e., contoured surfaces), and therefore references surfaces, faces, and edges on the model. For example, in Figure 6–1, the model displayed on the top can be machined using 2D toolpaths; however, the freeform shape shown on the bottom would require 3D toolpaths to machine it.

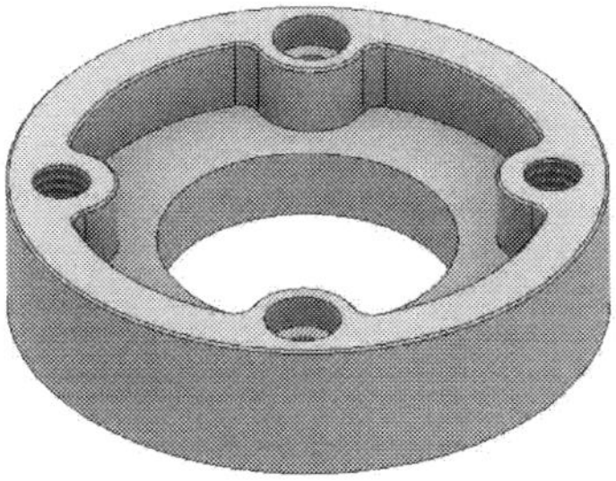

2D Milling strategies are used to generate the CNC code.

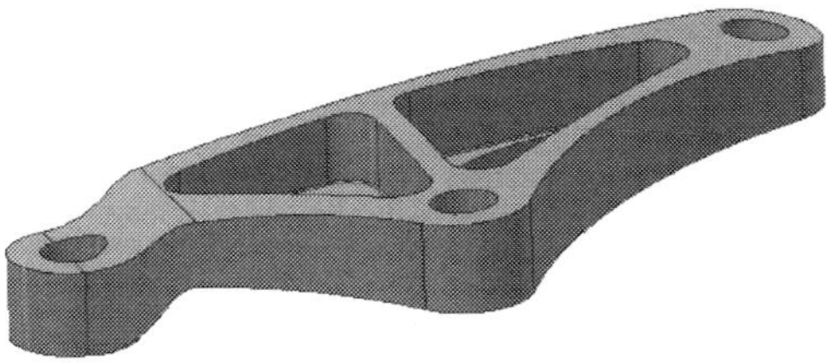

3D Milling strategies are used on contoured models like this to generate the CNC code.

Figure 6–1

In milling contoured surface, specific roughing and finishing toolpaths exist, as compared to in 2D milling where there are fewer toolpaths and the same type of toolpath can be used for both roughing and finishing. In general for 3D milling, the majority of the stock is removed with a roughing toolpath which leaves a poorer quality stepped surface. To finish the surface, more refined toolpaths are used that remove less material while leaving a higher quality contoured surface. It is common that multiple toolpaths with smaller and smaller tools may be required to mill the desired surface finish.

Figure 6–2 shows multiple stages of the milling process to obtain an acceptable surface finish for the top surface of the contoured model shown in Figure 6–1. Note that the toolpaths used to create the pockets and holes are not shown.

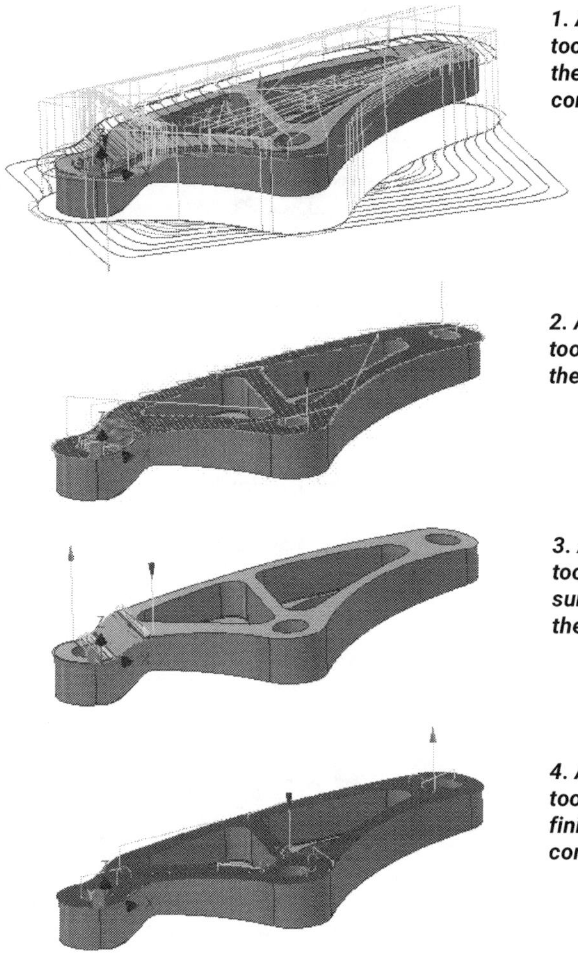

1. An Adaptive 3D Milling roughing toolpath is initially used to remove the majority of stock from the contoured model.

2. A Parallel 3D Milling finishing toolpath is used to further smooth the top of the contoured model.

3. A Contour 3D Milling finishing toolpath is used to refine the final surface on the steeper portion of the top of the contoured model.

4. A Scallop 3D Milling finishing toolpath is used for the final finishing pass on the top of the contoured model.

Figure 6–2

Inventor CAM provides functionality to allow for both 2D and 3D Milling Toolpaths. The interface for both are the same. In previous topics, you learned how to create a setup and use the toolpath palette interface to create toolpaths within your setup. For 3D, the process is the same. The main difference is specific to the options that are available in the 3D toolpath palettes. In this section, you will learn about the more commonly used 3D toolpaths. The main focus will be with respect to how the toolpaths are used (roughing/finishing), how to define the geometry to contain the tool to specific areas, as well as unique 3D milling options that you can consider when using these toolpaths.

Hint: Creating a 3D Toolpath

The default settings for many of the 3D Milling toolpaths may produce an acceptable result. When starting the creation of a new toolpath, it is recommended that you begin by defining the tool and geometry and then click **OK**. Simulate the result and review the required changes. Consider changing only one parameter at a time as you are working to refine the end result.

The following material describes the most commonly used 3D Milling toolpaths that are used in Inventor CAM. Figure 6–3 shows the available toolpaths on the 3D Milling panel.

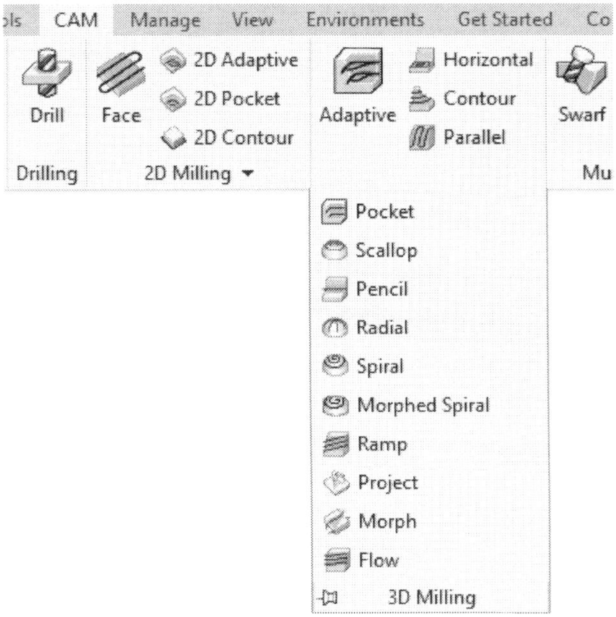

Figure 6–3

Adaptive

Similar to a 2D Adaptive toolpath, the **Adaptive** toolpath () for 3D Milling is best used for roughing and is considered a high-speed machining strategy. However, unlike a 2D Adaptive, this is done in three dimensions as the name implies. Compared to traditional CAM roughing toolpaths, where the focus is on maximum stepover distance, an **Adaptive** toolpath allows you to specify the optimal load of the cutter. This sets the maximum amount of engagement that the tool should maintain during the cutting path. The toolpath that is generated avoids abrupt direction changes and is automatically optimized to provide uniform and even tool load. The result is faster material removal while at the same time increasing the life of your tool.

In the example shown in Figure 6–4, an Adaptive toolpath was created to quickly remove large portions of stock over and around the contoured surfaces.

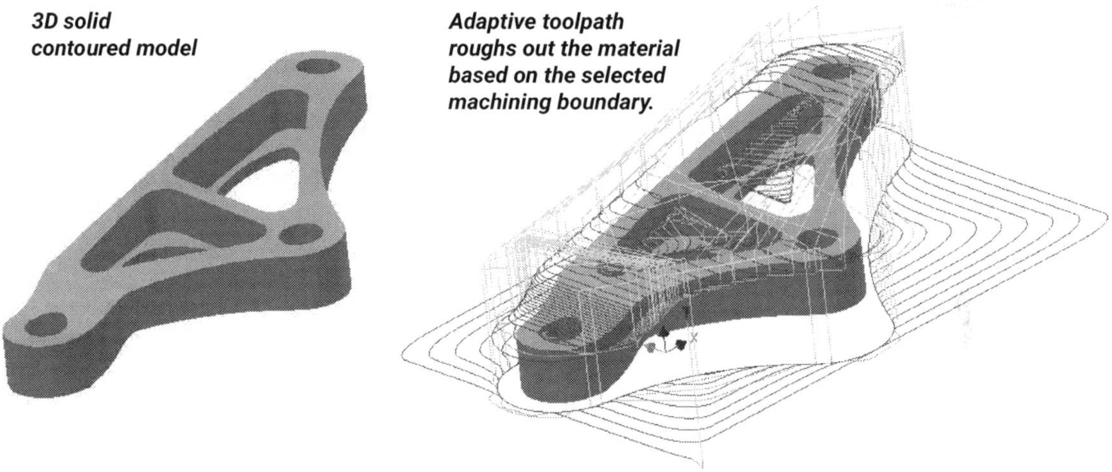

Figure 6–4

You are not required to select geometry to define the machining area for an Adaptive toolpath. It automatically recognizes the stock as the boundary and references the model geometry to determine the material that is to be cut. The geometry and tool containment can be modified, if needed. Consider the following:

- Define a machining boundary to define the stock to cut. The options include **Bounding Box**, **Silhouette**, or **Selection**. Leave the machining boundary set to None if you want the cutter to extend to the stock boundary. Silhouette is useful when you've already contoured the outer boundary of the part profile. Use Selection to assign 2D sketch lines as a boundary. They are described below and shown in Figure 6–5.
  - The **Bounding Box** option contains the toolpath within a box that encompasses the full extents of the model as viewed looking down the Z axis onto the XY plane.
  - The **Silhouette** option contains the toolpath within a boundary that is defined by the part shadow (silhouette) of the model on the XY plane.

- The **Selection** option contains the toolpath within a boundary that is defined by selected geometry (edge or surface).

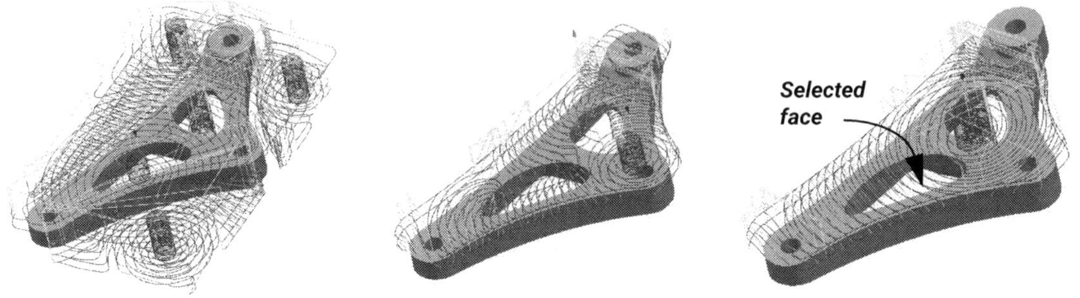

Machining Boundary is set as Bounding Box.

Machining Boundary is set as Silhouette.

Machining Boundary is set as Selection.

Figure 6–5

- The **Rest Machining** area (**Re**maining **St**ock) on the (Geometry) tab can be enabled to limit the toolpath so that it only removes material that was not removed in any previous toolpaths. Rest machining is typically used in secondary roughing operations. It limits the toolpath to only cut the remaining stock that a previous larger diameter tool couldn't cut.
- The **Model** area on the (Geometry) tab can be enabled and used to override the model geometry that was defined in the setup. Optionally, you can opt to remove or maintain the setup model in addition to a selected new model. This option is not available for a 2D Adaptive toolpath. This is primarily used when adding toolpaths to an assembly file where there are multiple solid bodies to choose from. It allows you to limit the toolpath to only the selected model and its surfaces.

The plane heights that are defined on the (Heights) tab can also be used to contain the tool to a specific area during an Adaptive toolpath.

The (Passes) tab also contains some options that should be considered to further control the 3D Adaptive path. These were not available for a 2D Adaptive path.

Note: *It is recommended that you review the toolpath using the default settings initially and then refine the parameters on the Passes tab one at a time.*

- Use the **Machine shallow areas** option to include additional Z-level passes in shallow areas on the surface. This allows for a smoother finish in the shallow area on the contoured surfaces. The tooltip image shown in Figure 6–6 shows the difference in the resulting toolpath when the option is enabled or not. The **Machine shallow areas** option is also available for Contour and Pocket 3D Milling toolpaths.

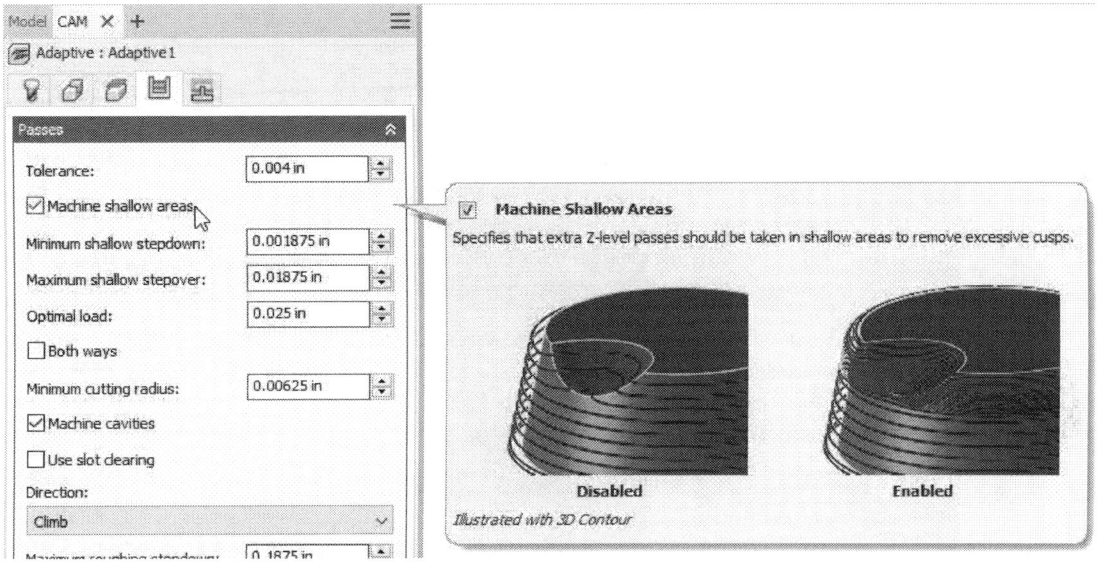

Figure 6–6

- Enable the **Machine cavities** option to include interior pockets in the 3D Adaptive toolpath. If this is left disabled, any pocket on the surface is left unmachined. If enabled, the additional **Use slot clearing** option is made available to further control the strategy on how the pocket is machined, as shown in the command's tooltip in Figure 6–7.

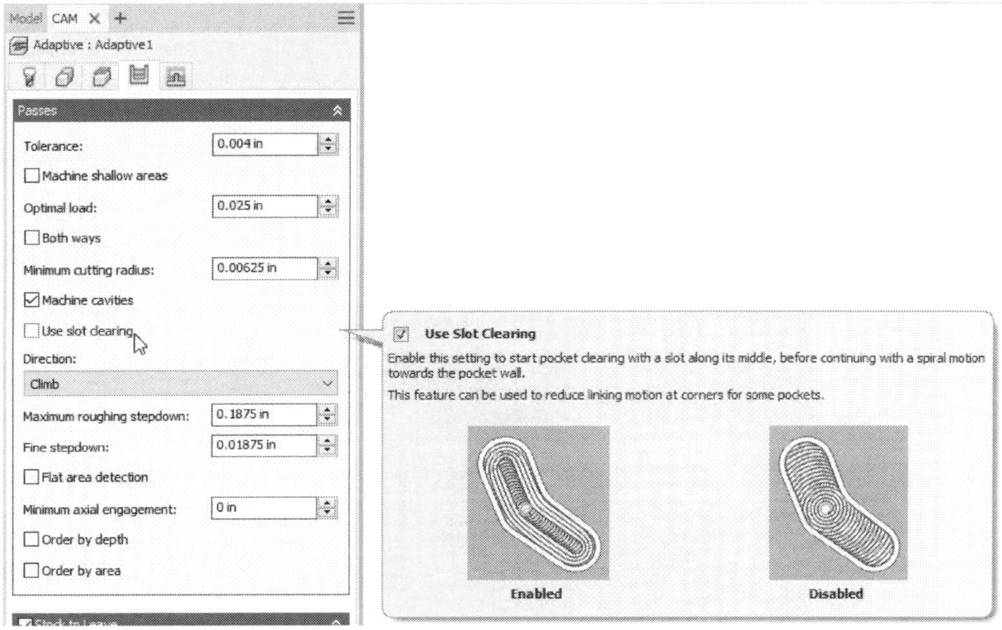

Figure 6–7

- A **Fine Stepdown** value can be assigned in a 3D Adaptive toolpath to control the stepdown size for intermediate steps that are between the roughing stepdown values. These steps are upwards in the direction of the tool axis. In other CAM softwares, this is sometimes referred to as "Step Cutting".
- Consider enabling the **Flat area detection** option in the *Passes* area to control how the toolpath is defined as it contacts flat areas and peaks. If disabled, the assigned stepdown value is used regardless of the geometry. If enabled, the toolpath attempts to detect the heights of the flats or peaks in the geometry and machines at that level. The use of the Flat area detection option can increase calculation time for the toolpath.
- Assign a **Minimum axial engagement** value to ensure that at least one flute stays engaged with the stock at all time when cutting at any intermediate steps. This can help reduce wear and chatter on the tool. Minimum axial engagement is important when using a small "Fine Stepdown" value. This keeps at least one flute engaged when stepping upward in the direction of the tool axis.
- The **Fillets** area can be enabled for a 3D Adaptive toolpath as well as all other 3D toolpaths. It enables you to include a toolpath fillet function within the path that avoids creating sharp corners. By assigning a fillet value the tool avoids sharp turns so that a higher feedrate can be maintained and it helps prevent marks on the machined model. Note that the fillet size overrides the Stock to Leave settings. Ensure that the necessary finishing toolpaths are included to remove any remaining stock.

Pocket

The **Pocket** toolpath for 3D Milling is a conventional roughing strategy (shown in Figure 6–8). Unlike a 2D Pocket, a 3D Pocket toolpath uses model surface recognition to determine areas that can be machined with the selected tool. Boundary selections are not required, but can be used to limit the area being milled. In contrast to Adaptive, 3D Pocket uses a traditional spiral stepover strategy that maintains the same stepover distance throughout. 3D Pocket isn't as efficient as Adaptive, but will leave a better surface finish on the floor of pocket features.

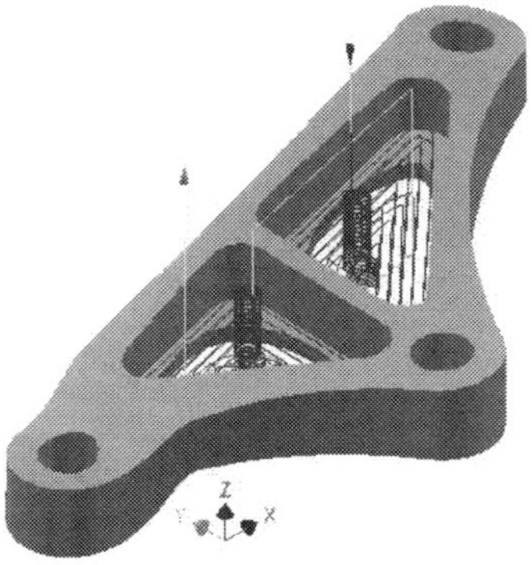

Figure 6–8

Contour

The (Contour) toolpath in the 3D Milling panel is recommended for use on steep or vertical faces similar to that shown in Figure 6–9. It can be used for either a semi-finishing or finishing cut. Many of the settings in the Contour palette are similar to other 3D Milling toolpaths.

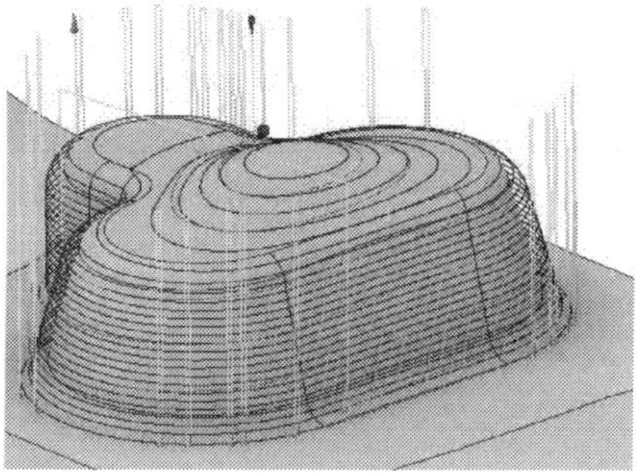

Figure 6–9

Consider the following specifically for the Contour toolpath:

- The cutting area for a Contour toolpath defaults to using the Silhouette option that is defined by the part shadow (silhouette) of the model on the XY plane. If this default doesn't appropriately define the machining area, you can refine the machining boundary using the **Bounding Box** or **Selection** options.

- A **Slope** area is included on the (Geometry) tab, to enable you to specify a range for the face steepness (angle) that will be included in the toolpath. The tooltip shown in Figure 6–10 shows how you can use the From and To slope angle values to control the faces that are included.

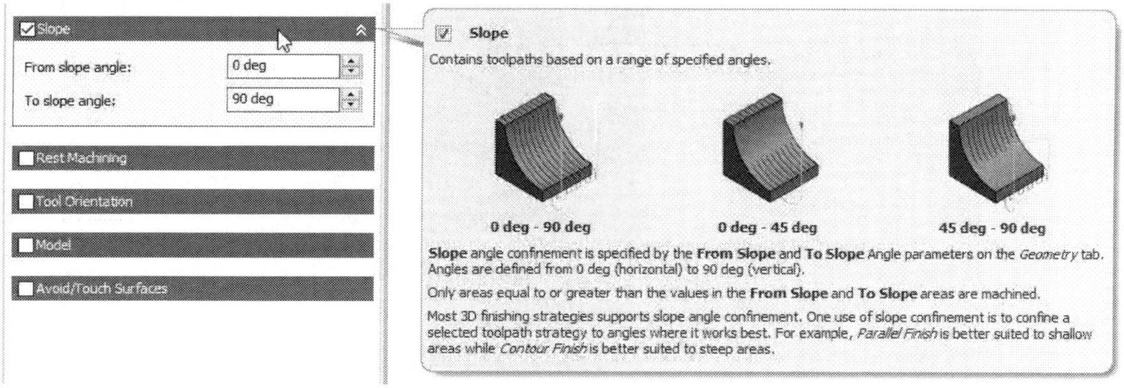

Figure 6–10

- The **Avoid/Touch Surfaces** area on the (Geometry) tab can be used to control whether surfaces are either included or not in the Contour toolpath. Using the selection tool select any surface(s) that are to be either avoided or included. With the Touch surfaces option disabled, the selected surfaces are avoided with the option enabled the selected surfaces are the only surfaces included, as shown in the tooltip image shown in Figure 6–11.

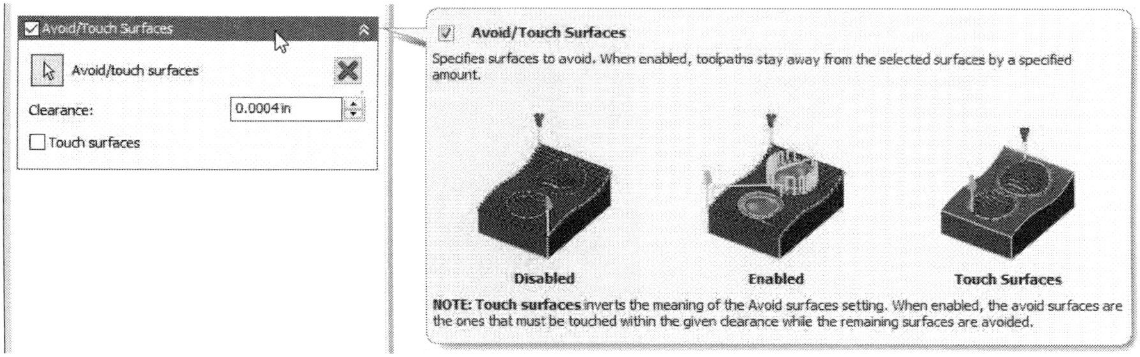

Figure 6–11

- The **Machine shallow areas** option on the (Passes) tab can also be used to include additional Z-level passes in shallow areas on the surface. This allows for a smoother finish in the shallow area on the contoured surfaces. Figure 6–12 shows the resulting toolpath when the option is enabled. In this case, the shallow surface is convex and provides for a cleaner finish at the top of the model.

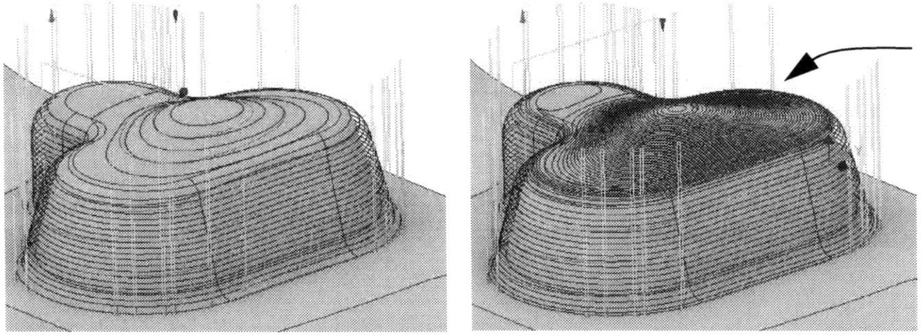

Machine shallow areas disabled ***Machine shallow areas enabled***

Figure 6–12

- A Contour toolpath should begin away from the part and ramp in to begin cutting. This can be defined in the *Leads & Transitions* area on the (Linking) tab, in the same way as was done for a 2D Contour. However, unlike a 2D Contour toolpath, the *Ramp* area (also on the Linking tab) is not optional for 3D Milling. You must specify how the tool will move down to cut each depth (Plunge, Profile, or Helix) and define how the toolpath should transition between each depth. The transition options include **No contact**, **Straight line**, **Shortest path**, and **Smooth** and can be used in conjunction with the other values to customize the toolpath.

Hint: Contour vs. Ramp

Similar to a Contour toolpath, the Ramp toolpath ( ) is also used for finishing on steep contoured surfaces. Unlike a Contour toolpath that machines each pass at a constraint Z, a Ramp toolpath maintains tool engagement at all times and ramps down as it cuts.

Horizontal

The (Horizontal) toolpath can be used on flat areas or shelved flat areas of the model geometry and is unique to 3D Milling. The flat areas are automatically recognized on the contoured model (as shown in Figure 6–13); however, if any automatically detected flat areas are not required, you must explicitly use the *Machining boundary* options to define the required flat areas.

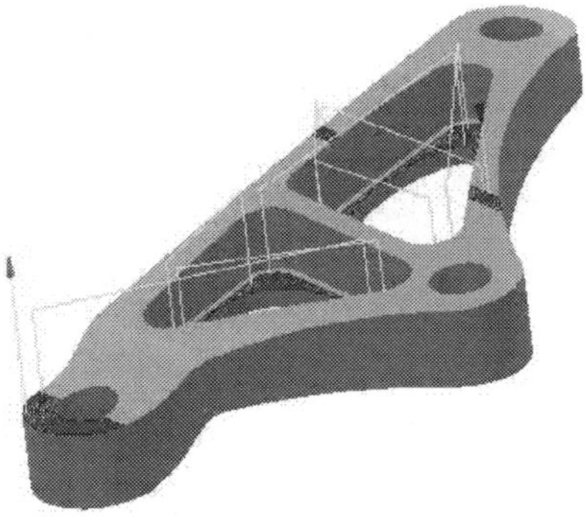

Figure 6–13

The toolpath is similar to a Pocket toolpath in that it cuts material with an offsetting path. The **Manual stepover** option on the (Passes) tab can be enabled to set the stepover size to manage the chip load on the tool. **Axial offset passes** is another option that enables you to manage the depth of cut and machine at several Z direction increments before the final depth.

Parallel

The (Parallel) toolpath is one of the most common finishing sequences that is used on the 3D Milling panel. The cutting paths are parallel to one another in the XY plane and follow the contoured surface in the Z direction, as shown in Figure 6–14.

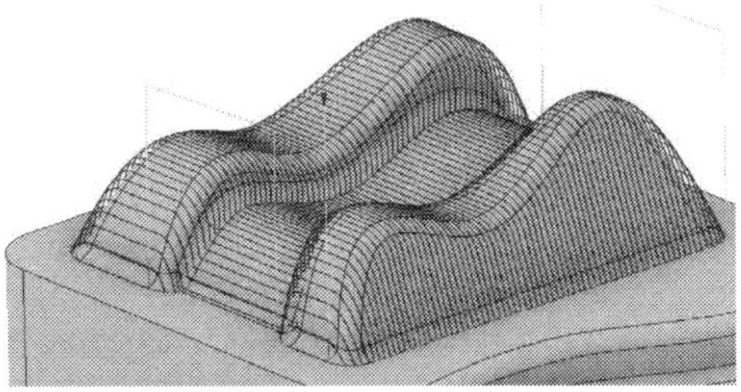

Figure 6–14

Many of the settings in the Parallel palette are similar to a Contour toolpath; however the main difference is that Parallel is primarily used for shallow areas, but can be used on any shape, where Contour is better suited for steep areas. Because the direction is limited, it is most commonly used as a semi-finish strategy prior to Scallop or Morphed Spiral.

The commonly edited parameters for the Parallel toolpath are focused on the (Passes) tab in the *Passes* area and include the following:

- The angular cutting direction in the XY plane can also be customized for the Parallel toolpath by entering a **Pass direction** angular value. Figure 6–15 shows two different results using different angular values.

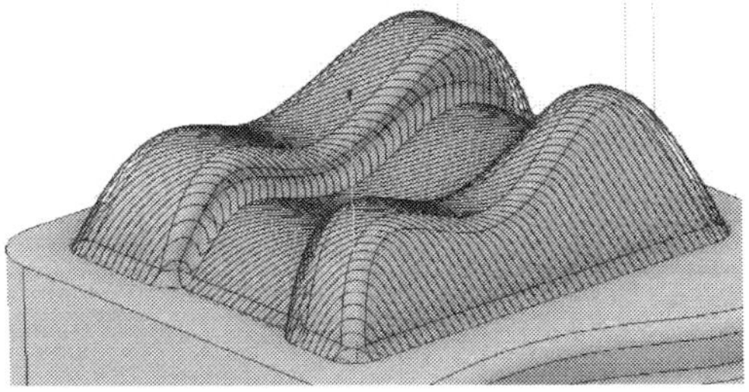

Pass Direction angle set at 45

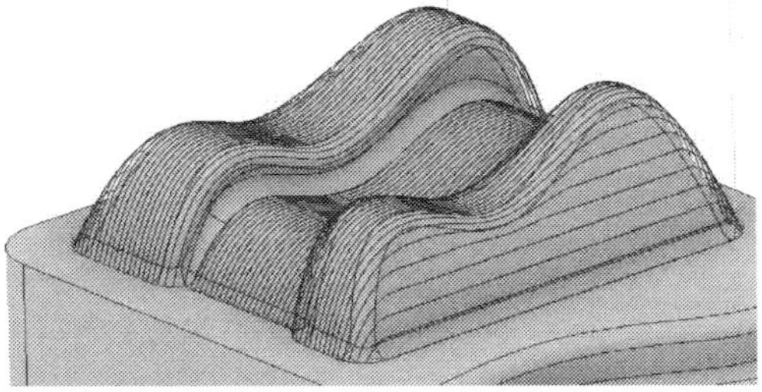

Pass Direction angle set at 90

Figure 6–15

- The **Machine steep areas** option has unique settings that allows you to use the Parallel toolpath to machine a steep area (Machine steep areas), if necessary. Otherwise, using a Contour toolpath is recommended. Once enabled, it allows you to add stepdown and stepover values to the cutting path (as shown in the steeper areas of Figure 6–16).

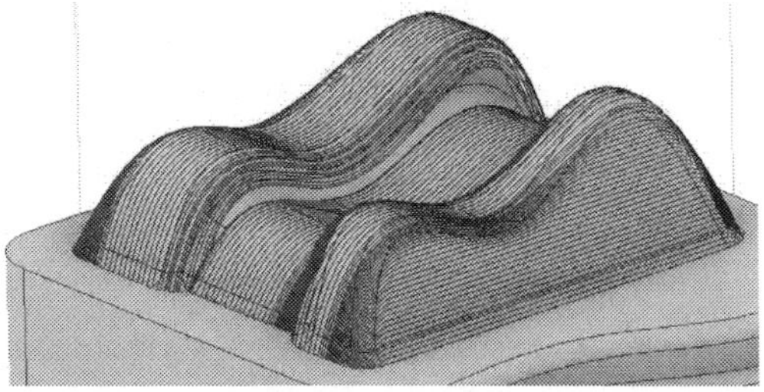

Figure 6–16

- The **Add perpendicular passes** option can also be set to include additional toolpaths that run perpendicular to the first direction. This helps reduce cusps being created as machined.
- The **Simple ordering** option enables the system to force ordering across the cutting direction, instead of ordering by shortest distance. This will increase time; however, it can help to eliminate marks on the machined surface.
- The *Direction* of each parallel cut can be customized using either the **One way**, **Other way**, or **Both ways** options. If **Both ways** is used, the system optimizes the path to generate the shortest toolpath.The tooltip shown in Figure 6–17 includes images of these cutting options. This setting is used if you want to maintain a consistent milling direction, either climb or conventional.

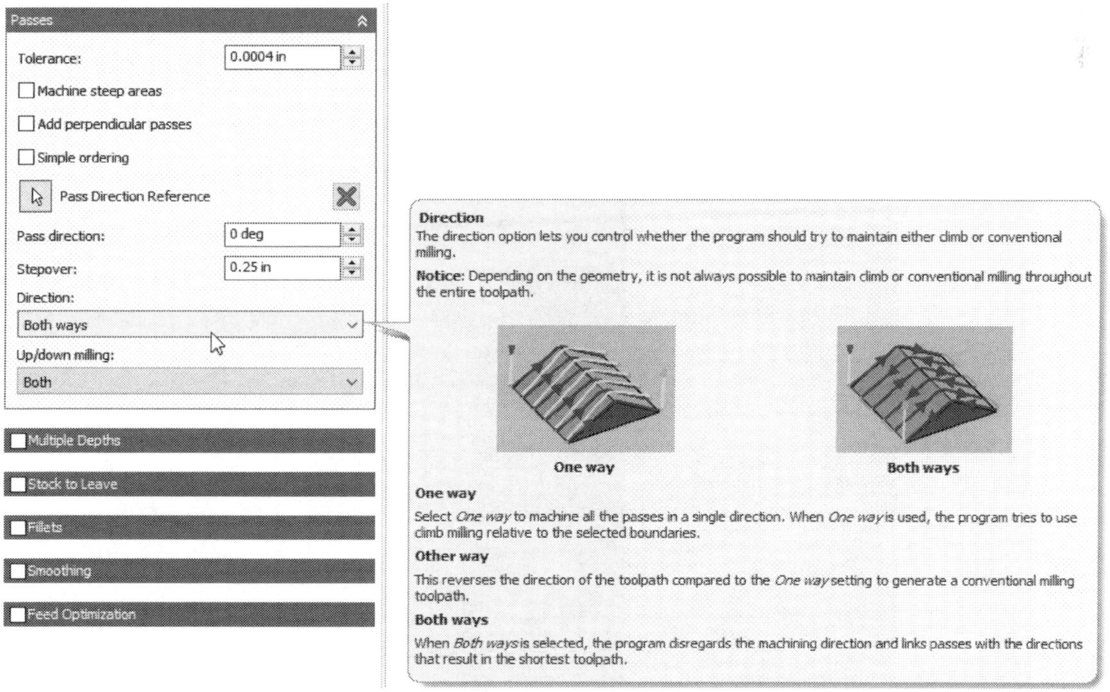

Figure 6–17

- The Up/down milling drop-down list enables you to customize whether the toolpath is generated using upwards toolpaths (**Up milling**), downwards (**Down milling**), or whichever generates the shortest toolpath (**Both**). This breaks up the passes so that the surface is only machined in upward or downward moves. This is helpful when using insert cutters that are restricted to a specific cutting direction.

Pencil

The (Pencil) toolpath is generally used as a final cleanup toolpath after other finishing strategies. It is used to create toolpaths along internal corners and fillets using single or multiple passes, as shown in Figure 6–18. The radii is smaller than or equal to the corner radius of the selected tool.

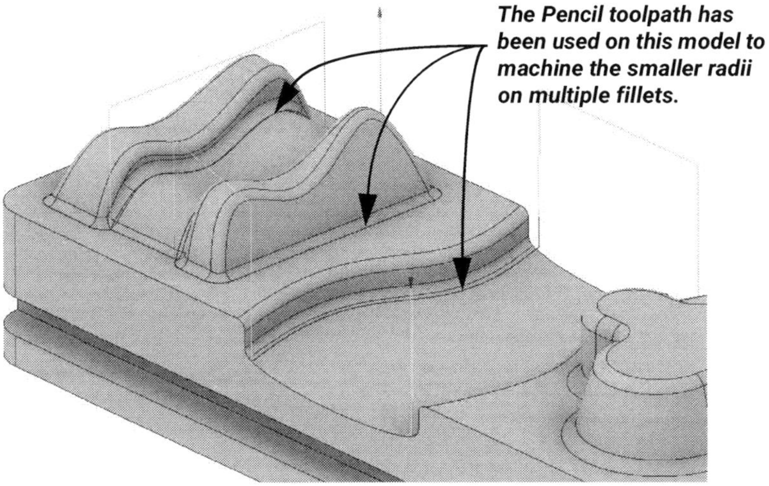

Figure 6–18

- Similar to the other 3D Milling toolpaths, the edges for the toolpath are automatically identified using the **Silhouette** option. This can be modified if necessary to define specific edges. For example, the Silhouette option will identify the edges in counterbore holes that are parallel with the XY plane. These should be removed from the selection set as these edges would normally be machined with drilling sequences.

  Note: *The remaining options on the (Geometry) tab are the same as the other 3D Milling toolpaths that were previously discussed.*

- The main parameter that controls the Pencil toolpath is the **Bitangency angle** option that is located on the (Passes) tab. It allows you to specify the angular measurement between the two points of contact for the final pass along the internal corner or fillet. Multiple passes may be needed until the tool's touch points reach the specified angle. This value also helps determine how small the internal corners and fillets are that are detected for machining. The tooltip shown in Figure 6–19 includes images of how the angle is measured.

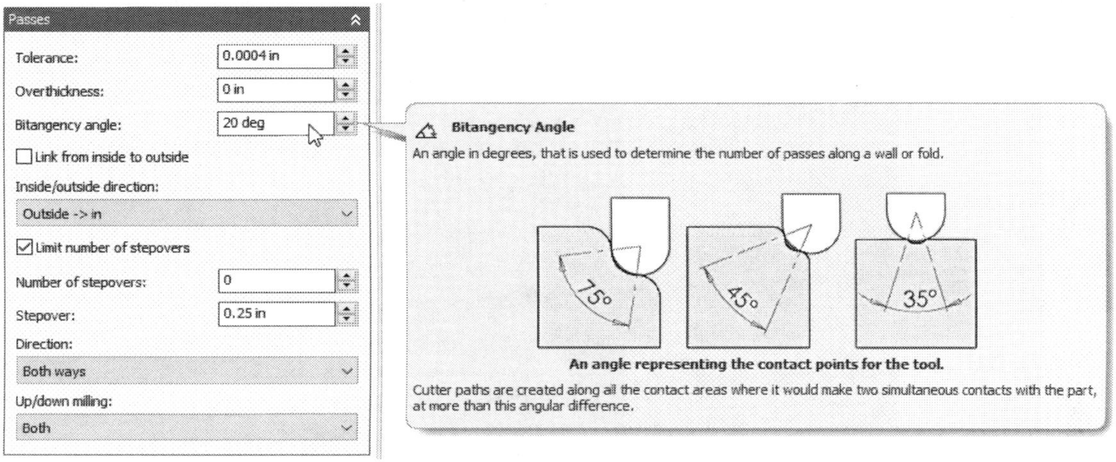

Figure 6–19

- The **Overthickness** value can also be incorporated to help control the number of passes. This value incorporates additional thickness to the tool radius to help calculating the number of passes. The Bitangency value is also maintained when an Overthickness value is incorporated. The tooltip shown in Figure 6–20 includes an image of how the overthickness is measured. This is used when the fillet radius is slightly greater than the tool radius. For example, when you have a fillet with a corner radius of 0.20" and you want to machine it with a tool 0.375" Ball Nose end mill.

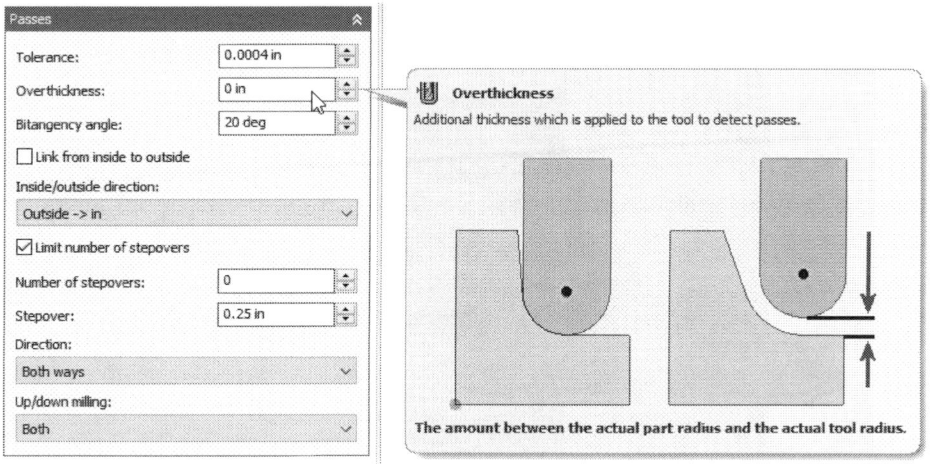

Figure 6–20

- The remaining options in the *Passes* area enable you to control the direction of the tool, step over, and milling strategy, similar to other 3D Milling toolpaths.

Scallop

Similar to a Pencil toolpath that is used for cleanup after another semi-finishing toolpath is run (i.e., Parallel or Contour), the (Scallop) toolpath is also a cleanup toolpath that provides the final finish on a contoured surface, as shown in Figure 6–21.

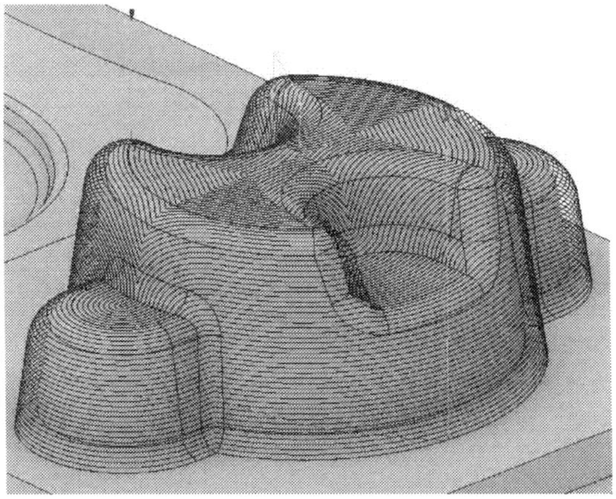

Figure 6–21

The Scallop toolpath is also commonly known as a Constant Stepover Finishing toolpath. It generates passes that are at a constant distance from one another (stepover) and works from the exterior to the interior maintaining the constant stepover. Similar to the Parallel and Contour toolpaths, it can also be limited by a Slope angular range.

Morphed Spiral

Scallop toolpaths are generally used for highly contoured, free-form surfaces; however, a (Morphed Spiral) toolpath can also be considered if the surfaces are not overly steep. This toolpath provides a smoother toolpath which helps in avoiding visible marks on the model that might be caused by sharp corners, changes in direction, and linking the generated passes when a Scallop toolpath is used.

Figure 6–22 shows the top view of a Morphed Spiral and Scallop toolpath for the model shown in Figure 6–22. Note that the Morphed Spiral toolpath has a smoother path and would leave fewer visible marks after machining.

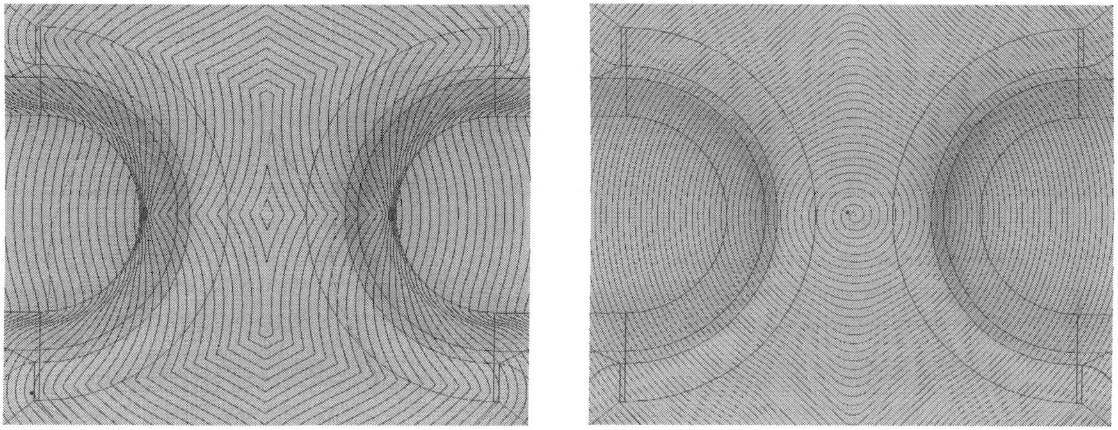

Scallop Toolpath ***Morphed Spiral***

Figure 6–22

For a Morphed Spiral toolpath, the (Passes) tab enables you to customize the pass settings to further refine the result:

- Select a cutting direction for the path by selecting the **Inside -> out**, **Outside -> in**, or **Shortest machining distance** options. The **Shortest machining distance** option minimizes the ordering by distance and will choose a direction that has the shortest travel distance and machining time.
- By default, the toolpath is set to cut counterclockwise. To change to a clockwise direction, enable **Clockwise**.
- Customize the stepover by entering a custom value.
- Similar to other toolpaths, you can also determine if climb or conventional milling or up/down milling is used.

Spiral

The (Spiral) toolpath generates a spiral toolpath similar to a Morphed Spiral. It is generally used to machine round areas that tend to be relatively flat, similar to the geometry and toolpath shown in Figure 6–23.

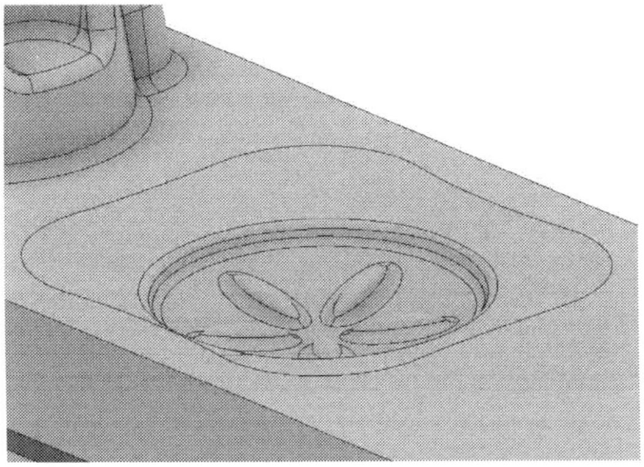

Spiral toolpaths are generally suited for round shallow areas.

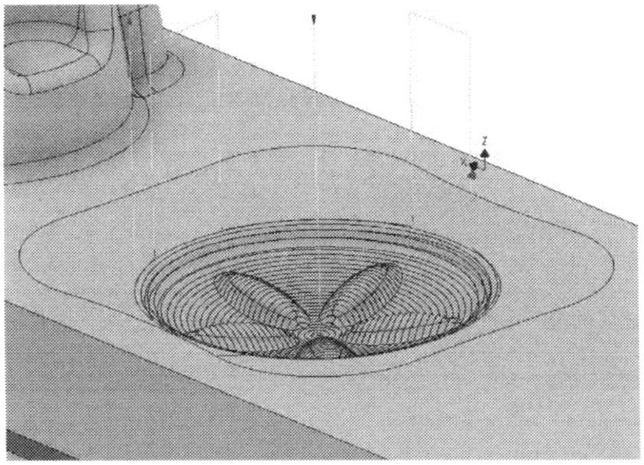

Spiral Toolpath

Figure 6–23

The following describe the main differences in the settings for Spiral versus the Morphed Spiral toolpath:

- A center point should be defined for the toolpath to define the point at which the tool initially contacts the model at the beginning of the path and from which the spiraling path will begin. If no centerpoint is defined, a default is assumed. This reference point is defined on the (Geometry) tab.

- The (Passes) tab provides additional options to define the Spiral Mode. The available options are shown in the tooltip image in Figure 6–24. Additionally, you can set inner and outer limits for the radius value of the spiral toolpath. For example, if the inner limit is set at 0, the spiral toolpath begins at the centerpoint; otherwise, the toolpath begins at the defined Inner Limit value.

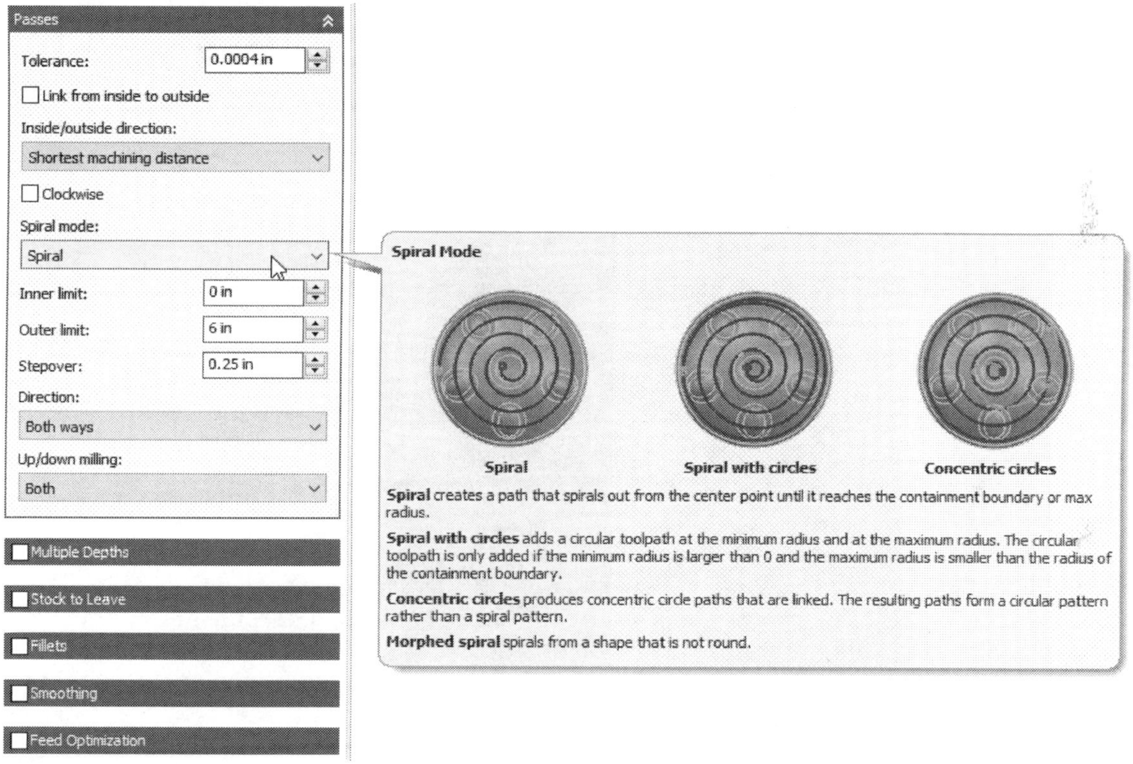

Figure 6–24

Radial

The (Radial) toolpath generates a toolpath that radiates along a contoured surface through a range of angles. Similar to how the Spiral toolpath uses a centerpoint reference to define the starting location for the path, a Radial toolpath also uses a centerpoint to define the angular motion. The Radial toolpath shown in Figure 6–25 is defined with a centerpoint and two selected boundaries, and passes through a full 360 degrees.

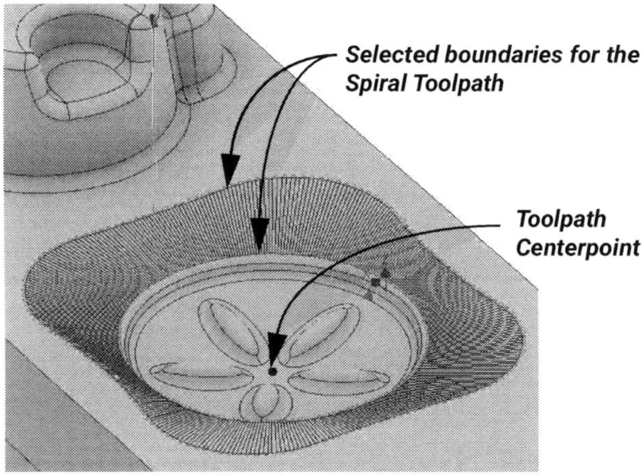

Figure 6–25

Similar to a Spiral toolpath, you can set inner and outer limits for the radius value for the resulting toolpath. This enables you to reduce the dense overlapping passes that would be created as the tool nears the starting centerpoint. Additionally, you can use settings in the *Passes* tab to define the angular stepover (in degrees), a start reference, and an angular range of from-to values (in degrees).

The Radial toolpath shown in Figure 6–26 has been modified such that the *Angle from* and *Angle to* values are specified from 180 to 360 deg and the *Angular step* was set at 2 deg.

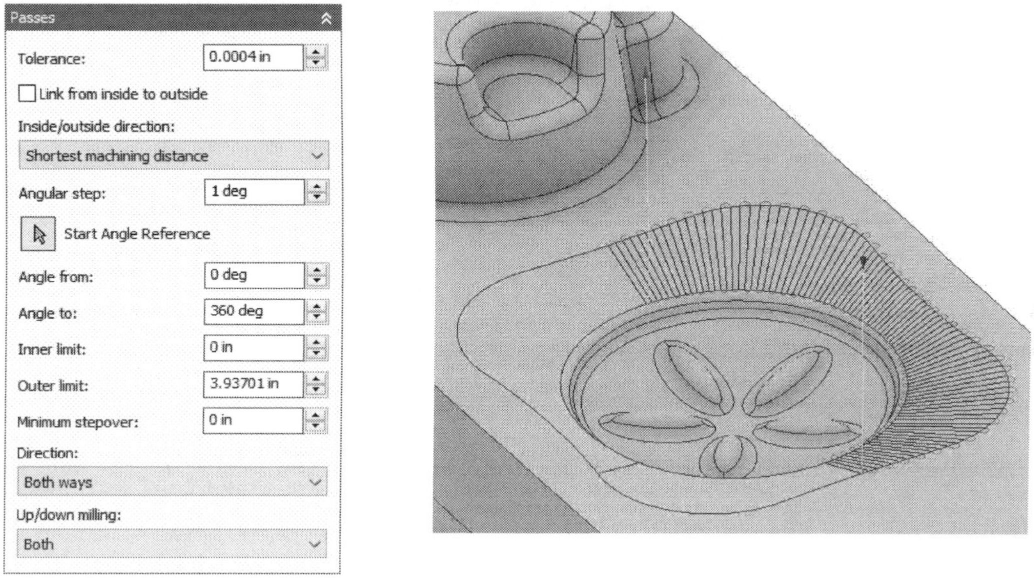

Figure 6–26

Hint: Additional 3D Milling Toolpaths

The following toolpaths are not as commonly used as the other 3D Milling finishing toolpaths described earlier in this content.

- The (Project) 3D Milling toolpath enables you to project a curve onto a contoured surface and assign the toolpath that will cut the resulting curve. This is generally used for engraving.
- The (Morph) 3D Milling toolpath enables you to machine the surface area between two selected curves.
- The (Flow) 3D Milling toolpath enables you to machine along the isocurves on a freeform type surface. Flow is typically used to machine outside fillets. It can also be used as a Multi-Axis strategy.

Practice 6a
Creating 3D Milling Toolpaths

Practice Objectives

- Create setups in a model that will allow for the machining of the top and bottom of the model.
- Create folders within a setup to organize roughing and finishing toolpaths.
- Create 3D Milling toolpaths to create the required roughing and finishing toolpaths to machine a contoured model.
- Use the Simulation tools in Inventor CAM to display operations.

In this practice, you will create 3D Milling and Drilling toolpaths to machine the top and bottom of a contoured model. All toolpaths will be broken into roughing and finishing sequences within two separate setups. The newly discussed 3D Milling toolpaths that will be used include Adaptive, Pocket, Horizontal, Pencil, Parallel, Contour, and Scallop.

Task 1: Open a model and review the existing setup and model geometry.

1. Open **Triangulo.ipt**. Select the CAM browser, if not already displayed. Rotate the model to view the model, as shown in Figure 6–27. This will be considered the top side of the model geometry. This model has a setup created for you called **Top Side**. It has two sub-folders to help organize the Roughing and Surface Finishing operations.

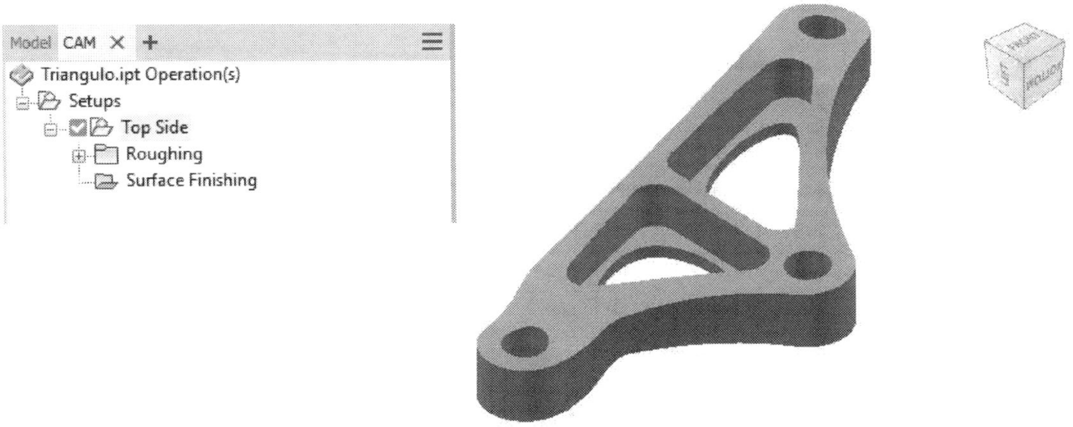

Figure 6–27

2. Select the **Top Side** setup to display the stock and WCS that was assigned in the setup. Note that the setup for a model that will be machined with 3D toolpaths is the same as that of a model that is machined solely using 2D toolpaths.

3. Expand the **Roughing** folder and note that a Facing toolpath has been created for you that machines the top of the stock and ensures that it is flat and free of irregularities. Double-click on the Facing toolpath to review it. Note that, on the (Heights) tab, the *Bottom Height* is set to **Stock top** and a value of **-0.05 in** was manually assigned to define how far below the stock top the material was to be removed. Close the Face palette.
4. Reorient the model using the ViewCube, as shown in Figure 6–28. Note how the stock is machined to where the tool first comes in contact with the model geometry and no stock is left at this location.

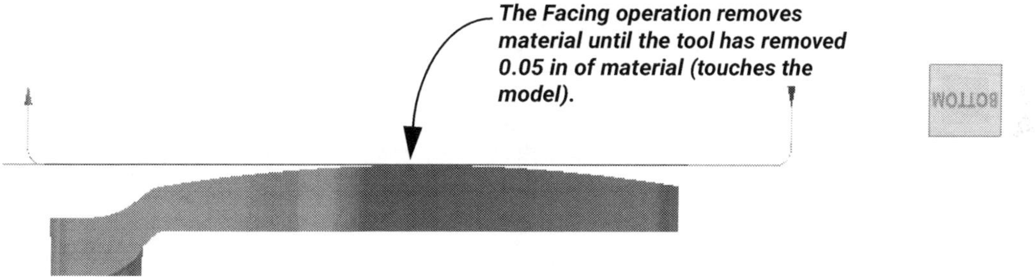

Figure 6–28

5. Right-click on the **Roughing** folder and select **Default Folder** to set it as the active folder, as shown in Figure 6–29. This ensures that any new operations will be added to this folder.

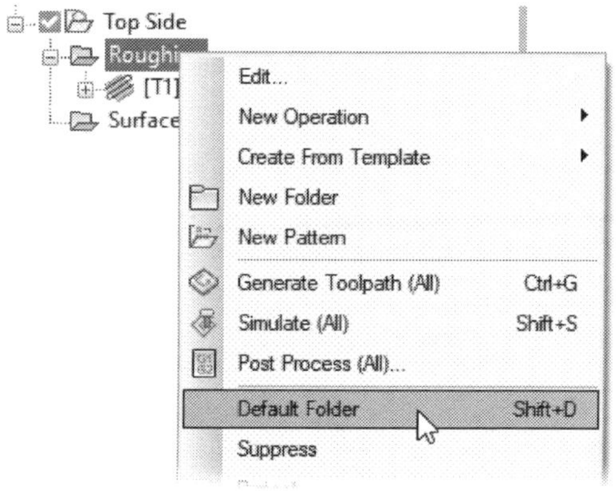

Figure 6–29

Task 2: Add an Adaptive toolpath to the Top Side of the model.

In this task, you will add an Adaptive roughing toolpath that will remove additional stock from the top side of the model. When setting up this toolpath, interior cavities will be manually avoided and machined using another strategy and tool.

1. In the 3D Milling panel, click (Adaptive). The Adaptive palette opens.

2. In the (Tool) tab, note that the currently assigned tool is the same tool that was used in the Facing toolpath. Open the Tool Library and select **#2 – 1/2" Flat Endmill** from the list and click **Select** to assign it to this Adaptive toolpath.

3. Select the (Geometry) tab. Ensure that the *Rest Machining* area is activated and change the *Rest material source* to **From previous operation(s)**. This enables you to limit the operation to remove material that wasn't previously removed in the last operation (in this case the Facing operation).

4. No changes are required on the (Heights) tab. Note that the *Bottom Height* option is set as **Model bottom**. This adaptive toolpath will remove stock all the way down to the bottom of the model.

5. Select the (Passes) tab and set the following (as shown in Figure 6–30).
   - Clear the checkbox for **Machine cavities**. This prevents the tool from removing material in the counterbores and the two internal pockets. Those will be machined later using a smaller tool and a different strategy.
   - Change the *Maximum roughing stepdown* to **2.0 in** and the *Fine stepdown* to **0.02 in**.
   - Check the box for **Order by depth**. This reduces the number of repositioning movements and the tool will work its way down the part.
   - Enable the *Stock to leave* area and maintain the default values of **0.02 in** to leave material both radially and axially for finishing operations.

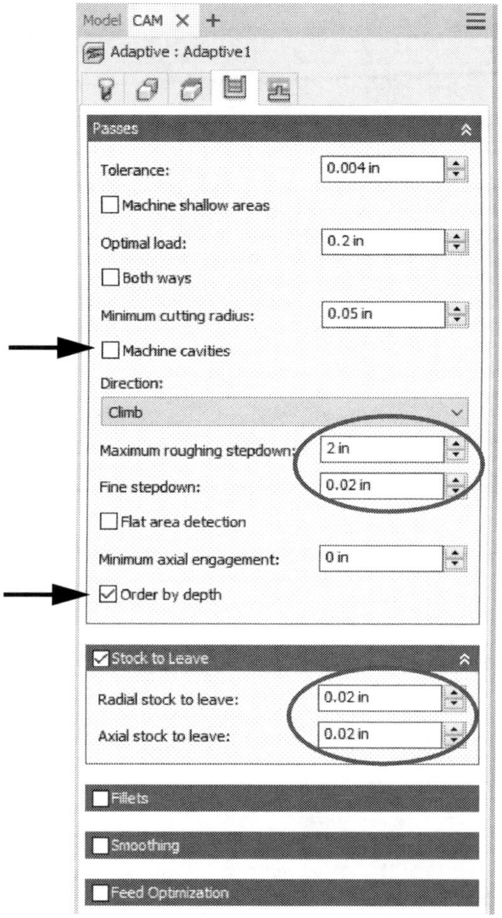
Model
CAM
Adaptive : Adaptive1
Passes
Tolerance:
0.004 in
Machine shallow areas
Optimal load:
0.2 in
Both ways
Minimum cutting radius:
0.05 in
Machine cavities
Direction:
Climb
Maximum roughing stepdown:
2 in
Fine stepdown:
0.02 in
Flat area detection
Minimum axial engagement:
0 in
Order by depth
Stock to Leave
Radial stock to leave:
0.02 in
Axial stock to leave:
0.02 in
Fillets
Smoothing
Feed Optimization

Figure 6–30

6. Select the (Linking) tab and set the following (as shown in Figure 6–31).
   - Set the *Retraction policy* to **Minimum retraction**.
   - Change the Stay-down level to **60%**. This will make the tool move straight up to the minimum clearance height between cutting passes. Changing the Stay-down level will create a more efficient toolpath but will add to the calculation time.
   - Maintain the remaining defaults on this tab.

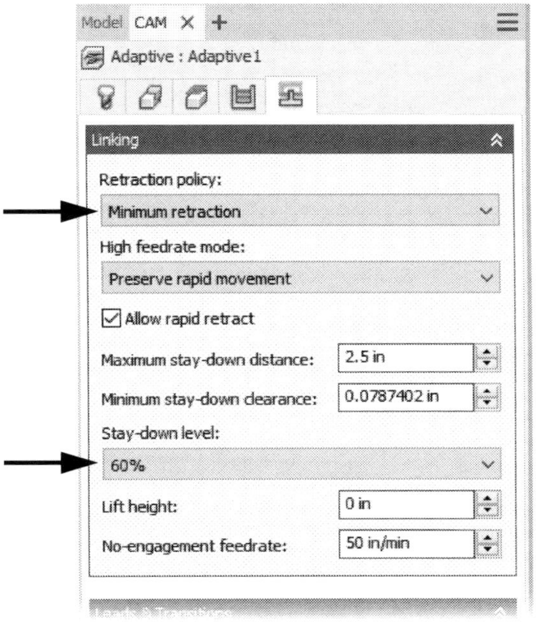

Figure 6–31

7. Click **OK** to complete the toolpath. It may take a few minutes to generate the toolpath.
8. View the toolpath and/or simulation of the new Adaptive toolpath and ensure that it removes material as expected. Figure 6–32 shows both the toolpath and completed simulation (with *Colorization* set to **Use material**).

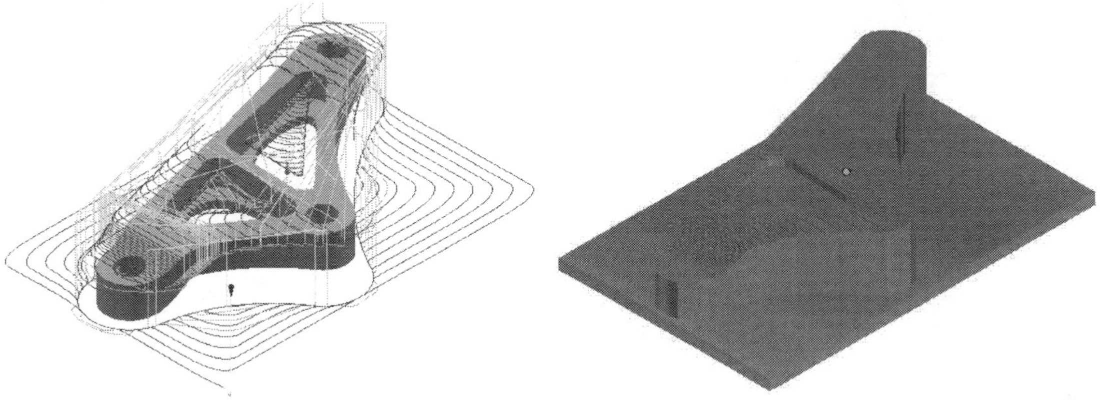

Figure 6–32

Task 3: Create a Pocket toolpath to rough out the pockets in the model.

In this task, you will create a Pocket toolpath to rough out the internal pockets.

1. In the expanded 3D Milling panel, click (Pocket). The Pocket palette opens.

2. In the (Tool) tab, assign the **#3 – 1/4" Bullnose Endmill** tool from the model's tool library.

3. Select the (Geometry) tab. Change the *Machining boundary* to **Selection** and the *Tool containment* to **Tool inside boundary**. Select on the top two edges of the pockets as shown in Figure 6–33 to define the machining boundary.

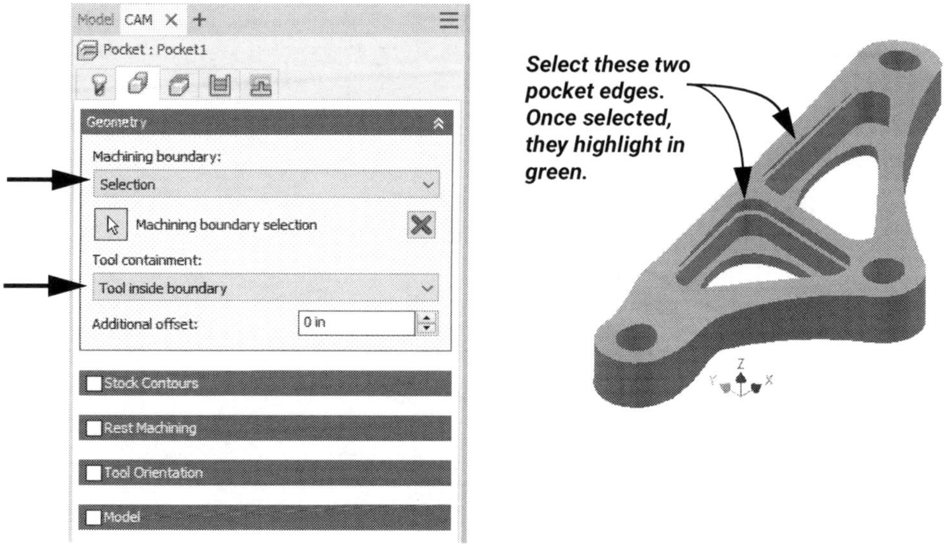

Figure 6–33

4. Ensure that the *Rest Machining* area is not selected. This is because the previous Adaptive toolpath did not previously remove any material within the pockets. Disabling, if it is not required, can help reduce calculation time.

5. Select the (Heights) tab and change the following settings:
   - Change the *Top Height* setting so that the new Pocket toolpath starts at the top of the model. In the *Top Height* area, select **Model top** from the drop-down list. The blue plane is repositioned, tangent to the top of the model.
   - Change the *Bottom Height* setting to **Selection** and select the flat face on the bottom of the models, as shown in Figure 6–34. Enter a *Bottom offset* of **-0.05 in**.

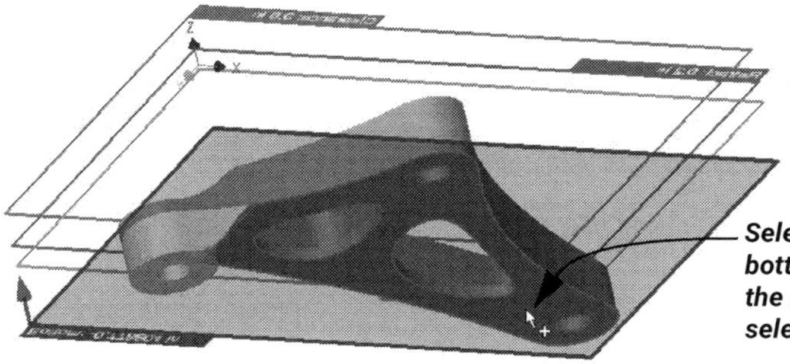

Figure 6–34

6. Select the (Passes) tab and set the following (as shown in Figure 6–35).
   - Enable **Manual stepover** and change the *Maximum stepover* value to **0.1 in** and the *Minimum stepover* value to **0.01 in**.
   - Change the Maximum roughing stepdown to **0.75 in**. (This is equal to the flute length of the bullnose endmill.)
   - In the *Stock to Leave* area, set both the axial and radial direction values as **0.01 in**.

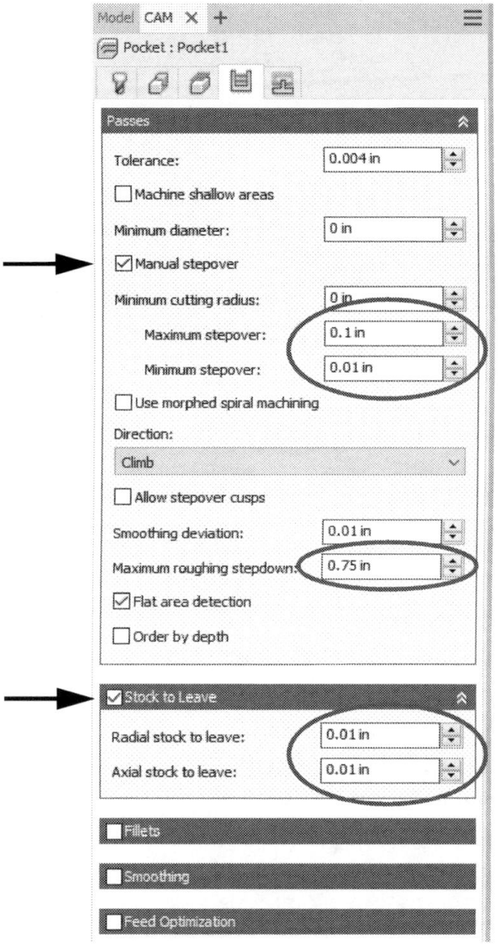

Figure 6–35

7. Select the (Linking) tab and change the *Retraction policy* to **Minimum Retraction**.

8. Click **OK** to complete the toolpath. The toolpath updates to show its path as shown in Figure 6–36.

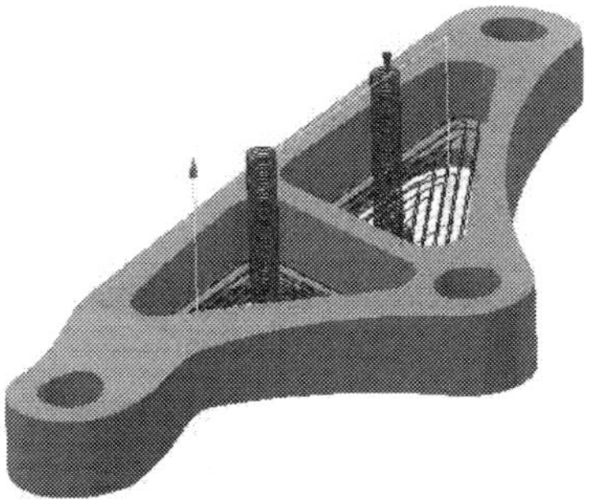

Figure 6–36

9. Note that the toolpath ramps into the pocket a considerable distance away from the model.

   To adjust this, right-click on the Pocket toolpath and select **Edit**. Select the (Linking) tab and change the *Ramp clearance height* value to **0.125 in**. Complete the toolpath and note that the tool now ramps into the pocket at a more reasonable height.

10. In the CAM browser, note that the icon for the new Pocket1 toolpath has a yellow checkmark overlayed ( ). This icon indicates a warning. Right-click on **Pocket1** and select **Show Log**. The Log Messages window appears displaying two warnings, as shown in Figure 6–37. The warnings are regarding the retract and clearance heights having been automatically changed to generate the toolpath. These heights do not automatically update in the toolpath.

11. To avoid these warnings in future, modify the toolpath and ensure that the heights are appropriate as compared to the Safe distance value set on the *Linking* tab. Modify these values to clear this error. For example, set the Retract and Clearance height offsets to **.8 in** (or a value greater than the Safe distance value).

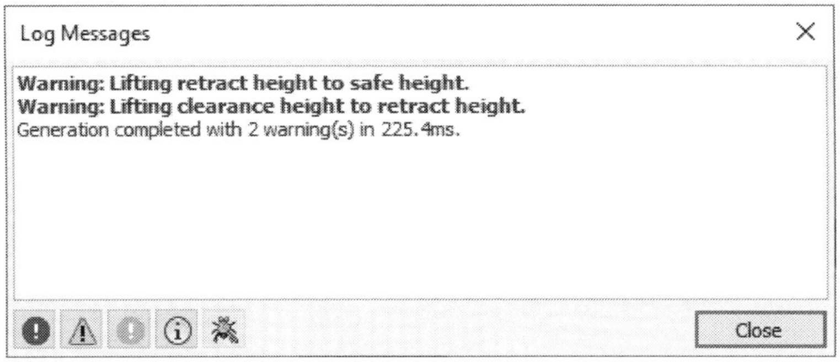

Figure 6–37

12. View the toolpath and/or simulation of the three toolpaths (Facing, 3D Adaptive, and 3D Pocket) and ensure that it removes material as expected. Figure 6–38 shows both the toolpath and completed simulation (with *Colorization* set to **Use material**).

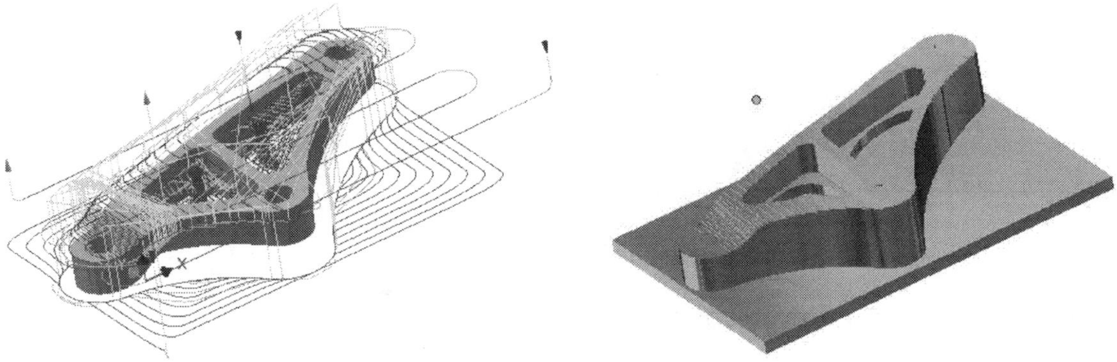

Figure 6–38

13. Close the Simulation palette.
14. Save the model.

Task 4: Create a Horizontal toolpath to create a finishing path in the pockets of the model.

In this task, you will create a Horizontal toolpath as the first of two paths that will be created to finish the internal pockets.

1. Right-click on the **Surface Finishing** folder in the Top Side operation and select **Default Folder**. All finishing operations will be organized into this folder.
2. In the 3D Milling panel, click (Horizontal). The Horizontal palette opens.
3. In the (Tool) tab, note that the **#3 1/4" Bullnose Endmill** tool is already assigned from the previous toolpath. You can use this tool for this toolpath so it does not have to be modified.

4. Select the (Geometry) tab and set the following, as shown in Figure 6–39. The geometry for a Horizontal toolpath can be automatically selected; however, if specific flat areas are not required, you must use the Machining Boundary options, as is done for this model.
   - Change the *Machining boundary* to **Selection** and the *Tool containment* to **Tool inside boundary**.
   - Select the same top two edges of the pockets that were previously selected.
   - Set the *Additional offset* value to **0 in**.

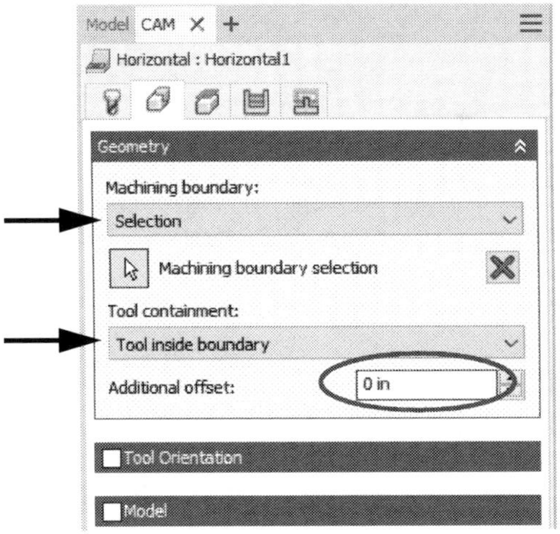

Figure 6–39

5. Select the (Heights) tab and change the following settings:
   - Set the *Bottom Height* setting to **Selection** and select the flat face on the inside of the model, as shown in Figure 6–40. The bottom of both pockets are planar so both can be included in the same toolpath.

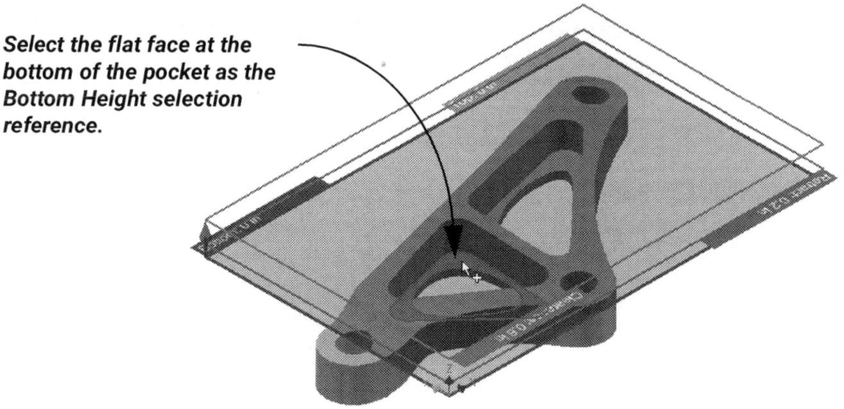

Figure 6–40

6. Select the (Passes) tab and enable the *Stock to Leave* area. Enter **0.005 in** for the *Radial stock to leave* and **0 in** for the *Axial stock to leave*. This will leave some material on the walls to finish with a final Pencil operation.
7. No changes are required on the (Linking) tab.
8. Click **OK** to complete the toolpath. The toolpath updates to show its path.
9. View the toolpath and/or simulation of the Top Side operations and ensure that it removes material as expected. Figure 6–41 shows both the Horizontal toolpath and completed full simulation.

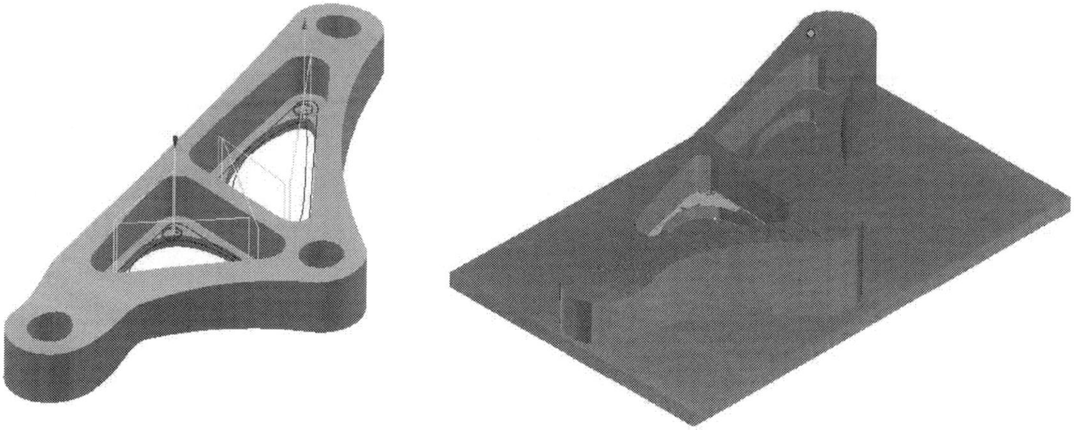

Figure 6–41

Task 5: Reuse the Horizontal toolpath to create an additional path to machine the end of the model.

1. Right-click on the **Horizontal1** toolpath that was previously created and select **Create Derived Operation>3D Milling> Horizontal**. A duplicate of the selected toolpath is created and its settings can be modified, as needed, to machine the new area. No changes are required for the tool.

2. On the (Geometry) tab, clear the previous Geometry selection and select the curve shown in Figure 6–42.

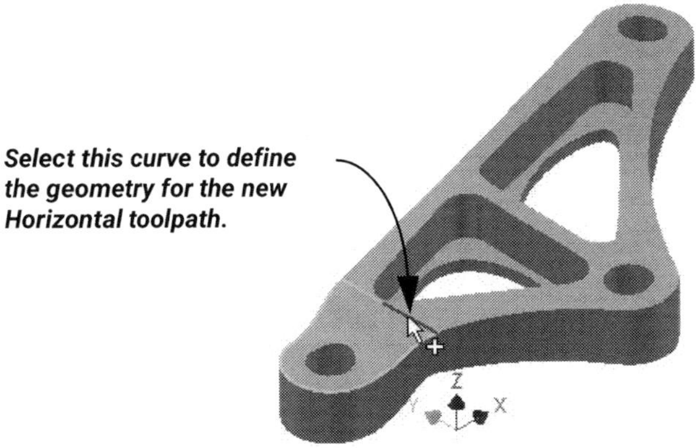

Figure 6–42

3. Select the (Passes) tab clear the *Stock to Leave* area as this will be the final pass made on this area of the model.
4. Click **OK** to complete the toolpath. The toolpath updates to show its path.
5. Rename *Horizontal1* to **Horizontal_Inside** and *Horizontal2* to **Horizontal_Outside**, as shown in Figure 6–43.

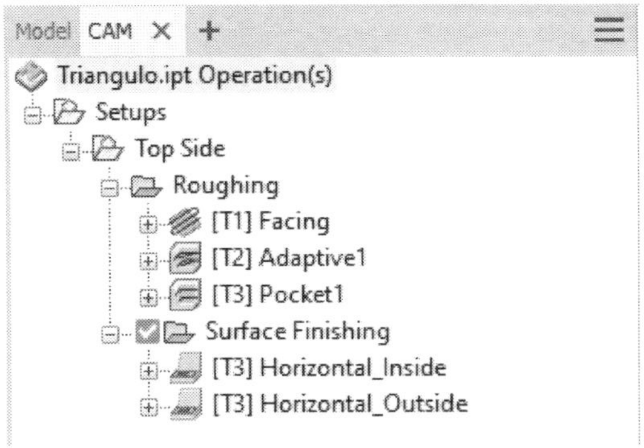

Figure 6–43

6. Select the two toolpaths in the Surface Finishing folder. The paths appear as shown in Figure 6–44. Note how the Horizontal toolpath only removes material on faces oriented normal to the Z-axis.

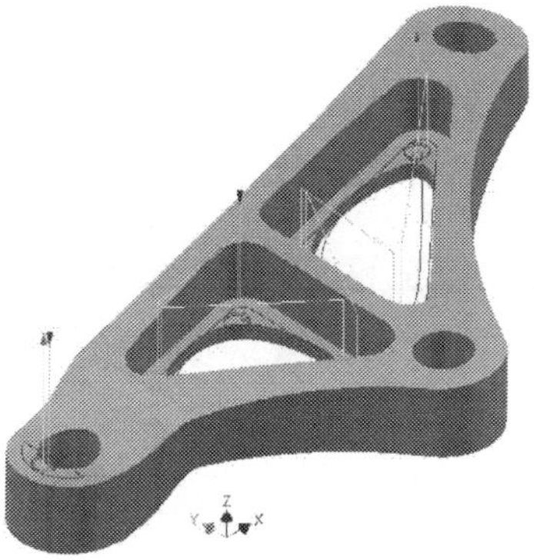

Figure 6–44

Task 6: Reuse a toolpath to generate a Pencil toolpath to finish the corners of the inside pockets.

1. Right-click on the **Horizontal_Inside** toolpath and select **Create Derived Operation>3D Milling> Pencil**. A duplicate of the selected toolpath is created. No changes are required to the tool, selected geometry, or the height definition.
2. Select the  (Passes) tab, clear the *Stock to Leave* area.
3. Click **OK** to complete the toolpath.
4. View the simulation of the Top Side operations and ensure that it removes material as expected without any collisions. Figure 6–45 shows the completed simulation.

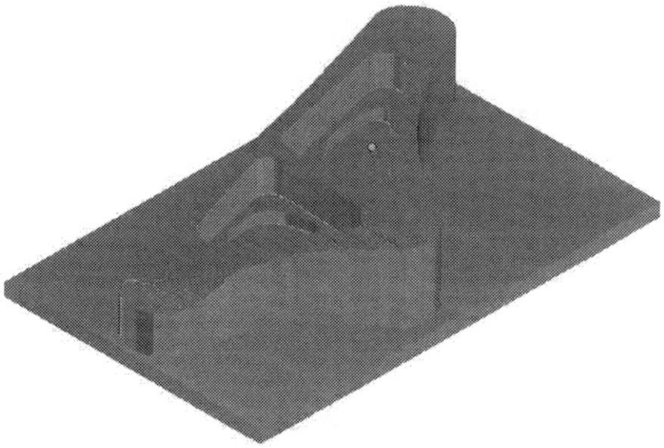

Figure 6–45

Task 7: Create a Parallel toolpath to machine the top face of the model.

1. Ensure that the **Surface Finishing** folder is still set as the **Default Folder**. If not, set it.

2. In the 3D Milling panel, click (Parallel). The Parallel palette opens.

3. In the (Tool) tab, set **#4 3/8" ball** as the tool for the operation.

4. Select the (Geometry) tab set the following as shown in Figure 6–46:
   - Change the *Machining boundary* to **Selection** and the *Tool containment* to **Tool center on boundary**.
   - Select the top six edges as shown.
   - Set the *Additional offset* value to **0.025 in**. This offset will extend the center of the Ball Mill tool, past the centerline of the boundary, to prevent cusps from being created along the edges of the part.

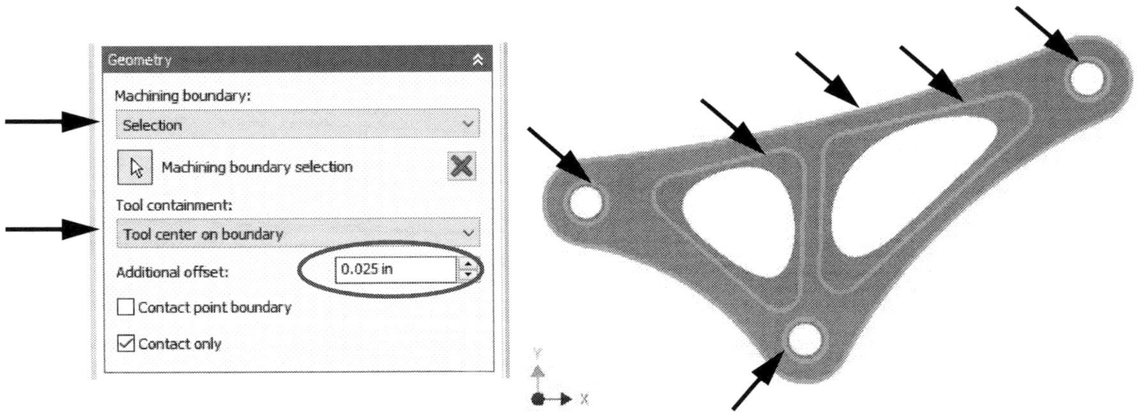

Figure 6–46

5. Select the (Passes) tab, and set the following:
   - Ensure the *Stock to Leave* area is cleared, as this is a finishing path on the top of the model.
   - Set the *Stepover* value to **0.05 in**.

6. Select the (Linking) tab and change the *Retraction policy* to **Minimum retraction**.
7. Click **OK** to complete the toolpath.

Task 8: Create a 3D Contouring toolpath to machine the top face of the model near the steep contour.

1. Ensure that the **Surface Finishing** folder is still set as the **Default Folder**. If not, set it.

2. In the 3D Milling panel, click (Contour). The Contour palette opens.

3. In the (Tool) tab, set **#8 1/8" Ball Endmill** as the tool for the operation.

4. Select the (Geometry) tab, and set the following, as shown in Figure 6–47:

   - Change the *Machining boundary* to **Selection** and the *Tool containment* to **Tool center on boundary**.
   - Select the two edges as shown.
   - Set the *Additional offset* value to **0.025 in**. This offset will extend the center of the Ball Mill tool, past the centerline of the boundary, to prevent cusps from being created along the edges.

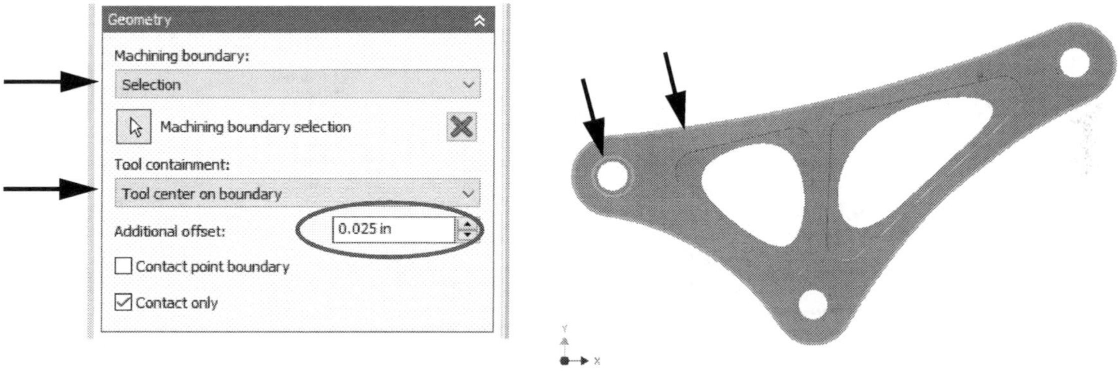

Figure 6–47

- Enable the *Avoid/Touch Surfaces* area and select **Touch surfaces**. Select the surfaces shown in Figure 6–48. This allows you to limit the toolpath to machine only the selected surfaces within the selected boundary. Set the *Clearance* value to **0 in**.

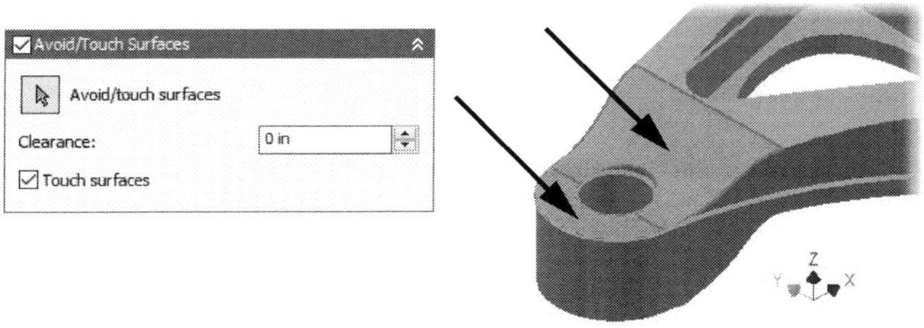

Figure 6–48

5. Select the (Passes) tab and set the following:
   - Set the *Maximum stepdown* value to **0.005 in**.
   - Enable the **Order by depth** option. This ensures that the machining is done from the top down.
6. Select the (Linking) tab and set the following:
   - Change the *Retraction policy* to **Minimum retraction**.
   - Change the *Ramp type* to **Plunge**.
7. Click **OK** to complete the toolpath. Select the new toolpath and zoom in on the path. Note how the contour toolpath uses smaller stepdowns on the steep areas.

Task 9: Reuse an existing toolpath to create a Scallop toolpath.

1. Right-click on the **Parallel1** toolpath that was previously created and select **Create Derived Operation>3D Milling> Scallop**. A duplicate of the selected toolpath is created. No changes are required for the tool, geometry, and height settings.
2. Select the (Passes) and change the *Stepover* to **0.005 in**. This smaller stepover value will help create a smooth surface finish.
3. Click **OK** to complete the toolpath.

Task 10: Create operations that will drill the three counterbore holes on the top side of the model.

In this task, you will complete the toolpath operations on the top of the model by adding the final three counterbore holes. Detailed step-by-step instructions are not included and it relies on the drilling instructions taught in an earlier chapter. As an alternative to adding each drilling operation individually you can also use the template that has been provided.

1. Right-click on the Top Side setup and select **New Folder**. Rename the new folder **Drilling Operations**.
2. Set the **Drilling Operations** folder as the Default Folder.
3. Create two drilling (a spot and a drill toolpath that drills through the entire 3/8" hole) and a bore toolpath to create the three counterbore holes on the top of the model. As an alternative you can import the **.375in Counterbore. invhsm-template** that has been provided for you to quickly create the holes. Hint: To import a toolpath right-click on the folder and select **Create from Template**. Navigate to and open the required template to use it as a basis for new toolpaths in your model.
4. If you used the template, modify the geometry references as needed to properly generate all the drilling toolpaths.
5. Run a simulation of all the toolpaths that have been created. Figure 6–49 shows completed simulation.

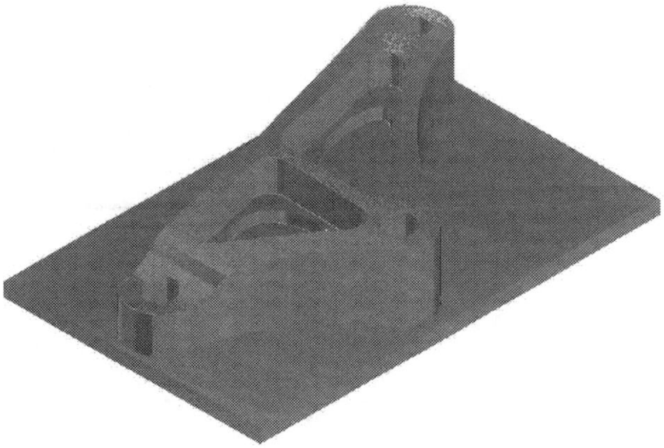

Figure 6–49

Task 11: Create a new setup to create the toolpaths for the bottom of the model.

1. Create a new setup for the bottom of the model geometry. Consider the following:
   - On the Setup tab, assign the **Generic 3-axis** machine and set **Milling** as the operation type. Ensure the WCS is set as shown in Figure 6–50.

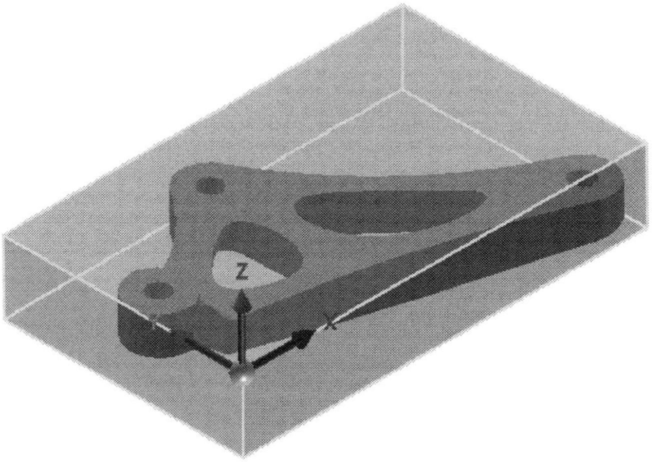

Figure 6–50

   - On the *Stock* tab, ensure the stock mode is **Fixed size box**. Similar to the top setup, by default, the Width is set to 7 in and Depth to 4.5 in. After the facing toolpath that removed the stock of irregularities, the *Height* should be **1.45 in**. Modify the *Model position* to **Offset from bottom (-Z)** with a **0 in** *Offset* value.
   - Complete the setup and rename the setup **Bottom Side**.
2. Ensure that the new setup is set as the Default Folder and reorient the model to view the bottom side of the model.

Task 12: Add an Adaptive roughing toolpath to the Bottom Side of the model to remove the majority of stock.

1. In the 3D Milling panel, click  (Adaptive). The Adaptive palette opens. Consider the following settings:
   - Assign the **#2 – 1/2" Flat Endmill** as the tool for the toolpath.
   - Maintain the default geometry selection, where no machining boundary is defined and REST Machining is set to **From setup stock**.

- Set the Bottom Height to **Selection**, and select the flat face (as shown in Figure 6–51) as the reference. The top setup previously removed the stock from within the pockets and holes.

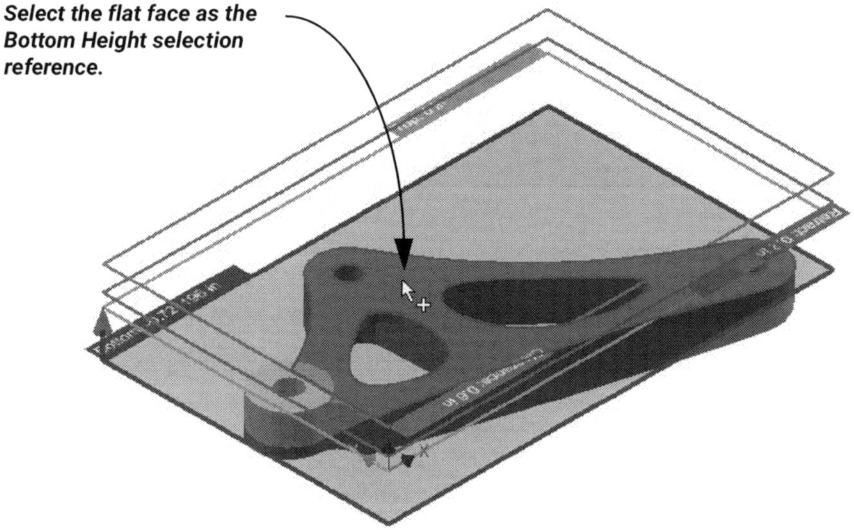

Figure 6–51

- Change the *Maximum roughing stepdown* to **2.0 in** and the *Fine stepdown* to **0.02 in**.
- Leave stock at **0.02 in** both radially and axially for finishing operations.
- Set the *Retraction policy* to **Minimum retraction**.
- Change the Stay-down level to **60%,** as was done in the Adaptive toolpath in the Top Side setup.

Note: *Changing the Stay-down percentage makes the tool move straight up to the minimum clearance height between cutting passes. Changing the Stay-down level will create a more efficient toolpath but will add to the calculation time.*

- Click **OK** to complete the toolpath.

2. View the toolpath and/or simulation of the new toolpath and ensure that it removes material as expected. Figure 6–52 shows both the toolpath and completed simulation.

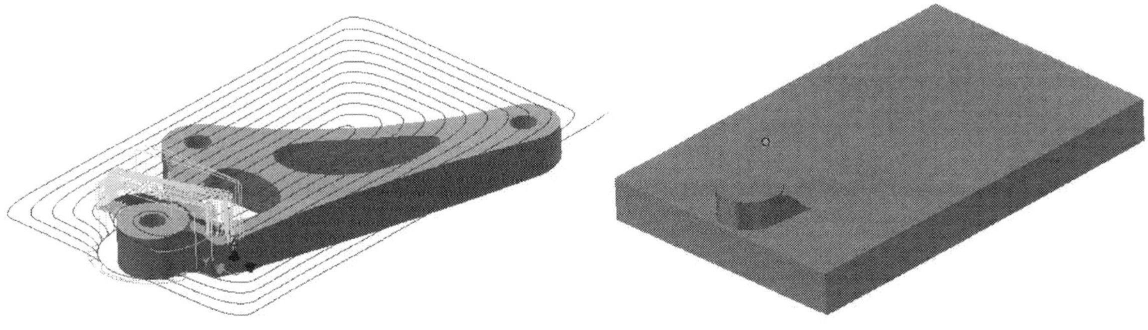

Figure 6–52

Task 13: Create Horizontal, Contour, and Pencil toolpaths to finish the faces for the Bottom Setup.

In this task, you will create three additional toolpaths that will finish the horizontal surfaces (faces parallel to the XY plane), and the contoured surfaces that join them.

1. In the 3D Milling panel, click  (Horizontal). The Horizontal palette opens. Consider the following settings to create the finishing pass for the horizontal faces:
   - Maintain the same tool used in the previous toolpath (**#2 – 1/2" Flat Endmill)** as the tool for the toolpath.
   - Maintain the default geometry selection. All horizontal faces will be machined with this toolpath.
   - Set the *Bottom Height* setting to **Selection** and select the same flat face as was selected for the Adaptive toolpath. This is the lower of the two horizontal faces.
   - On the  (Passes) tab, enable **Use morphed spiral machining** to provide a smoother finish. Morphed spiral machining adapts to the shape of the model helping to produce fewer sharp corners with a smoother finish.
   - Also set the machining strategy for the cutting *Direction* to be **Both Ways** for the toolpath, allowing for the tool to run smoother on the smaller area.
   - Set the *Retraction policy* to **Minimum retraction**. Additionally, set the *Safe distance* to **0.02 in** and the *Maximum stay-down distance* to **6 in**.
   - Click **OK** to complete the toolpath.

2. View the toolpaths and/or simulation of the two Bottom Side toolpaths. Ensure that it removes material as expected, as shown in Figure 6–53.

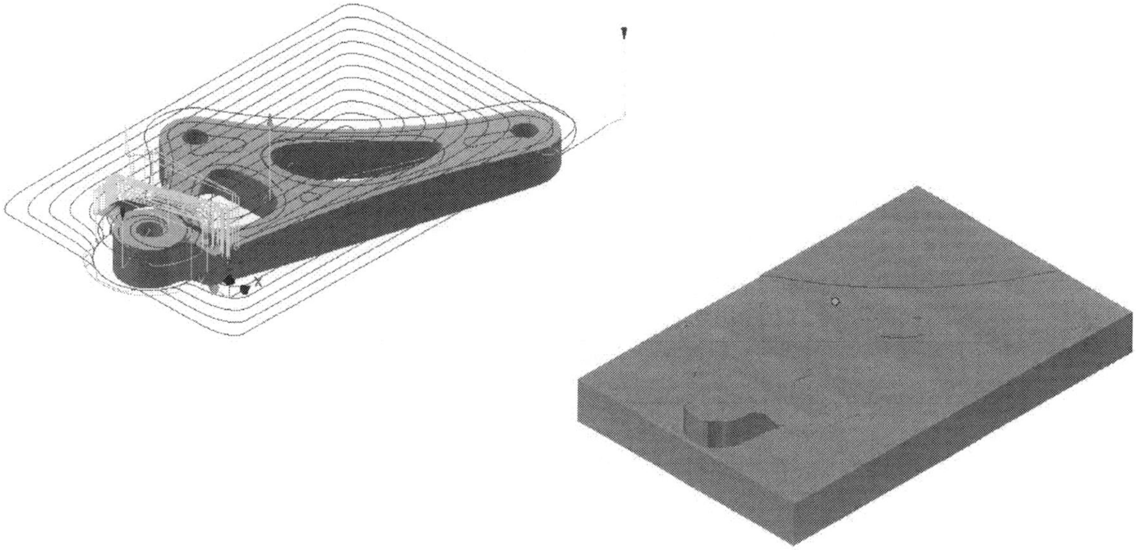

Figure 6–53

3. In the 3D Milling panel, click (Contour). Consider the following settings for the Contour toolpath:
   - Assign the **#9 1/8" Bullnose Endmill** as the tool for the toolpath.
   - Maintain the default Silhouette machining boundary geometry option. Enable the *Avoid/ Touch Surfaces* area and select the contoured surface shown in Figure 6–54 to include as the touch surface reference. Enable **Touch surfaces** to ensure only this selected surface is machined. Maintain the default *Clearance* value.

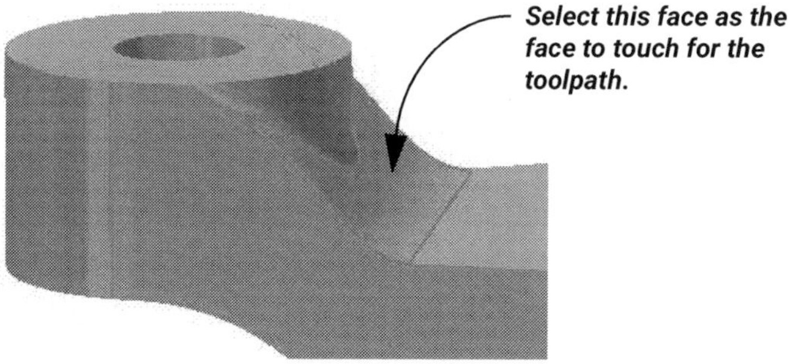

Figure 6–54

- On the *Passes* tab, enable **Order by depth**, to ensure the system does not attempt to optimize the cutting path by machining different areas of the surface separately which would lead to unwanted tool retracts for such a small area. Change the *Maximum stepdown* to **0.005 in** to create a smooth finish for this final pass.
- Set the *Retraction policy* to **Minimum retraction** and the *Ramp type* to **Plunge**. Enter **0.00525 in** as the Ramp clearance height for the toolpath.
- Click **OK** to complete the toolpath. The Contour toolpath is shown in Figure 6–55:

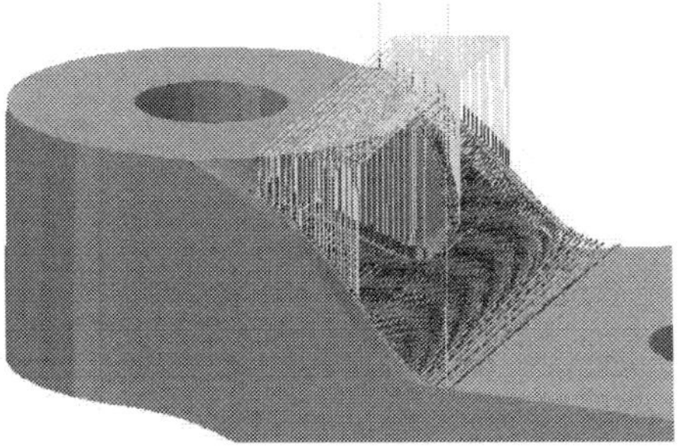

Figure 6–55

4. In the 3D Milling panel, click  (Pencil). Consider the following settings for the Pencil toolpath:

   - Assign the **#10 3/16" Ball Endmill** as the tool for the toolpath.
   - Maintain the default Silhouette machining boundary geometry option. Enable the *Avoid/ Touch Surfaces* area and select the contoured surface shown in Figure 6–56 to include as the touch surface reference. Enable **Touch surfaces** to ensure only this selected surface is machined. Maintain the default *Clearance* value.

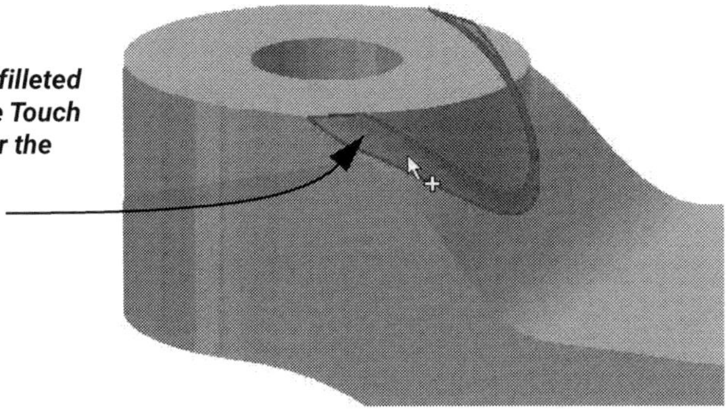

Figure 6–56

   - On the *Passes* tab, clear the **Limit number of stepovers** option and enter **0.01 in** as the *Stepover* value.
   - Set the *Retraction policy* to **Minimum retraction**.

- Click **OK** to complete the toolpath. The Pencil toolpath is shown in Figure 6–57:

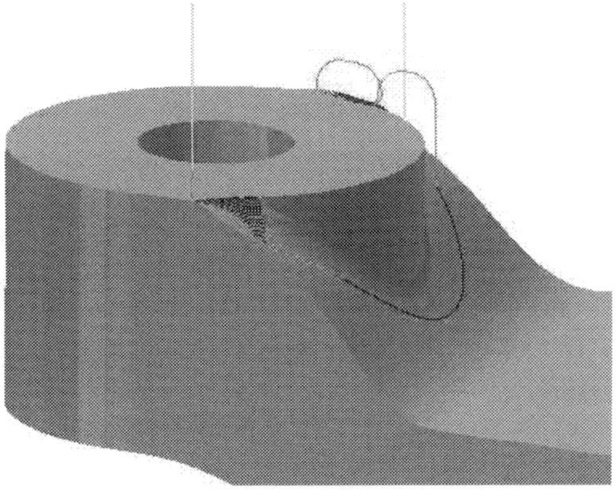

Figure 6–57

Task 14: Create a 2D Contour toolpath to complete the machining of the model.

In this task, you will return to the 2D Milling panel and use the 2D Contour option to generate a toolpath that will ensure all material is removed around the profile.

1. Add a 2D Contour toolpath () to define the finishing pass around the exterior of the model, as shown in Figure 6–58.
    - Ensure the **#2 1/2" Flat Endmill** is set as the tool.
    - Select the edge shown in Figure 6–58 as the contour selection.

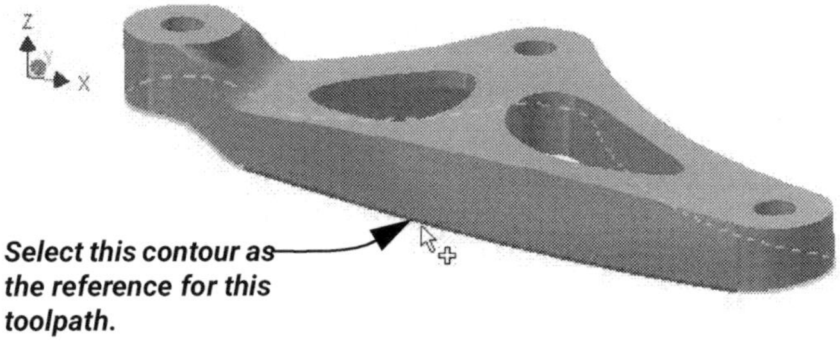

Figure 6–58

- For the Bottom Height, enter an offset value of **-0.01 in** from the selected contour.
- On the *Passes* tab, enable **Multiple finishing passes** and ensure that the *Number of finishing Passes* is set to **2** with a *Stepover* of **0.05 in**.
- No changes are required to the options on the Linking tab.

- Click **OK** to complete the toolpath. The 2D Contour toolpath is shown in Figure 6–59:

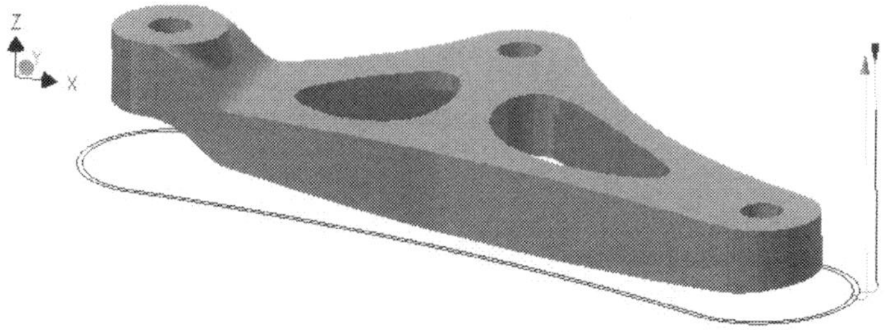

Figure 6–59

2. View the toolpath and/or simulation of the top and bottom setups and ensure that they remove material as expected.
3. Save the model. A completed model (**Triangulo_Final.ipt**) has been provided for review purposes in the class files folder, if required.

End of practice

Chapter Review Questions

1. Which of the following are true statements regarding the difference between the 2D Milling and 3D Milling Adaptive toolpaths? (Select all that apply.)
   a. The 2D Adaptive toolpath should be used for roughing and the 3D Adaptive toolpath should be used for finishing only.
   b. Both the 2D and 3D Adaptive toolpaths allow you to define the machining boundary using the Silhouette of the model projected onto the XY plane.
   c. The Fillets area can only be enabled for 3D Adaptive toolpaths to avoid sharp turns, to allow for maintaining a higher feed rate, and to help prevent marks on the model.
   d. The options on the (Linking) tab are the same for both 2D and 3D Adaptive toolpaths.

2. Which of the following toolpaths would be best suited to finish the faces selected in Figure 6–60?

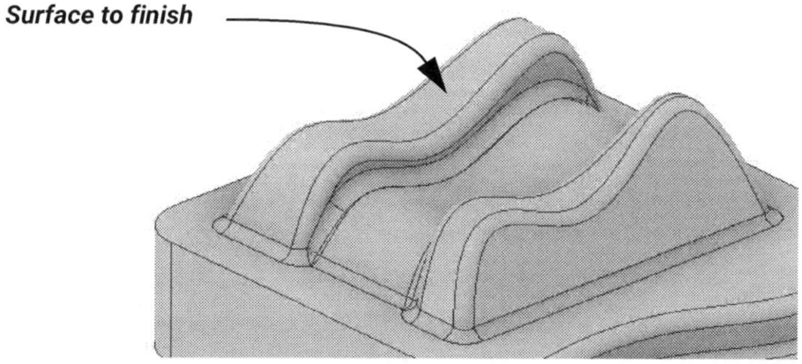

Figure 6–60

   a. Parallel
   b. Scallop
   c. Horizontal
   d. Ramp

3. When defining a 3D Milling Contour () toolpath, which of the areas on the  (Geometry) tab can be used to define a steepness angular range to refine the surfaces that are automatically selected for inclusion?

a. Geometry

b. Slope

c. Model

d. Avoid/Touch Surfaces

4. The *Avoid/Touch Surfaces* area on the  (Geometry) tab enables you to identify specific surfaces that should be the only ones touched during the toolpath. To ensure selected surfaces are machined and not avoided, the **Touch surfaces** option should be disabled.

a. True

b. False

5. The  (Horizontal) toolpath can only be used to machine flat areas that are parallel to the XY plane and the

 (Parallel) toolpath can only be used to machine flat areas that are perpendicular to the XY plane.

a. True

b. False

6. Which of the following 3D Milling toolpaths can be used to finish internal corners and fillets?

a. Contour

b. Pencil

c. Scallop

d. Radial

7. Which of the following 3D Milling toolpaths use a centerpoint geometry reference point to define how the path is created? (Select all that apply.)
   a. Spiral
   b. Morphed Spiral
   c. Scallop
   d. Radial

8. Similar to the  (Radial) toolpath, a  (Spiral) toolpath's stepover is defined in degrees.
   a. True
   b. False

Command Summary

Button	Command	Location
	**Adaptive**	• **Ribbon:** *CAM* tab>3D Milling panel
	**Contour**	• **Ribbon:** *CAM* tab>3D Milling panel
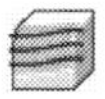	**Flow**	• **Ribbon:** *CAM* tab>3D Milling panel
	**Horizontal**	• **Ribbon:** *CAM* tab>3D Milling panel
	**Morph**	• **Ribbon:** *CAM* tab>3D Milling panel
	**Morphed Spiral**	• **Ribbon:** *CAM* tab>3D Milling panel
	**Parallel**	• **Ribbon:** *CAM* tab>3D Milling panel
	**Pencil**	• **Ribbon:** *CAM* tab>3D Milling panel
	**Pocket**	• **Ribbon:** *CAM* tab>3D Milling panel
	**Project**	• **Ribbon:** *CAM* tab>3D Milling panel
	**Radial**	• **Ribbon:** *CAM* tab>3D Milling panel
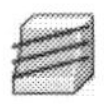	**Ramp**	• **Ribbon:** *CAM* tab>3D Milling panel
	**Scallop**	• **Ribbon:** *CAM* tab>3D Milling panel
	**Spiral**	• **Ribbon:** *CAM* tab>3D Milling panel

Chapter 7

Project Exercises II

In this chapter, you will be provided with two project exercises that allow you to practice setting up and defining the 3D milling toolpaths needed to machine contoured solid part models. These project exercises assume that you have completed the previous exercises and understand the general Inventor CAM workflow for both setting up milling operations and adding 3D toolpaths. Detailed instructions will not be provided. For more detailed instructions, refer to the steps in the previous exercises.

Learning Objectives

- Import tool libraries.
- Create setups that includes toolpaths to machine two practice models.
- Create folders within the setup to organize the toolpaths.
- Post process the Inventor CAM setup to output the CNC code to machine the two practice models.

Practice 7a
Generating Toolpaths III

Practice Objectives

- Import a tool library.
- Create a setup that includes toolpaths to machine the model.
- Create folders within the setup to organize the created toolpaths.
- Post process the Inventor CAM setup to output the CNC code to machine the model.

In this practice, you will create a single setup that will contain all the toolpaths to create the CNC code required to machine the top of the model. To help organize the roughing, finishing and drilling toolpaths you will create and use folders.

Task 1: Open the model and review its geometry.

1. Open **Wheel Hub.ipt** from the practice files folder. Switch to the Model browser, if not already active. The model and Model browser display as shown in Figure 7–1. Review the model geometry that will be machined. Note that all machining toolpaths can be machined on one side of the model (BACK on the ViewCube).

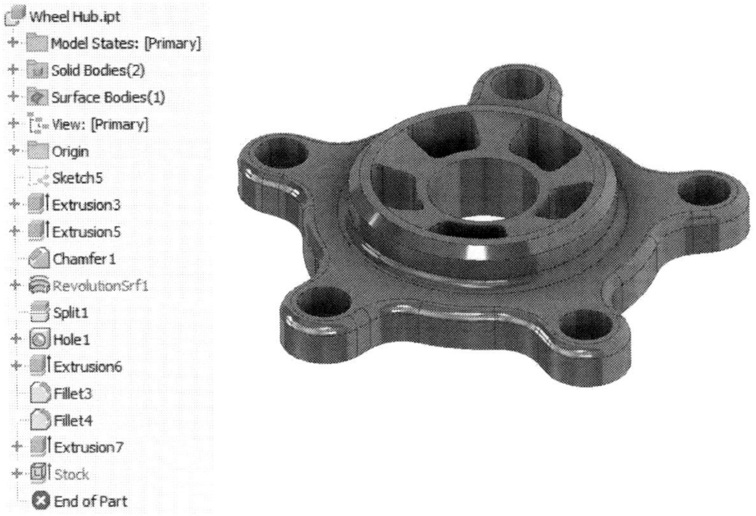

Figure 7–1

Note: *A completed model (**Wheel Hub_Final.ipt**) has been provided in the practice files. This model contains all completed setups and toolpaths that will be created in this project.*

2. Expand the **Solid Bodies** node in the Model browser. Further expand the **Solid3** body. Select **Stock**. A solid cylindrical body, with visibility disabled, is highlighted in the model. This will be used as the stock model in the model's CAM setup.
3. Right-click **Stock** and select **Edit Sketch**. The circular sketch in the model was created aligned to the center of model and is offset (.05 in) from a construction circle. The construction circle was created tangent to the outer diameter of the model. By creating the sketch in this way and then using it to create the solid geometry that will represent the stock, it allows for flexibility if changes are made to the extents of the wheel diameter. This will be shown at the end of this exercise once all toolpaths are defined.

   Note: *As an alternative, the stock could have been created in the CAM environment relative to the size of the model. Changes to the overall model size will also reflect in stock created using this method.*

4. Click **Finish Sketch** in the *Sketch* tab to close the sketch without making any changes.
5. Expand the **Surface Bodies** node. A surface called **Interior Cavity** has been created. Turn on its visibility and review its shape. Note that it lies on the surface of the interior cavity and does not have openings for each of the pockets. This surface will be used to efficiently define a future toolpath such that it avoids machining all of the pockets. Prior to continuing, clear the surface's visibility.

Task 2: Import a tool library.

To help simplify the tool selection process, you can import a tool library that has been provided for you.

1. In the *CAM* tab, open the Tool Library.
2. To import a library into the model, right-click on the **Wheel Hub** name in the *Open Documents* area and select **Import Tools from Library**.
3. Locate, select, and open the **Wheel Hub.hsmlib** file from the top-level practice files folder. Tools are added to your tool library. These will be used throughout this project.

Task 3: Define the setup for the model.

1. In the Inventor CAM environment, begin the setup for the model. Consider the following:

   - On the *Stock* tab, change the stock mode to **From solid** and select the **Solid3** (Stock) cylindrical geometry that was created in the model. The geometry can be selected by returning to the Model browser and selecting it from there. Once selected, return to the CAM browser.

- On the *Setup* tab, assign the **Generic 3-axis** machine and set **Milling** as the operation type. Ensure the WCS is set at the center (top) of the bounding box for the stock using the **Stock box point** Origin setting. Orient the WCS as shown in Figure 7–2.

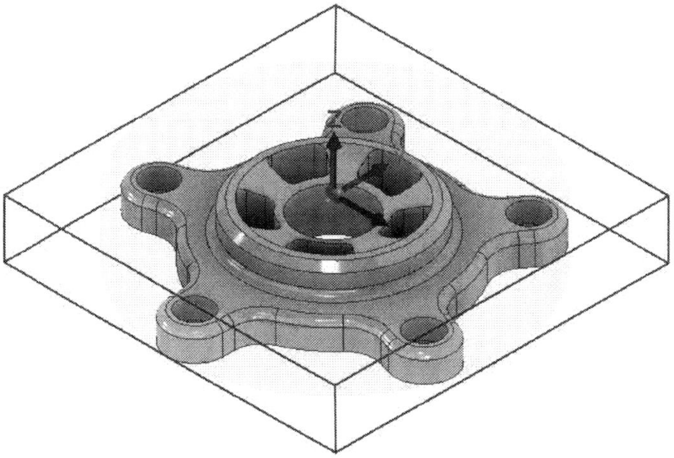

Figure 7–2

- The model that is to be machined must be explicitly selected because the model contains multiple bodies.
- Complete the setup and rename the setup **OP1**.

Task 4: Add the initial facing and roughing toolpaths to the model.

1. Add a Face toolpath to machine the top of the stock. The stock was designed offset from the top to ensure that a cutting pass was required to machine the top of the stock and clear it of any irregularities.
   - Assign the **#1 2" Face Mill** tool that was imported as one of the provided library tools.
   - Note that the preselected stock contour defaults to a bounding box that encompasses the selected stock. This pre-selection will create an appropriate toolpath; however, you could also remove this selection and reselect the top edge of the cylindrical stock, if desired. Hint: The stock's visibility must be on to select the edge.
   - Ensure the *Bottom Height* for the cut is set to **Model top**.
   - Set the *Pass extension* value to **1 in** so that the tool clears the stock before turning for the next cutting pass.
   - Set the *Maximum stepdown* to **0.0625 in**, in the *Multiple Depths* area.
   - Accept the remaining defaults and complete the toolpath.
   - Play the simulation and verify that there is no stock remaining on the top of the model.

2. Create a new folder called **Adaptive Roughing** and make it the default folder.
3. Create two separate 3D Adaptive toolpaths to rough out the majority of the stock on the top of the model, one for the outside and one for the inside, similar to those shown in Figure 7–3. Doing this as two separate paths allows for you to use two different tools and control the strategy differently for both.

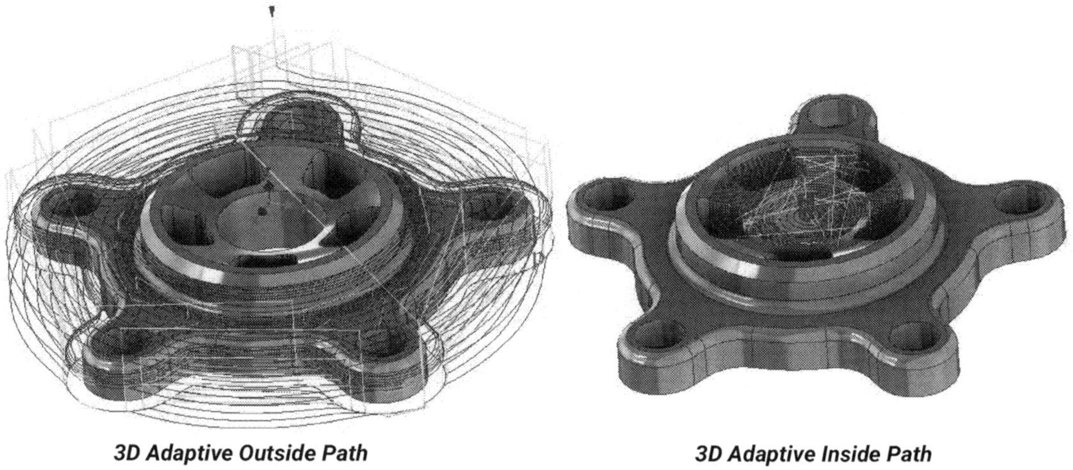

Figure 7–3

For the toolpath that will machine the outside of the model, consider the following:

- Assign tool **#6 3/4" Bullnose** for the toolpath.
- Select the bottom edge of the model as the stock contour to machine, as shown in Figure 7–4.

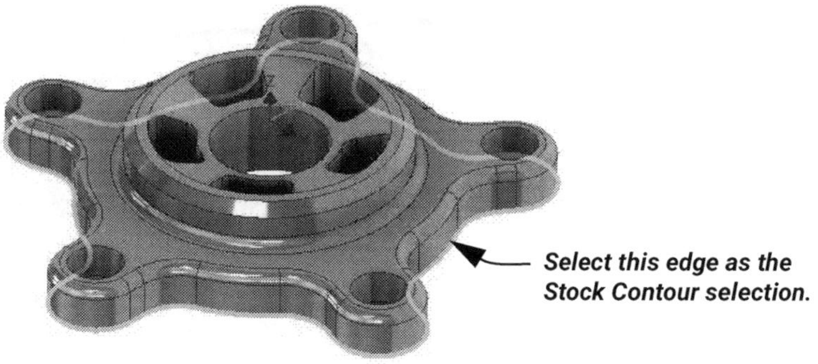

Figure 7–4

- Incorporate Rest Machining such that it machines from the previous operation.
- Ensure that the Bottom Height is set to machine **-0.05 in** past the bottom of the model.

- This roughing path will be ignoring all machine cavities. By disabling the **Machine cavities** option, the interior concave cavity will be ignored in this toolpath. This will be machined in future toolpaths.
- The Maximum roughing stepdown should be **0.75 in** and the Fine stepdown **0.05 in**.
- This roughing cut should remove all but **0.02 in** of stock both radially and axially. A finishing toolpath will be added later to finish the outside of the model.
- Change the Retraction Policy to **Minimum retraction**. This sets the retract so that on each cutting motion, the tool is prevented from a full retraction and simply retracts to clear the stock. This helps reduce cutting time, especially on larger models.
- Complete the toolpath and rename it as **Adaptive Outside**.

For the toolpath that will rough out the inside cavity of the model consider the following:

- Assign tool **#7 1/2" Bullnose** for the toolpath.
- Select the top edge of the cavity to define a custom machining boundary, as shown in Figure 7–5.

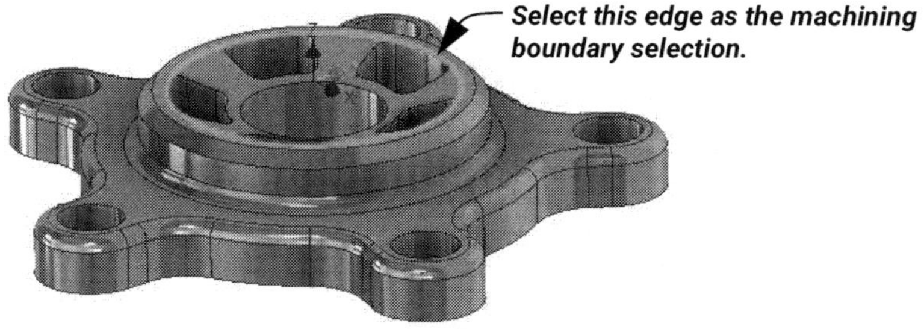

Figure 7–5

- Incorporate Rest Machining such that it machines from the previous operation.
- With the default machining boundary selection, this adaptive toolpath will machine all of the six interior pockets, requiring a large number of tool retracts. To obtain a smoother finish on the concave interior cavity, you will remove the pockets from the toolpath, and select the **Interior Cavity** surface that was created in the model (reviewed earlier in this exercise). This surface should be assigned as the model surface in the *Model* area.
- Ensure that the Bottom Height selection reference is the edge shown in Figure 7–6, and set the offset to machine **-0.05 in** past this reference. Set the Top Height as **Model top**.

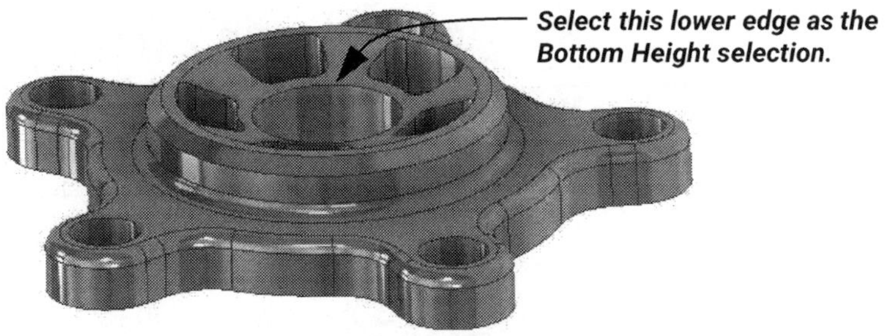

Figure 7–6

- Ensure that the **Machine cavities** option is enabled to machine all material inside the area defined by the Interior Surface model geometry.
- Set the Maximum roughing stepdown to **0.5 in** and the Fine stepdown **0.02 in**. Also enable **Order by Depth** to ensure that the system does not attempt to optimize the cutting path by machining different areas of the surface producing unwanted tool retracts.
- This roughing cut should remove all but **0.02 in** of stock both radially and axially. A finishing toolpath will be added later to finish the outside of the model.
- Change the Retraction Policy to **Minimum retraction**.
- Complete the toolpath and rename it as **Adaptive Inside**.

4. Play a simulation that includes the three new toolpaths and verify that stock has been removed as expected, as shown in Figure 7–7.

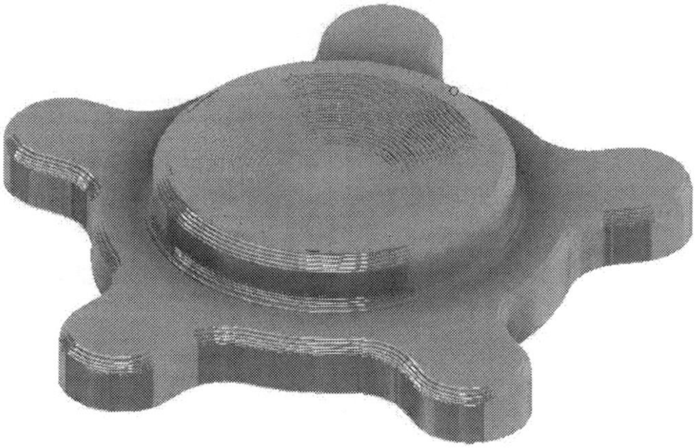

Figure 7–7

Task 5: Add the toolpaths to complete the interior cavity of the model.

The toolpaths that will be created in this task will finish the interior cavity and rough and finish the six interior pockets. To begin, you will create a Radial and Spiral toolpath to finish the concave area. This will also use the Interior Cavity surface as the machining boundary. These two are used in combination with one another to ensure that no cusps are generated and it will create a smoother finished surface.

1. Create a new folder called **Interior Cavities** and make it the default folder. Ensure that the folder is at the top-level and is not created as a subfolder to the existing folder.
2. Create a Radial toolpath as the first of two finishing paths that will be added to the concave interior cavity. Consider the following settings:
   - Assign tool **#4 3/8" Ball Endmill** for the toolpath.
   - Select the Center point (select the smaller lower circular edge) and the two circular edges shown in Figure 7–8 as the machining boundaries for the toolpath. Hint: Select the **Selection** Machining boundary option.

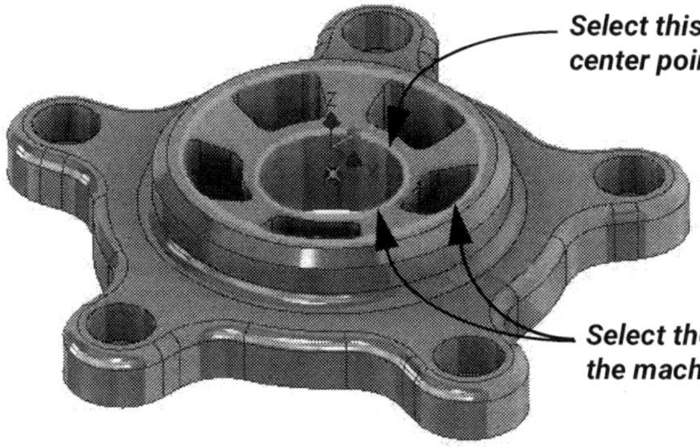

Figure 7–8

   - Ensure that the **Contact only** setting is cleared in the *Geometry* area. This is required to make sure that the entire cavity is machined, even where there are five pockets. This is being done to ensure that the tool stays engaged with the model to create a smoother finish.
   - Similar to the adaptive toolpath that was created, select the **Interior Cavity** surface as the selected Model surface.
   - No changes are required to the Height settings.
   - The radial path will begin on the selected inner boundary, so the **Inner limit** should be **0 in**. Ensure that the **Outer limit** is larger than the radius of the larger selected boundary (i.e. 2.5 in). This ensures that the toolpath will machine the entire surface between the two boundaries. The surface on top of the hole will be machined in another toolpath so does not need to be finished in this toolpath.

- Change the Retraction Policy to **Shortest path**, to move the tool in straight lines between passes.
- Complete the toolpath and rename it **Radial - Interior Cavity**. It should appear as shown in Figure 7–9.

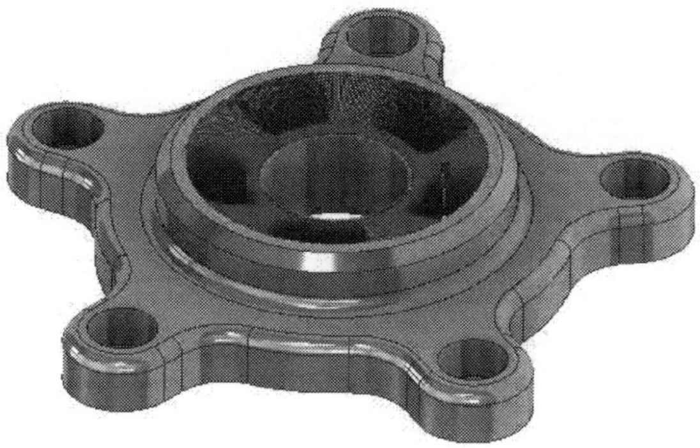

Figure 7–9

3. Create a Spiral toolpath to machine the same area in a perpendicular direction. Many of the settings used to create the Radial toolpath can be reused, including the tool and geometry selection. For ease of toolpath creation, consider deriving the new Spiral toolpath and consider the following changes to the new toolpath:
   - Change the Stepover value to **0.01 in**.
   - Complete the toolpath and rename it **Spiral - Interior Cavity**.

   Note: *In this exercise, Spiral and Radial toolpaths were selected as the machining strategy. As an alternative, you could have also used Scallop and Contour toolpaths.*

4. Select both the **Radial - Interior Cavity** and **Spiral - Interior Cavity toolpaths**. Zoom into the model and compare the Spiral and Radial toolpaths. Note how the paths are perpendicular to one another. This was done to help produce a smoother finish on this concave area.

5. Add a 3D Pocket toolpath to rough out the stock from the six interior pockets.
    - Assign the **#7 1/2" Bullnose** tool for the toolpath.
    - Select the edge shown in Figure 7–10 to select the machining boundary.

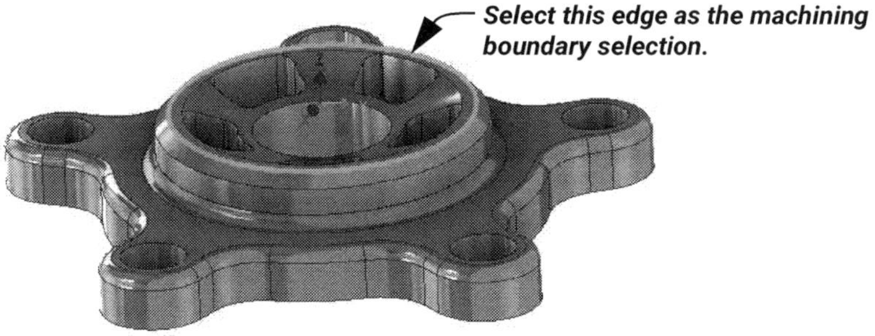

Figure 7–10

- Incorporate Rest Machining such that it machines from the previous operation.

Note: *The Interior Cavity surface is not going to be used in this toolpath because the pockets are being machined. That surface was used in previous toolpaths to avoid the pockets.*

- The top and bottom heights should be set to the Model top and Model bottom respectively. Also set a **-0.05 in** offset to ensure that the tool extends past the bottom of the model.
- Enable a **Manual stepover** such that the maximum and minimum values are **0.2 in** and **0.02 in**, respectively.
- The **Maximum roughing stepdown** can be set to **0.5 in**.
- This roughing cut should remove all but **0.02 in** of stock both radially and axially. A finishing toolpath will be added later to finish the outside of the model.
- Change the *Retraction Policy* to **Minimum retraction**.
- Set the *Ramp clearance height* to **0.1 in**.
- Complete the toolpath and rename it **Pocket - Interior Pockets**.

6. Review the new pocket toolpath's browser icon. If it has a yellow checkmark overlayed ( ), it indicates that there is a warning regarding this toolpath. Right-click on the toolpath and select **Show Log**. The warning indicates the retract height was automatically changed to generate the toolpath. To fix this, modify the toolpath and ensure that the Retract Height is larger than the Safe distance value assigned on the Linking tab.

7. Display the toolpath on the model. It should appear as shown in Figure 7–11.

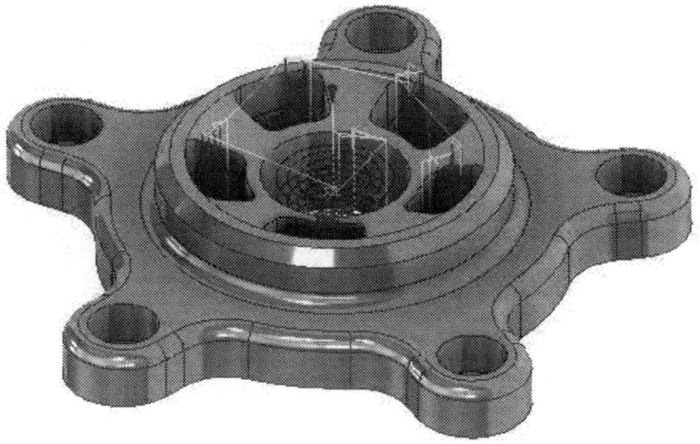

Figure 7–11

8. To finish the vertical walls of the six interior pockets, create a 2D Contour toolpath.
   - Assign the **#2 1/2" Flat** tool for the toolpath.
   - Reorient the model as shown in Figure 7–12. Select the six closed edges shown to define the contour geometry.

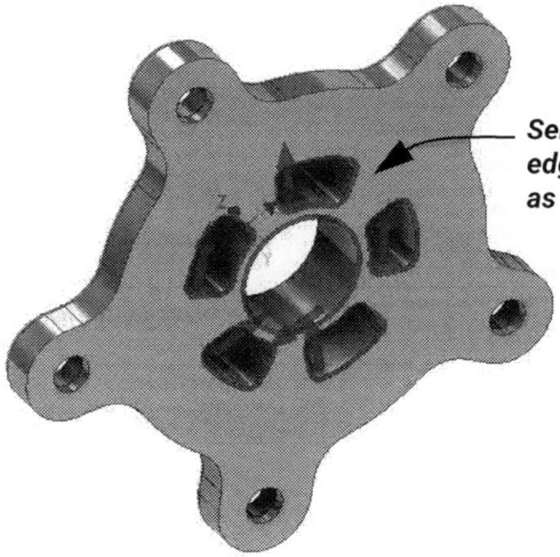

Figure 7–12

   - Change the *Top Height* reference to the top of the model and assign an offset of **0.05 in** from the Bottom Height selected contour.
   - Ensure that the *Multiple Depths* area is enabled and that the *Maximum roughing stepdown* is set as **0.25 in**, the *Finishing stepdowns* is **1**, the *Finishing stepdown* is **0.125 in**.
   - Since this is a finishing toolpath, ensure that no stock is left axially or radially.
   - Complete the toolpath and rename it as **2D Contour - Interior Pockets**.

9. Play a simulation that includes all toolpaths and verify that the stock has been removed as expected, as shown in Figure 7–13.

Figure 7–13

Task 6: Add the toolpaths to complete the exterior of the model.

The toolpaths that will be created in this task will finish the exterior of the model. You will use a combination of Horizontal, 2D Contour, Trace, and 3D Contour toolpaths to finish the surfaces shown in Figure 7–14.

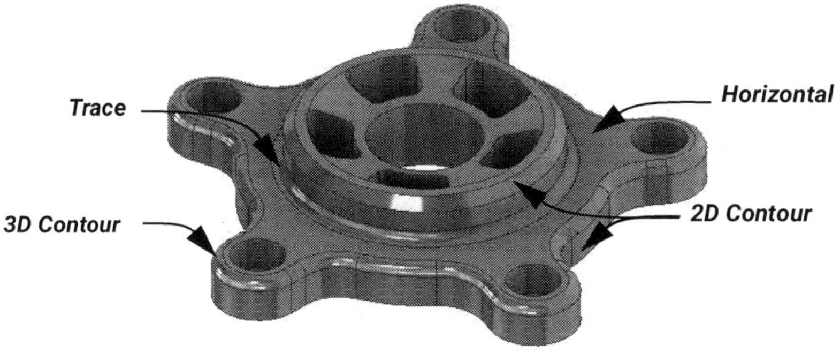

Figure 7–14

1. Create a new folder called **Exterior Finishing** and set it as the Default folder.
2. Create a Horizontal toolpath and consider the following settings:
    - Assign tool **#2 1/2" Flat** for the toolpath.
    - Select the edges shown in Figure 7–15 as the machining boundaries for the toolpath. Set the *Additional offset* value to **0 in** as you do not need to machine past these references.

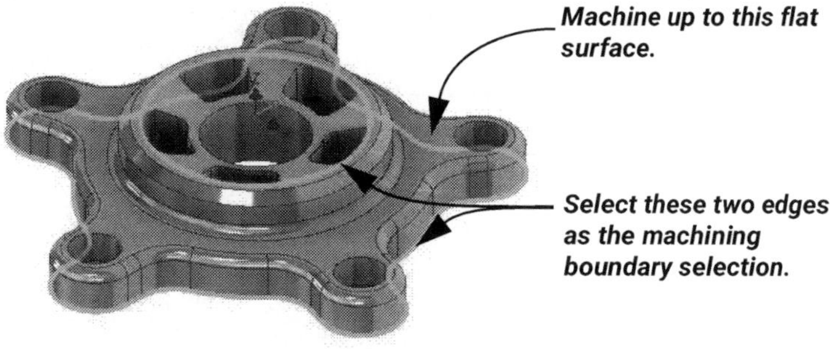

Figure 7–15

- Set the *Bottom Height* setting to **Selection** and select the flat face shown in Figure 7–15.
- No further changes are required to this toolpath. Complete the toolpath and review it. Rename it as **Horizontal Surfaces**.

3. To finish the exterior vertical wall, create a 2D Contour toolpath. Consider the following:
    - Assign tool **#2 1/2" Flat** for the toolpath.
    - Define the contour so that it machines around the bottom edge of the model.
    - Set the Height options as appropriate to machine from the horizontal exterior surface to -0.05 in below the contoured edge reference/bottom of the model.
    - Create the contour so that it cuts in **Multiple Depths** with a *Maximum roughing stepdown* of **1 in**, the *Finishing stepdowns* is **0**, the *Finishing stepdown* is **0.125 in**.
    - Complete the toolpath and rename it as **2D Contour - Exterior**.
4. Create a 3D Contour toolpath to machine the rounded surface between the vertical wall and the top of the horizontal face. This will create a finishing path similar to that shown in Figure 7–16.

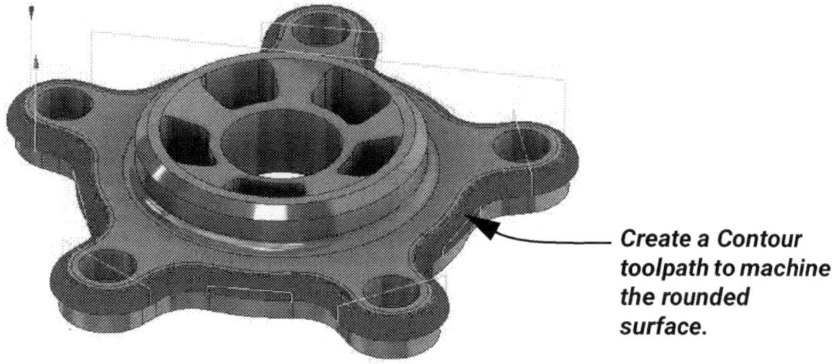

Figure 7–16

Consider the following when creating the toolpath:

- Assign tool **#4 3/8" Ball Endmill** for the toolpath.

- To define the geometry for a Contour toolpath, you must select the top and bottom edges that fully enclose the surface being machined. Using the **Selection** option to define the Machining boundary, select the two edges shown in Figure 7–17. Set the Tool containment option to **Tool outside boundary**.

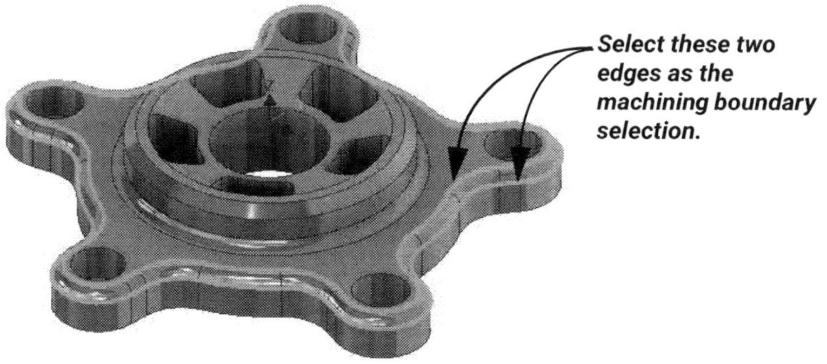

Figure 7–17

- Set the *Maximum stepdown* as **0.01 in** to obtain a smooth finish on the surfaces.
- Change the *Retraction Policy* to **Minimum retraction**.
- Complete the toolpath and rename it as **Contour - Exterior Round**.

5. Create a 2D Contour toolpath to finish the chamfered edge at the top edge of the model, as shown in Figure 7–18.

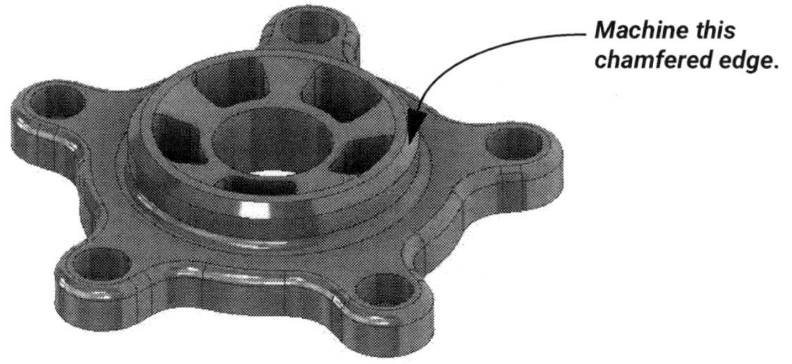

Figure 7–18

Consider the following:

- Assign tool **#5 1" 45° chamfer** for the toolpath.
- Select the lower edge of the chamfer as the selection for the geometry to machine.
- Set the tip of the tool to offset **0.05 in** below the selected contoured edge.
- Complete the toolpath and rename it as **2D Contour - Chamfer**.

6. To finish the machining of the horizontal surface, create a final 2D Trace toolpath to finish the rounded edge shown in Figure 7–19.

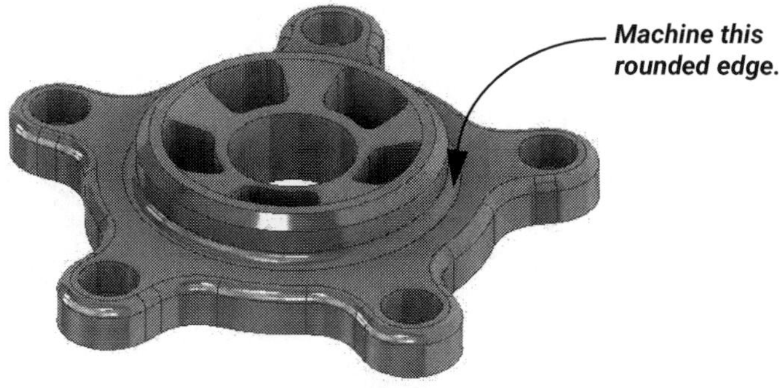

Figure 7–19

Consider the following:

- Assign tool **#3 1/2" Ball Endmill** for the toolpath.
- Select the lower edge that lies on the horizontal surface as the reference geometry for this toolpath.
- Change the *Retraction Policy* to **Minimum retraction**.
- Complete the toolpath and rename it as **Trace - Round**.

7. Play a simulation that includes all toolpaths and verify that stock has been removed as expected, as shown in Figure 7–20. The Model browser should also be similar to that shown.

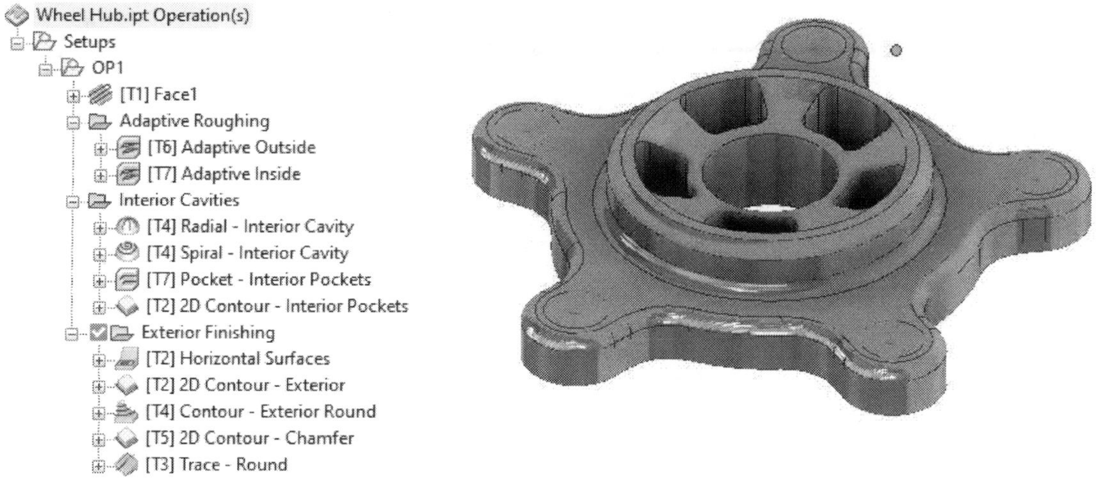

Figure 7–20

Task 7: Create the final drilling operations on the outer spokes of the wheel.

In this task, you will complete the toolpath operations on the top of the model by adding the final five counterbore holes. Detailed step-by-step instructions are not included and it relies on the drilling instructions taught in an earlier chapter.

1. Using the tools provided in the imported tool library, create a spot drill to locate the holes, a drilling toolpath to machine through the model, and complete the drilling operation with a Bore operation. Add all of these toolpaths in a folder called Drilling.
2. Run a simulation of all the toolpaths that have been created. Figure 7–21 shows the completed simulation.

Figure 7–21

3. Save the model.

Task 8: Modify the overall diameter of the model and update the CAM toolpaths.

1. In the Model browser, right-click on **Sketch5** and select **Edit Sketch**. The sketch opens as shown in Figure 7–22. This sketch was used to create the overall geometry for the model.

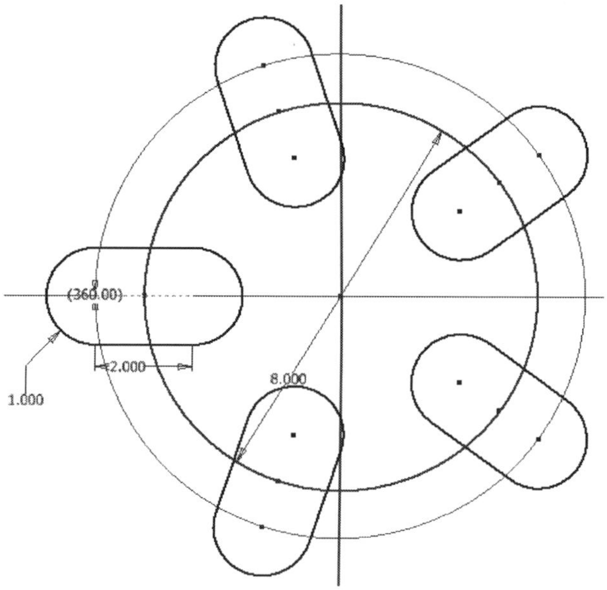

Figure 7–22

2. Double-click on the 2.000 dimension value, enter **2.5 in**, and press **Enter** on your keyboard. Note how the overall extent of the diameter of the model has enlarged.
3. Click **Finish Sketch** in the *Sketch* tab to close the sketch and update the model with the new size change.
4. Return to the *CAM* tab.
5. Select the **OP1** setup to display the stock that was defined in the setup, if not already displayed.

6. Reorient the model to the BACK view on the ViewCube and note how the stock has updated to the correct size for the modified model geometry (as shown in Figure 7–23). The stock updated because of the design intent that was incorporated into the stock's sketch. A construction circle was created tangent with the spokes of the wheel geometry and the sketched circle is .05 in offset from it.

   Note: *If the stock's diameter didn't automatically update to reflect the size change, edit Sketch10 to open the sketch and then close it again to force the regeneration.*

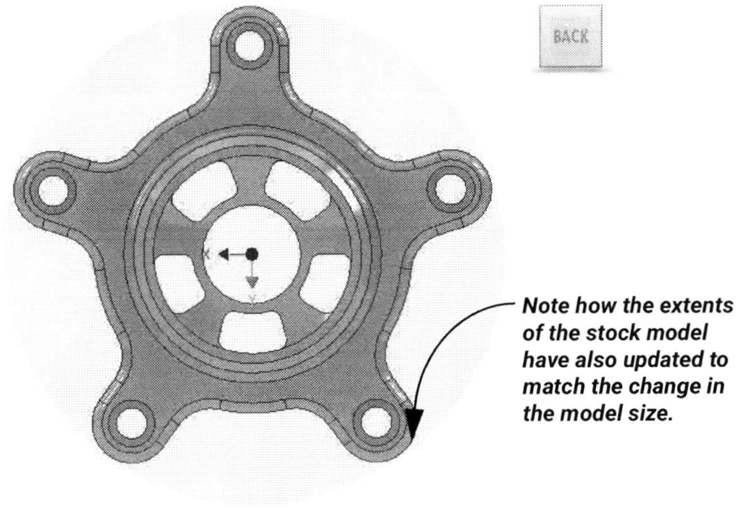

Figure 7–23

7. Note that all the toolpaths are now out of date due to the dimension change. Generate the paths again to update the toolpaths.

Had the stock been assigned in the setup by defining the actual size of the Cylinder, it would have had to have been updated manually to take into effect the dimension change in the model. If the Relative size cylinder mode option been used, this would have also automatically updated the model.

8. Save the model.
9. A completed model called **Wheel Hub_Final.ipt** has been provided in the practice files folder. This model contains all completed setups and toolpaths that will be created in this project. If you did not complete the previous tasks, you can open and use this model to complete the exercise.

Task 9: Generate the CNC code required to machine the model.

In this task, you will post process the toolpaths to create the code required by the CNC machine. This task does not teach you how to edit the file as that is considered an advanced functionality that is outside the scope of this learning content.

1. In the Toolpath panel, click (Post Process). The Post Process dialog box opens. Define the following settings (as shown in Figure 7–24):
   - Select **HAAS (pre-NGC) / haas** as the post process configurator to be used.
   - Change the *Output folder* to your practice files folder, if not already set.
   - Note that the *Program name or number* is set by default to 1001. This was the value that was assigned by default when the Top setup was created.
   - Enter **Project Exercise Wheel Hub** as the *Program comment* value to help identify the program.

Note: *When post processing, Inventor CAM maintains the previously selected options for the fields in the Post Process dialog box.*

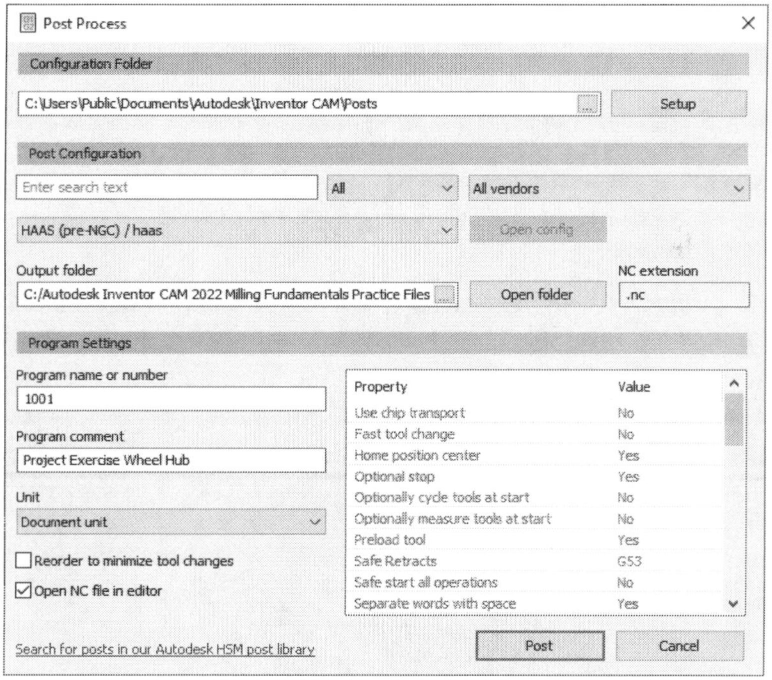

Figure 7–24

2. Click **Post**, then click **Save** to accept the default **1001.nc** file name. If you post processed the previous project, you will be prompted to overwrite the existing file. Rename it or overwrite it, as needed.
3. Once complete, the post processed machine code will open in an editor. Scroll through the N-code to review it. Close the file without making changes.
4. Return to Inventor and save and close the model.

End of practice

Practice 7b
Generating Toolpaths IV

Practice Objectives

- Import a tool library.
- Create a setup that includes toolpaths to machine the model.
- Post process an Inventor CAM setup to output the CNC code to machine the model.

In this practice, you will create four setups that will be used to define the operations to machine the model. A combination of 2D Milling, 3D Milling, and Drilling toolpaths will be used. To complete the project, you will post process the CAM data to create the CNC code required to machine the final model.

Task 1: Open and review the casting model.

1. Open **Sample Model.ipt**. Rotate the model to review the geometry on all sides of the model. The orientation shown in Figure 7–25 identifies the four sides of the model that will need to be machined. The naming of the sides corresponds to the orientation of the ViewCube.
   - The FRONT contains the contoured path that represents half of a model toy casting as well as the bottom of four counterbore holes. This side will require 3D Milling toolpaths.
   - The BACK will require drilling for the four counterbore holes.
   - The BOTTOM and RIGHT side cutouts create half of a flange for the mold. These cutouts could be machined from the FRONT side using 3D toolpaths; however, it is easier to use 2D paths directly on these sides.

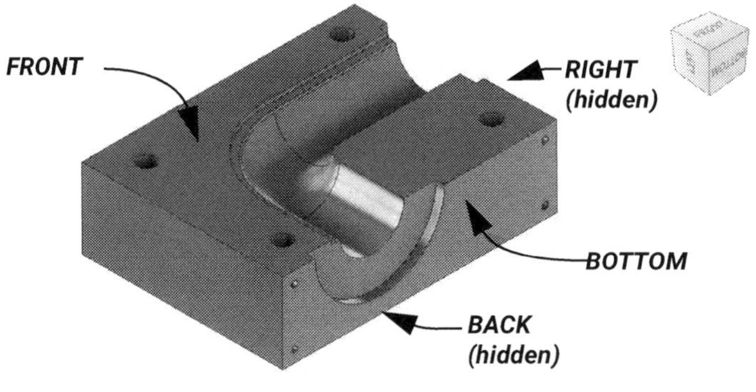

Figure 7–25

__Note:__ A completed model (__Sample Model_Final.ipt__) has been provided in the practice files. This model contains all completed setups and toolpaths that will be created.

Task 2: Sketch a CAM Boundary.

1. To prevent the 3D toolpath that will be created on the FRONT from including the flanges on the two ends, you will need to create a custom CAM Boundary that can be selected as the geometry reference for the toolpath. This is done by creating a sketch in the model.
2. Select the *Model* tab at the top of the browser to return to the Model browser display.
3. If not already active, select the *3D Model* tab on the ribbon.
4. In the Sketch panel, click (Start 2D Sketch) and select the face shown in Figure 7–26 as the sketch plane.

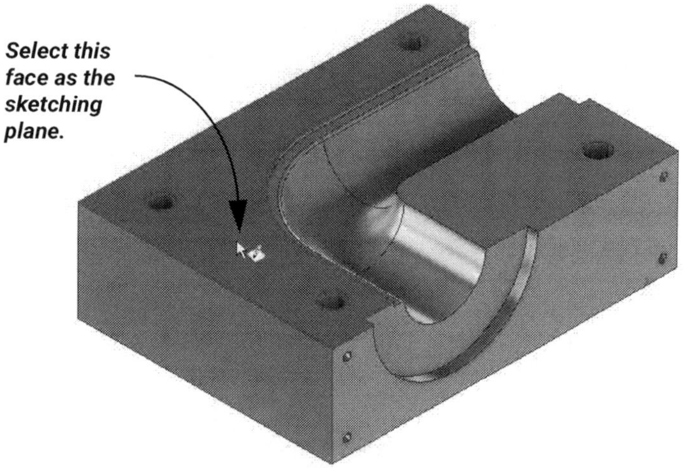

Figure 7–26

5. The sketch will reorient automatically into a 2D orientation and the *Sketch* tab becomes active in the ribbon.
6. To create the sketch for the boundary, you will reference existing edges of the model. This is done so that if changes are made to the model's overall size, the sketched boundary will also update to reflect these changes. In the Create panel, click (Project Geometry).

7. Select the four edges shown in Figure 7–27. The projected edges display as yellow.

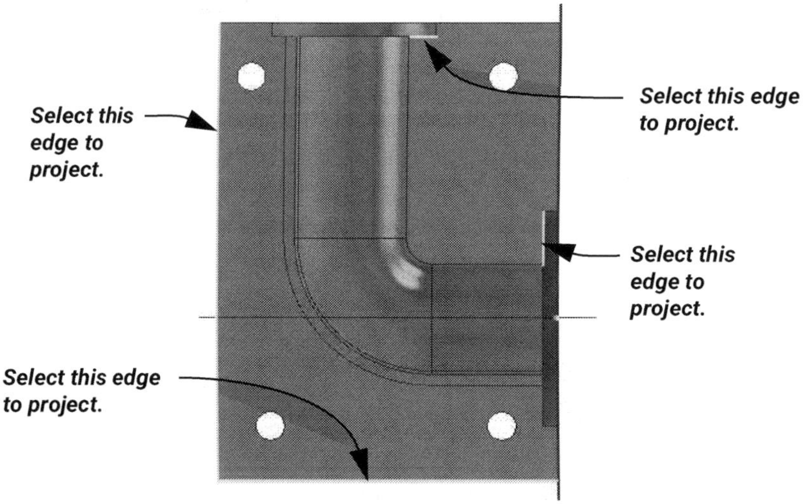

Figure 7–27

8. In the Create panel, click (Rectangle). Complete the following:

- Place your cursor over the bottom left-hand corner of the model (shown in Figure 7–28). A green circle appears indicating that the start point is snapping to the projected edges. Press and release the left mouse button to select this point.
- Drag the rectangular sketch to a location similar to that shown in Figure 7–28 and press and release the left mouse button to select this point.

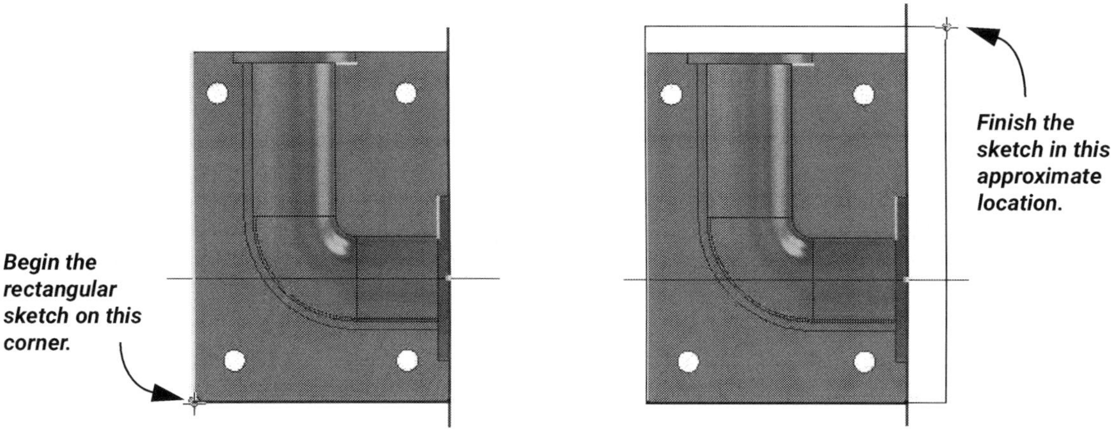

Figure 7–28

9. Review the bottom right-hand corner of the graphics window and note that the rectangular sketch requires 2 dimensions to be fully constrained.

10. In the Constrain panel, click (Collinear Constraint). This constraint will be used to align the sketched edges with the two projected smaller edges. Complete the following:

- Select the top horizontal sketched line and then select the smaller projected horizontal edge. The sketched line should snap to the projected edge. Only 1 dimension is now required to fully constrain the sketch.
- Select the right-hand vertical sketched line and then select the smaller projected vertical edge. The sketched line should snap to the projected edge. The sketch is now fully constrained, as shown in Figure 7–29.

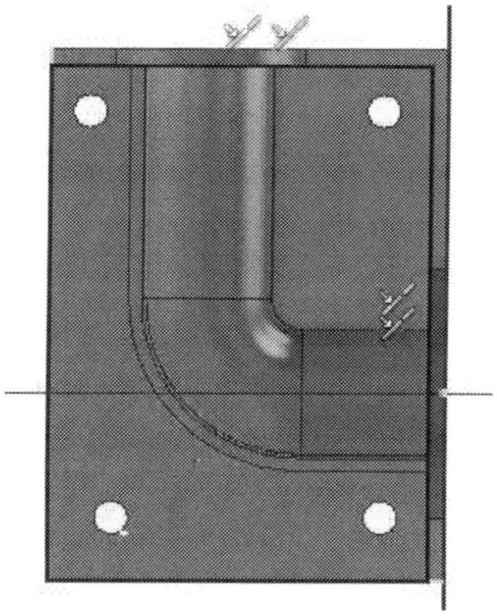

Figure 7–29

11. In the Exit panel, click (Finish Sketch). Rename the sketch in the Model browser to **CAM Boundary**. This is done by slowly double-clicking on the sketch name directly in the browser. The sketch appears on the FRONT face, as shown in Figure 7–30. A model that includes the completed sketch (**Sample Model_with_Sketch.ipt**) has been provided in the practice files folder if you were unable to successfully create the sketch.

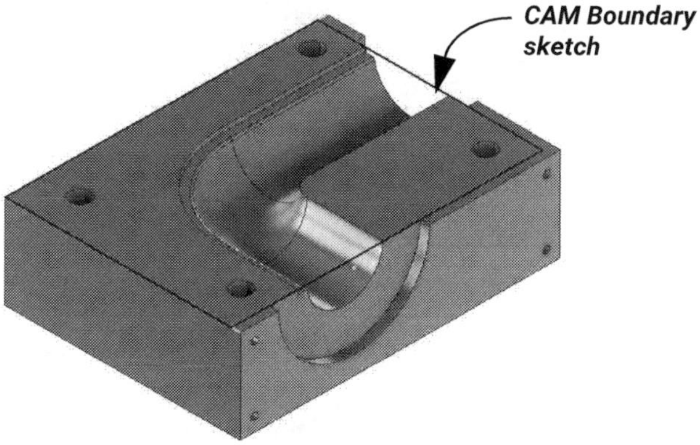

Figure 7–30

Task 3: Import a tool library.

To help simplify the tool selection process, you can import a tool library that has been provided for you.

1. In the *CAM* tab, open the Tool Library.
2. To import a library into the model, right-click on the **Sample Model** name in the *Open Documents* area and select **Import Tools from Library**.
3. Locate, select, and open the **Sample Model.hsmlib** file from the top-level practice files folder. Tools are added to your tool library. These will be used throughout this project.

Task 4: Define the first setup and toolpaths for the top of the model.

1. In the Inventor CAM environment, begin the setup for the FRONT side of the model. Consider the following:
   - On the *Stock* tab, change the stock mode to **Relative size box**. For simplicity in this exercise, no additional stock will be added to any of the sides. This is done to eliminate the need for creating facing operations on all sides. When setting up your own models, ensure that the stock assignment matches the stock that will be used in your machine.
   - On the *Setup* tab, assign the **Generic 3-axis** machine and set **Milling** as the operation type. Ensure that WCS is set at the center of the bounding box for the stock and oriented, as shown in Figure 7–31.

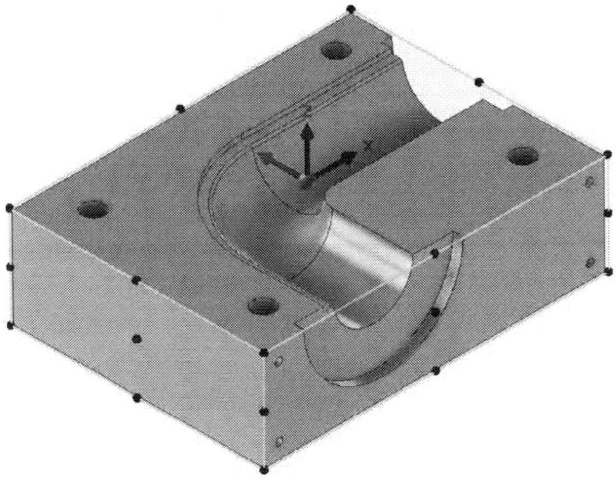

Figure 7–31

   - Verify that the model was automatically assigned, if not, select it.
   - Complete the setup and rename the setup **OP1 - FRONT**.
2. Create a **Roughing** folder and ensure that it is set as the Default folder.

3. Add a Face toolpath to machine the top of the stock (FRONT side of the model). The cutting pass machines the top of the stock, to clear it of any irregularities, as this will be a mating face with the other side of the mold.
   - Assign the **#1 2" Face Mill** tool that was imported as one of the provided library tools.
   - Ensure that the entire top of the stock is preselected.
   - Ensure that the *Bottom Height* for the cut is set to **Model top**.
   - Set the *Pass extension* value to **1 in** so that the tool clears the stock before turning for the next cutting pass.
   - Accept the remaining defaults and complete the toolpath.
   - Play the simulation and verify the path.
4. Create a 3D Adaptive toolpath to rough out the stock along contour on the top of the model (FRONT side). The CAM Boundary sketch that you created earlier will be used as the Machining Boundary selection.
   - Assign tool **#3 1/2"R 00.625 Bullnose** for the toolpath.
   - Select the **CAM Boundary** sketch as the Machining Boundary selection. Set the Tool containment boundary to **Tool outside boundary** and include a **0.25 in** *Additional offset* value.
   - Clear the use of the *Stock Contours* area.
   - Incorporate Rest Machining such that it machines from the previous operation.
   - The Maximum roughing stepdown should be **0.75 in** and the Fine stepdown **0.05 in**.
   - This roughing cut should remove all but **0.02 in** of stock both radially and axially. A finishing toolpath will be added later to finish the outside of the model.
   - Change the Retraction Policy to **Minimum retraction**.
   - Complete the toolpath. It should appear similar to that shown in Figure 7–32.

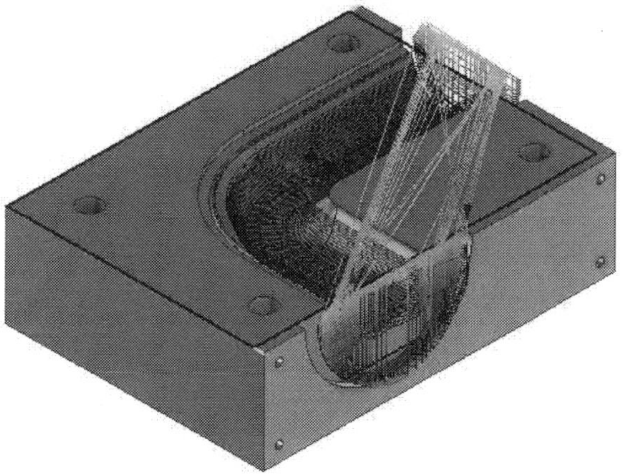

Figure 7–32

5. Create a **Finishing** folder and ensure that it is set as the Default folder. Three finishing toolpaths will be added to complete the contoured path.
6. Create a Horizontal toolpath along the top edge of the contour and consider the following settings:
   - Assign tool **#7 1/4" Flat End Mill** for the toolpath.
   - Select the face shown in Figure 7–33 as the machining boundary for the toolpath.

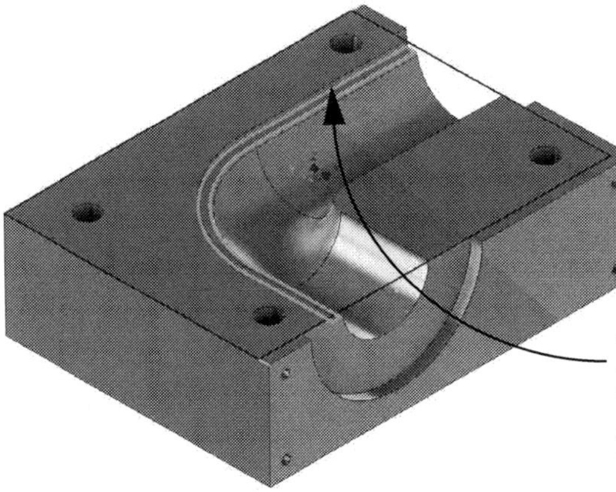

Figure 7–33

   - Set the *Top Height* setting to **Selection** and select the same face shown in the Figure 7–33. Assign a **0.1 in** *Top Offset* value.
   - No further changes are required to this toolpath. Complete the toolpath and review it.
7. Two toolpaths will be added to finish the contoured surface. To begin, add a 3D Contour toolpath and consider the following settings:
   - Assign tool **#2 1/4" Ball End Mill** for the toolpath.
   - Select the **CAM Boundary** sketch as the Machining Boundary selection and set the *Tool containment* to **Tool center on boundary**.
   - Enable the *Avoid/Touch Surfaces* area and select **Touch surfaces**. This allows you to limit the toolpath to machine only the selected surfaces. Select the six surfaces shown in Figure 7–34. Maintain the default *Clearance* value.

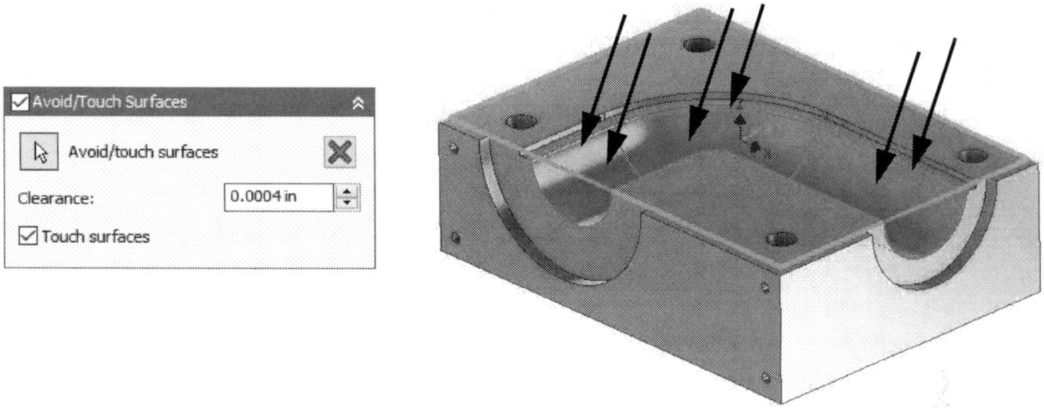

Figure 7–34

- Set the *Maximum stepdown* value to **0.005 in**.
- Change the *Retraction policy* to **Minimum retraction**.
- Change the *Ramp type* to **Plunge**.
- No further changes are required to this toolpath. Complete the toolpath and review it.

8. Create a Scallop toolpath as the final finishing toolpath. Many of the settings will be similar, so consider deriving the new toolpath using the Contour toolpath. The only change that is required is to reduce the *Stepover* value to **0.01 in**.
9. Return to the Model browser, right-click on the CAM Boundary sketch, and clear the **Visibility** setting. This removes the sketch from the display. It will not be required throughout the remainder of the tasks.
10. Play a simulation that includes all toolpaths in the **OP1 - FRONT** setup and verify that stock has been removed as expected, as shown in Figure 7–35. The Model browser should also be similar to that shown.

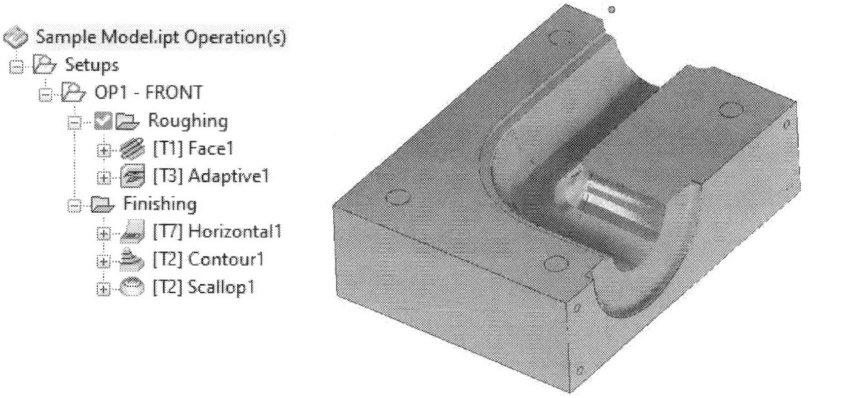

Figure 7–35

Task 5: Define the setup for the RIGHT side of the model and its toolpaths.

1. In the Inventor CAM environment, begin the setup for the RIGHT side of the model. Consider the following:
   - On the *Stock* tab, change the stock mode to **Relative size box**. Similar to the previous setup, no additional stock will be added to any of the sides.
   - On the *Setup* tab, assign the **Generic 3-axis** machine and set **Milling** as the operation type. Ensure that WCS is set at the center of the bounding box for the stock and oriented, as shown in Figure 7–36.

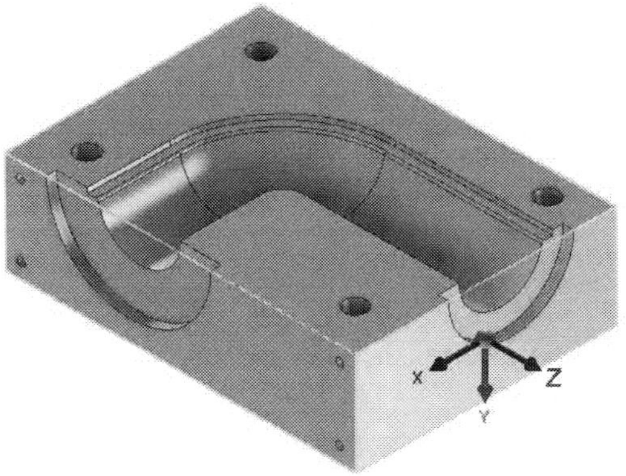

Figure 7–36

   - Verify that the model was automatically assigned, if not, select it.
   - Complete the setup and rename the setup **OP2 - RIGHT**.
2. Set the **OP2 - RIGHT** setup as the Default folder.

   Note: *Folders can be used in a setup to help easily identify the toolpaths. However, in this setup, as there are only two toolpaths being created, the organization of the two is not required.*

3. A single 2D roughing and finishing toolpath will be added to machine this side of the model. To begin, add a 2D Adaptive toolpath to clear the stock.
   - Assign the **#3 1/2" R 0.0626" Bullnose** tool that was imported as one of the provided library tools.
   - Select the face shown in Figure 7–37 as the geometry reference for the toolpath.

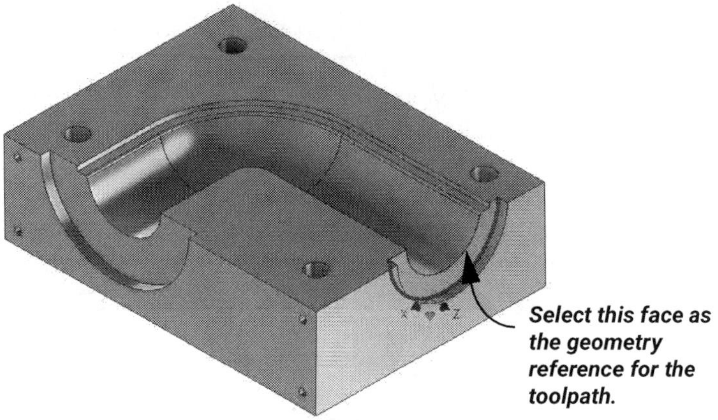

Figure 7–37

- This roughing cut should remove all but **0.02 in** of stock both radially and axially. A finishing toolpath will be added later to finish this area of the model.
- No further changes are required to this toolpath. Complete the toolpath and review it.

4. Create a 2D Contour toolpath to finish the RIGHT side of the model and consider the following settings:
   - Assign the **#7 1/4" Flat Endmill** tool that was imported as one of the provided library tools.
   - Select the edge shown in Figure 7–38 as the geometry reference for the toolpath.

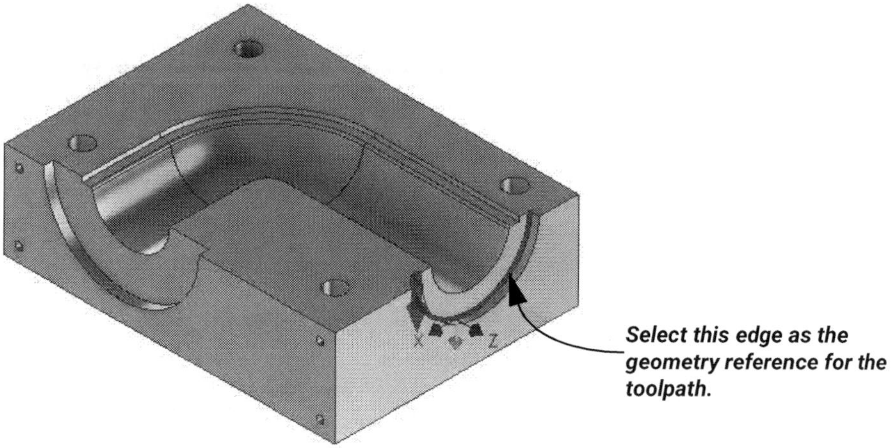

Figure 7–38

   - Enable the *Roughing Passes* area and set the *Maximum stepover* value to **0.1 in** and the *Number of stepovers* to **6**.
   - No further changes are required to this toolpath. Complete the toolpath and review it.

Task 6: Define the setup for the BOTTOM side of the model and its toolpaths.

The setup and toolpaths for the BOTTOM side is very similar to that which was just completed for the RIGHT side. For efficiency, you can duplicate that setup and make the necessary changes.

1. Right-click on the **OP2 - RIGHT** setup in the CAM browser and select **Duplicate**. A copy of the setup and the two toolpaths are generated.
2. Complete the following to modify the new setup and toolpaths for the RIGHT side.
   - Rename the setup to **OP3 - BOTTOM**.
   - Modify the stock point and its orientation.
   - Select the appropriate faces and edges to accurately define both the 2D Adaptive and 2D Contour toolpaths. Hint: Be sure to delete the original references before selecting new ones; otherwise, the new ones are simply added to the existing selection.
   - Review the two toolpaths. They should appear similar to that shown in Figure 7–39.

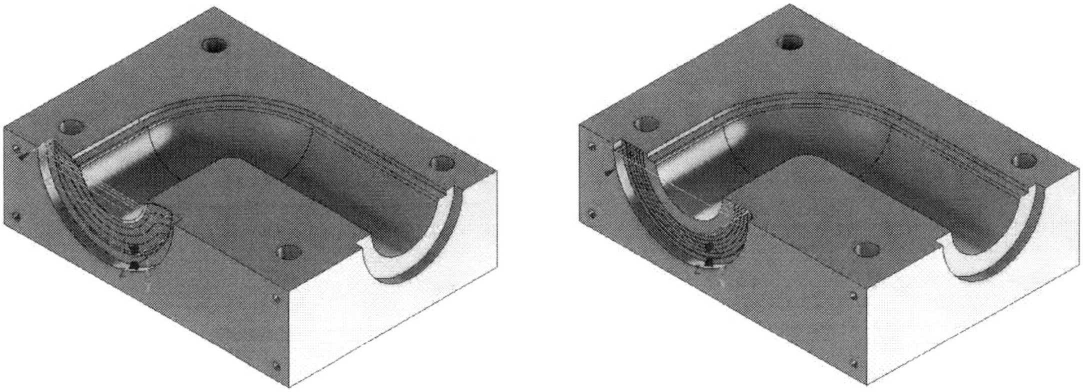

2D Adaptive1 (2) ***2D Contour1 (2)***

Figure 7–39

Note: *If the new toolpaths were created in the OP2 - RIGHT setup you can drag and drop them into the OP3 - BOTTOM setup using the CAM browser. Duplicating setups does not set the new folder as Default. You must manually do this after the toolpath is copied.*

3. Using the tools provided in the imported tool library, create a spot drill to locate the holes, a drilling toolpath to the bottom of the hole, and a tapping toolpath to complete the drilling operations. The CAM browser should appear as shown in Figure 7–40, once the drilling toolpaths are created.

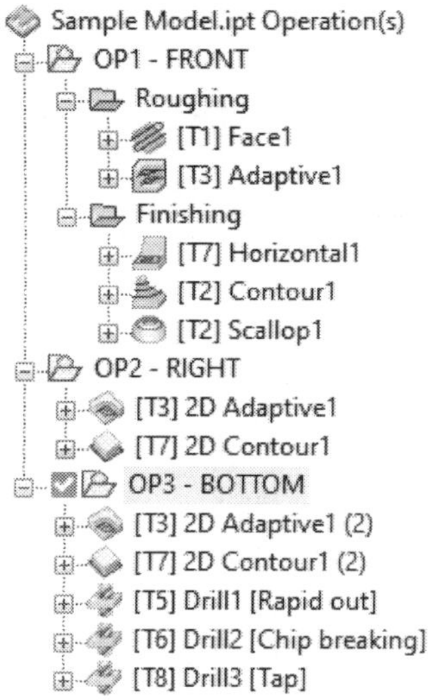

Figure 7–40

Task 7: Define the setup for the BACK side of the model and its toolpaths.

In this task, you will complete the operation setup and toolpaths on the last side of the model (BACK) by adding the final four counterbore holes. Detailed step-by-step instructions are not included and it relies on instructions taught earlier in this learning guide.

1. Create the setup similar to the methods used for all of the other setups that already exist in the model. Assign the Stock point and its orientation, as required.

2. Using the tools provided in the imported tool library, create a spot drill to locate the holes, a drilling toolpath to machine through the model, and complete the drilling operation with a Bore operation. The CAM browser should appear as shown in Figure 7–41 once the drilling toolpaths are created.

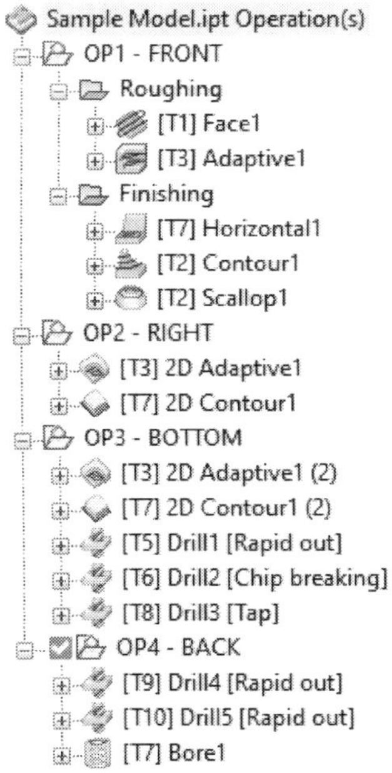

Figure 7–41

3. Run a simulation of all the toolpaths that have been created. Figure 7–42 shows the completed simulation in two different view orientations. Do not close the Simulation palette.

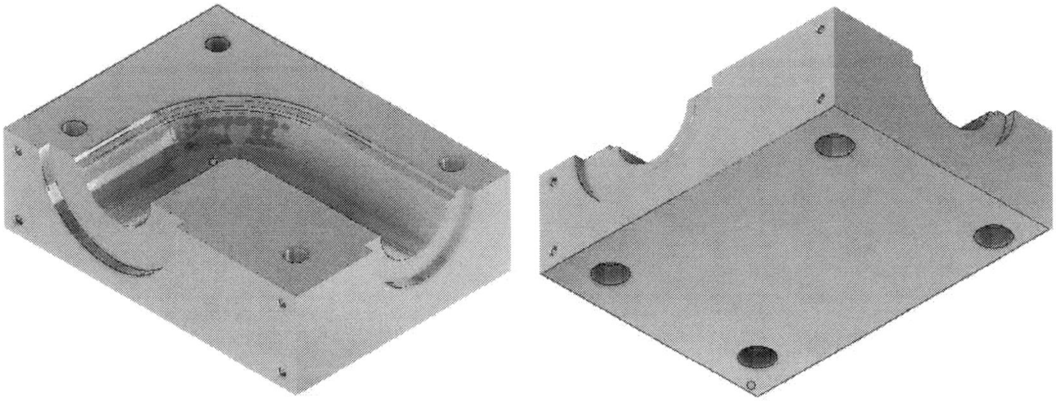

Figure 7–42

4. Select the (Statistics) tab and review the Machining time for the entire model. Recall that as you were watching the simulation the majority of time was spent on the Contour and Scallop finishing toolpaths. Close the Simulation palette.
5. Select the **[T2] Contour1** toolpath. The path displays and you can see that the entire contoured surface is touched during this toolpath. Review **[T2] Scallop1** and note the same thing.
6. To reduce the overall machining time, modify both the [T2] Contour1 and [T2] Scallop1 toolpaths to incorporate a slope range. The Contour toolpath will be used on the steeper faces and the Scallop will be used on the shallow portion of the geometry.
   - Edit **[T2] Contour1** and, on the (Geometry) tab, enable the *Slope* area. Enter a *From slope angle* value of **20 deg** and a *To slope angle* value of **90 deg**, as shown in Figure 7–43.
   - Edit **[T2] Scallop1** and, on the (Geometry) tab, enable the *Slope* area. Enter a *From slope angle* value of **0 deg** and a *To slope angle* value of **25 deg**, as shown in Figure 7–43.

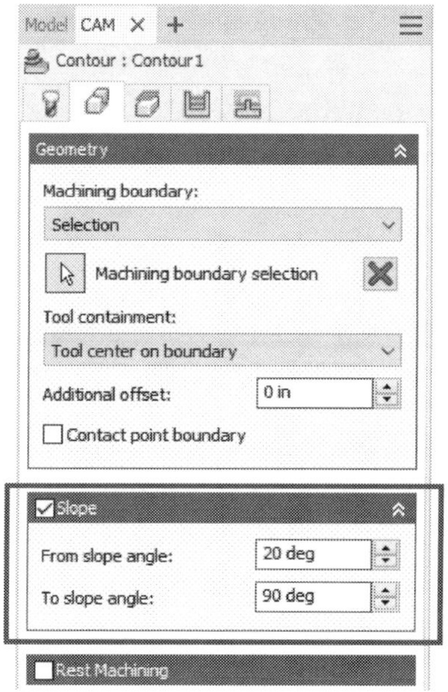

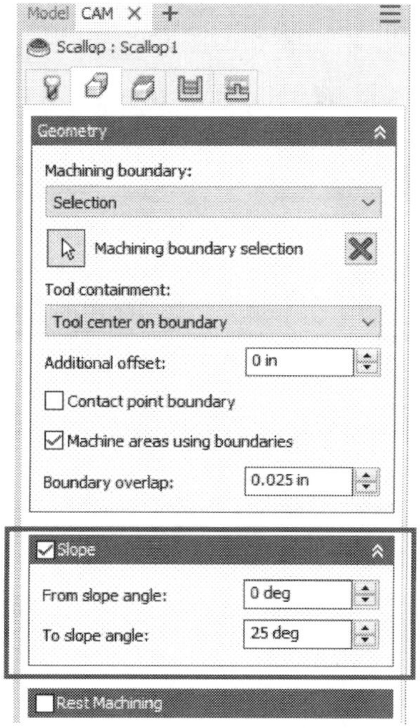

Figure 7–43

7. Once the two modification are made, select the two toolpaths individually to review the toolpath preview. Note how the cutting areas have changed.

8. Once again, run a simulation of all the toolpaths that have been created. Once complete, review the Machining Time statistic and note that the changes have saved over 30 minutes of cutting time. Close the Simulation palette.
9. Save the model.

Task 8: Generate the CNC code required to machine the model.

In this task, you will post process the toolpaths to create the code required by the CNC machine. Each setup must be run and stored separately because they each have unique WCS settings. This task does not teach you how to edit the files as that is considered an advanced functionality that is outside the scope of this learning content.

1. Set the **OP1 - FRONT** folder as the Default folder.
2. In the Toolpath panel, click (Post Process). The Post Process dialog box opens. Define the following settings (as shown in Figure 7–44):
    - Select **HAAS (pre-NGC) / haas** as the post process configurator to be used.
    - Change the *Output folder* to your practice files folder, if not already set.
    - Note that the *Program name or number* is set by default to **1001**. This was the value that was assigned by default when the OP1 - FRONT setup was created.
    - Enter **Project Exercise Sample Model - FRONT** as the *Program comment* value to help identify the program.

    Note: *When post processing, Inventor CAM maintains the previously selected options for the fields in the Post Process dialog box.*

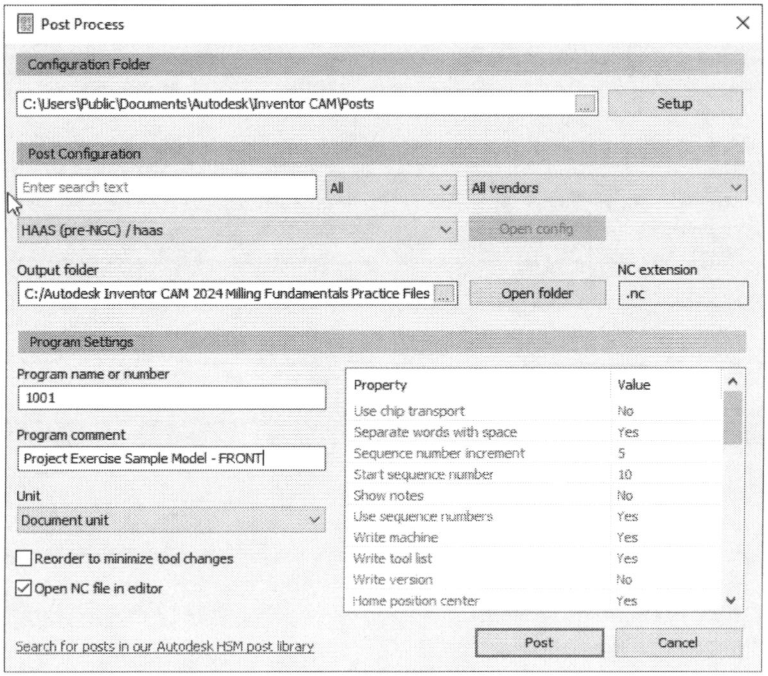

Figure 7–44

3. Click **Post**, then click **Save** to accept the default **1001.nc** file name. If you post processed the previous project, you will be prompted to overwrite the existing file. Rename it or overwrite it, as needed.
4. Once complete, the post processed machine code will open in an editor. Scroll through the N-code to review it. Close the file without making changes.
5. Return to Inventor and continue to post process the other three setup operations, if time permits. Consider naming the files such that each indicates the setup name to help identify them.
6. Save and close the model.

End of practice

Index

Made in the USA
Coppell, TX
05 November 2026

11306033R00168